Art
and the
War at Sea
1914–45

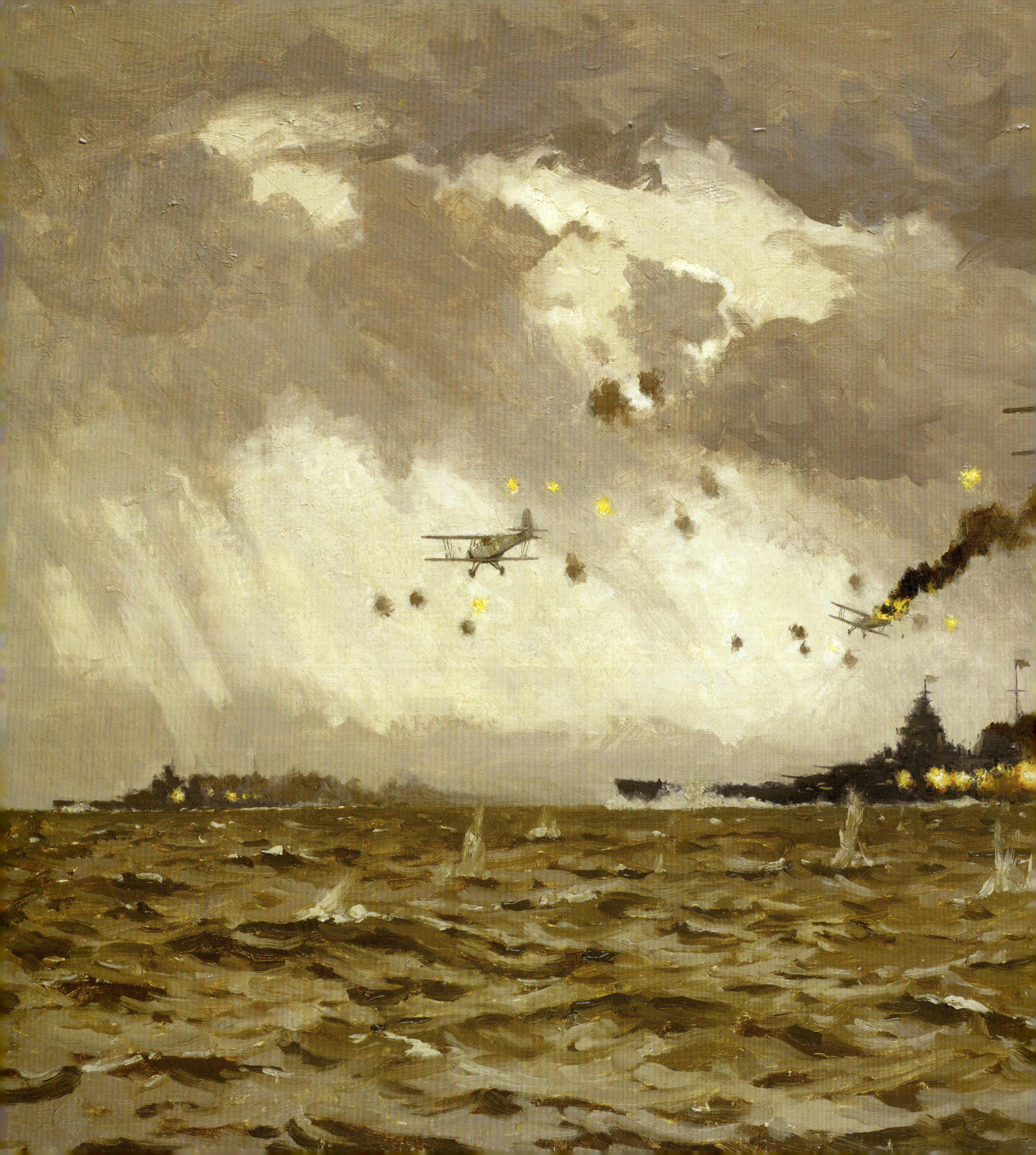

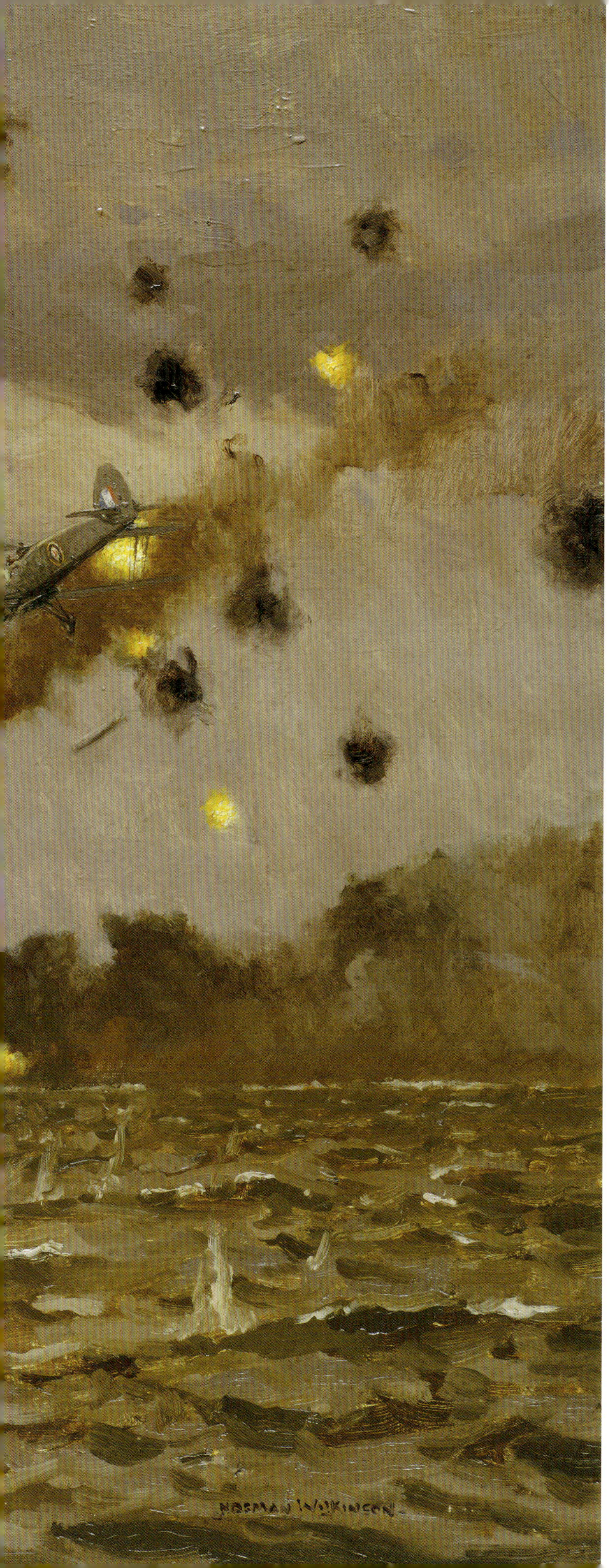

Edited by
Christine Riding

Art and the War at Sea 1914–45

Lund Humphries
in association with the
National Maritime Museum

First published in 2015 by Lund Humphries in association
with Royal Museums Greenwich, the group name for the
National Maritime Museum, Royal Observatory Greenwich,
Queen's House and *Cutty Sark*
www.rmg.co.uk

Lund Humphries
140-142 St John Street
London
EC1V 4UB
UK

www.lundhumphries.com

A Cataloguing-in-Publication record for this book is available from
the British Library

Library of Congress Cataloging-in-Publication Data (hardback edition)

Art and the war at sea : 1914-1945 / Edited by Christine Riding.
pages cm
Includes bibliographical references and index.
ISBN 978-1-84822-168-0 (hardcover : alk. paper) 1. War in art.
2. Naval battles in art. 3. World War, 1914-1918--Art and the war.
4. World War, 1939-1945--Art and the war. I. Riding, Christine, editor.
N8260.A755 2015
704.9'49940545--dc23
2015008166

Hardback ISBN: 978-1-84822-168-0
Paperback ISBN: 978-1-906367-58-9

Editor: Howard Watson
Designer: Adrian Hunt
Set in Futura and Plantin
Printed in Slovenia

Frontispiece
Norman Wilkinson
Air Attack on the 'Scharnhorst' and 'Gneisenau', 11–12 February 1942,
c.1942–4
Oil on canvas
76.2 × 101.6 cm (30 × 40 in)
BHC1625

Contents

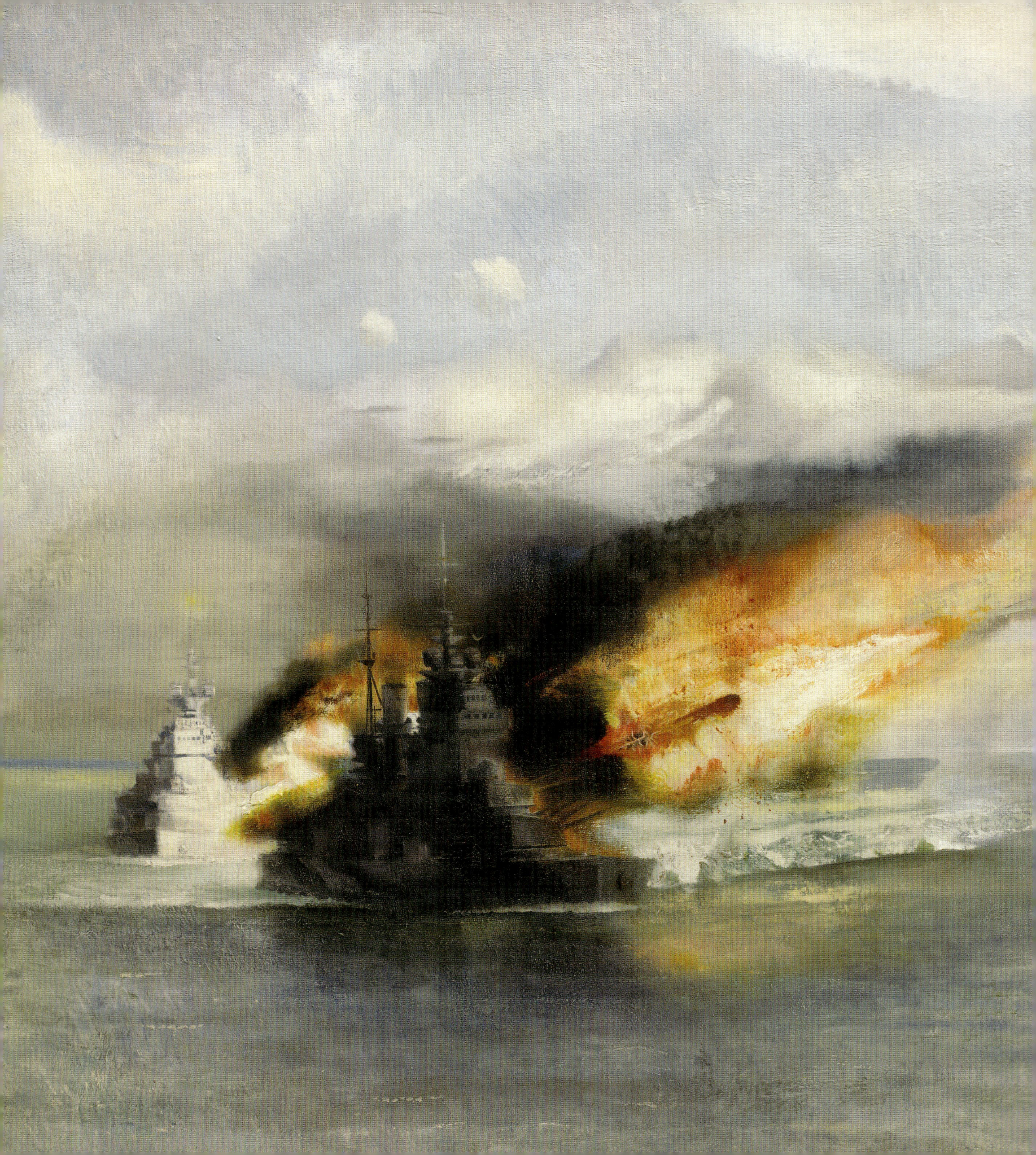

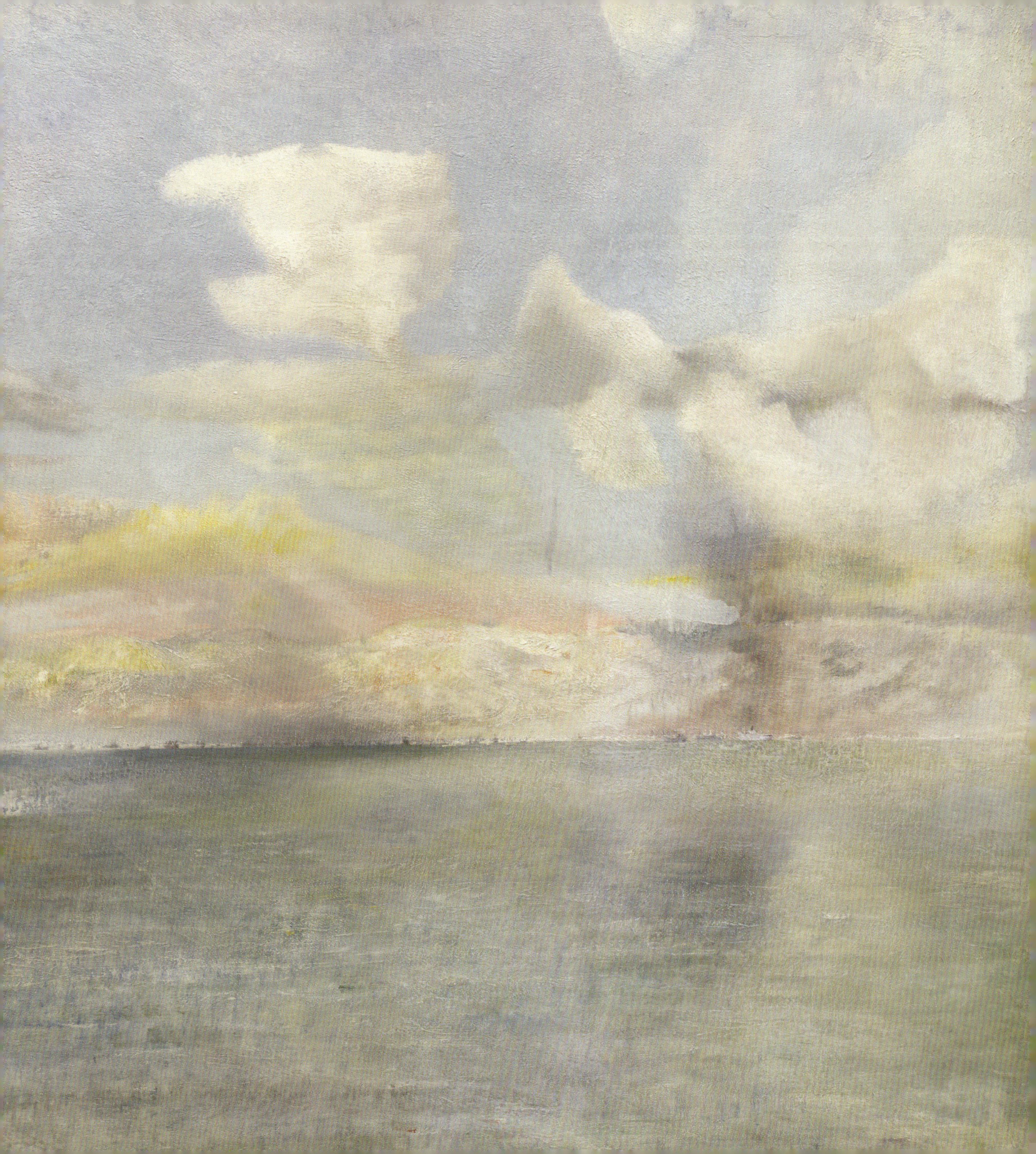

Art and the War at Sea, 1914–45

Christine Riding

Previous pages:
Richard Eurich
Bombardment of the Coast near Trapani, 1943
Oil on canvas
76.2 x 127 cm (30 x 50 in)
BHC1566

Forgotten Fighters?

In August 2014, as part of the First World War centenary commemorations, the National Maritime Museum (NMM) opened a gallery called 'Forgotten Fighters'. The premise of the display was that, despite the critical role played by the Royal and Merchant Navies in the progress and outcome of the conflict, the war at sea had been largely ignored in more recent times, or viewed as a sideshow to the primary theatre of conflict, the Western Front, with its iconic battles and attendant horrors. However, setting aside the Navy and merchant fleet's transportation of British and Imperial troops, armaments and reinforcements both across the Channel and around the globe between 1914 and 1918, Britain itself would have starved during those years without its joint naval and mercantile power at sea. Moreover, the Battle of Jutland (1916), the largest fleet action in the Royal Navy's long history – and the most significant since the legendary Battle of Trafalgar (1805) – was one that the nation simply could not have afforded to lose.

In attempting to explain the apparent disconnect between actual events and popular memory, it is important to note that a general tendency to underrate the role of the Navy, let alone that of the Merchant Navy, was acknowledged after 1918. In his revised third edition of *Peeps at the Royal Navy*, published in 1921, the Reverend James Baikie admitted that the First World War had been 'unique most of all in this, that never before was a conflict waged with absolutely decisive results, in which the fighting between fleets concerned occupied so small a place comparatively, and was attended by results apparently so indecisive'. 'So much was this the case,' he continues, 'that the general feeling of the British public towards the work of the Navy, whether avowed or, more generally, only silently felt, was one of disappointment.'[1] Baikie's comments simultaneously underline that Jutland was no Trafalgar, and that the nature of war at sea, as with the war on land, had changed fundamentally, whether the public appreciated it or not. This was demonstrated above all by the introduction of such transformative and increasingly devastating technologies as submarines and aeroplanes, as well as the extraordinary advances in battleship design and long-range firepower, first heralded by the launch of HMS *Dreadnought* in 1906. Thus, in both World Wars, conflict at sea was no longer defined by the set-piece, potentially decisive battles characteristic of the past – as made familiar to twentieth-century audiences by countless published histories, images and so on – but by the less 'heroic' strategies of bombardment and counter bombardment, and the extensive deployment of convoys of merchant ships sailing across oceans, mostly under the protection of the Navy. A government poster from the Second World War, *A Few Careless Words May End in This* (fig.1), shows the survivors in a lifeboat watching a steamer sink, the subtitle stating that 'Many lives were lost in the last war through careless talk / Be on your guard! Don't discuss movements of ships or troops.' The Battle of the Atlantic, to which this poster broadly refers, began a few hours after Britain declared war on Nazi Germany in September 1939 and ended in May 1945. It therefore spanned almost the entire war, and hinged primarily on the outcome posed by one simple yet fundamental question: could Britain and its allies 'build, fill with cargoes and man more merchant ships than the Axis could sink?'[2]

Perhaps another difficulty in grasping the World Wars at sea (and the art relating to them) results from their geographical reach. After all, the Western Front represents a relatively concentrated area of land, where the devastation and loss of life were evident for all to see. In contrast, the global nature of maritime conflict in both wars makes for a fragmented and – one might even say – nebulous subject, for the enemy (in the form of submarines and mines) was often concealed beneath the waterline, or in the sky thousands of feet above, and countless ships – and their human casualties – were sunk without physical trace. The gargantuan task of doing justice to the complex pattern of events, locations and technologies employed in the Second World War, in particular, may well explain Norman

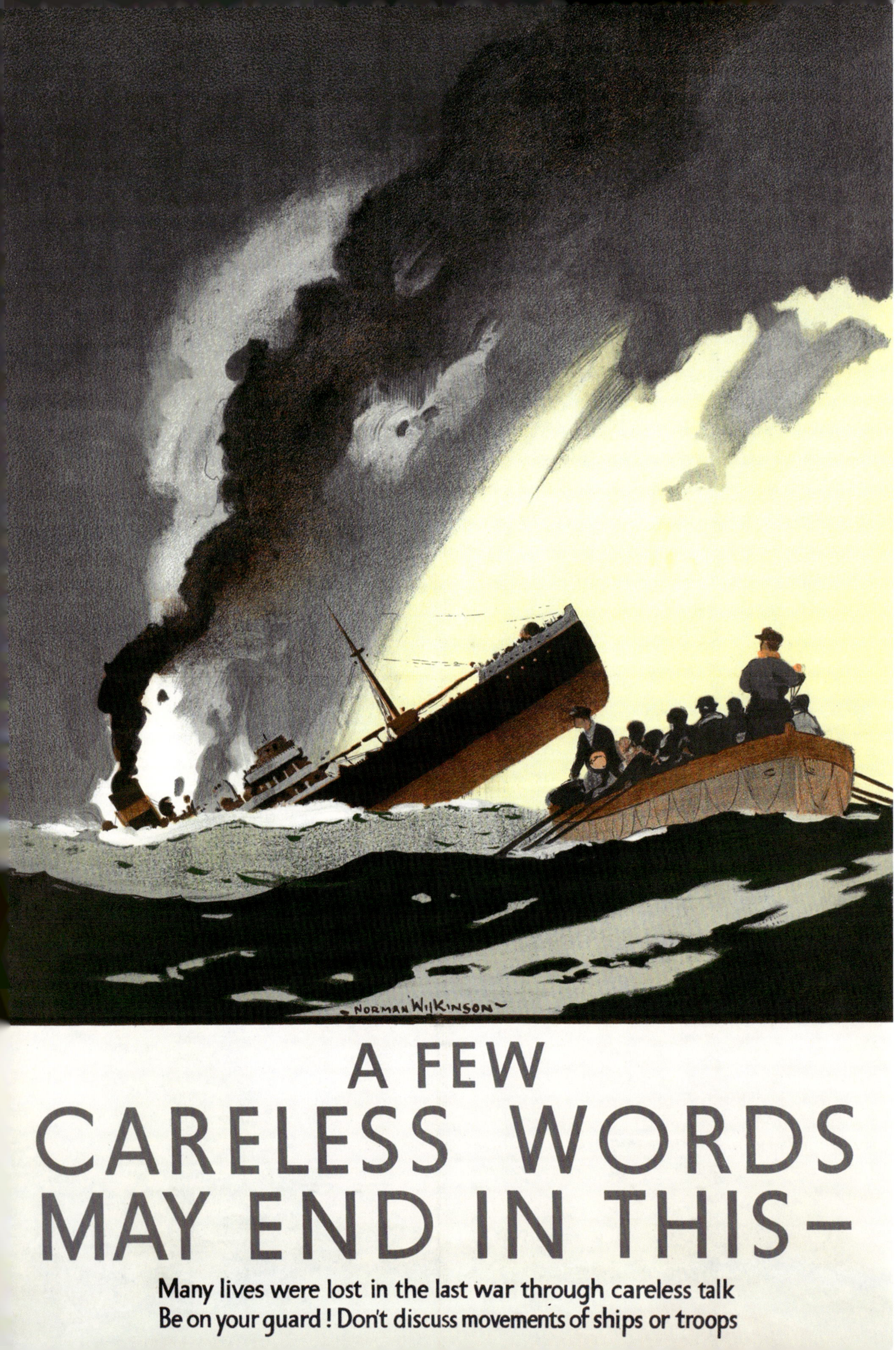
NORMAN WILKINSON
A FEW
CARELESS WORDS
MAY END IN THIS–
Many lives were lost in the last war through careless talk
Be on your guard! Don't discuss movements of ships or troops

Fig.1
Norman Wilkinson
A Few Careless Words May End in This,
British Government poster, *c.*1941
Lithograph
76.1 × 50.5 cm (30 × 19 ⅞ in)
Imperial War Museums
ART.IWM PST 13957

Wilkinson's rationale behind his series of 54 paintings entitled *The War at Sea* (1942–4, see figs 14–15 and plates 8–12), embracing the work of the Royal Navy, the Merchant Navy and RAF Coastal Command, and why he was adamant that the whole group should be presented to one museum rather than broken up (see Chapter 1: Pictorial Narratives of the War at Sea): presumably he was of the opinion that the synergy between the canvases created a whole that was greater than the sum of its parts. In any case, the format of multiple or sequential images employed by Wilkinson and others was a highly effective way of visualising the war at sea, especially for 'land-locked' audiences back at home.

Another challenge for artists was tackling, in pictorial terms, the subject of modern naval sea fights. This is especially significant given the prominence of battle paintings, whether major fleet actions or one-to-one confrontations, within the tradition of European marine painting. In his 1942 introduction to *War at Sea*, the first of the *War Pictures by British Artists* series published by the Ministry of Information, Admiral Sir Herbert Richmond (1871–1946) acknowledged the ongoing significance of changes in naval technology and tactics, noting that artists of the past had a 'task easier' than that of modern artists because their subjects 'lent themselves to compositions better than those of the widespread engagements of the long-range modern battle'. Hence, with 'a legitimate employment of licence', artists of the seventeenth and eighteenth centuries could 'show the whole scene of two fleets or squadrons in combat'. Conversely, in more modern times, 'If [the artist] be on board one of the engaged ships all that he can see in the first stage is the masts of the enemy above the horizon, and even in the later phases the enemy's hulls appear so small that no "picture" can be made of them.'[3] The difficulties of scale and range highlighted by Richmond are perhaps demonstrated by two paintings, W.L. Wyllie's *HMS 'Iron Duke' at the Battle of Jutland* (*c.*1919, fig.29) and Richard Eurich's *Bombardment of the Coast near Trapani* (1943, fig.2), which show battleships dominating

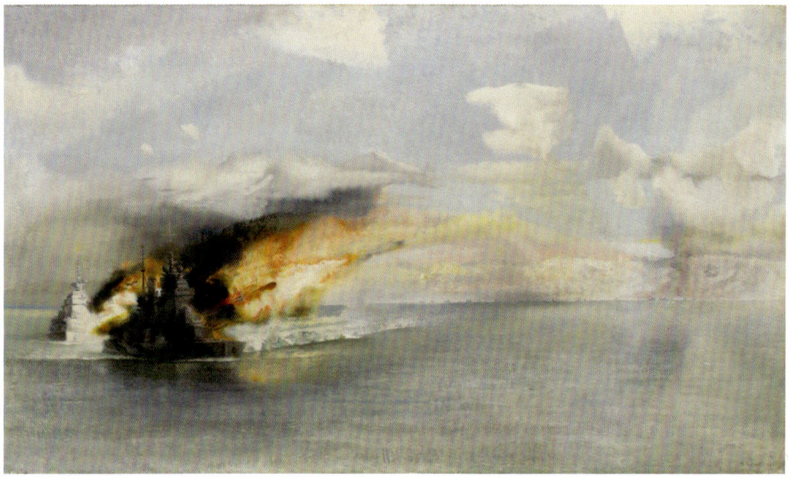

Fig.2
Richard Eurich
Bombardment of the Coast near Trapani, 1943
Oil on canvas
76.2 × 127 cm (30 × 50 in)
BHC1566

the composition and firing, respectively, into an unseen or indistinguishable distance. An alternative interpretation of these works, however, bearing in mind the absence of a defined target, may be that both were conceived to focus the viewer entirely on the overwhelming power of British ships of war. Given that such ships were perceived at the time as potent symbols of national identity and international prestige, it is worth noting that the name 'Iron Duke' is, in this context, a loaded reference to the Duke of Wellington, victor of the Battle of Waterloo (1815), and that one of the ships in Eurich's painting is HMS *King George V*. As we shall see, the real, the historic and the symbolic inevitably blended in artistic representations of the Navy, just as they did more widely within British culture.

In grappling with such vast distances, Wyllie, Eurich and Wilkinson also utilised the all-embracing potential of aerial perspective in some

Fig.3
John Worsley
A young trawler Quartermaster, 1941
Crayon on paper
48 × 38 cm (18 7/8 × 15 in)
PAJ3511

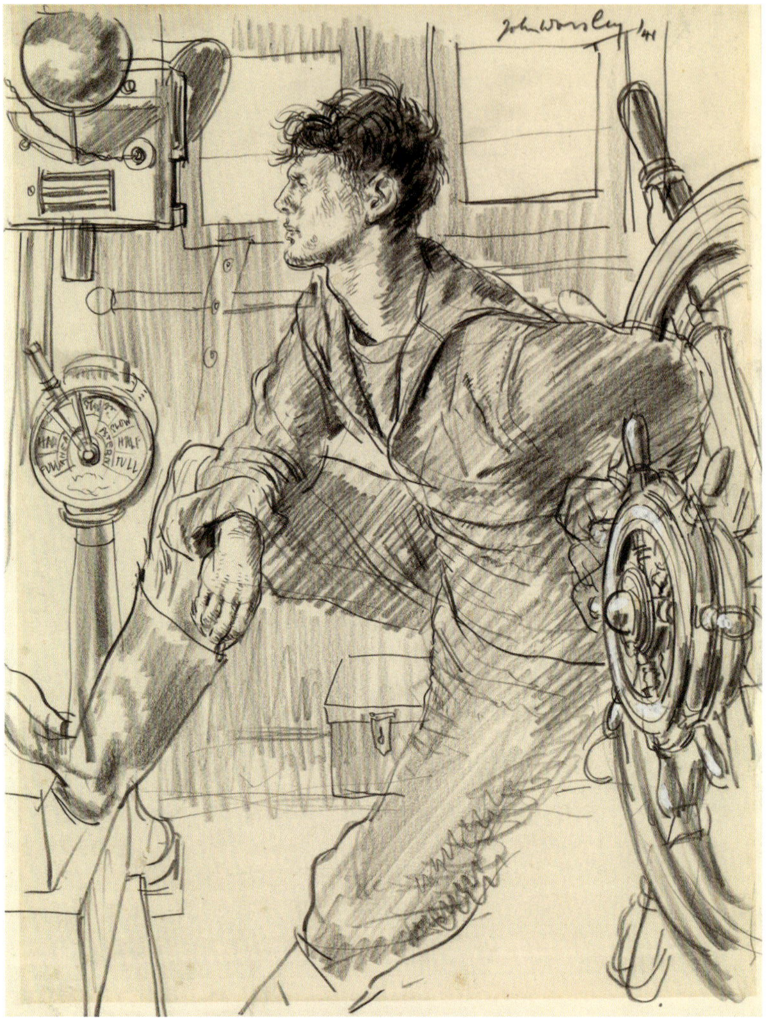

of their works, whether representing battles, fleets or convoys. This had the advantage of being a device associated with revered marine painters of the past, a fact that all three artists knew well, and a viewpoint that was now exploitable in ways unimaginable before the advent of modern aviation. Tradition and modernity therefore could, and did, effectively co-exist in contemporary marine painting, rather than being in tension with each other.

Art, War and the Sea

As these and other works of art in this publication show, many artists adapted and developed their practice to engage with new realities and the challenges, as well as the opportunities, that they presented for image making. Now that we are in the centenary period of the First World War (1914–18) and the 75th anniversary of the Second (1939–45), the time is ripe to foreground both wars at sea – thus reconnecting with the people, services and events that defined each conflict – and to re-evaluate the NMM's outstanding (but largely unknown) collection of modern British art that relates to them: a substantial number of works from it are published here for the first time. Furthermore, *Art and the War at Sea: 1914–45* is the only study to focus on the war art of this period from a purely naval and maritime perspective. Many publications have engaged with the events, artists and poets associated with the Western Front in particular, but the cultural history of the two wars at sea remains a largely neglected aspect, above all that of the 1914–18 conflict. This is despite such well-known events as the sinking of RMS *Lusitania* by a German U-boat in 1915, the Gallipoli Campaign in 1915–16 and the formation of the Women's Royal Naval Service (WRNS) in 1917.

With regards to the Second World War, the War Artists Advisory Committee (WAAC) was formed in 1939 under the direction of Sir Kenneth Clark (1903–83) largely in response to the significant role played by British artists during the First World War. The products of its many commissions are well known today in areas such as the war effort on land and the home front, views of bombed cities and underground shelters, and the seminal Battle of Britain (1940). However, if perhaps excepting representations of the Allied evacuation from Dunkirk in 1940 (plate 5) and the 'D-Day' Normandy landings in 1944 (fig.15), the vast majority of marine-related art created under the Committee's auspices – battle and convoy paintings, portraits of commissioned officers and ratings, and scenes above and below deck – awaits popular rediscovery.

In order to cover significant and often uncharted territory the main essays here take a major theme or genre in art – pictorial narratives, portraiture, scenes on board ship, artists as prisoners of war, the home front and commemoration – that further indicate the breadth and diversity of artistic responses to the two World Wars at sea. These essays are followed by supplementary essays that aim to give the reader further information concerning seminal events, developments and themes that, in turn, offer further context

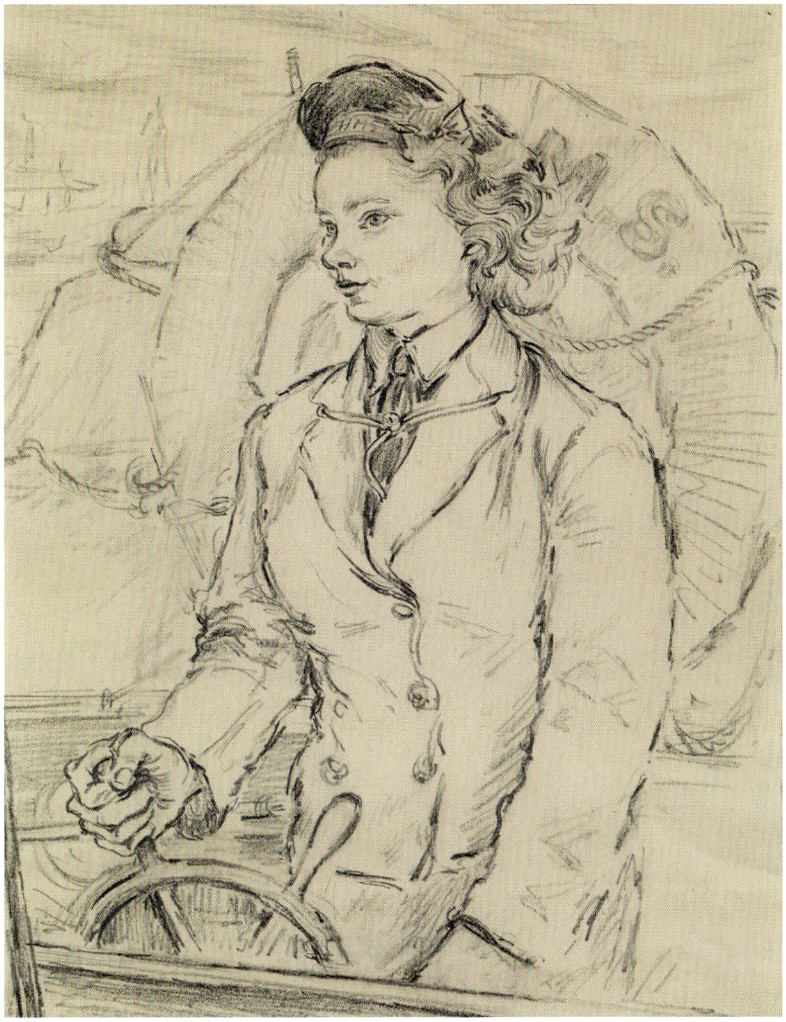

Fig.4
Gladys E. Reed
Wren boat's crew HMS 'Hornet', c.1943–4
Graphite on paper
33 × 24.8 cm (13 × 9 3/5 in)
PAH0097

and potential insights into the art relating to them. In addition to a thematic focus, each main essay also concentrates on a selection of artists, with relevant biographical details, in the context of a particular body of work represented in the NMM collections. Some of these artists are well known. Others are being reintroduced after many decades of relative obscurity. Thus Eric Kennington, Edward Wadsworth, Jacob Epstein and Eric Ravilious are familiar names in the present. Much less so are Richard Eurich and Charles Wheeler; and W.L. Wyllie, John Everett, Charles Pears, William Dring, Stephen Bone and John Worsley (fig.3) may hardly register at all, at least as war artists. Despite his prolific output – mostly sea-related – across both conflicts, Norman Wilkinson only really features in relevant publications as the inventor of 'dazzle' camouflage, while, as Sue Malvern has noted, Muirhead Bone (1876–1953) 'is now mostly remembered, if at all', as Britain's first official war artist.[4]

Admittedly, much of Bone's published work on naval and maritime themes forms part of larger projects, whether as the sole contributor or collaborating with others. These were initiated as propaganda by Wellington House (Britain's War Propaganda Bureau, established in 1914 and rolled into the Ministry of Information in early 1918) and attempted to cover all aspects of 'total' war. They include Bone's *The Western Front* series (1917), which incorporates naval imagery, and *Britain's Efforts and Ideals* (1918), comprising 66 prints by 18 artists, with two relevant sub-groups – *Making Sailors* by Frank Brangwyn and *Transport by Sea* by Charles Pears (fig.49).[5] Rather than being viewed as a 'stand-alone' subject, it could be argued that here the war at sea simply becomes absorbed into broader pictorial narratives, with the effect of positioning it as an integral aspect of the whole conflict, while conversely tempering its impact and thus potentially its particular character and significance within popular memory. Selecting from *The Western Front* images Bone also created a naval-subject portfolio, *With the Grand Fleet* (1917), which ranges from shipbuilding and post-battle repairs in dry-dock to battle and on-board scenes (see Chapter 3: Above and Below Deck). While little known today, this discrete group is important here because it foregrounds the Navy's centrality to Britain's war effort and acknowledges the enormous public interest at the time in all matters relating to the so-called 'Senior Service'. Bone's imposing representation of HMS *Lion* (fig.5), shown being repaired post-Jutland, demonstrates how naval ships could also be the focus for patriotic pride and wartime defiance. The *Lion* served as the flagship of the Grand Fleet's battle-cruisers (except when being repaired and refitted) throughout the First World War and was Vice-Admiral Beatty's flagship at the Battle of Jutland. The image was reproduced in *Country Life* magazine in May 1917 accompanied by the following bullish lines by the journalist C.E. Montague: 'The great hull we see here has seen more battling in the present war than any other of our "capital" ships. Officially "sunk" by the Germans, she will yet prove a troublesome ghost to them.'[6]

Muirhead Bone was not only employed as a war artist in both conflicts (fig.6), along with Pears, Kennington and others, but also

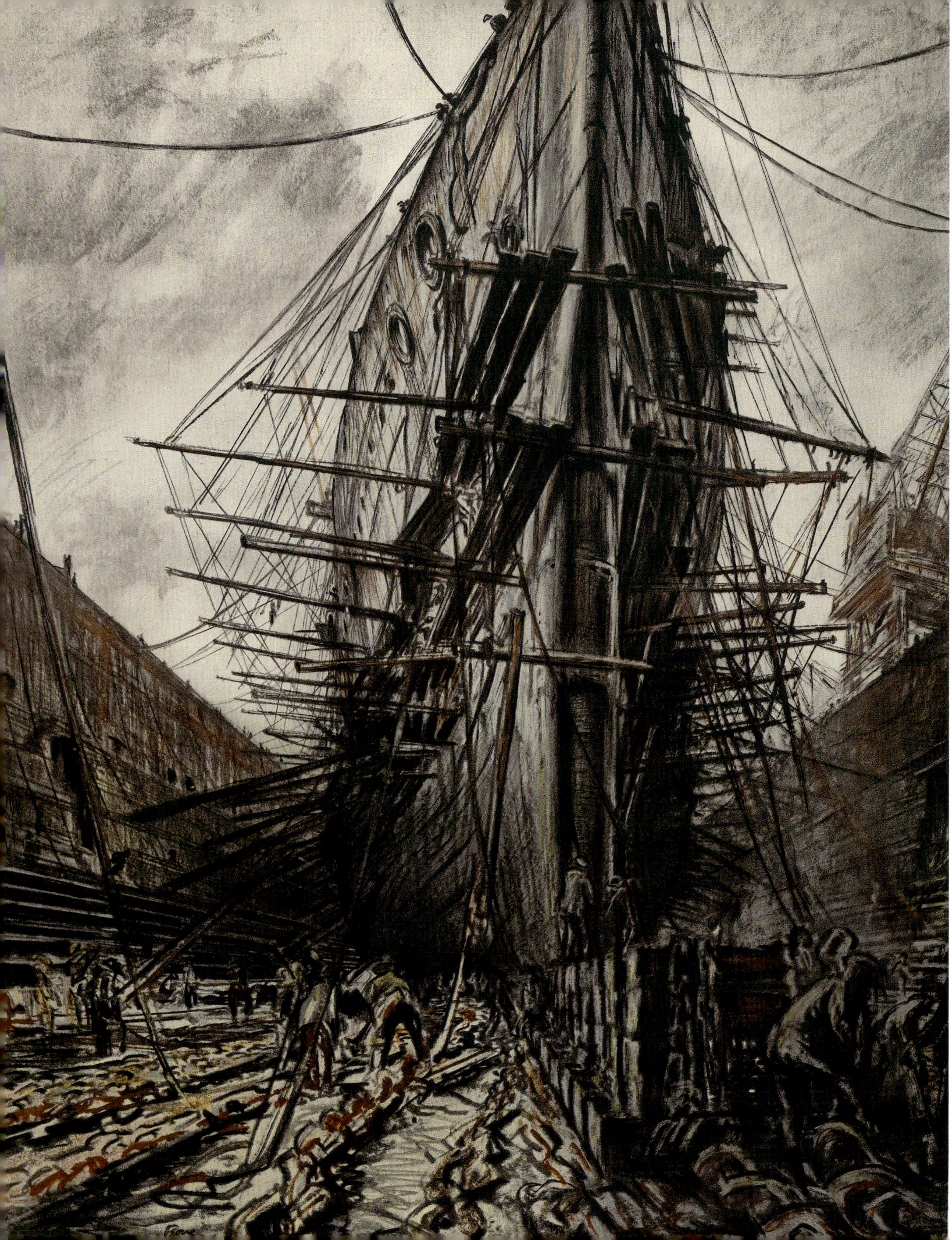

Fig.5 (opposite)
Muirhead Bone
With the Grand Fleet – HMS 'Lion' in Dry Dock, 1917
Coloured lithograph
79.7 × 55.7 cm (31 3/8 × 21 7/8 in)
PAI0681

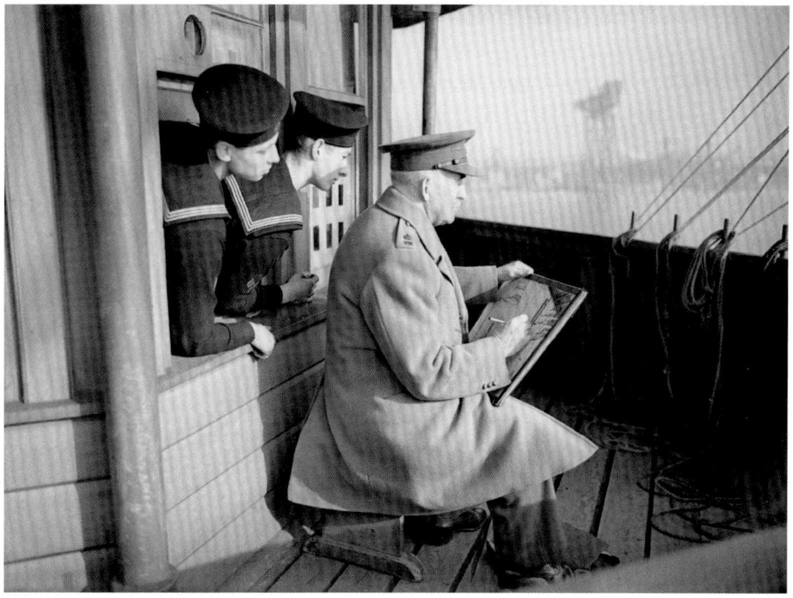

Fig.6
Lt S.J. Beadell
Sir Muirhead Bone at work, on board one of HM ships in harbour, 1940
Admiralty official collection,
Imperial War Museums
A 1341

championed the work of fellow artists, particularly those of the younger generation, through his membership of the British War Memorial Committee (and later the WAAC), through his own art fund, and via other less formal avenues.[7] Many of them, Kennington and Epstein to name but two, had 'a very different idea of art to his own'.[8] In fact, embracing and encouraging a wide variety of artistic responses, whether land-, sea- or air-related, came to be viewed at an official level and beyond as emblematic of British values of liberty and freedom of expression, in direct opposition to the tighter control exerted on artists by German authorities, whether under Kaiser Wilhelm or Adolf Hitler.[9] This in part explains the range of styles and approaches represented here (albeit that the more abstract and experimental art of pre-1914 tends not to feature).[10] And while a cursory glance at the list of First World War artists reveals how relatively few were engaged in sea-themed projects,[11] the same is not true of the Second, as this publication affirms. The recent rediscovery of the war art of Wren Gladys E. Reed (fig.4), naval nurse Rosemary Rutherford and merchant seaman John Kingsley Cook, all of whom were trained artists and had WAAC permission to record their observations and experiences, suggests that there is much more material and many more practitioners waiting to be recovered.

What role did the Admiralty play concerning art in both World Wars? Clearly aware of its propaganda value, the Admiralty employed artists from early days – Geoffrey Allfree, Philip Connard, Nelson Dawson, John Lavery, Ambrose McEvoy, Charles Pears, Glyn Philpot and Norman Wilkinson were approached from June 1917 onwards – and took advice from the Tate Gallery, National Gallery and the Victoria and Albert Museum in its choice of them.[12] It participated in art commissions, including providing privileged access to naval ships, high-ranking officers, crews and naval bases (more so during the Second World War), and in national commemorative projects, such as the formation of the Imperial War Museum (IWM) and the work of the Imperial (now Commonwealth) War Graves Commission (IWGC), in particular the naval memorials in London, Chatham, Portsmouth and Plymouth. The symbiotic relationship between art and the war at sea is neatly demonstrated by the *Sea Power Exhibition*, which was organised by the IWM with the blessing of the Admiralty and held at the Grosvenor Galleries in 1918–19 in aid of King George's Fund for Sailors. A comparable sea-focused exhibition of Second World War art was the *Naval Art Exhibition* held at the Suffolk Street galleries of the Royal Society of British Artists in 1946.

The Admiralty's active involvement in war-related projects continued into the 1930s with the establishment of the National Maritime Museum at Greenwich and, of course, the programme of the WAAC. The aforementioned publication of 1942, *War at Sea*, contains a selection of WAAC drawings and paintings made 'under the official direction of the Admiralty' by Muirhead Bone, Eurich, Ravilious, Kennington, Pears and Worsley, as well as John Nash and Stanley Spencer. Perhaps some measure of its amenability towards war art and artists during the Second World War can be gleaned from the Admiralty's employment of the sculptor Charles Wheeler, who made seven portraits of naval officers from the rank of captain to admiral, during 1941–4 (plate 15). As Wheeler himself noted, the sitters 'were of course deeply involved in the war and I could get them for only half-an-hour during their lunch time'. 'Therefore,' he continues:

> I had an improvised studio set up in Admiralty Arch over its middle and the captains would come and sit. The most difficult to get was Admiral of the Fleet Lord Mountbatten; in fact I never secured him. Several times appointments were made only to be cancelled almost at the last minute. I think he was working 22 hours out of every 24 in those tragic days.[13]

Fig.7
Muirhead Bone
Officers dining in the Painted Hall during the Second World War, c.1942
Pastel on paper
88 × 136 cm (34 5/8 × 53 1/2 in)
PAJ2843

Over and above any propaganda value (or, as in the case of 'dazzle' camouflage, practical value) the Admiralty's involvement in war-art schemes must have stemmed, at least in part, from its long-standing (if somewhat ad hoc) tradition of art patronage, both on an institutional and on a private individual basis. In tandem with this, the Navy also had a far older and well-documented history of painters and latterly photographers being included in Admiralty-funded or otherwise-supported ventures, such as the Pacific voyages (1768–80) of Captain James Cook and the early twentieth-century Antarctic expeditions of Robert Falcon Scott (himself a Royal Naval captain) and Ernest Shackleton.[14] This almost customary participation by artists in naval or maritime matters also relates to the long-standing reputation of European marine painters as experienced seafarers – including some who served in state and merchant navies – and by extension their role as 'eyewitnesses'.[15] In his introduction to *War at Sea*, Admiral Richmond records that the eminent Dutch marine painters, Willem van de Velde the Elder (*c*.1611–93) and the Younger (1633–1707) were 'eye-witnesses of many great battles', that both were 'admirable draughtsmen', and that the elder had served at sea before he became a painter and 'had that "feeling" for a ship which only one who has lived in a ship can fully enjoy'. Extending this characterisation to the likes of Nicholas Pocock (1740–1821) – a former merchant captain – and other eighteenth-century British marine painters, Richmond concludes that 'these painters of the war at sea combined nautical experience, technical knowledge, powers of observation and most skilled draughtsmanship – see how beautifully and with what perfect truth they render the curve of a swelling sail or the outline of a ship's form'.[16] Such criteria were thought to be just as pertinent, if only within naval circles, to the work of modern artists. As a result, in his published history of the Royal Navy of 1907, Henry Lawrence Swinburne could claim that Wilkinson's accompanying illustrations were valuable, simultaneously, because 'their artistic value' was 'of the highest' and because 'their accuracy and completeness in detail' spoke volumes for the artist's 'technical knowledge of the Royal Navy and of naval history'.[17]

Art, Identity and the Navy: Continuity and Change

Of course, the premium placed on the artist 'being there' was of enormous relevance to the various war-artist schemes discussed here, and for exactly the same reasons: such first-hand experience was thought to give their works greater authenticity and, imbued with a kind of personal testimony, greater authority. This was especially true of those artists, like Wilkinson, who had seen active service in the armed forces, and it is perhaps worth mentioning here that Geoffrey Allfree, a lieutenant in the Royal Naval Volunteer Reserve who was assigned to the Admiralty in December 1917, was the only official war artist killed during the First World War.[18]

While this aspect of war art is as relevant to the Army and the Air Force, what makes the war at sea exceptional is the dynamic interrelationship between the past and the present. Furthermore, as far as the Royal Navy was concerned, its history was an integral part of its modern identity. This is clearly represented by the naval and maritime associations of Greenwich and, by extension, the historic and modern art collections at the NMM. The observations of Admiral Richmond are a case in point. At the time he was writing for the *War at Sea* publication, Richmond was an eminent naval historian and (significantly enough) was himself grandson of the portrait painter, George Richmond, and the son of another, Sir William Blake Richmond. He was also very familiar with the Royal Naval College at Greenwich, where he had lectured in naval history in 1907, and had as a result been surrounded with the visual evidence of just how powerful the relationship between art and the Navy had been from the seventeenth century onwards.

At that time the College occupied the magnificent architecture designed by Sir Christopher Wren and used until 1869 as the Royal Hospital for Seamen (Greenwich Hospital), the naval equivalent to the Army's at Chelsea. From 1824 to 1936, firmly spanning the transition change from Hospital to College, it also held the 'National Gallery of Naval Art' (or 'Naval Gallery'), an impressive display of eventually some 300 paintings. These were primarily portraits of

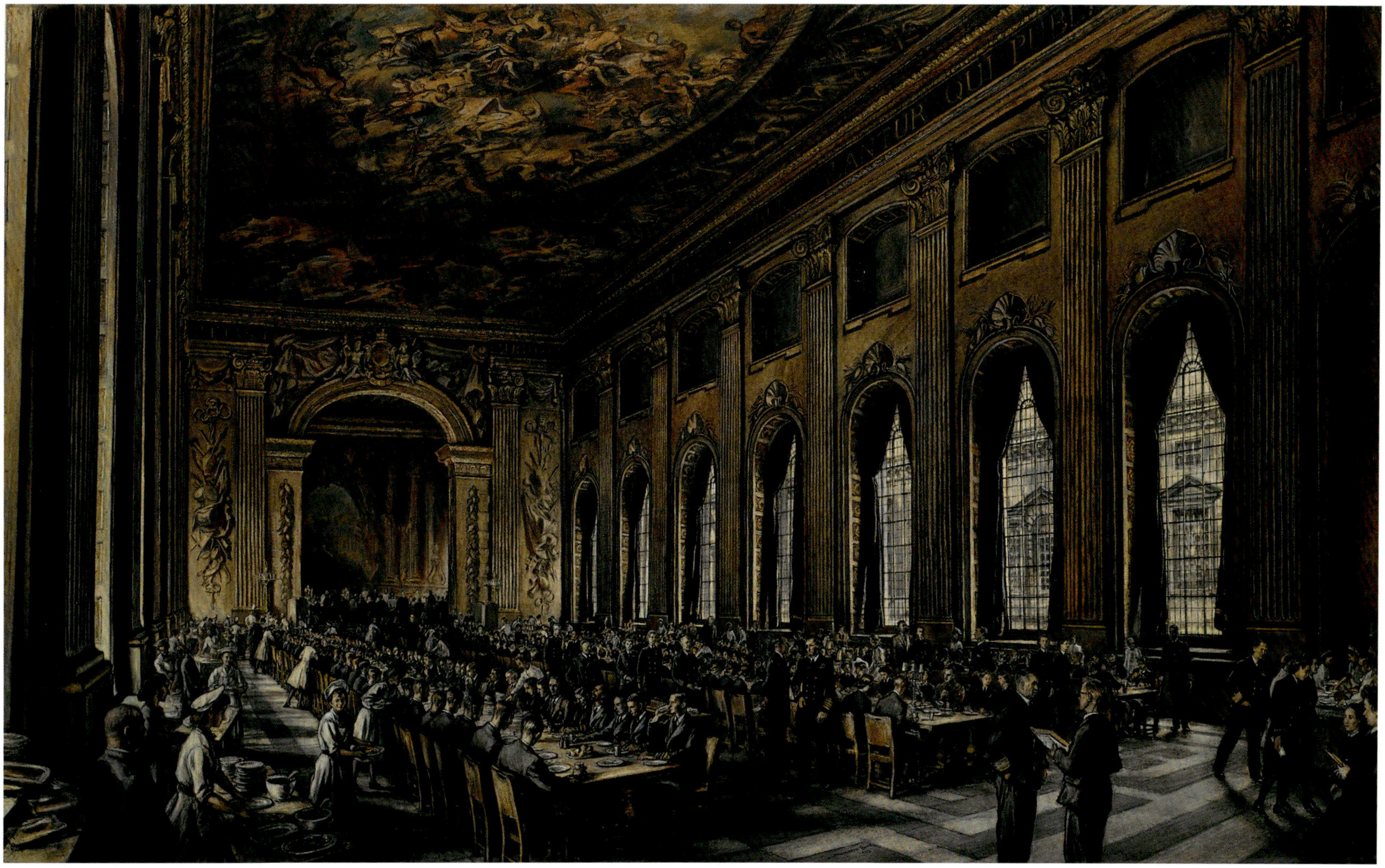

admirals, other naval officers and major battle scenes, with some pieces of sculpture, that collectively represented a grand historical narrative of the Royal Navy and, at the same time, emphatically underscored the leadership rights of social and naval rank, a concept that was relevant even during the first half of the twentieth century. The works of art were, moreover, exhibited together in Sir James Thornhill's monumental Painted Hall, itself decorated between 1708 and 1726 with a scheme that still celebrates British sea power of that era as the prime bastion of national liberty and prosperity against European (Catholic) tyranny. As Richard Johns has noted, the triumphal symbolism of Thornhill's programme – incorporating royal allegories, classical gods, mythological creatures and personifications, and the almost life-size stern of a Royal Naval ship – in essence co-opted the 'conventional language of courtly painting' to create a spectacle that combined 'royal greatness' with a powerful visualisation of Britain's maritime identity.[19] That this interior continued to resonate during the first half of the twentieth century, in terms of the nation's relationship to the Navy, is underlined by Muirhead Bone's large-scale drawing entitled *Officers dining in the Painted Hall during the Second World War* (fig.7): this was the centrepiece of a room of drawings, arranged by Sir Kenneth Clark, in a rolling display of war art at the National Gallery in February 1943 and, on the 13th of the same month, appeared in the *Illustrated London News* with the caption 'The Great Jewel of the Naval Crown'.

More than simply a splendid historical backdrop, however, one might suggest that the visual language represented in the Painted Hall also formed part of the iconography of the modern Navy. This would explain the range of symbols, personifications and mythological creatures that were to feature on the naval war memorials of both World Wars, and why the Admiralty wholeheartedly endorsed the idea of 'Baroque themes',[20] of mermaids, tritons and dolphins, for the memorial fountains to Admirals Jellicoe and Beatty, unveiled in Trafalgar Square in 1948

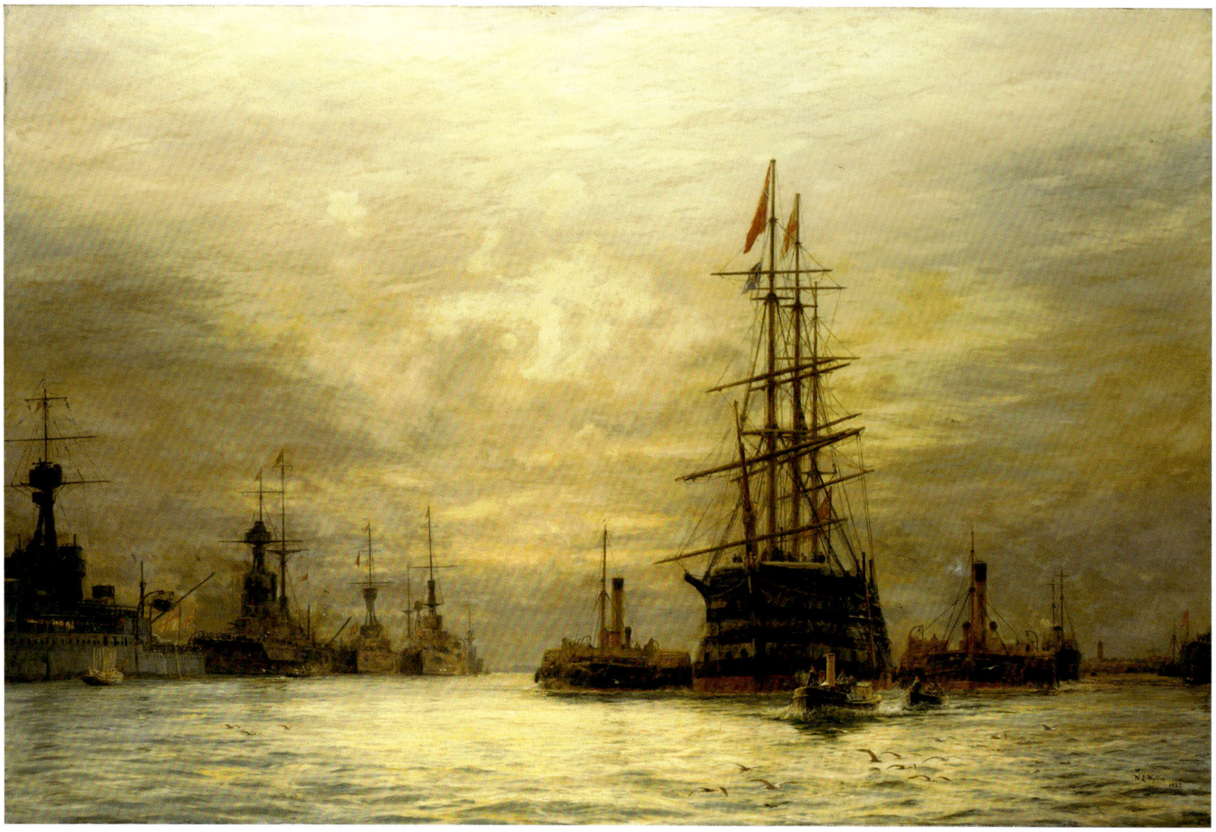

Fig.8
William Lionel Wyllie
With Drums and Rolling Music, Like a Queen: Ships of the Atlantic Fleet Play 'Victory' into Dock, 1922
Oil on canvas
127 × 185.4 cm (50 × 73 in)
BHC3700

(see Chapter 6: Public Memorials, Symbolic Spaces). Importantly the term 'baroque' was in regular use throughout the twentieth century to describe Wren's buildings and their interiors.

In 1936, the art works in the Naval Gallery (which are still owned by the Crown naval charity that is today simply called Greenwich Hospital) were transferred to the care of the NMM, itself founded in 1934. By this time much more had also been amassed for the new Museum – including the most important collection of work by the van de Veldes anywhere in the world – by its major benefactor, James Caird, under the guidance of Geoffrey Callender, formerly Professor of History at the College and, from 1934, first Director of the NMM. Admiral Richmond was fully aware of all these developments and his comments, which are both insightful and partial, are therefore informed by his extensive practical and intellectual knowledge of the Navy and its history, and the long role that Greenwich has played in both as a major theatre of naval welfare, education and commemoration. It was thus an entirely appropriate consequence that, in 1947, some 385 WAAC paintings and 6 sculptures by Wheeler (plate 15) and Frank Dobson (fig.23) were presented to the Museum at Greenwich, as the modern national institution continuing the former role of the Naval Gallery.[21]

The rationale behind the WAAC – that is, to direct and commission art in ways that served the war effort through documenting the conflict, raising morale and promoting national culture and values at home and abroad – itself offers a fascinating context to explore issues surrounding Britain's relationship with, and attitude towards, the war at sea. But given the historical significance of Greenwich, whose national (and indeed global) importance is wholly a product of its historic royal, naval and navigational associations over half a millennium, the WAAC donation of such a large group of sea-related works was much more than Whitehall generosity to bolster the twentieth-century art holdings of a still very new national museum. In this sense we can see how Greenwich represented a living history, as underlined by the officers populating Muirhead Bone's image of the Painted Hall, and secondly, how the site participated in the development and prolongation of what was described from the late nineteenth century as the 'cult of the navy'. This was founded on the idea that the Royal Navy, as Jan Rüger has demonstrated, was not only 'a political and military instrument' but 'a powerful cultural symbol'.[22] Rüger's thesis primarily focuses on the kind of 'naval theatre' represented by fleet reviews and the launch of battleships, which were attended by hundreds of thousands of people, as part of the pre-First World War naval arms race with Germany.

Another powerful and enduring element of this 'cult' was the Navy's most celebrated hero, Vice-Admiral Horatio Nelson (1758–1805). And here too there are strong links with Greenwich. These

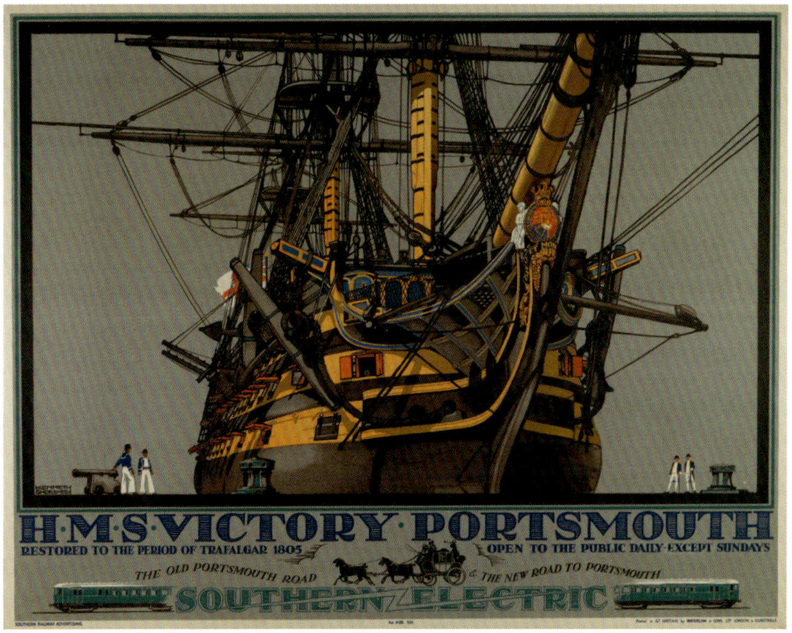

Fig.9
Kenneth Shoesmith
HMS 'Victory', 1936
Lithograph
107.2 × 133 cm (42 ¼ × 52 ⅜ in)
ZBA2203

began soon after Nelson's 'death in victory' at Trafalgar, when his body lay in state in the Painted Hall, prior to his state funeral at St Paul's Cathedral on 9 January 1806. Nelson's apotheosis during the nineteenth century was established and reinforced by a number of commemorative schemes, the best known being the installation of Nelson's Column in Trafalgar Square in 1843. But his celebration at Greenwich was far earlier, starting with the installation of the magnificent 50-foot Coade-stone 'Nelson pediment', designed by Benjamin West, in the Wren and Hawksmoor courtyard flanking the Painted Hall in 1812, and the numerous art works and personal relics which accrued, all by gift, to the Naval Gallery from the 1820s on. These included A.W. Devis' iconic painting of the hero's death, below decks on HMS *Victory*, and the bullet-holed uniform coat he was wearing when shot at Trafalgar, purchased and presented by Prince Albert in 1845.[23] By this time the Hall was a Nelson shrine, and so much so that a special Nelson Room was subsequently arranged off the Upper Hall for smaller pictures and other items.

That Nelson was a constant touchstone for British sailors during the first half of the twentieth century is borne out by the countless references to him in publications. To give two representative examples; in Swinburne's 1907 history of the Navy he is referred to as 'the immortal Nelson', and in the juvenile publication *Stirring Deeds of Britain's Sea-dogs in the Great War*, published in 1916, he is 'the uncanonized patron saint of the Navy'.[24] The almost compulsive nature of this Nelsonic referencing continued into the Second World War period, albeit with a markedly less reverential but nonetheless affectionate tone. In his *British Women Go to War* publication of 1944, J.B. Priestley notes about the Wrens, 'it is difficult to imagine which would have astonished and delighted Nelson's sailors more – the guns or the girls';[25] and he is mentioned in the popular naval war films, *In Which We Serve* (1943) and *The Cruel Sea* (1953).

In this context, the permanent dry-docking and restoration during the 1920s of HMS *Victory*, Nelson's flagship at Trafalgar, after the effects of a century afloat at Portsmouth, was of great historical and symbolic significance. Geoffrey Callender stated that *Victory* had been preserved 'as a perpetual monument to Nelson's memory', the ship's value being 'not only as a visible link to the past, but as a visible reminder of Service and Sacrifice and an incentive to fresh endeavour'.[26] The idea of the ship as both a 'link' and an 'incentive' seems to be the theme of Wyllie's painting entitled *With Drums and Rolling Music, Like a Queen: Ships of the Atlantic Fleet Play 'Victory' into Dock* of 1922 (fig.8). The composition deliberately reverses J.M.W. Turner's celebrated painting, *The Fighting Temeraire* (1839, National Gallery), which poignantly marks the final journey to a breakers yard in 1838 of a 'ship of the line' that had fought at Trafalgar. In 1839, the author and art critic William Thackeray described Turner's painting specifically as 'memorial art', and further opined that old warships, such as *Victory*, 'ought to be sacred relics, for Englishmen to worship almost'.[27] That this hope was to a degree fulfilled is demonstrated by Muirhead Bone's print *HMS 'Victory' in War Time*, executed under the auspices of the WAAC and the Admiralty, and reproduced in the *War at Sea* publication of 1942 with the caption 'Nelson's Flagship stands as a symbol of the greatness of the Royal Navy'.[28] Even earlier, in the 1930s, the fact that *Victory* was the subject of a poster by Kenneth Shoesmith for the Southern Electric Railway (fig.9) shows the degree to which the ship had become as much a national as a naval symbol, though by then against the background of the widely publicised 'Save the Victory' campaign and fundraising that had ensured the ship's preservation, restoration and celebrity over the previous decade.

A final point to make here concerns the character of the Navy itself during the early to mid-twentieth century. Essentially, it was promoted as a steadfast, dutiful and patriotic community, displaying the same characteristics as British sailors of the past, despite the radical changes that the Navy, and society more broadly, were experiencing. In 1913, the Reverend James Baikie published the following comment, the sentiment of which was often repeated in the decades to come:

> Only one thing has remained the same through all the centuries – the cool, steady courage of the men who manned the ships and fought the battles for the sake of the land they loved. That, we are sure, remains as unquestionable to-day as it was when Nelson led his ships into action at Trafalgar, or when Grenville in the little *Revenge* defied the whole fleet of Spain.[29]

As Mary Conley has argued in *From Jack Tar to Union Jack*, such sentiments not only underline a kind of masculinity that the 'Senior Service' was thought to represent but also how central this 'naval manliness' was to 'both the success of the navy and the expansion of the empire'. Furthermore, Conley identifies a transformation in the popular image of the sailor, from the late nineteenth century to the close of the First World War, away from the 'brave but bawdy' Jack Tar of the Georgian Navy towards a more idealised representation of the British 'Bluejacket', as both 'a patriotic defender' and 'a dutiful husband and father'. While this transformation clearly chimed with the cultural values of late Victorian and Edwardian Britain, it was also linked to greater professionalisation within the lower ranks of the Navy, such as the introduction of regulation uniform for ratings in 1857 and the establishment of continual service from 1853. The result was a more stable working environment than before, and a more specifically 'British' (that is, racially white) make up to the personnel.[30] In fact, both the naval authority and ratings perpetuated the idea of the rollicking Nelsonian sailor, for their own ends, and at various junctures. But what emerged during this time was a more powerfully defined identity of the ordinary sailor as a respectable and highly skilled professional. Such a change offers an important lens through which observations and evaluations can be made concerning portraits and other naval representations in this publication.

In this regard, an equally important point to emphasise is how status- and class-conscious, and thus hierarchical, the Navy was throughout this period. Acknowledging that at the turn of the twentieth century, naval officers were still being appointed 'from the old aristocracy of the British Isles', Christopher McKee has noted that 'increasingly they originated from the ranks of the financially secure and the affluent middle classes, whose numbers and whose wealth had been fuelled by nineteenth-century industrialization and a sun-never-sets empire'. 'Distinct in birth, education, and the route by which they entered the Royal Navy,' he continues, 'officers were as remote from the ratings as it was possible to be in the restricted world of a ship [...] Most important, they knew they were entitled to be officers because a deep and unbridged social gulf set them apart from the men of the lower deck.'[31] That this 'difference' could manifest itself in physical terms is suggested by the following quote from 1916, where Admiral Sir John Jellicoe's innate leadership qualities are not only likened to those of Nelson, but visible in his general appearance, which 'bespeaks a commanding personality [...] The nose is large, the mouth and jaw that of a man of decision [...] With Nelson, Jellicoe might well and truly say: "I had the happiness to command a band of brothers."'[32]

As Quintin Colville has argued, the role of uniform was both subtle and powerful in visualising this hierarchy into the 1930s and arguably beyond.[33] On the one hand, all sailors were clearly demarked from the rest of society by their uniforms, whether officers or ratings, and there was huge social cachet to be had in the adoption of both types of costume (albeit within different constituencies). On the other, the essential difference between officers and ratings was codified by the dark suit of the middle-class professional and gentleman, worn by those in command, which contrasted with the 'square rig' of ordinary sailors, who were thus

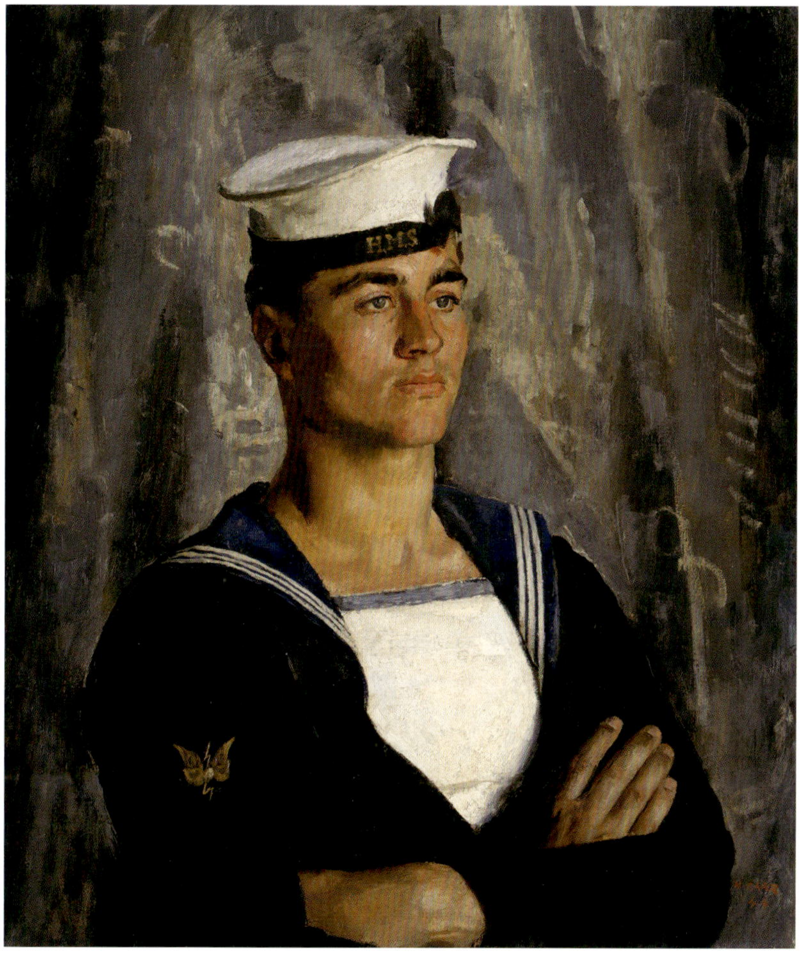

Fig.10
Henry Carr
The Sailor (Maurice Alan Easton), 1944
Oil on canvas
76.2 × 63.5 cm (30 × 25 in)
BHC2675

commanded. Naturally the concept of deference and hierarchy was essential to the well-ordered running of a ship of war, and was broadly accepted by ordinary sailors, who invariably came from the working classes.[34] That sailor suits (specifically the square rig) remained a popular dress for children is perhaps another indication, as Colville suggests, of the subordinate status of the ordinary sailor within the professional and social hierarchy of the Navy.[35]

Of course, society does not remain static. Thus by the Second World War, to quote Christopher McKee, 'the pressures of finding men to command the much enlarged Royal Navy' would result in a 'more democratically recruited officer corps'.[36] And, in parallel, the status of ordinary sailors, not to mention that of women (whether in the WRNS or other auxiliary services) also improved (see Chapter 5: Art, Artists and the Home Front). In terms of war art, these changes were marked by the greater visibility of those who had been marginalised, relatively speaking, during the First World War. One example of this is the Admiralty-endorsed images by Lee Miller, an accredited war photographer with the US Army (previously employed as a fashion photographer for *Vogue* magazine) of the Wrens 'at work and leisure'. Some of the photographs were published as an article, 'Seaworthy and Semi Seagoing', in the September 1943 issue of *Vogue* magazine, and the whole series as a stand-alone publication, *Wrens in Camera*, in 1945. Another indication is the far higher number of WAAC portraits of ordinary sailors, from both the Royal and Merchant navies, which (to use Brian Foss' calculation) achieved a ratio of one for every three representing officers.[37] Indeed, by 1943 Admiral Richmond could comment that the creation of images of ordinary sailors, as well as scenes of everyday life and the war effort on the home front, was not just desirable but absolutely imperative.[38] Perhaps for this reason, Henry Carr's portrait of Maurice Alan Easton (fig.10) was not only included in the *Naval Art Exhibition* of 1946, but was used as the poster image to advertise the event, much to the astonishment of the sitter, who had returned from abroad to find his image pasted on numerous walls and billboards across London. Rather than capture 'an individual', however, Carr clearly meant to portray a type of 'naval manliness', handsome, professional, direct and steadfast, that would appeal to a British public. Hence the portrait was exhibited with the generic title *The Sailor*. But the actual identity of Maurice Easton only came to light many years later.[39]

1

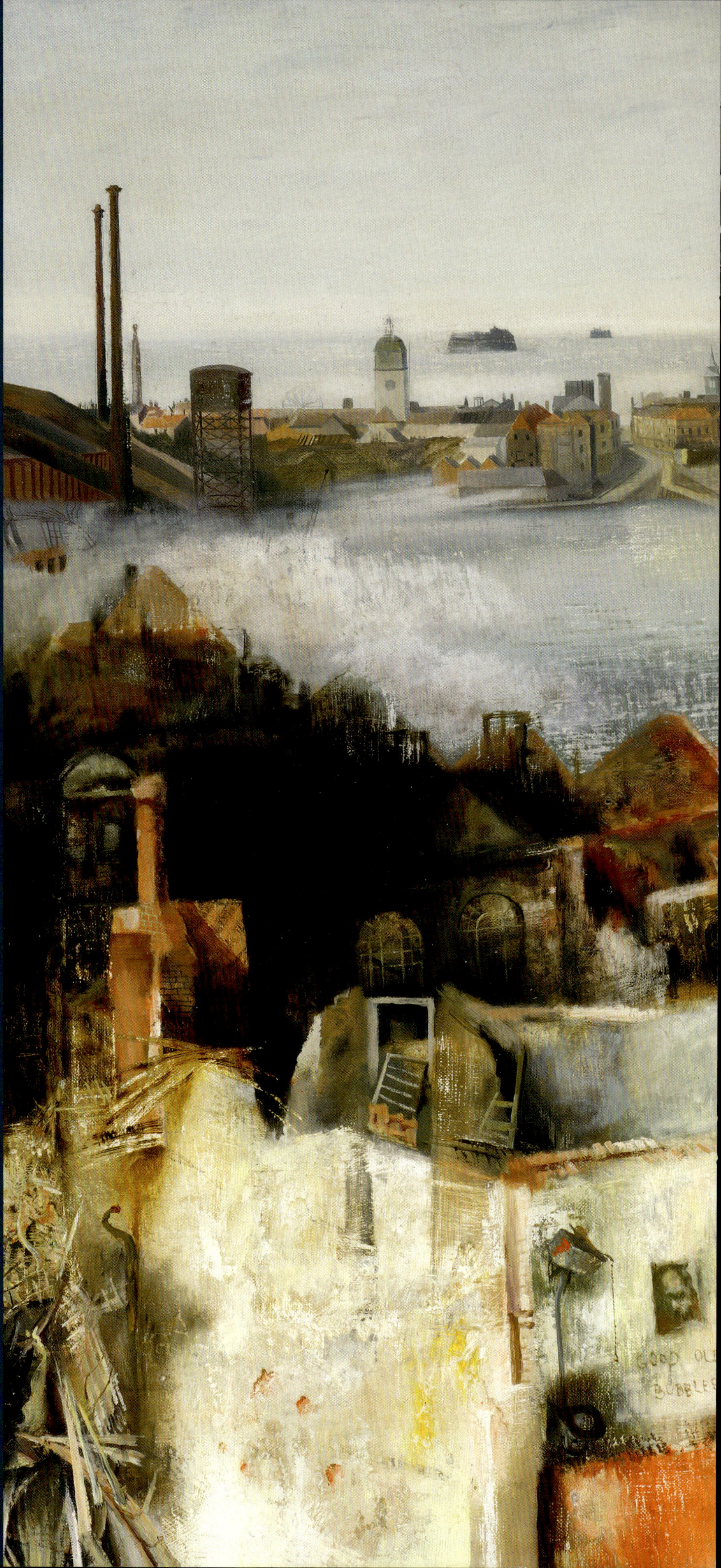

Richard Eurich
HMS 'Revenge' Leaving Harbour, 1942
Oil on canvas
76.2 × 127 cm (30 × 50 in)
BHC1571

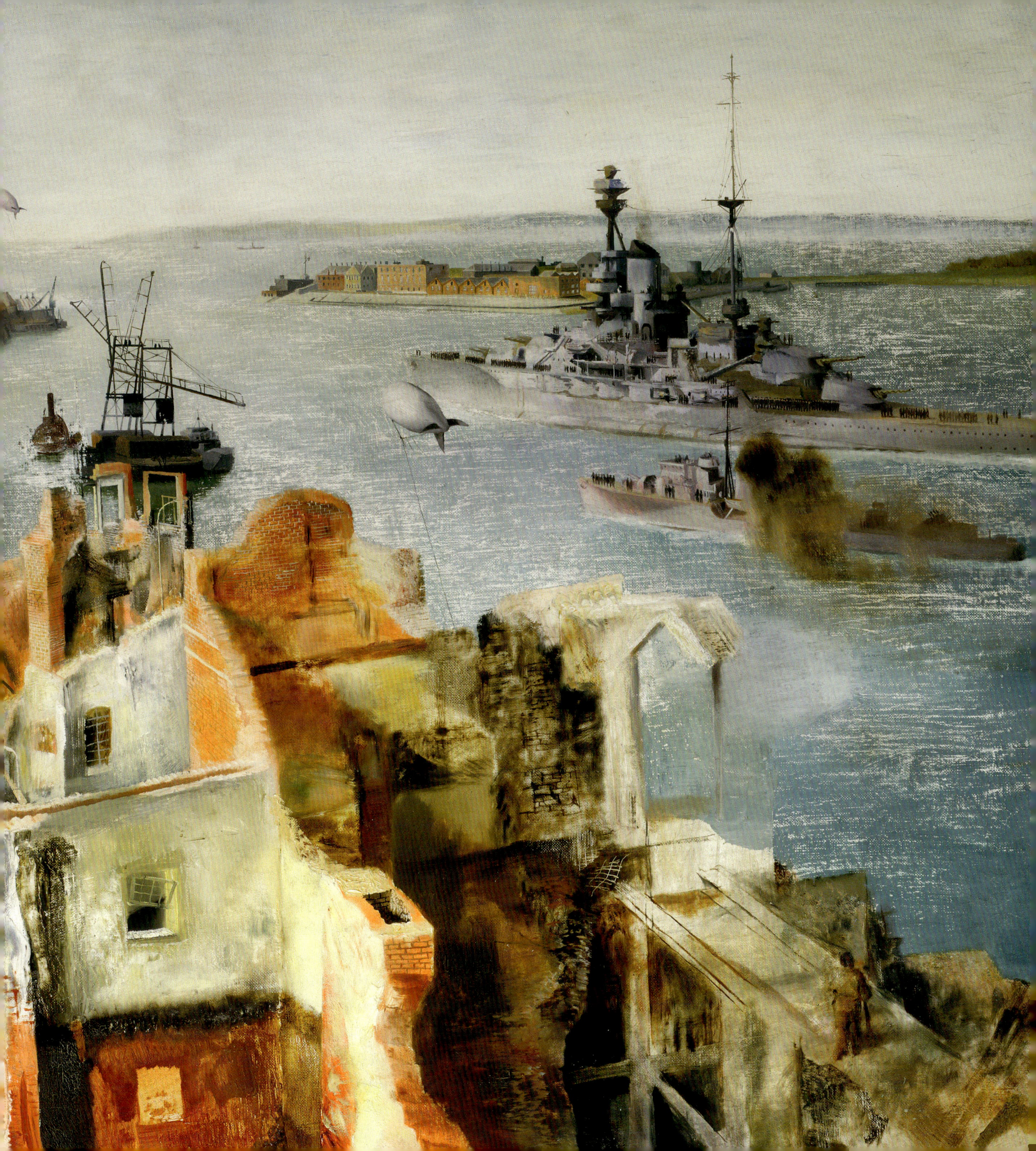

1

Pictorial Narratives of the War at Sea: Wyllie, Eurich and Wilkinson

Pieter van der Merwe

Theatres of War, 1914–18

The First and Second World Wars, as their names imply, covered an unprecedented scope by sea as by land. The 1914–18 conflict had long been feared but arrived at unexpected speed, with less than six weeks from the assassination of the Archduke Franz Ferdinand of Austria on 28 June, which triggered it, to Britain declaring war on Germany on 4 August. Consequently there was little time to reconfigure pre-war naval dispositions in preparation for the conflict. This led to the destruction of Rear-Admiral Cradock's small Pacific Ocean squadron by Vice-Admiral von Spee off Coronel, Chile, in November; Cradock's two principal ships, both armoured cruisers, were sunk with all hands. By that December, lessons had already been learned and the British immolation of von Spee at the Falkland Islands in December was as calculated as it was swift. The naval effort was then briefly focused on the Eastern Mediterranean in the ill-conceived Dardanelles campaign (25 April 1915–9 January 1916).[1] Fought off and around the Gallipoli peninsula of Turkey against Germany's Ottoman allies, its failure ultimately cost Winston Churchill his job as First Lord of the Admiralty.

That aside, the arena for potentially decisive fleet action throughout the war was the North Sea. Conflict there, which started immediately from the declaration, included German naval bombardment of English east-coast towns – Hartlepool, Hull, Scarborough and Whitby – while the main operational bases of the British battle fleet were not in the traditional southern centres of Portsmouth or Plymouth but in Scotland, principally the Firth of Forth and Scapa Flow, Orkney. From there, with generally lighter forces operating off the east coast (from Harwich, the Thames and Dover) and in the English Channel, Britain's strategy was to prevent shipping reaching or leaving German-held ports, contain the High Seas Fleet in its home bases at Kiel and Wilhelmshaven and ideally, should it emerge, destroy it.[2]

Two early actions by small squadrons took place in the Heligoland Bight on 28 August 1914 and on the Dogger Bank, on 24 January 1915, in which battle-cruisers were the largest units involved. Their combined outcome was heavy German losses in ships and men, confirming that effective German fleet action would have to be much more substantial. It was in this context that the Battle of Jutland on 30 May–1 June 1916, by far the largest naval engagement of the war, disabused both the Royal Navy and the British nation of any illusion of ongoing 'Nelsonic' superiority. As Churchill wrote later, Admiral Sir John Jellicoe, the British commander-in-chief, was 'the only man on either side who could lose the war in an afternoon' and that prospect became imaginable as superior German technology exacted unexpectedly high losses on the much larger British Grand Fleet.[3] In the event, German retreat to port left Britain still well in control of the North Sea, with no later renewal of challenge on that scale. Nevertheless, as a critical engagement in which the Royal Navy's loss of men was double that of the enemy and its loss of major ships also greater, Jutland was no cause for self-congratulation (see Chapter 2: The Battle of Jutland).

Britain managed, early in the war, to overrun German colonial bases on the African coast, in the Indian Ocean and the Pacific, and to neutralise the various detached cruising warships linked to those stations. Thereafter, and especially post-Jutland, the nation found itself slowly relearning age-old lessons of the merits of using convoys to protect merchant shipping against German U-boats (from *unterseeboot* / under-sea boat), which had little difficulty eluding British attempts to enforce a blockade in the North Sea. These became, in effect, the principal means that the German Navy could continue an offensive campaign against shipping. From the outbreak of war, they gave devastating proof of their effectiveness in a series of attacks against both British warships and merchantmen, at first in the North Sea and as minelayers, but increasingly against Britain's transatlantic supply lines from Canada down to South America.

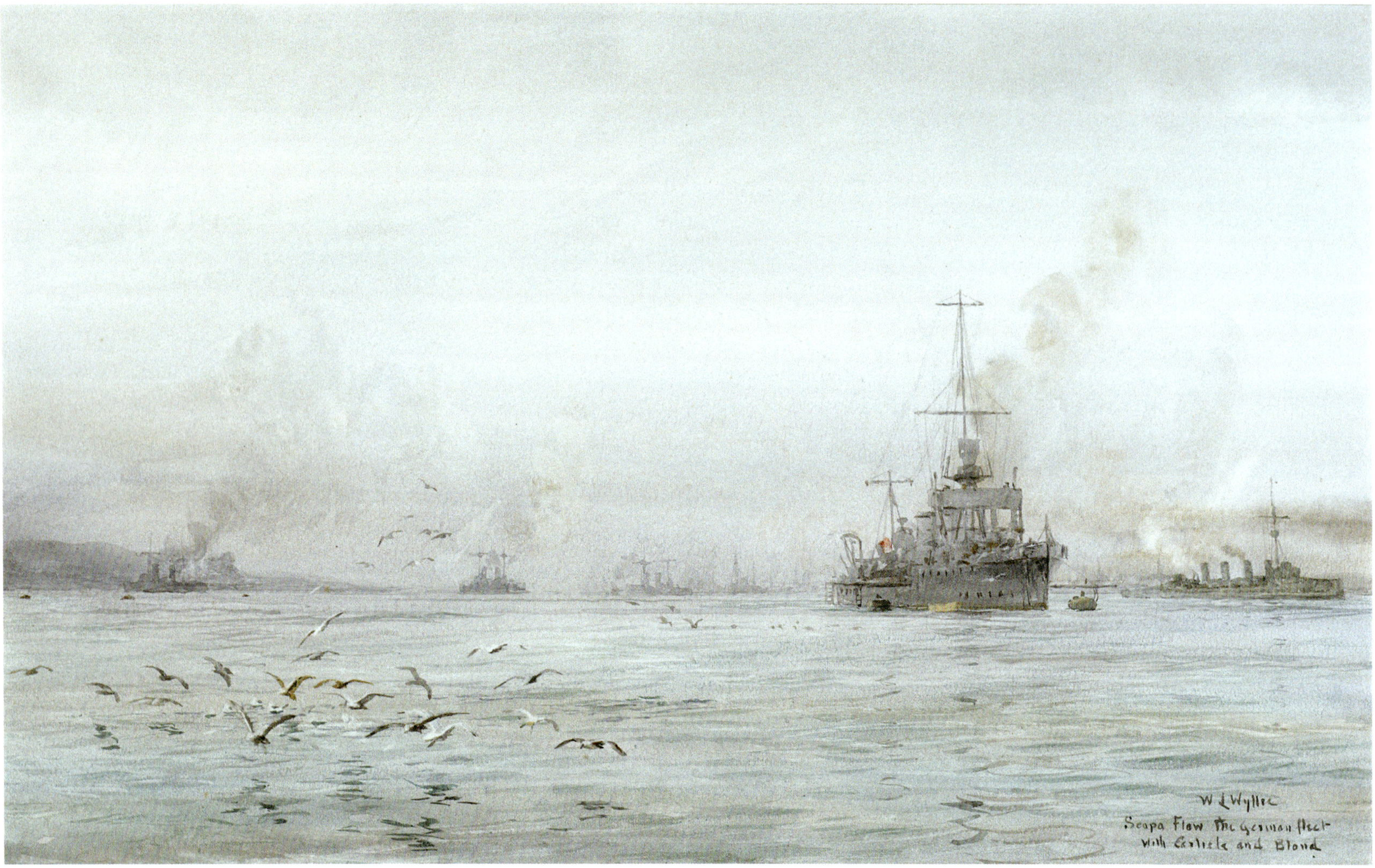

When Germany declared unrestricted submarine warfare against all vessels supplying Britain in February 1915, this raised the losses – in ships and lives – of neutral nations, of which the most significant was still the USA. May that year saw one of the most notorious 'atrocities' – as such acts were represented – when the homeward-bound transatlantic liner, *Lusitania*, was torpedoed and sunk off southern Ireland: out of its 1,959 civilian passengers and crew, 1,198 were killed. Many were Americans, including some wealthy and publicly known figures. Further intensification of the German submarine campaign after Jutland, adding to American losses in ships and men, was a major factor in bringing the USA into war in April 1917.

Early British submarines, by contrast, had mainly been designed for coastal defence and these were still the majority in service, although the new D- and E-types built from 1908 were for longer-range offensive use and four commanders in them won Victoria Crosses in the Dardanelles campaign. Countermeasures against German submarines were also initially limited: effective depth charges, for example, only slowly became available from 1916 and mines proved more successful. However, measures included the ingenious Q-ship system of decoy vessels – small merchant ships with concealed weaponry – whose exploits also garnered some artistic commemoration and a number of Victoria Crosses.[4] Larger German Q-ship equivalents were briefly successful as commerce raiders, the most remarkable being Count Felix von Luckner's *Seeadler* – a sailing ship in which he broke the North Sea blockade in 1916 and, without killing anyone, picked off lone British vessels round into the Pacific until wrecked there the following year.

The last significant – or at least significantly painted – sea operation of the First World War was the British raid on Zeebrugge in support of the final Western Front efforts that led to the Armistice of 11 November 1918 (W.L. Wyllie, Charles John de Lacey and Donald Maxwell all did dramatic treatments of the raid). The unique and visually impressive seaborne finale was the surrender

Fig.11
William Lionel Wyllie
The interned German High Seas Fleet at Scapa Flow, with HMS 'Carlisle' and 'Blonde', c.1918–19
Watercolour on paper
28.4 × 44.4 cm (11 1/8 × 17 1/2 in)
PAF2124

of Germany's High Seas Fleet in the Firth of Forth, a week after the Armistice. Artists William Lionel Wyllie (1851–1931), Norman Wilkinson (1878–1971) and Montague Dawson (1890–1973) recorded this event directly (fig.11). Subsequently the German fleet, after months of increasingly stressful internment in Scapa Flow (and much to the embarrassment of the British), scuttled itself there on 21 June 1919 rather than be divided among the victorious allies. Nine Germans, shot as the Navy tried to restore control, were among the last casualties of the war.

Wyllie's War

Wyllie's vantage point for recording such events was exceptional since at its outbreak, when he was aged 63, he was already a highly regarded marine painter and a Royal Academician, with wide practical sea experience. He had lived overlooking Portsmouth harbour from 1906 to 1907, and his work celebrated Navy and merchant-shipping, including through advertising projects.[5] Though never an official war artist he quickly became a semi-official one, easily obtaining access to Navy vessels on home stations and on short sea trips, and to other military or naval properties.[6] He appears to have visited the east-coast base at Harwich and, in the summer of 1915, spent a period with the Grand Fleet in Scottish waters, from Scapa Flow to the Firth of Forth, and at sea on gunnery exercises. From the Forth he also went out in a C-class submarine being used for testing hydrophone listening devices.[7] His presence at the internment of the German fleet in the Forth, and then at Scapa, was as a guest – for a month – of Admiral Sir Charles Madden in HMS *Revenge*.[8]

While never in battle, his experiences placed him in an eyewitness tradition, going back to the Willem van de Veldes in the seventeenth century, as an officially sanctioned naval artist recording the activities of the fleet. Influenced by J.M.W. Turner – of whom he wrote a biography in 1905 – Wyllie also had historical marine interests and was one of several distinguished founder members of the Society for Nautical Research in 1910. Through this he became a champion of the preservation of HMS *Victory* at Portsmouth after the war and the establishment of the related Victory Museum, and more indirectly of the National Maritime Museum, Greenwich (NMM).[9] He did not live to see the opening of the NMM but knew its forerunners, the Naval Museum and Naval Gallery in the Royal Naval College, where Turner's huge *Battle of Trafalgar* (1823–4) hung from 1829 until both collections passed into the new institution's care in 1936.[10] After his death in 1931, his Society friend and colleague, James Caird – a generous benefactor of both the *Victory* project and the NMM – bought his studio archive (over 5,000 items) for the latter's collection, partly to help his family.

In his voluminous sketches for magazine illustrations, watercolours and set-piece oil paintings, and etched versions of these, Wyllie covered all aspects of the war at sea.[11] Like many others, such as his younger contemporaries Wilkinson and Dawson, his career began as a commercial news illustrator. He worked predominantly for the *Graphic* from the 1870s, while Wilkinson worked for the *Illustrated London News* and Dawson for the *Sphere* in the pre-war years, each continuing through the conflict to varying degrees. The speed at which such work had to be done, much in monochrome (all that was needed for block-making), encouraged both facility and accuracy, either from life or much more often from reported description, sketches by others or photographs. Wyllie, on principle, only used the last when there was no alternative.[12]

He planned complex works in great detail and was skilled at aerial, bird's-eye perspectives – a tradition in marine battle painting associated with the van de Veldes. He was able to arrange to have ships' guns trained and elevated in harbour so he could sketch them and accurately portray the battle actions he wished to capture in his paintings. Although he and others were no nearer the battles they represented than most of their historical predecessors,[13] his studies and more worked-up compositions on paper have vivid immediacy,

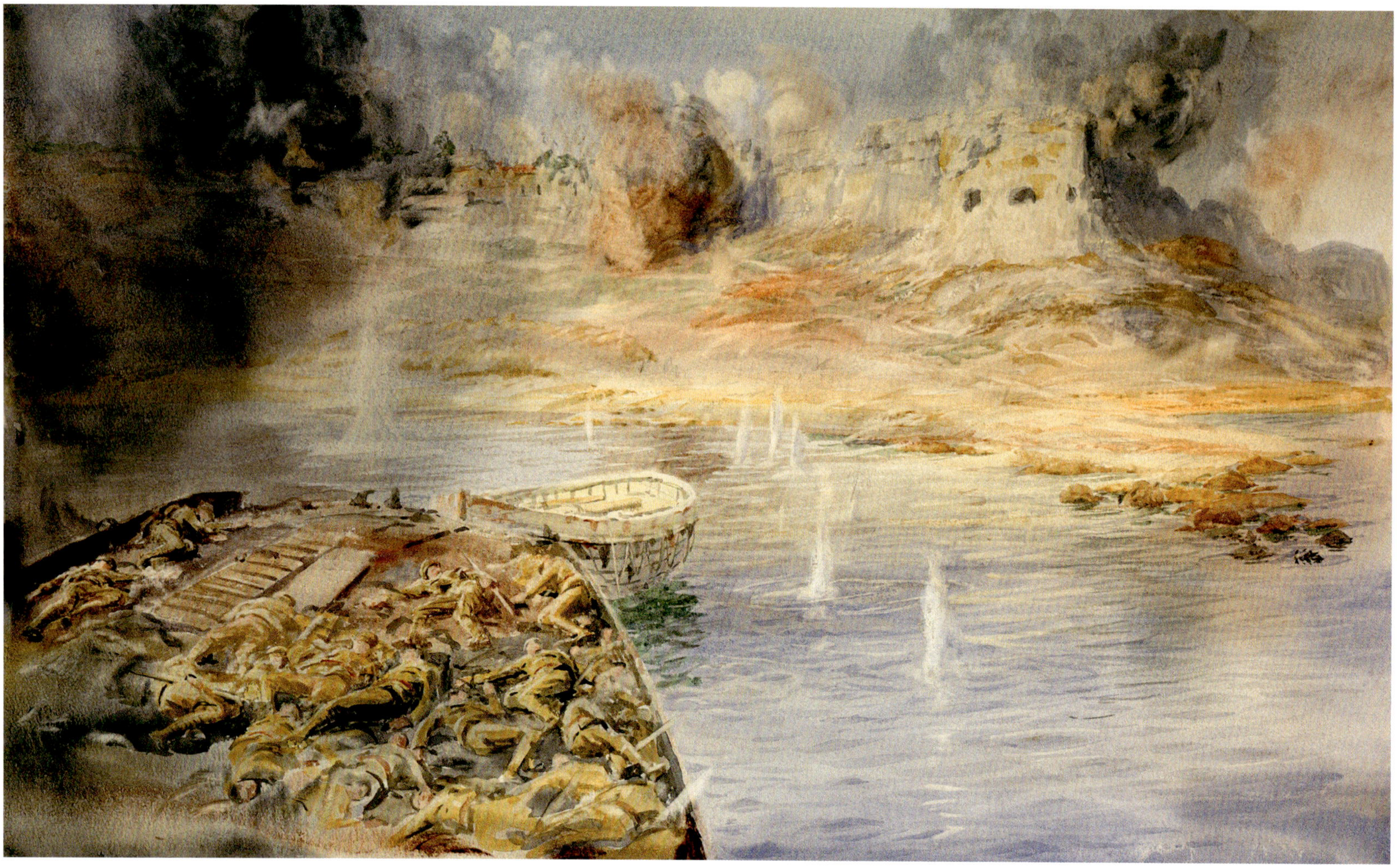

as well as technical accuracy, the latter being of particular importance to the Navy. While the recording aspect of his First World War oils is similar, their aesthetic quality is more variable: all were done in his 60s and 70s and, especially on a large scale, often have a more laborious quality than the freer, romantic, peacetime marine subjects of his earlier years.

Wyllie sold a considerable output of war work in oils, watercolours and his very popular etchings, which were the regular product of his long association (from 1883) with the London print dealer and publisher, Robert Dunthorne. He also co-authored two books, *Sea Fights of the Great War: Naval Incidents during the First Nine Months* and *More Sea Fights of the Great War, including the Battle of Jutland.*[14] The first of these covers worldwide events to May 1915 (which itself indicates how soon German action on the global scale was curtailed) and appeared in September 1918. The second, published in 1919, was apparently a planned sequel focusing on the main battle-fleet operations in the North Sea and neighbouring waters, from 1914 to the Battle of Jutland in mid-1916: after that it just stops, apart from brief mention of the final German fleet surrender and a couple of incidents in 1917 earlier in the book. Each volume was illustrated with 100 pictures (24 in colour), of which a good number were done expressly for them – though in both there are few direct text references to any – but others seem to be just decorative additions of ships and more general views taken from Wyllie's studio archive.[15] Indeed, the earliest pictures in the 1918 book go back to the 1890s to cover the pre-war arms-race years, including reference to Wyllie's experience as a guest of the Kaiser on his racing yacht, *Meteor*, at the Cowes regatta of 1893 (which he covered for the *Illustrated London News*). A few also directly reproduce or relate to works he exhibited during the war and his separately published etchings.[16]

Though credit is often given to German gallantry, the books' tone – verbally and in the illustration – is patriotic and propagandistic: in the first book the floating remains of an unnamed sailing ship, including dead bodies and entitled *Track of the Hun*, are echoed in the sequel by *The Brutal Hun* – a similar view of a U-boat

Fig.12
William Lionel Wyllie
Gallipoli: V-Beach and the fort of Sedd-el-Bahr, seen from the 'River Clyde', 25 April 1915, c.1915
Watercolour on paper
30.1 × 47 cm (11 7/8 × 18 1/2 in)
PAE0974

torpedoing a merchantman – and the corpse-strewn *Track of the 'Lusitania'* (fig.16). German warships are shown sinking, British are not, and Dardanelles operations are safely represented by views of offshore bombardment and landing manoeuvres, not the slaughter of Allied troops on the Gallipoli beaches. Wyllie did not ignore that subject (fig.12) but, if he put one forward for inclusion, the publisher presumably disagreed. Overall the books are good and often detailed general summaries of the naval war, published with opportunistic commercial acumen as it concluded. One cannot be sure exactly how many images he drew expressly for them, but by also exploiting his studio stock and sharing subjects with his exhibited oils and etchings, the books were resource-efficient in both labour and promotional terms. The success of the first volume, at least, is shown by its rapid reprinting in October 1918, before the war's end. Cassell's, the publisher, advertised the second (at 15 shillings) in a list of 'presentation' volumes just before Christmas the following year.[17]

Wyllie continued to paint images of the First World War, including commissions, to the end of his life. All twenty of his Royal Academy exhibits from 1915 to 1919 were war subjects (six, including two aviation paintings, being of the Western Front) and at least nine of the 44 thereafter. His large canvas of the storming of the Zeebrugge Mole in April 1918 – done for the RN Engineering College, Keyham, but today at HMS *Excellent*, Portsmouth – was among his last exhibits at the Royal Academy in 1931. He died suddenly, a few weeks short of his eightieth birthday, while in London to oversee them being hung.

Theatres of War, 1939–45

For Britain, the Second World War at sea (setting aside here the Pacific theatre) was very different, for both operational and technological reasons. These included the speed of the Nazi advance on land in all directions and the development since 1918 of land- and sea-based fighter, bomber and auxiliary air power, and of submarines and communications. By June 1940, Hitler had seized almost the entire north-western European coast from Norway to the Pyrenees: Franco's Spain was a hostile neutral, fascist Italy a German ally, and the Mediterranean rapidly became a field of battle at sea, across most of North Africa, in the Balkans and Greece.

In effect, Britain was under siege, both at home and at key strongpoints of her wider maritime empire. Gibraltar held firm, and (miraculously) Malta; Singapore and Hong Kong rapidly fell to the Japanese after they unexpectedly demonstrated almost unimagined strategic understanding of seaborne airpower in attacking the US Pacific Fleet at Pearl Harbour on 7 December 1941, thereby bringing themselves and a hitherto reluctant USA into the war. The Royal Navy was no luckier with isolated capital ships: three days after Pearl Harbour, HMS *Prince of Wales* and *Repulse* were sunk by Japanese air attacks while trying to interdict their landings in Malaya.[18]

Air power thus made the big-gun capital ship obsolescent, or at least proved that the aircraft carrier would be its likely replacement. That apart, the 1919 peace treaty had prevented Germany rebuilding a fleet for gunnery battles like Jutland. The only such British action – the last ever fought by the Royal Navy (with Australian units) – was against the Italians south of Cape Matapan, Greece, on 27–29 March 1941, when three British battleships, a carrier and light cruisers, engaged one Italian battleship and six heavy cruisers: the Italians lost 2,300 men and three cruisers, with other heavy damage, in contrast to three dead and minor injury to ships on the British side.

Hitler's most effective strategy at sea, both before and after the United States joined the conflict, became the so-called Battle of the Atlantic: the long-running 'convoy war' that cost heavy losses in merchant ships and men to keep Britain supplied with the necessities of daily life and to prosecute the struggle from the Mediterranean to Arctic Russia, and further afield. In this, the supreme German weapon was again the U-boat, now unhampered by a British blockade and operating in coordinated 'wolf-packs',

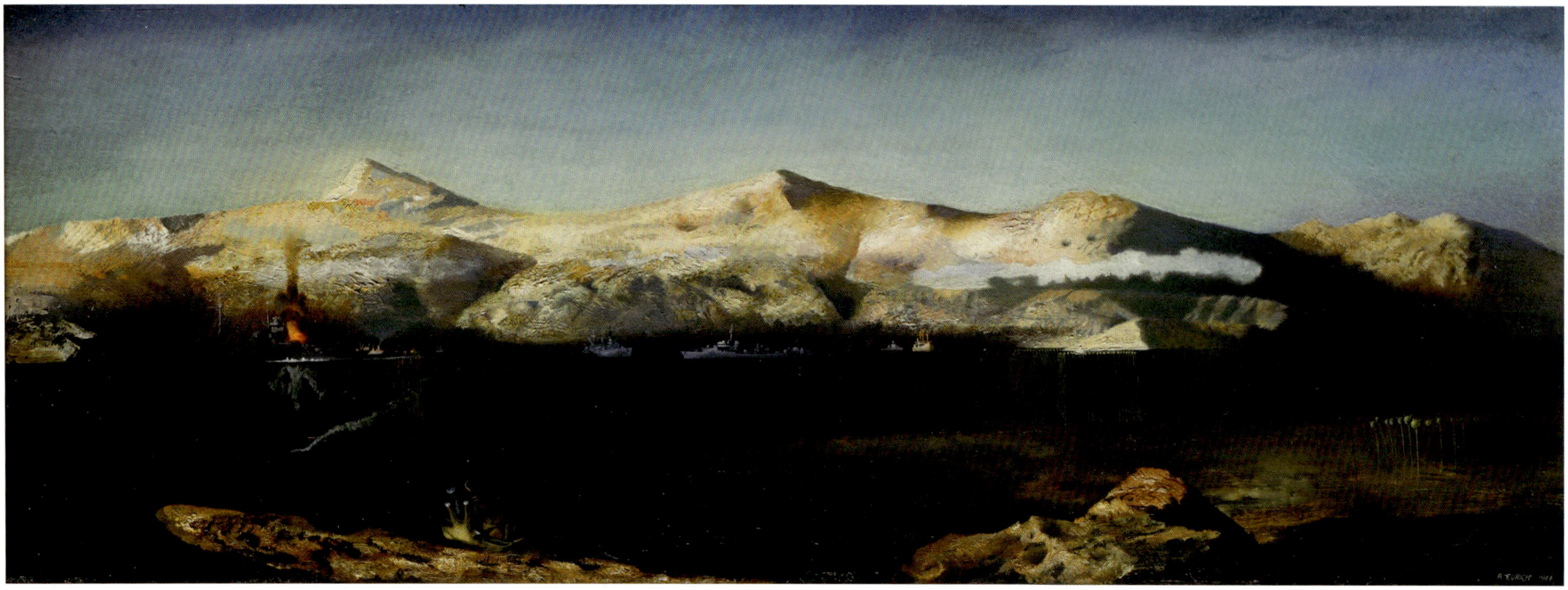

Fig.13 (above)
Richard Eurich
Midget submarine attack on the 'Tirpitz', 22 September 1943, 1944
Oil on panel
40.6 × 106.7 cm (16 × 42 in)
BHC0684

Fig.14 (opposite)
Norman Wilkinson
A Sunderland attacking a wolf pack, c.1942–4
Oil on canvas
76.2 × 101.6 cm (30 × 40 in)
BHC1596

supported from well-defended advance bases in occupied territory, such as those of Atlantic France.

As before, German surface raiders had some early success against merchant shipping, but that soon ended. The Reichsmarine's heavy cruiser, *Admiral Graf Spee*, was in the South Atlantic when war broke out and, after damage at the Battle of the River Plate in December 1939, was scuttled in the Plate estuary off Montevideo, Uruguay, rather than suicidally re-engaging the overwhelming force being summoned against it (or so the Germans were cleverly persuaded to believe). The battleship *Bismarck* broke out into the Atlantic in 1941 and again showed the inadequacy of British First World War ship design by blowing up HMS *Hood*, before itself being crippled by almost equally obsolete British aircraft in the first-ever carrier-borne torpedo attacks on a capital ship at sea. Also lucky for the British was the subsequent sighting of *Bismarck* by air reconnaissance, sealing its fate by superior fleet firepower. The mere presence of its sister ship, *Tirpitz*, lurking in Norwegian fjords, menaced the Arctic convoys to Russia until, after costly air and miniature-submarine attacks, it was finally capsized by bombing in November 1944 (fig.13). *Scharnhorst* and *Gneisenau*, also sister battleships, did some serious damage in two Atlantic forays and during the German occupation of Norway. After they made a daring 'Channel dash' directly back from occupied Brest to Wilhelmshaven early in 1942, *Scharnhorst* was turned against the Arctic convoys until sunk at the Battle of North Cape later in the year. Of all the large German surface raiders, *Admiral Scheer* (a sister of *Graf Spee*) was easily the most successful and was only eliminated by bombing at Kiel early in 1945 when having its guns replaced: they were by then worn out from sinking ships in the Atlantic and Indian Oceans, and sharing the convoy raiding from occupied Norway. This included the infamous PQ17 episode of July 1942, when that Russia-bound convoy was ordered to scatter in fear of a surface attack that had already been called off: no longer under unified escort, 24 of its 35 ships were sunk, largely by U-boats.

The worst hand dealt to those at sea was where the threat of land-based enemy aircraft and submarines were combined, especially in lethal natural conditions such as on the freezing Arctic convoy route. However, the situation was little better in the warmer confines of the Mediterranean, as epitomised in the desperate and very costly relief of Malta by Operation Pedestal, also in summer 1942.[19] The one positive factor was that U-boats proved vulnerable to aircraft, including land-based, long-range patrol bombers like the Hudson and the Sunderland flying-boat (fig.14). German airpower, however, in terms of massive bombing, took a heavy toll on British ports and coastal towns. The strategically planned 'Blitz' of September 1940 to May 1941 hit not only London but also Liverpool, Southampton, Bristol, Portsmouth, Plymouth, Hull and elsewhere, before RAF Bomber Command got into its stride and repaid the compliment on Germany's industrial heartland and ports.

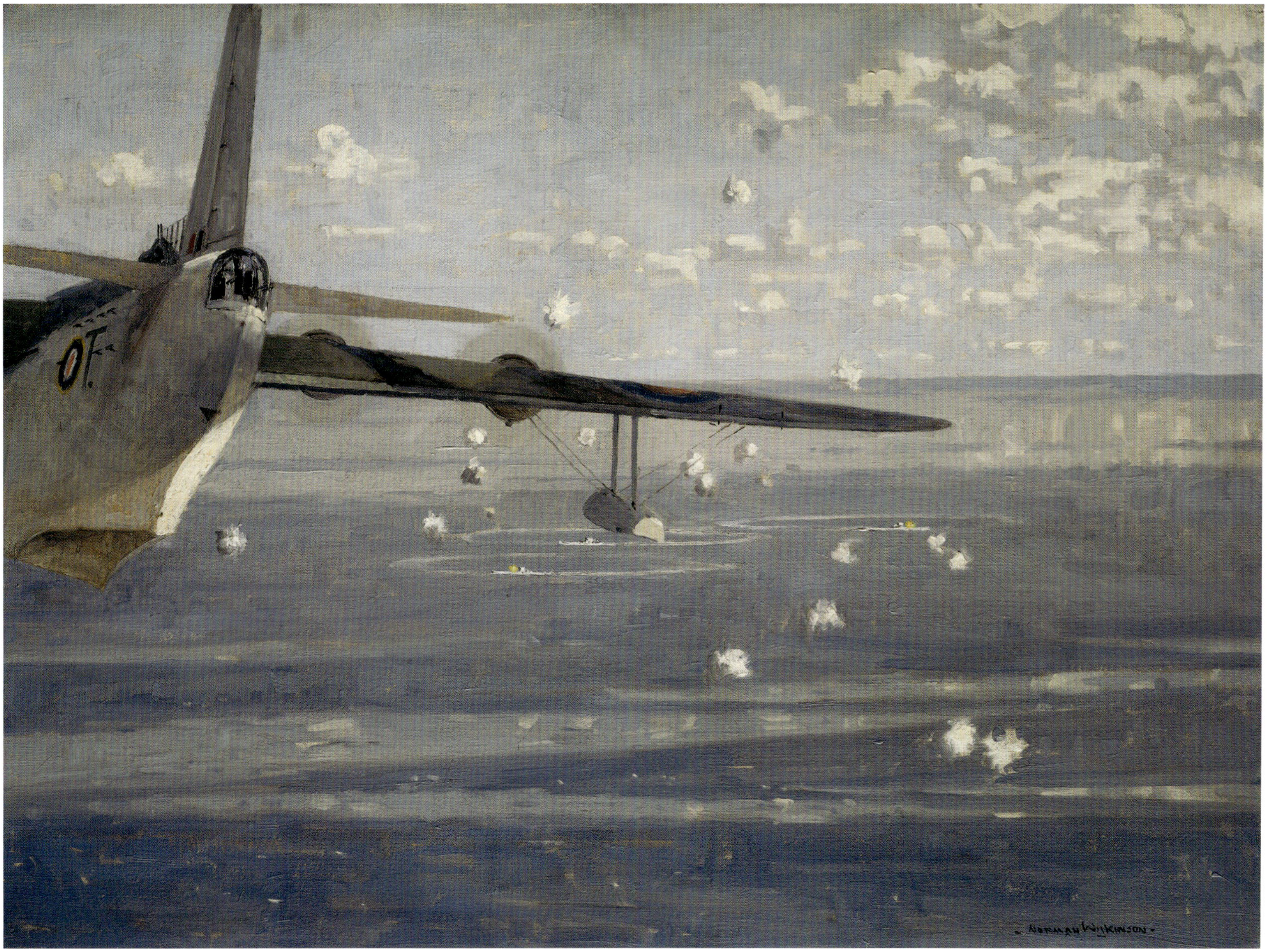

Labours Paid and Unpaid: Eurich and Wilkinson

During the Second World War, the War Artists Advisory Committee (WAAC) commissioned artists to cover general naval and maritime experiences, including areas of support operations and life on the home front, and was a focus for others to make proposals or gifts. Under the chairmanship of its founder, Sir Kenneth Clark, the Committee also supported patriotic morale by showing the results on a rolling basis in the National Gallery, of which Clark was director.

In treating war subjects in home ports and incidents at sea, Richard Eurich (1903–92) was perhaps the most significant modern marine painter to cover the 1939–45 conflict. No less than Wyllie, Eurich saw himself as an heir to van de Velde the Younger and Turner, whose tradition he thought 'should be carried on to enrich and record our heritage'.[20] However, he was also influenced by his contemporaries, notably Christopher Wood (1901–30), and his spacious composition, use of colour and varied manner of painting is striking and distinctive, catching moments of wartime mood as much as transforming received information into his own imaginatively detailed re-creations of events, often with a surreal, toy-like quality. His *Withdrawal from Dunkirk, June 1940* (plate 5), using the traditional device of an aerial perspective, as he frequently did, is one of the best-known examples and brought him instantly into the wartime public eye. Recognising the Dunkirk episode as the epic subject he sought, and with many of the 'little ships' bringing exhausted troops into Southampton where he lived, he secured the commission (for £50) from the WAAC in July 1940. Six weeks later, on 19 August, he delivered the picture for hanging in the National Gallery. The critics singled out Paul Nash's studies of crashed bombers from the new submissions for 'their intuitive grip and sensitive yet powerful presentation',[21] but it was Eurich's menacing cloud of smoke rising from Dunkirk's port, as back-scene to a deeply receding panorama of evacuation from the beaches, that the *Illustrated London News* (7 September) chose to represent the updated display. Although the whole exhibition was dismissed as 'superficial' and 'totally unsatisfactory' by a lofty critic in the *Burlington Magazine*,[22] *Withdrawal from Dunkirk, June 1940* was a sensation at a popular level, with reproductions on sale at the gallery and the image used as the Navy's Christmas card for 1940. In 1941, for the *Britain at War* exhibition at the Museum of Modern Art, New York, it was both the dust-cover image and the frontispiece of the catalogue.[23]

Eurich became an official, salaried Admiralty artist in March 1941 and was elected an Associate of the Royal Academy in 1942, but his labours during the remaining war years left him physically exhausted. He was also greatly affected by the death of both his father and infant daughter within weeks of each other in 1945. Later wartime works by him now at Greenwich that were also reproduced in the *Illustrated London News* (on 21 August 1943) were the survivor subject, *A Ship's Boat at Sea* (fig.37), and *HMS 'Revenge' Leaving Harbour* (plate 6). Four works that were featured in the same publication on 11 March 1944 included two versions of *The great convoy to North Africa, November 1942*: one of these is in the National Maritime Museum collection (plate 7) but the more surreal version, a panorama partly seen enlarged through binoculars at dead centre, is in the Imperial War Museum. The accompanying *Illustrated London News* comment called this 'strikingly original in conception' and Eurich's work 'perhaps the most notable contribution' to the ongoing National Gallery display.[24] Responding to his group there, the *Yorkshire Post* of 4 March 1944 – with pardonable local bias – observed that 'Richard Eurich, of Bradford [his birthplace], continues his brilliant series of sea pictures.'

One remarkable group of paintings accepted by the WAAC was unique in being the only one that attempted to document the entire Royal and Merchant Navy war, along with RAF Coastal Command elements. This was undertaken from early 1942 by Norman Wilkinson, who by the 1930s was a successful and well-known painter, not least through public familiarity with his work done for railway posters.[25] Wilkinson served as a junior Volunteer Reserve naval officer in the First World War, including in the Gallipoli campaign, where he claimed (late in 1917) to have been the only professional artist present. At the suggestion of Admiral A.H. Christian, he had painted watercolours covering the early amphibious aspects of the campaign.[26] These were exhibited at the Fine Art Society in November 1915, when eight appeared in colour in the *Illustrated London News* as 'by an eye-witness':[27] thirty-six, interleaved with related line vignettes, appeared in his handsome book *The Dardanelles, Colour Sketches from Gallipoli*, published on 8 December, for which he also wrote a seven-chapter introduction.[28] Produced at the same time that calls for the appointment of 'official war artists' were growing (Muirhead Bone was the first appointed in May 1916), its opening paragraphs lamented 'the lack of pictorial records of this war – records made by artists of experience, who actually witness the scenes they portray. Our descendants will surely regret the omission'.[29]

Back in England Wilkinson then briefly commanded a minesweeping launch in the Channel but, in early 1917, invented and thereafter successfully developed wartime 'dazzle-painting' (see Chapter 5: Art, Artists and the Home Front), for which he was awarded an OBE and, later, £2,000.[30] In October 1917, when it was hanging in the Royal Institute of Oil Painters exhibition, the Imperial

War Museum purchased his painting of HMS *Queen Elizabeth* at Gallipoli and (at his suggestion) went on to commission a set of 12 of other naval events of the war, and a set of dazzle subjects.[31]

From 1939 to 1942, with the high rank of honorary air commodore, Wilkinson was the RAF's Inspector of Camouflage but subsequently turned his illustrative and naval experience to creating his painting series known as *The War at Sea*. It was an entirely personal project and, while he also did other war subjects and further versions from the set, apparently sprang from the same belief in making wartime 'pictorial records' that he mentioned in 1915. This time, for most of the series, he had to work from secondary sources and information supplied: for instance, Admiral Sir Bruce Fraser, who directed the night-time sinking of the *Scharnhorst*, sent him personal notes on that event, including on the distinctive colours of British and German star-shell and tracer fire.[32] He also claimed, though unreliably, to be the only painter present on D-Day, but at 65 he was certainly the oldest such witness to the Normandy invasion from seaward: Anthony Gross (1905–84), an official war artist since 1941, waded ashore with the troops, and Albert Richards (1919–45) parachuted in and fought as a Royal Engineer as well as painting.

Wilkinson's presence resulted from a well-sanctioned personal invitation to join the destroyer *Jervis* before it was reassigned to D-Day and, in this way, he made studies of the naval side of the landings on 6 June 1944 and for some days afterwards. By summer of that year he had, by his own account, completed 56 canvases and, after discussion with Sir Kenneth Clark and a little havering from the WAAC – partly since donation, at least on this scale, was unprecedented – offered them all to the Committee as a gift for the nation.[33] They were first shown at the National Gallery in September 1944 (as *The War at Sea*) to general critical and public approval. The set was by then 54 but one was omitted, possibly for practical reasons.[34]

While some have greater painterly and compositional quality than others, the series gives a comprehensive and often dramatic impression of the overall nature of British sea operations, excluding (as Wilkinson acknowledged) the important role of submarines. That nine cover what he saw on and around D-Day is understandable (fig.15); that 13 focus on aspects of the convoy war and 11 (some overlapping) show the impact of air power at sea underlines the differences already mentioned between the nature of the 1939–45 conflict and its predecessor, including its 'total' aspect in making so many civilian seamen enemy targets from the start. Only seven treat duels of any sort between naval surface vessels, and grandiose images of British capital ships are notably few compared to those of the smaller units of a fleet in which 'hostilities only' citizen-sailors had an equal claim to commemoration as admirals. In five examples U-boats are depth-charged, sunk or surrendered (to flying-boat attack) but aircraft carriers are largely absent. The only 'portrait' instance is not of a British vessel but a fine horizon view of the USS *Hornet* launching the Doolittle raid against Tokyo in 1942, which, with a more obviously photo-based image of Pearl Harbour (plate 9), makes the set's only nod towards the war in the Pacific.

In making his original offer, Wilkinson later claimed that he 'stated in the strongest terms [that] the pictures should remain as a single collection and not be split up'.[35] However, after they returned from an exhibition tour in Australia and New Zealand in 1947, 14 were allocated to the Imperial War Museum, one to the Royal United Services Institute, and 39 to the National Maritime Museum. Wilkinson objected and began a campaign for those sent to the IWM to be re-allocated to the NMM, which was keen to have the whole set. When this got nowhere, he appealed directly to the Prime Minister, Clement Attlee, and his intervention saw all reunited at Greenwich except *Convoy*, the first in the National Gallery show, which remains with the Royal United Service Institute.

Wilkinson's OBE was elevated to a CBE in 1948, recognising his RAF work and his artistic generosity. He presumably also restored peace with the IWM, to which he later gave other items, including his Dardanelles sketchbook.

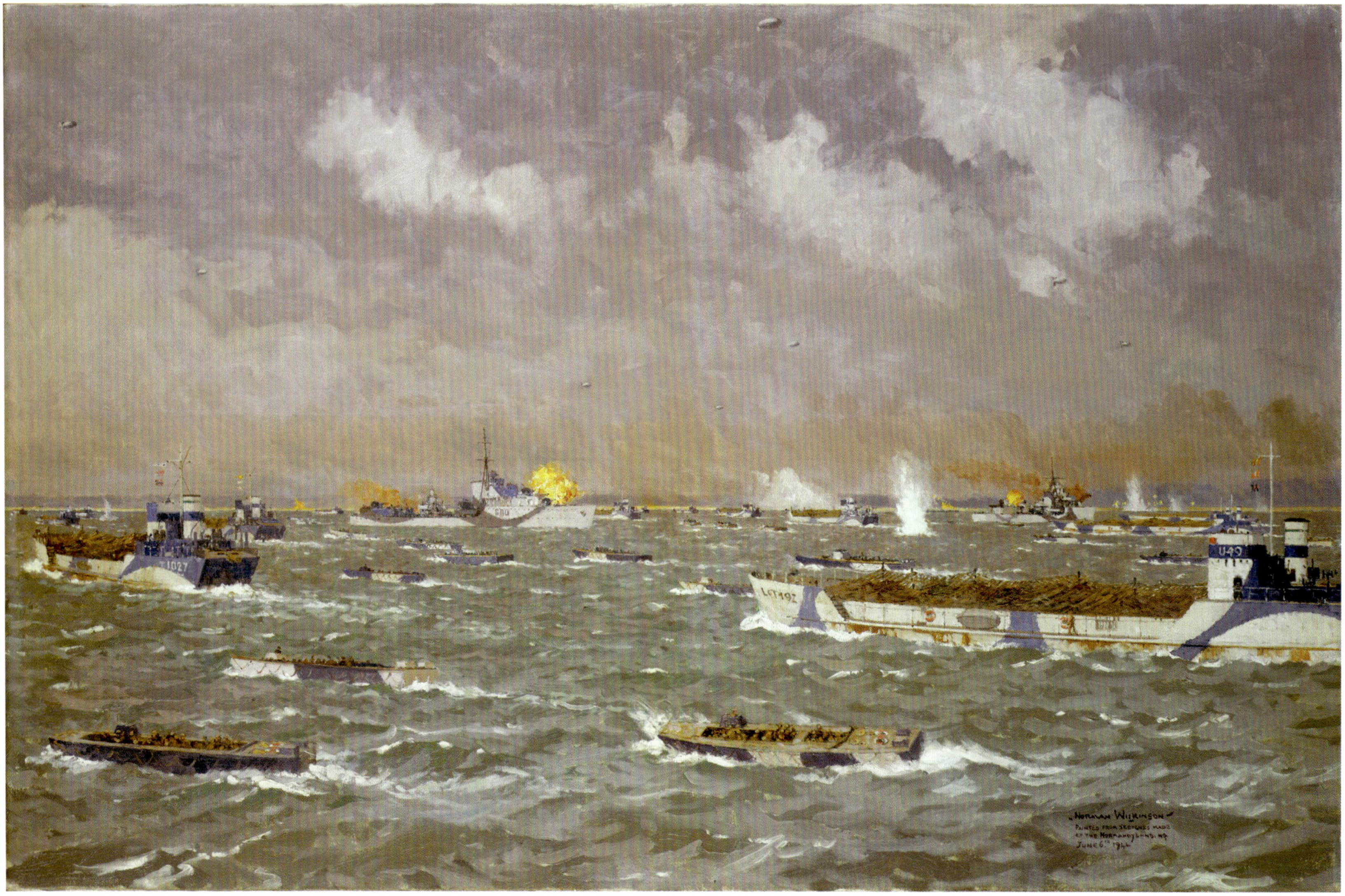
NORMAN WILKINSON
JUNE 6th 1944

Part of the value of both Wyllie's and Wilkinson's streams of production is that they steer a comprehensive if stylistically conservative course through the main events at sea in both the World Wars. From that baseline one can view other areas (portraiture, for example, being neither artist's field) and more overtly 'modern' modes of representation, among which Edward Wadsworth's 'dazzle' subjects, in oil and print, and Eric Ravilious' *Submarine* lithographs and other similarly stylised war work are perhaps supreme examples. Richard Eurich was a much more 'contemporary' artist than Wyllie or Wilkinson in terms of manner and the influences on him, but he had difficulty in selling work after the Second World War as his idiosyncratic representational style fell out of favour (though it saw a strong revival from the late 1960s). Consequently, the tendency is to place these artists together in the 'documentary' tradition of marine painting going back to the seventeenth century. While all three would have acknowledged this inheritance it may explain, given the more abstract main directions of twentieth-century art, why they and most of their wartime colleagues command specialist and popular admiration rather than being generally regarded, like Paul Nash, Edward Wadsworth and Henry Moore, as among the great artistic names of their time. That does not diminish their merits, in the case of Wyllie and Wilkinson as notable figures at the end of a long 'reportage' tradition before it was fully overtaken by photography, and, in the case of all three artists, for the talents they brought to interpreting wartime events. Their war work, moreover, occupied only a short period in three otherwise long working lives: taken together, their joint history of Royal Academy exhibition alone spans well over a century, from Wyllie's first appearance there in 1868 to Eurich's last in 1989.[36]

Fig.15
Norman Wilkinson
June 6th: landing craft going in to the beaches (D-Day), 1944
Oil on canvas
101.6 × 152.4 cm (40 × 60 in)
BHC1635

The Sinking of the *Lusitania*

Robert J. Blyth

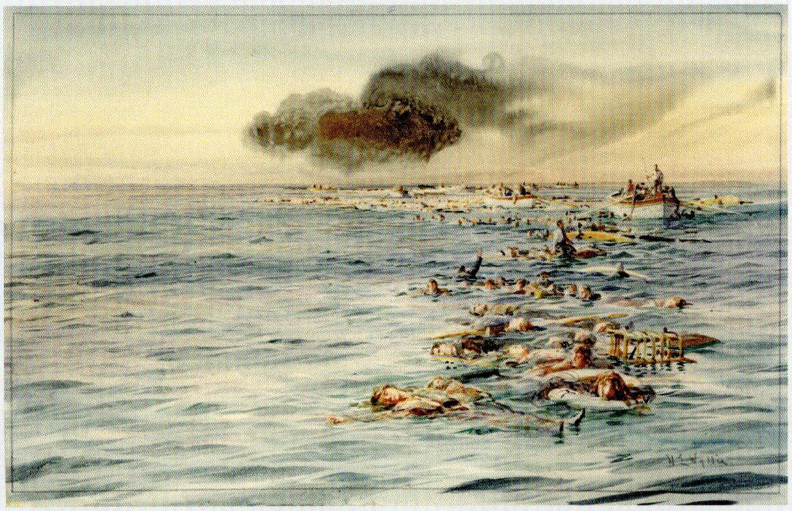

Fig.16
William Lionel Wyllie
The Track of the 'Lusitania', c.1915–19
Watercolour on paper
28.6 × 44.3 cm (11 ¼ × 17 ½ in)
PAF1553

Linking the old world with the new and typifying the excitement of the Edwardian age, the great transatlantic liners of the early twentieth century were technological triumphs, embodying speed, luxury and modernity. These vessels of individual opportunity and collective optimism were potent statements of national pride and achievement. The sinking of the RMS *Titanic* on 14–15 April 1912, following the White Star Line ship's fateful collision with an iceberg en route to New York, was a major blow to this confidence. That a huge, prestigious and 'unsinkable' ship could founder mid-ocean on its maiden voyage with such enormous loss of life was, therefore, a profound shock and one with a lasting legacy. Just three years later, however, the RMS *Lusitania*, another renowned liner, sank in the Atlantic, not as a result of improvident misadventure but as a consequence of an act of war.

In 1915, the Cunard Line advertised its transatlantic crossings in the American press as usual. Next to this unremarkable timetable the German embassy in Washington, DC, placed an ominous warning dated 22 April. It read:

> Notice! Travellers intending to embark on the Atlantic voyage are reminded that a state of war exists between Germany and her allies and Great Britain and her allies; that the zone of war includes the waters adjacent to the British Isles; that, in accordance with formal notice given by the Imperial German Government, vessels flying the flag of Great Britain, or any of her allies, are liable to destruction in those waters and that travellers sailing in the war zone on the ships of Great Britain or her allies do so at their own risk.[37]

Despite the evident danger, 1,959 passengers and crew embarked and the *Lusitania* began its scheduled run to Liverpool, leaving New York on 1 May. There was general confidence that the liner's speed would protect it from U-boat attack.

The previous day, *U-20* left Emden on a mission against Allied shipping. It had some success in the seas around the south-west coast of Ireland, sinking a schooner, the *Earl of Lathom*, and two British freighters, *Candidate* and *Centurion*. With fuel running low, the U-boat's captain, Lieutenant-Commander Walther Schwieger, decided to return to base. Early in the afternoon of 7 May, however, the crew spotted a large ship off the Old Head of Kinsale: it was the *Lusitania*. Schwieger resolved to intercept but, following a standard zigzag, anti-submarine course, the ship turned and steamed away in the opposite direction. The captain had no hope of bringing the much faster liner within range but his disappointment was short-lived: the *Lusitania* turned again, making a perfect target for *U-20*. On board the ship, passengers had finished lunch and were at leisure, enjoying the calm seas. At 2.10 PM and at a distance of 700 metres, Schwieger fired a torpedo that struck the ship and exploded, tearing a hole in the starboard side. The great liner was doomed.

The initial explosion was quickly followed by a huge internal blast as high-pressure steam pipes ruptured, causing further destruction and falsely leading some to believe that a second torpedo had hit.[38] Electrical power failed almost immediately and, in the pitch-black interior of the ship, panic ensued. Bulkhead doors could not be opened, some passengers were trapped in the lifts and a number of other technical issues exacerbated the huge loss of life. It also took the *Lusitania* ten minutes to slow to a speed at which it was possible to launch the lifeboats. In the meantime, with water flooding through the gaping hole in her hull, the ship listed severely to starboard. As a result, lifeboats on the starboard side swung out of easy reach, making boarding very risky and slow. On the port side, they were difficult to launch without seriously damaging or overturning them on the protruding rivets of the hull. In any case, there was almost no time to organise an evacuation. After the torpedo detonated, the ship sank in just 18 minutes: 1,198 passengers and crew died – over 60 per cent of those on board – leaving 761 survivors of what

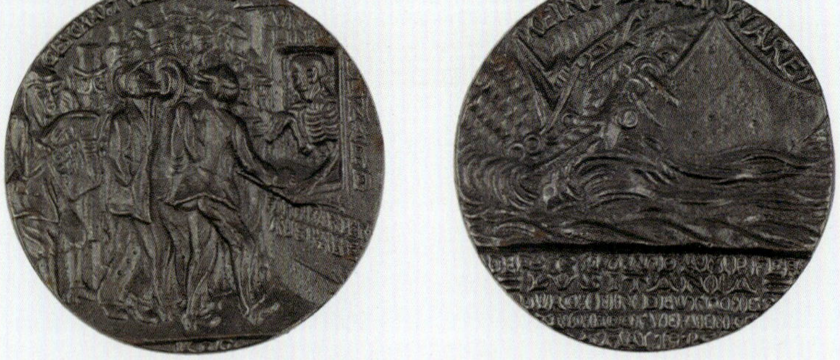

Fig.17 (far left)
After Karl Goetz
Medal commemorating the sinking of the RMS *Lusitania*, 1915
Iron
5.5 cm (2 ⅛ in) diam.
MEC2677

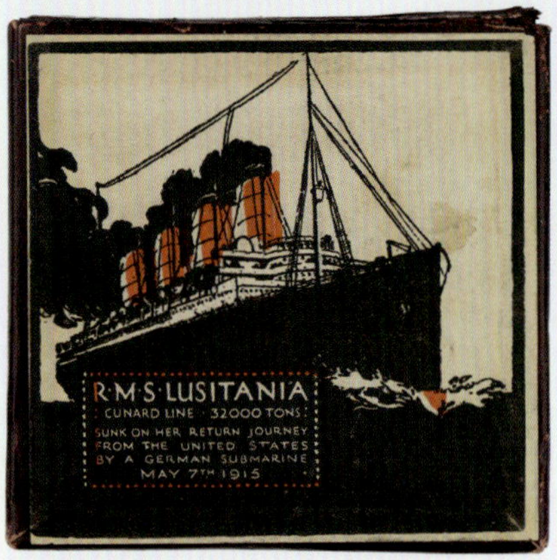

Fig.18 (left)
Presentation box for medal commemorating the sinking of the RMS *Lusitania*, 1915
MEC2677.2

became one of the most notorious incidents in the history of the First World War at sea.[39]

News of the sinking was met with shock on both sides of the Atlantic. *The Times* reported that it 'was received throughout the United States with a hush of horror'.[40] In the days that followed, further details emerged as survivors recounted their experiences. The paper's correspondent in Ireland wrote movingly of the scene ashore:

> those survivors who had friends and family on the ship could not rest. Women appealed piteously for news of husbands and children, and now and then a distraught mother, hearing that a little boy or girl had been taken to this or that house, would go to ask, with dread and hope fighting for the mastery, 'Is it my boy?' or 'Is it my little girl?' Unhappily in hardly any case was hope justified.
>
> Behind [the] broader facts of the disaster lie hundreds of individual experiences which will never be forgotten – however much they may wish to forget – by those who have lived to remember. Who shall tell of the last leave-takings of husband and wife, parent and child, friend and friend, in the moments before the ship went down? These are locked in the hearts of those who were spared, far too sacred to be spoken.[41]

One person told of seeing the ship in its final seconds as it sank beneath the waves: 'I heard no screaming at the last, but a long, wailing, mournful, despairing, beseeching cry'.[42] Many survivors were taken to Liverpool, the *Lusitania*'s home port and ultimate destination. Here, and elsewhere, anti-German feeling boiled over; localised rioting broke out and German-owned shops and businesses (or those thought to be) were attacked.[43] As the days passed more and more bodies were washed ashore, some identified, others not. Many were never recovered through being trapped forever, deep in the *Lusitania*, or otherwise lost to the vagaries of the ocean.

On 8 May, in the immediate aftermath of the sinking, the German authorities issued a statement declaring the liner was carrying contraband of war and was a legitimate target, being classified as an armed auxiliary warship. Indeed, on the same day the *New York Times* published the ship's manifest, which categorically showed that the *Lusitania* was carrying munitions (4,200 cases of rifle cartridges, amounting to 4.2 million rounds) and other war supplies. This report was suppressed in Britain, heightening the propaganda impact of the event as a dastardly German attack on a vessel innocently conveying passengers – non-combatant men, women and children – with a cargo unconnected to the war effort.[44]

The most famous, or perhaps infamous, artistic response to the sinking was the satirical German medal struck by Karl Goetz (1875–1950). Under the legend '*KEINE BANNWARE!*' ('No contraband!'), the obverse shows the liner in its final moments descending into the deep, with the incident mistakenly dated 5 May 1915. The reverse depicts a skeletal Death in the Cunard ticket office taking passengers' fares, while the legend reads '*GESCHÄFT ÜBER ALLES*' ('Business above all'). In arriving at such a macabre representation, Goetz was, like many German artists of the time, reworking the medieval 'Dance of Death' motif to reflect on the horrors of contemporary warfare. However, according to Goetz, the blame on this occasion lay firmly at the feet of the Cunard Line, supported by the hypocritical outrage of the Allies. News of the medal's production found its way into the Allied press (presumably for propaganda purposes) on the first anniversary of the sinking. It was met with disbelief and disgust in Britain and the United States. When, for example, the *American Art News* carried details of the medal, readers expressed 'doubt as to the truth of the story and [voiced] indignant protests against its publication', necessitating the inclusion of images the following week to confirm its existence.[45] Responding to the mass of German commemorative war medals, Arthur Evans, the president of the Royal Numismatic Society, wrote to editors of the *Burlington Magazine*, noting Goetz's use of

Fig.19
Fred Spear
Enlist, US recruitment poster, 1916
Lithograph
82.3 × 58.7 cm (32 3/8 × 23 1/8 in)
Imperial War Museums
ART.IWM PST 3284

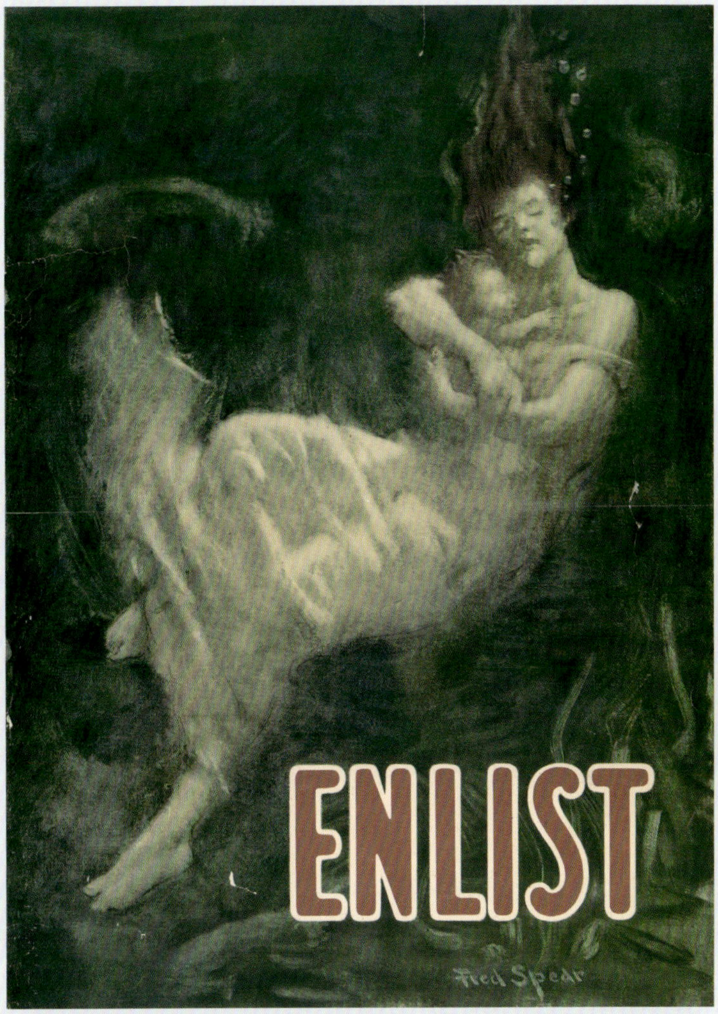

'deliberately falsified information' and a 'sentiment perverted by the cult of hate'.[46] Some 300,000 copies of the medal were produced in Britain (fig.17) on the instructions of Captain Reginald Hall, Director of Naval Intelligence, as anti-German propaganda and sold with an explanatory leaflet, *A German Naval Victory*. Analysing the symbolism of the reverse side, the leaflet notes that 'This picture seeks apparently to propound the theory that if a murderer warns his victim of his intention, the guilt of the crime will rest with the victim, not the murderer'. The text included on the lid of the presentation box (fig.18) concludes that the medal itself is 'proof positive that such crimes are not merely regarded favourably, but are given encouragement in the land of Kultur'.[47]

In W.L. Wyllie's powerful and affecting watercolour, *The Track of the 'Lusitania'* (*c*.1915–19, fig.16), the bodies of men, women and children are strewn across the smooth, blue-grey water, marking the fateful course of the liner. Many are dead; some cling to wreckage; others, a lucky few, are in lifeboats helping survivors. The composition draws the eye around this arc of death and despair to a distant plume of drifting black smoke on the horizon, an ephemeral memorial for the vanished ship and hundreds of dead within. Wyllie reproduced, and most probably expressly drew, the image as a colour plate in the second of his two volumes on the war at sea.[48]

The shock of the event was also exploited by the military as a persuasive subject for recruitment posters, both in Britain and, later, in the United States. The British Army was still a volunteer force when the *Lusitania* was sunk; conscription was not introduced until March 1916. Maintaining mass recruitment in the face of mounting losses on the Western Front and elsewhere was a top priority. Posters urging men to join up were seen across the country and played on patriotic sentiment and anti-German fervour. For propagandists, the sinking of the *Lusitania*, like the executions of the British nurse Edith Cavell and the merchant sea captain, Charles Fryatt, in October 1915 and July 1916 respectively, provided an unequivocal example of German barbarism and the threat it posed to civilisation. One poster appealed to Irishmen to 'avenge the *Lusitania*' and another implored recruits 'to take up the sword of justice'. In a powerfully emotive image, the artist Fred Spear depicted a drowned mother – descending into the deep while cradling her infant child – with a single word: 'ENLIST' (fig.19). This chilling poster was also used in the United States when it joined the Allies in April 1917.

The sinking of the *Lusitania* was just one event in the long and costly war at sea. Over and above the many thousands of lives lost, nearly 7,000 Allied and neutral ships were sunk, totalling more than 13 million tons. At its height in 1917, the sheer scale of German U-boat activity threatened to starve Britain of vital food and resources. The crisis demanded a speedy and effective response from the Royal Navy. The introduction of convoys escorted by warships and more sophisticated methods of anti-submarine warfare eventually turned the tide, allowing the Allies to sustain and increase the pressure on the Western Front that eventually secured victory. Schwieger himself was a victim of this more determined policy when his U-boat was chased by a British warship and destroyed by a mine in September 1917.

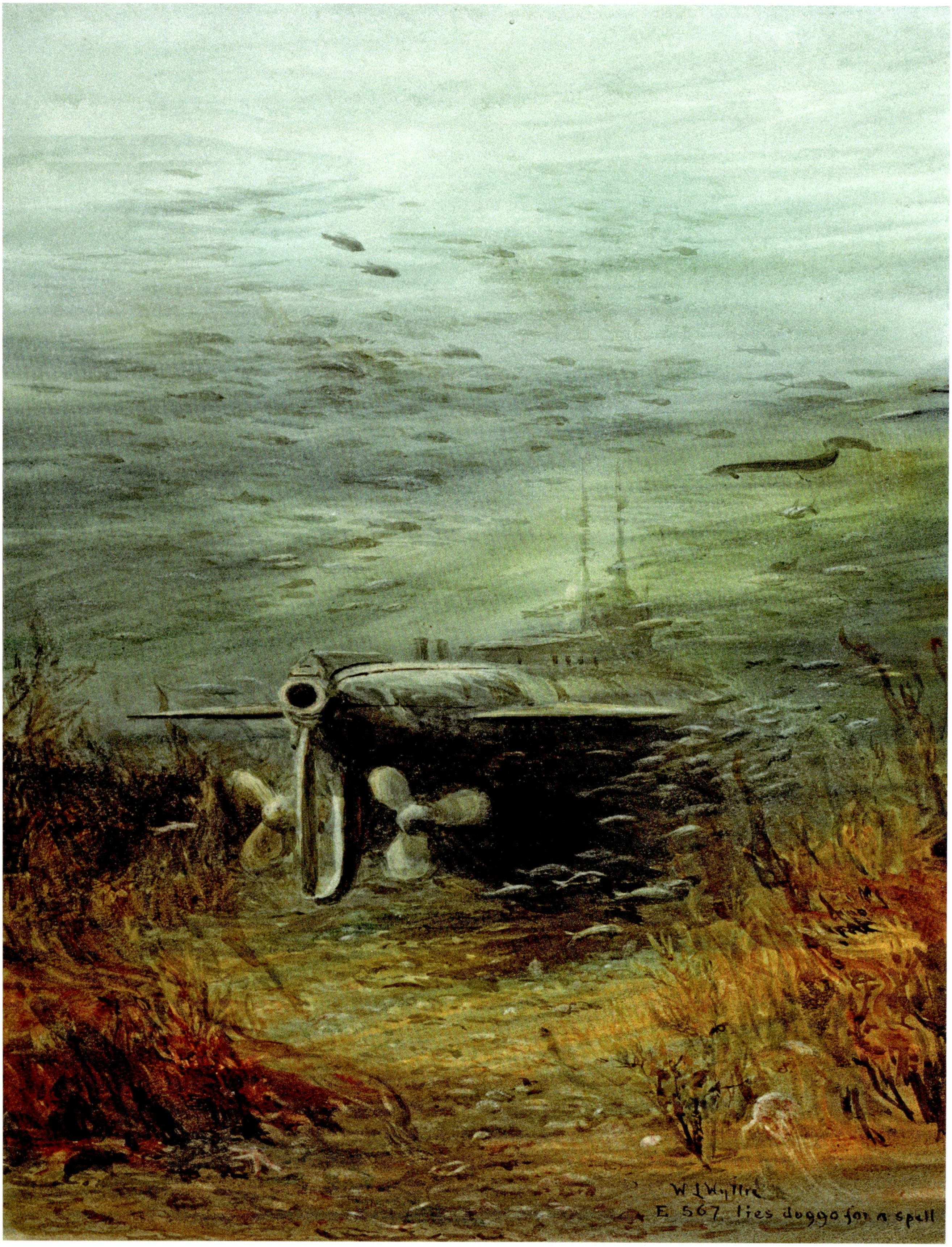
W L Wyllie
E 567 lies doggo for a spell

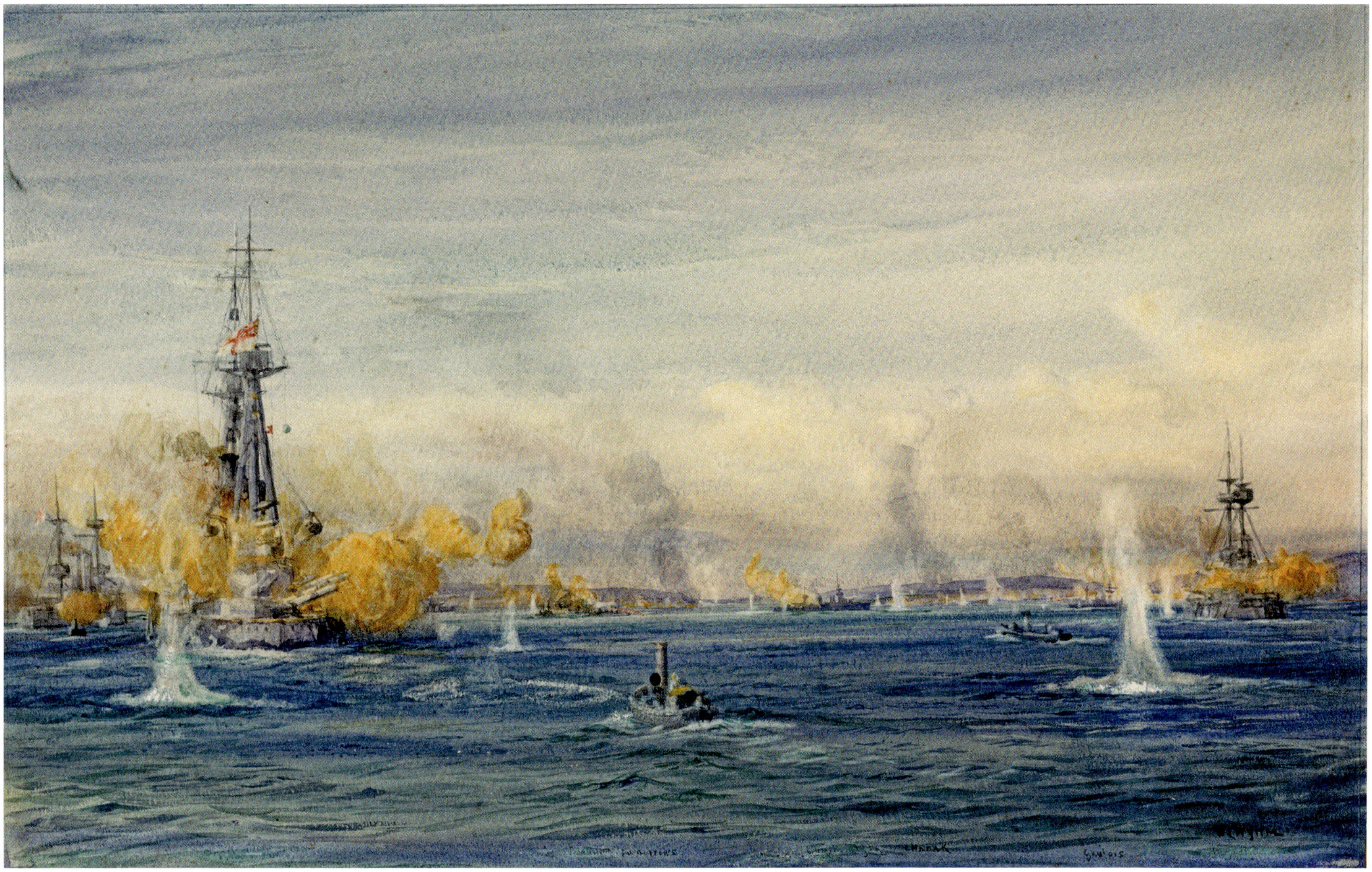

Plate 1 (opposite)
William Lionel Wyllie
'E 567 lies doggo for a spell': a submarine on the sea-bed, c.1917
Watercolour on paper
43.1 × 26.8 cm (17 × 10 ½ in)
PAF1786

Plate 2 (above)
William Lionel Wyllie
Bombarding Turkish Batteries at Chanak, c.1915–18
Watercolour on paper
28.9 × 43.9 cm (11 ⅜ × 17 ¼ in)
PAF0900

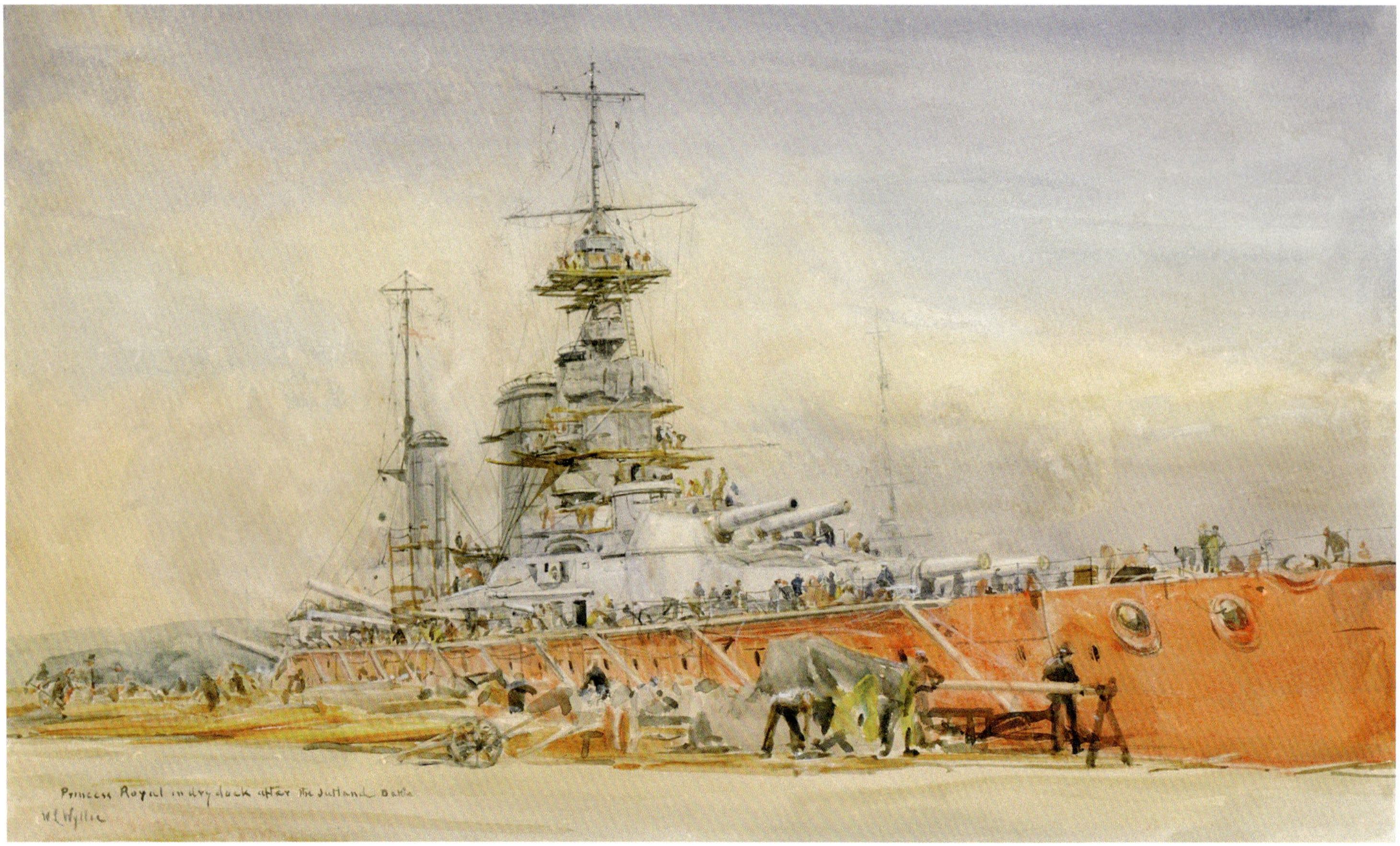
Princess Royal in dry dock after the Jutland Battle
W L Wyllie

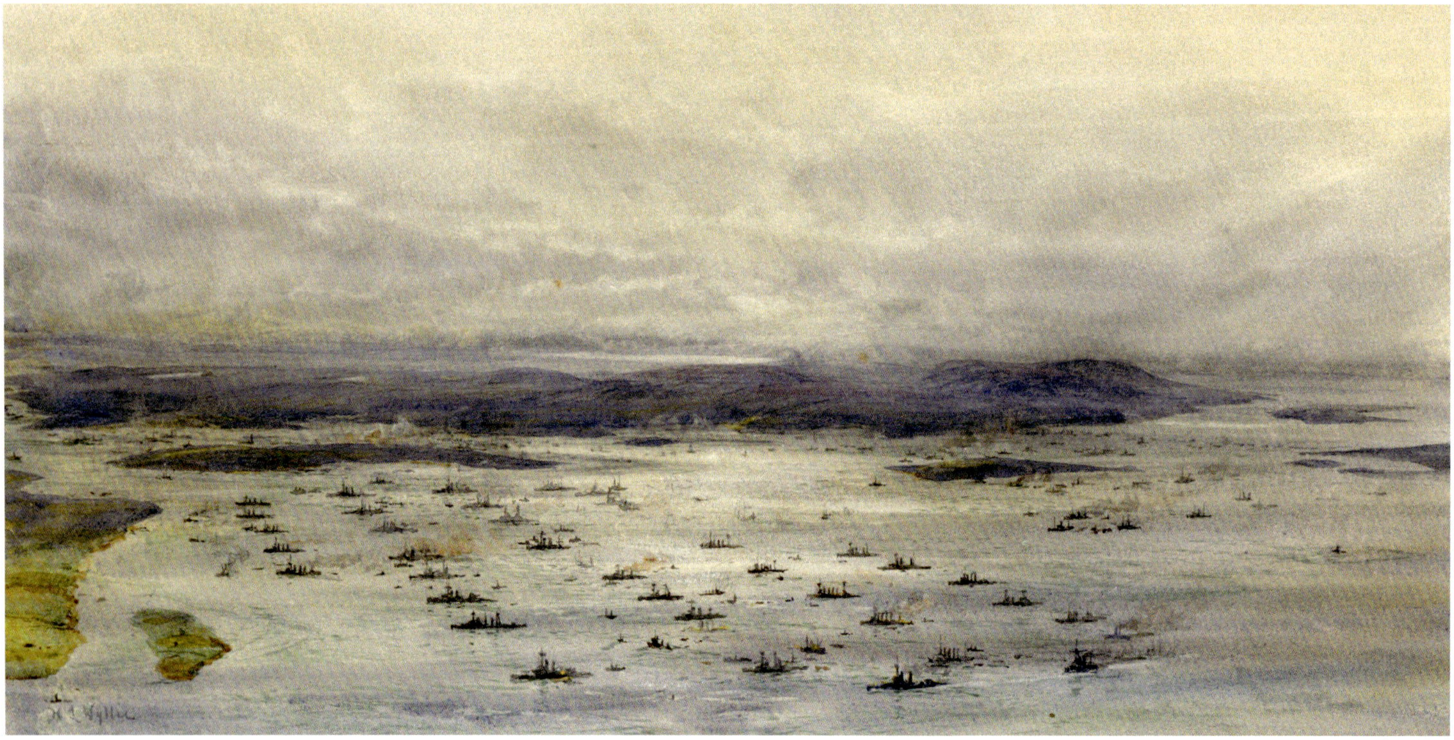

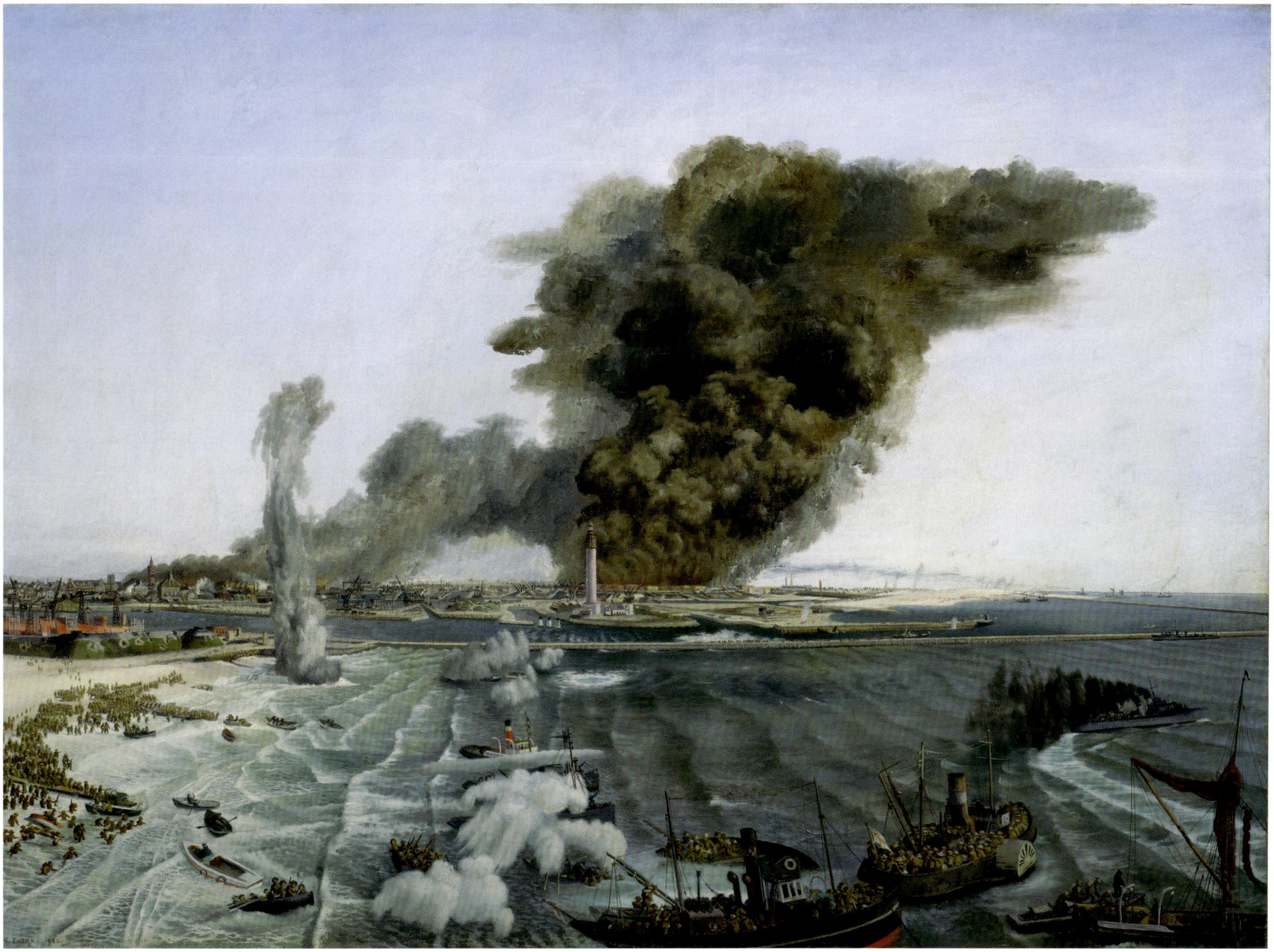

Plate 3 (opposite, above)
William Lionel Wyllie
'Princess Royal' in dry dock after the Jutland Battle, 1916
Watercolour on paper
26.9 × 43.2 cm (10 5⁄8 × 17 in)
PAF1805

Plate 4 (opposite, below)
William Lionel Wyllie
The Grand Fleet in Scapa Flow, c.1918
Watercolour on paper
29.5 × 47.8 cm (11 5⁄8 × 18 7⁄8 in)
PAF1756

Plate 5
Richard Eurich
Withdrawal from Dunkirk, June 1940, 1940
Oil on canvas
76.2 × 101.6 cm (30 × 40 in)
BHC0672

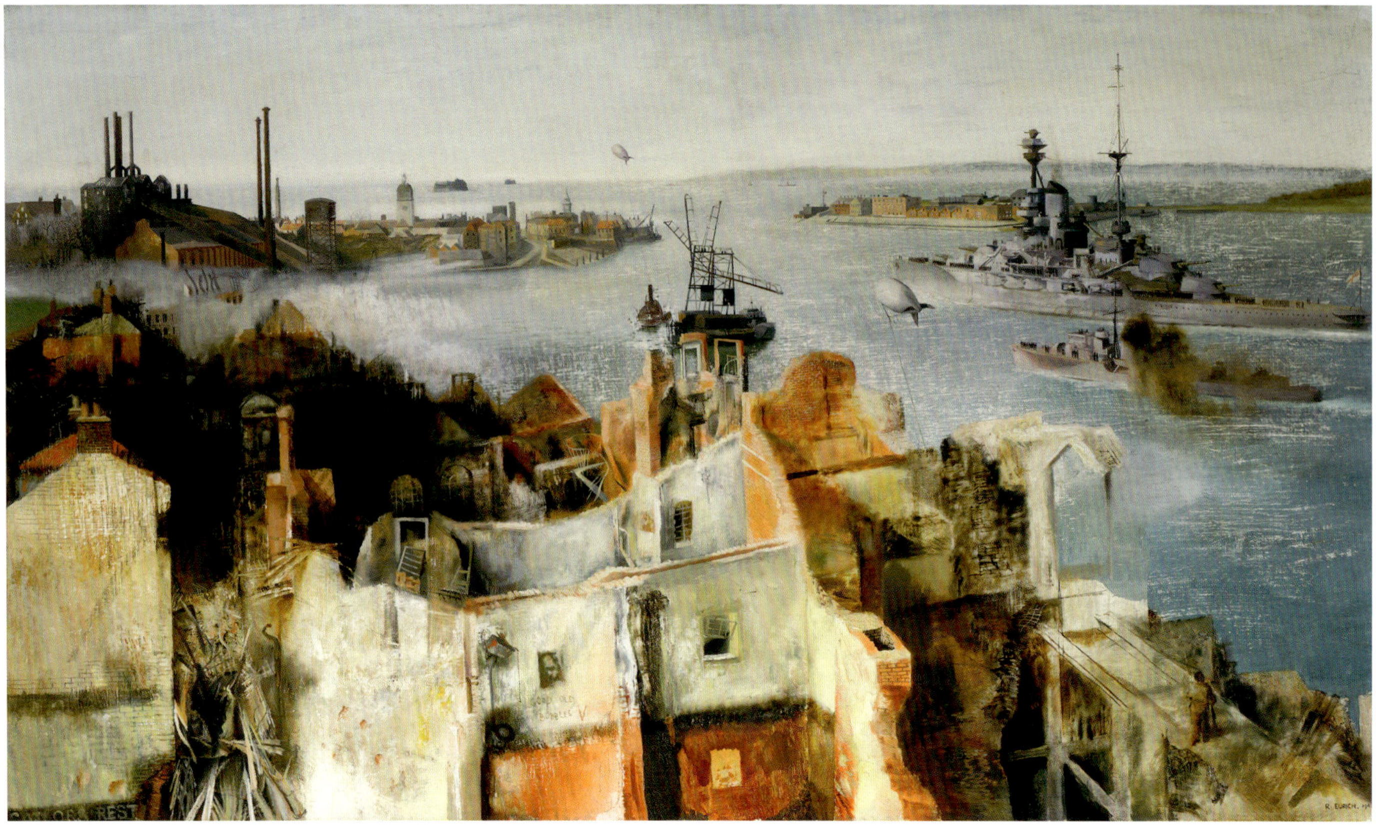

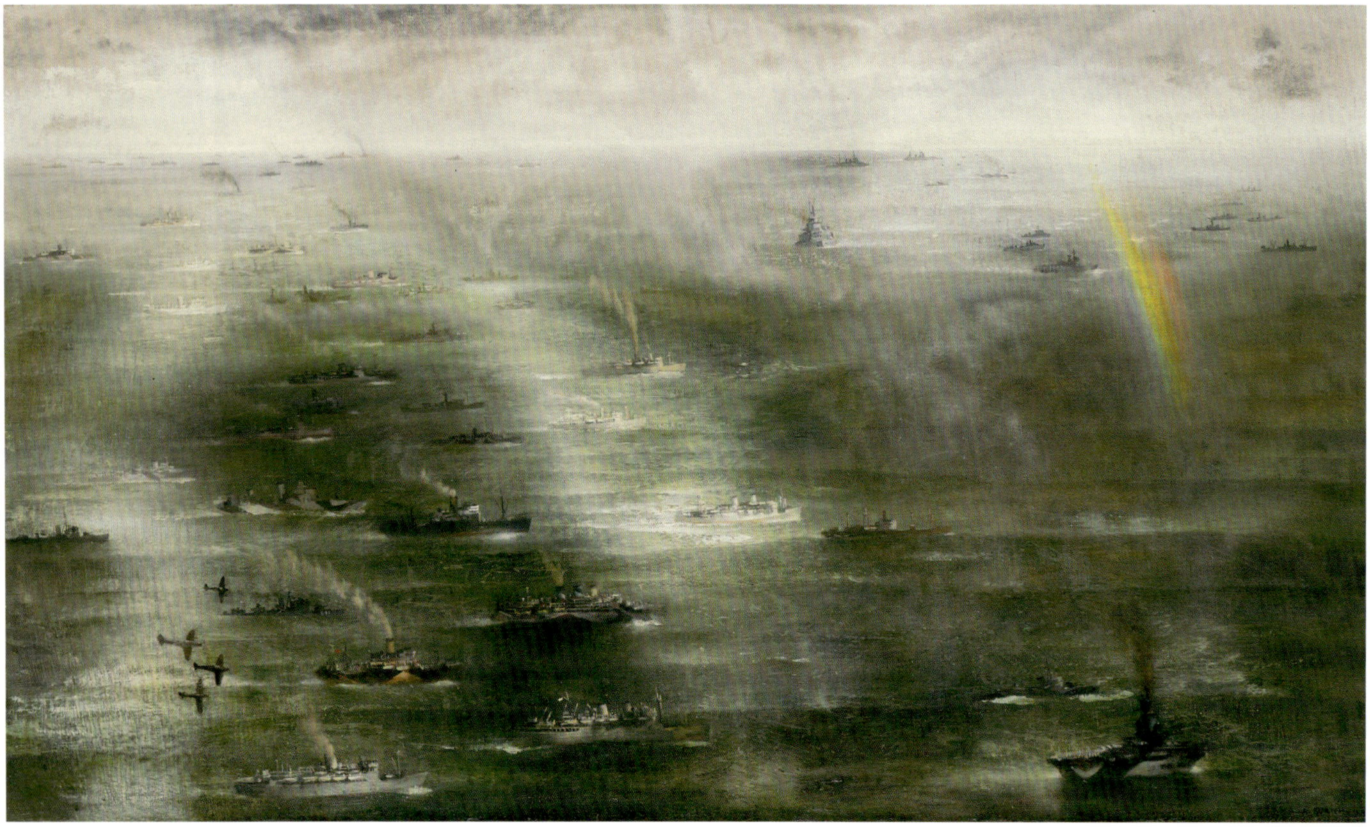

Plate 6 (opposite, above)
Richard Eurich
HMS 'Revenge' Leaving Harbour, 1942
Oil on canvas
76.2 × 127 cm (30 × 50 in)
BHC1571

Plate 7 (opposite, below)
Richard Eurich
The great convoy to North Africa, November 1942, 1943
Oil on canvas
76 × 127 cm (29 7/8 × 50 in)
BHC1565

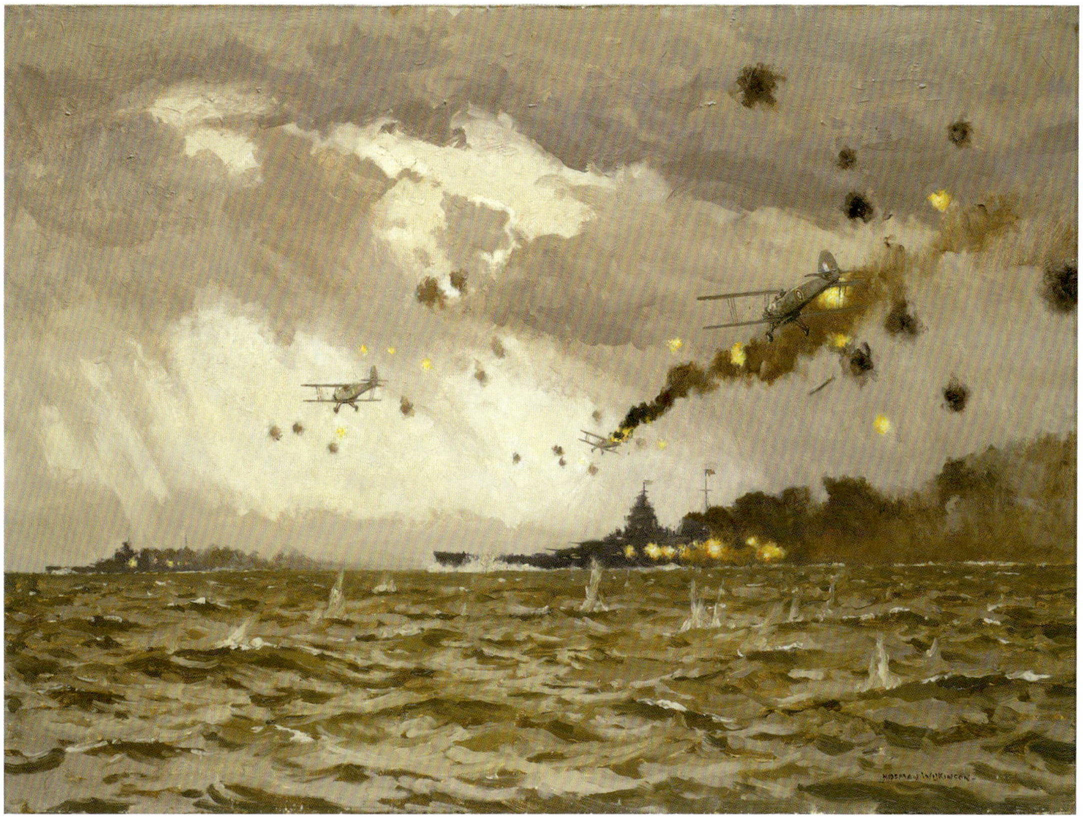

Plate 8 (above)
Norman Wilkinson
Air Attack on the 'Scharnhorst' and 'Gneisenau', 11–12 February 1942, c.1942–4
Oil on canvas
76.2 × 101.6 cm (30 × 40 in)
BHC1625

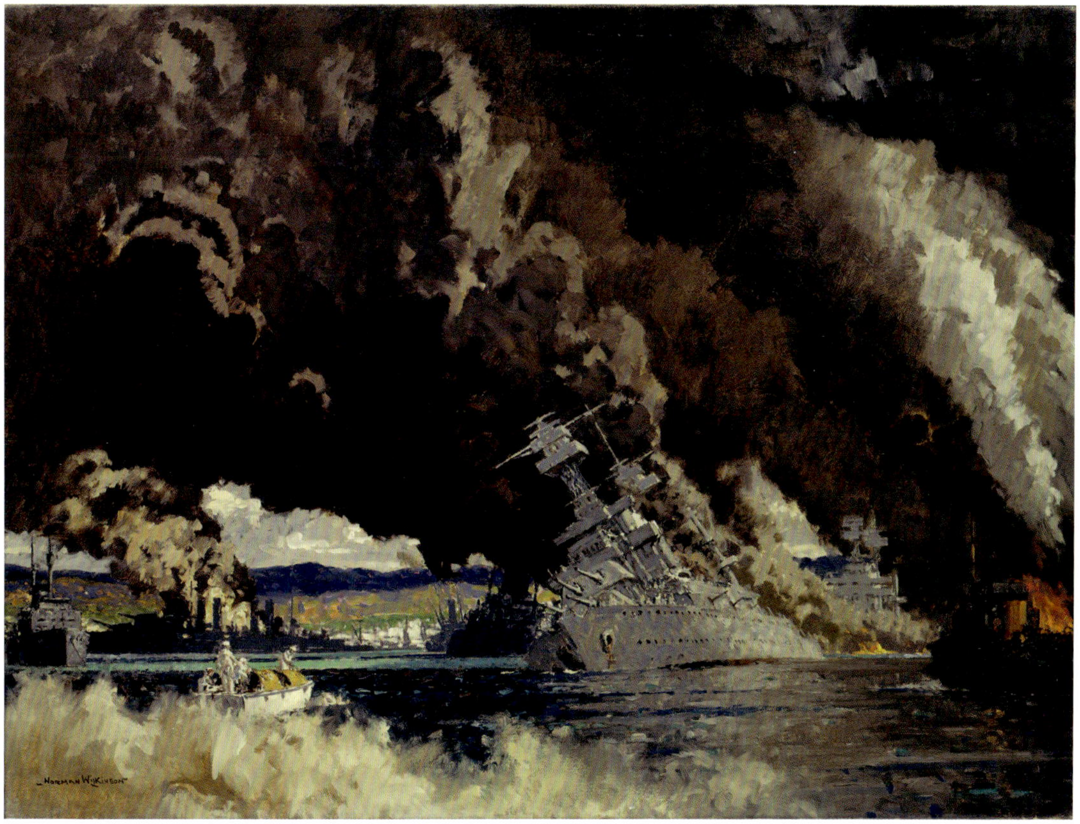

Plate 9 (below)
Norman Wilkinson
Japan signs her own death warrant: attack on Pearl Harbour, 7 December 1941, c.1942
Oil on canvas
76.2 × 101.6 cm (30 × 40 in)
BHC1634

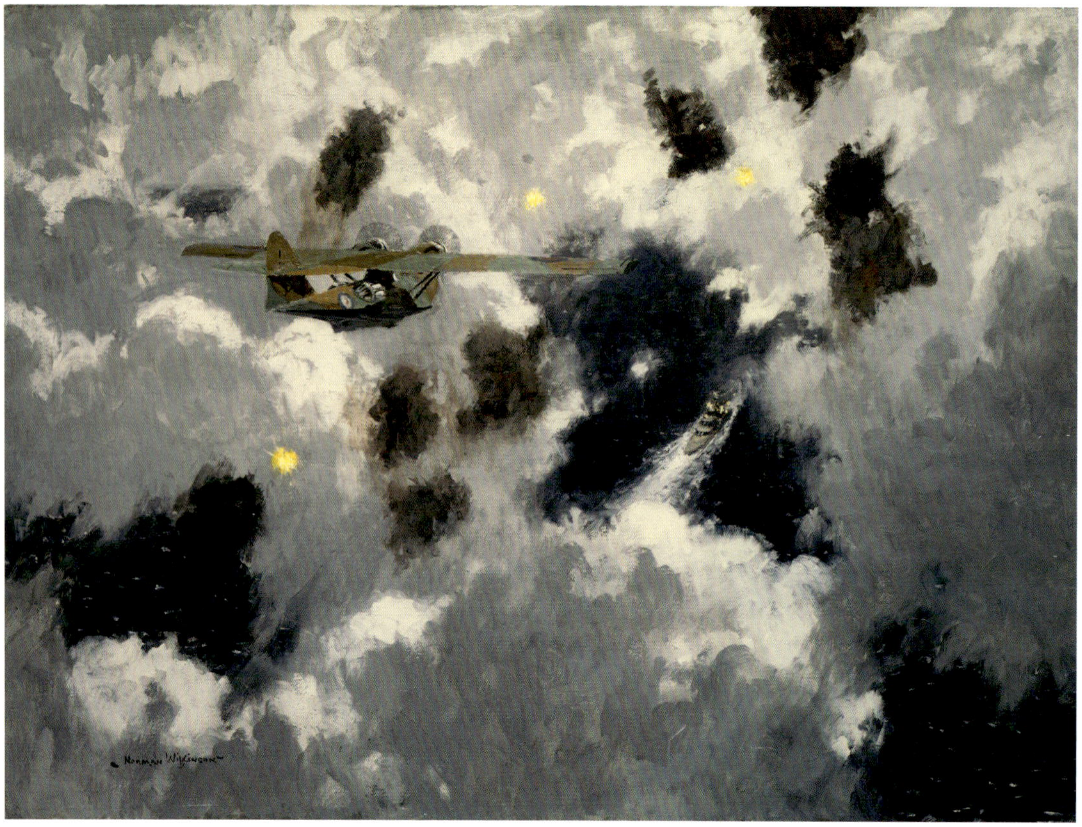

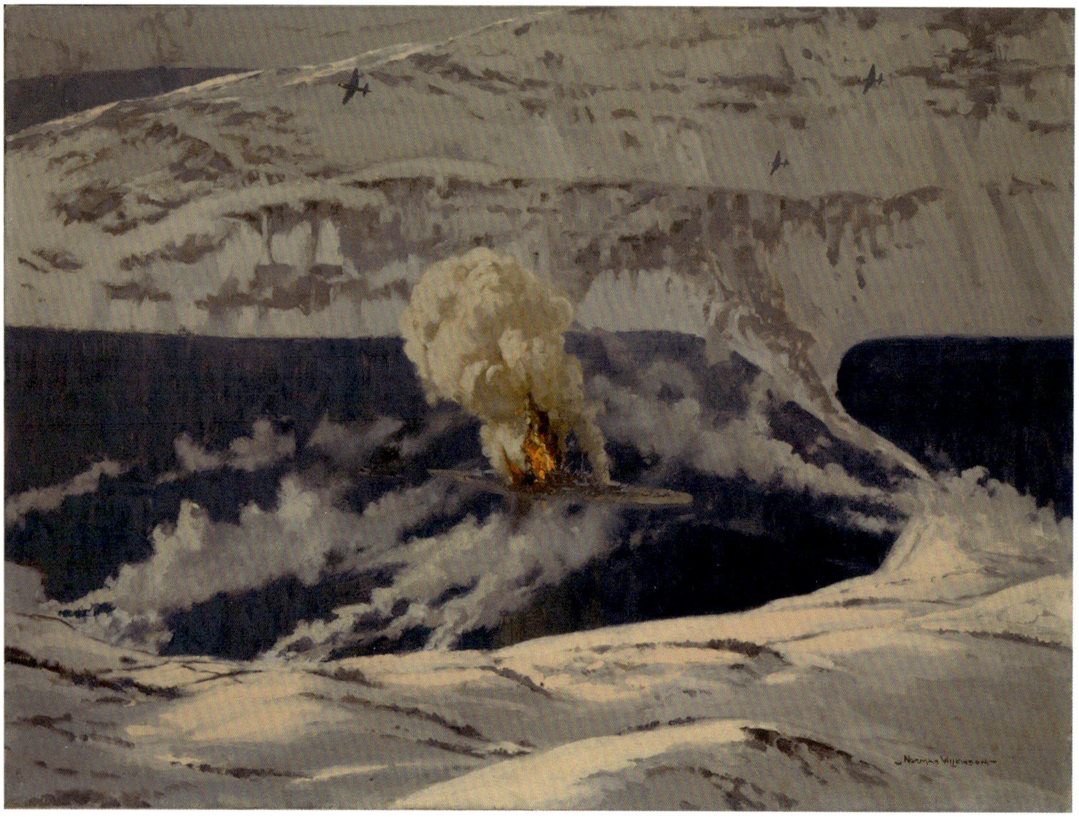

Plate 10 (above)
Norman Wilkinson
A Catalina flying boat sighting the 'Bismarck', 26 May 1941, 1942–4
Oil on canvas
76.2 × 101.6 cm (30 × 40 in)
BHC1604

Plate 11 (below)
Norman Wilkinson
Barracudas bombing the 'Tirpitz', 3 April 1944, 1944
Oil on canvas
76.2 × 101.6 cm (30 × 40 in)
BHC1606

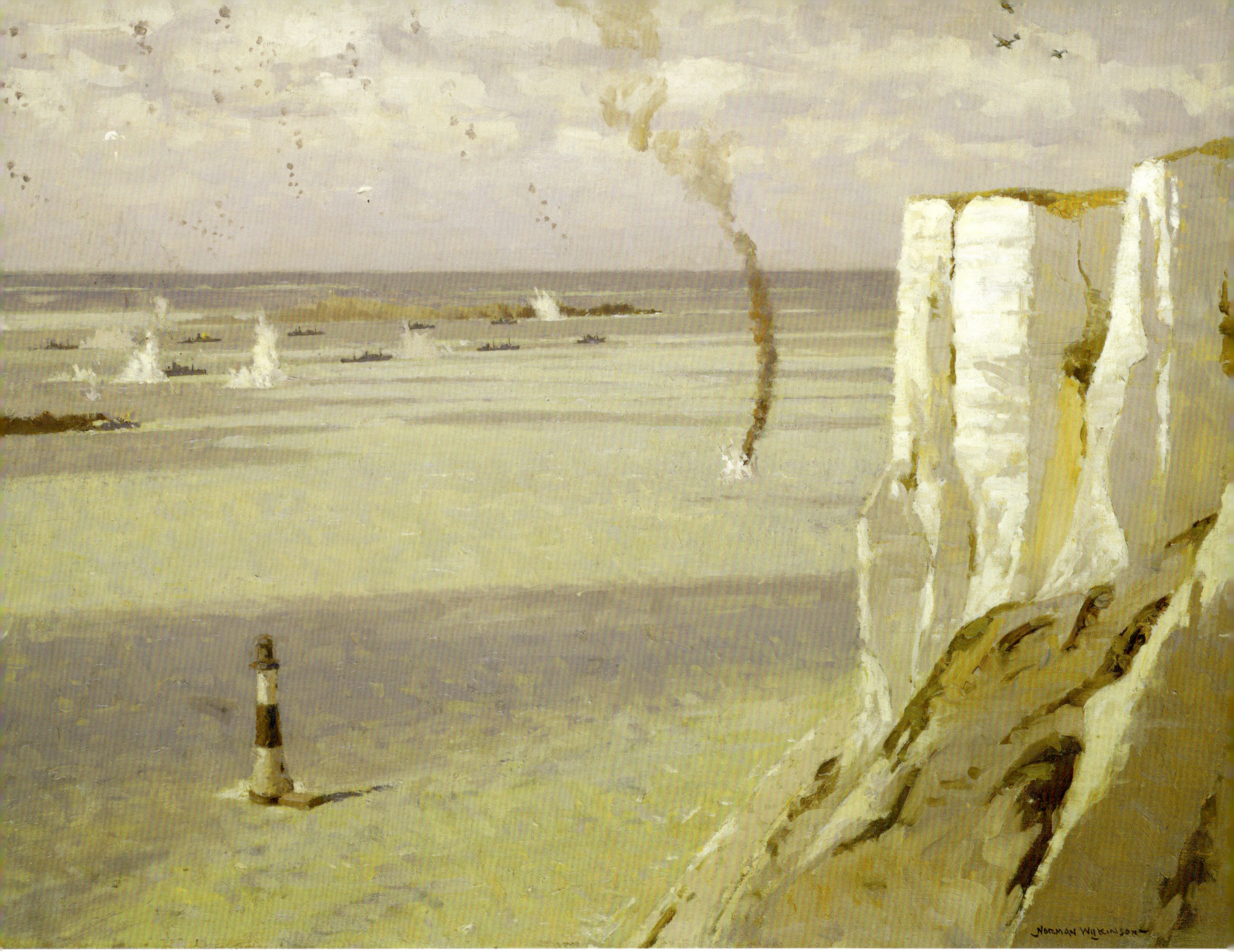

Plate 12
Norman Wilkinson
Beachy Head: Attack on a Convoy, c.1942–4
Oil on canvas
76.2 × 101.6 cm (30 × 40 in)
BHC1599

2

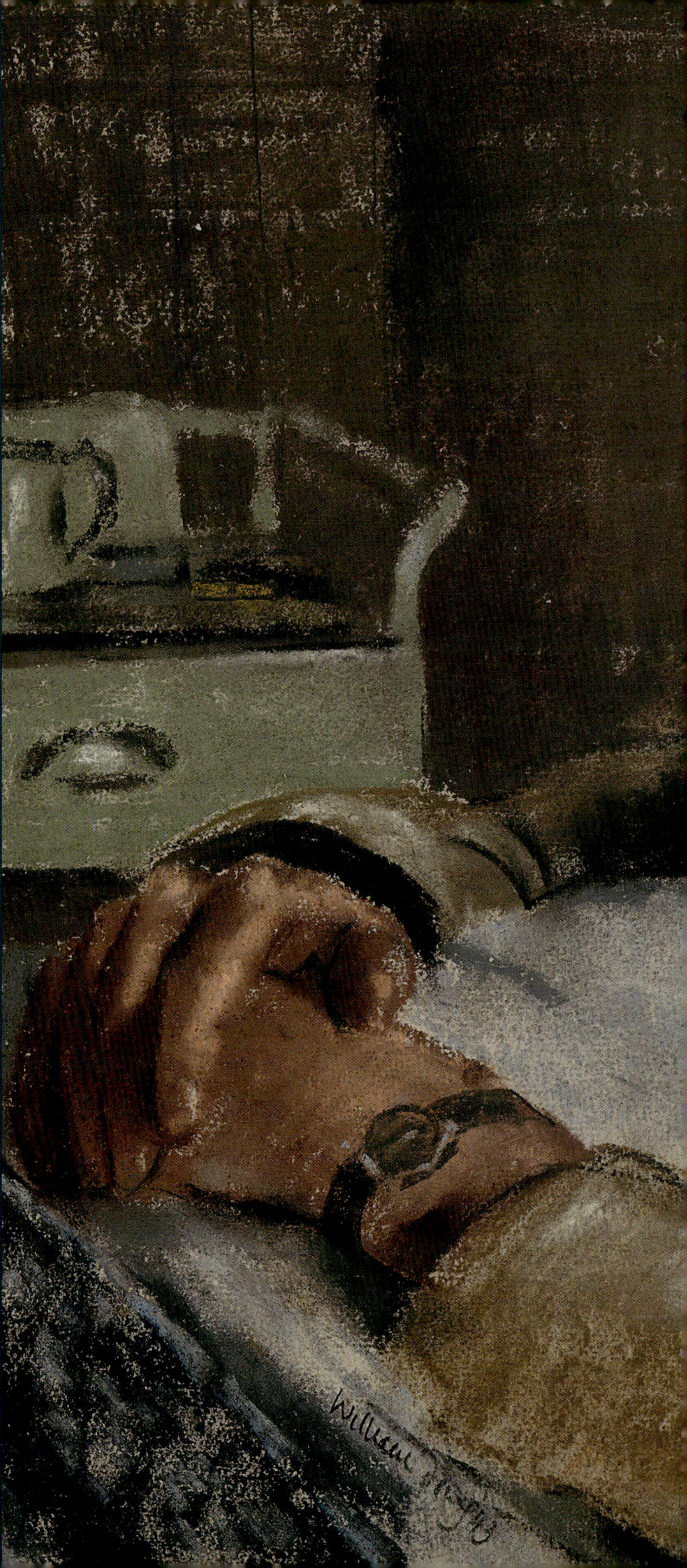

William Dring
Lieutenant-Surgeon Philip R.C. Evans, GC [GM] RNVR, 1943
Pastel on paper
33.5 x 48 cm (13 ¼ x 18 ⅞ in)
PAJ2986

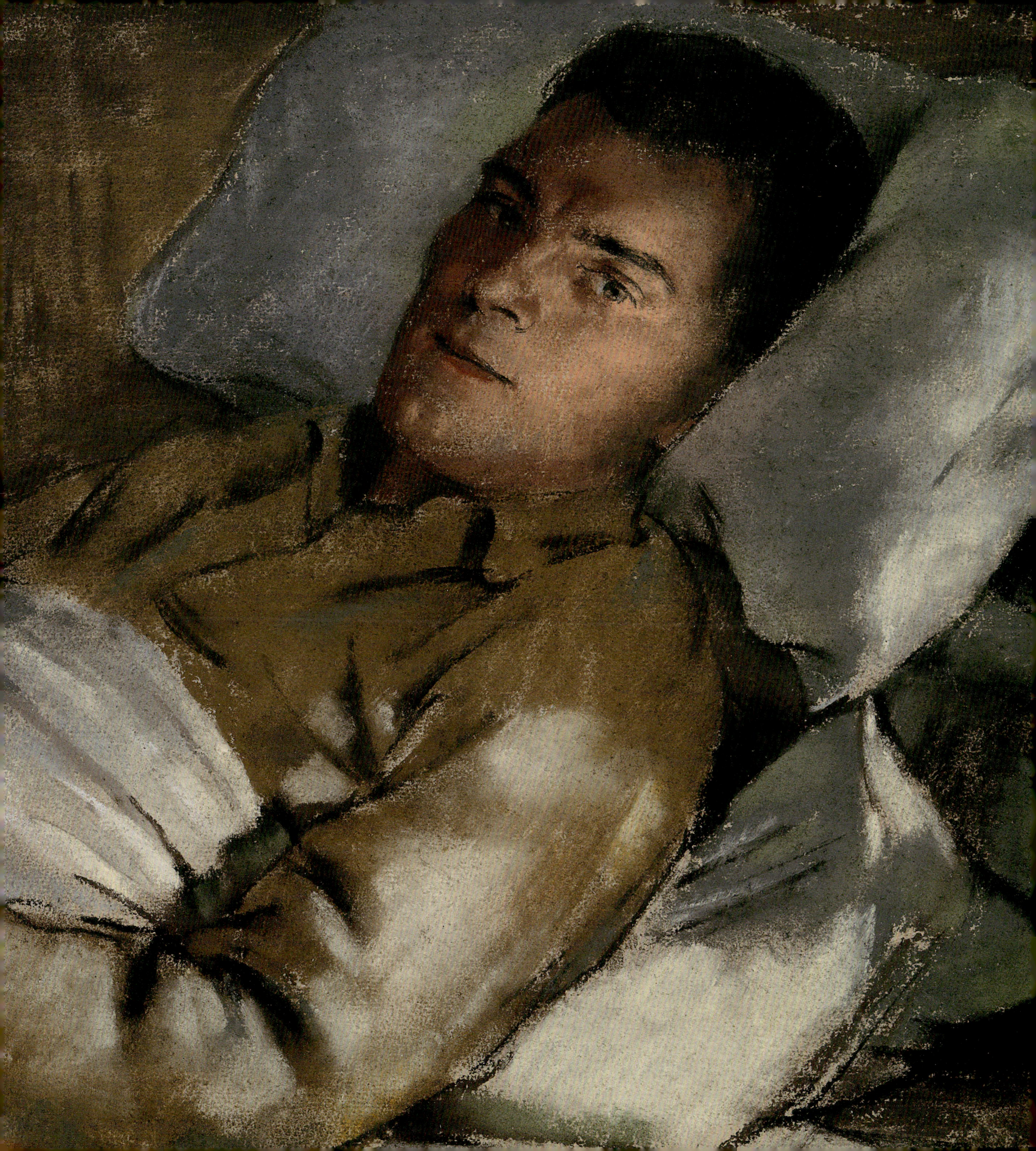

2

The Face of War: Officers and Ratings

Melanie Vandenbrouck

The tragic toll of the war was something our generation had not experienced before [...] The whole nation was stirred by the story of a boy in the Battle of Jutland, where a lad from our slums leapt into immortality by a courage that has never been surpassed.[1]

Frank O. Salisbury, *Sarum Chase*, 1944

A Working-class Hero

One of the simplest yet most poignant images from the First World War is *John Travers Cornwell, Boy First Class, VC (1900–1916)* by Ambrose McEvoy (1878–1927; plate 13). Sixteen-year-old Cornwell's boyish features contrast with the maturity of his expression. Resolutely staring out of the picture plane, he seems to be facing his destiny. As a sight-setter on the cruiser HMS *Chester* at the Battle of Jutland, on 31 May 1916, Cornwell was stationed at the forward deck-gun on the ship's forecastle. His position was shelled four times by German cruisers and he was hit in the chest by shrapnel. In his official despatch of the battle, published in July, Vice-Admiral Sir David Beatty described how, despite fatal injuries, the boy seaman 'remained standing alone ... quietly awaiting orders till the end of the action, with the gun's crew dead and wounded all round him'.[2] The media and public reaction to Cornwell's fate was overwhelming. Indeed, the drive to memorialise his character, actions and ultimate sacrifice was stoked by another equally poignant revelation that Cornwell, who died on 2 June, had been buried in an unmarked grave at Manor Park, not far from his home in East Ham, London.[3] The Admiralty bowed to growing public pressure and arranged for Cornwell's body to be reburied on 29 July in the same cemetery, this time with full naval honours, and the funeral procession and ceremony was attended by thousands of mourners, all of which was captured on film by British Pathé.[4]

By the summer of 1916, the outcome of the war was far from certain. Britain had not only sustained considerable casualties at the Battle of Jutland (see Chapter 2: The Battle of Jutland), but also embarked on the Battle of the Somme (1 July–18 November), which would claim a devastating number of lives. Young 'Jack' Cornwell came to symbolise, at a critical moment, the sacrifice of a generation cut down by the most mechanised conflict mankind had until then experienced. On a popular level his tragic end – or, rather, the widespread publicity it was given for propaganda and commercial press reasons – generated a profound sense of community loss. He was posthumously awarded the Victoria Cross, becoming the youngest-ever naval holder of one, and was honoured across Britain as a national hero, a working-class example of selflessness, duty and courage. Cornwell's youth was, of course, central to the power of his narrative. His features were reproduced extensively in print, on penny stamps, commemorative medals, even cigarette cards. In August 1916, a memorial to 'boy Cornwell' was erected at St Botolph's, Broadgate, London, and in September that year the Navy League's 'Jack Cornwell Day' was celebrated in many British schools.[5] Journalists in the *Spectator* and *The Times* suggested that his portrait photograph, taken when a naval trainee, should be displayed

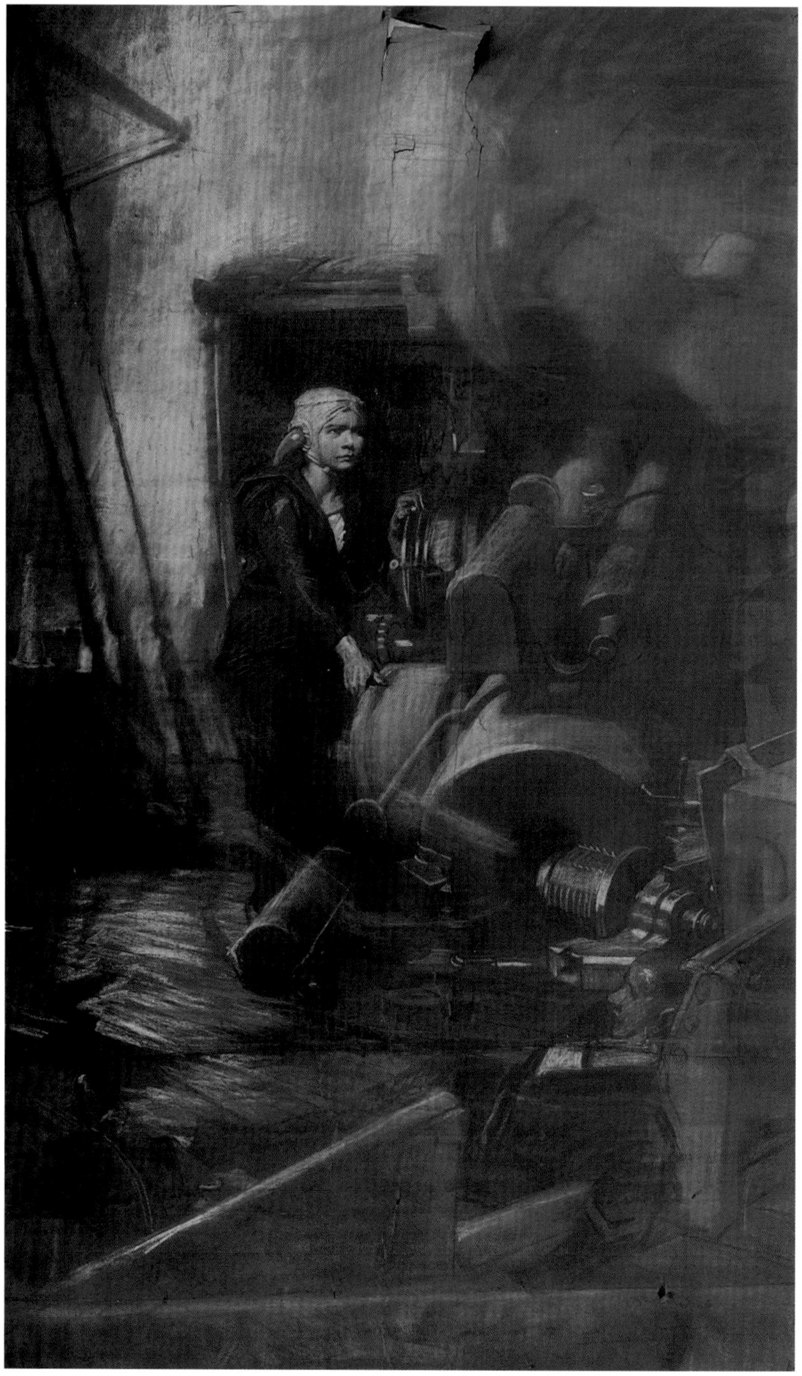

Fig.20
Frank O. Salisbury
Preparatory sketch for the painting of Jack Cornwell, 1917
Charcoal and pastel on paper
271 x 151.5 cm (106 3/4 x 59 5/8 in)
Private collection

in every elementary school, 'so that the lustre of his deed may shine where boys and girls are quick to catch the reflection of lofty and honourable conduct'.[6]

Following Cornwell's public funeral, donations were collected across the British Empire to raise money for the newly created Jack Cornwell Ward of the Star and Garter Home for Disabled Servicemen at Richmond. Part of the proceeds was used for a representation of Cornwell (fig.20), executed by Frank O. Salisbury (1874–1962), a well-known society portraitist of the day.[7] The finished picture was exhibited in a position of honour at the Royal Academy in May 1917 and was presented to the Admiralty, today being at the Royal Navy's training centre, HMS *Raleigh*, in Cornwall; during that spring reproductions were also distributed to schools across Britain and the Empire. Surrounded by the carnage exacted by modern naval warfare, Cornwell's small, vulnerable figure is shown standing at his post, leaning on the gun mount, his left hand gripping the elevating wheel. His face is bathed in light and seems drained of blood, while his expression mixes anxiety with stoical resolution. Despite the thoroughly modern subject and setting, the timeless, quasi-religious resonances of this image are evident, both from Cornwell's delicate features – his younger brother served as Salisbury's model – and from the overall composition, the whole utilising artistic conventions associated with Christian martyrdom. In this way, Salisbury's highly romanticised representation forms part of a major commemorative theme of the First World War; that the sacrifice of the individual was akin to the sacrifice of Jesus Christ.[8]

In contrast, McEvoy's more 'straightforward' portrait was not to be seen until long after the war had ended. Serving in the Royal Naval Division in France, he had been commissioned to produce portraits of both living and posthumous Royal Naval Victoria Cross holders, to be displayed in the proposed Hall of Honour, also known as the 'Gallery of Heroes', for the newly created Imperial War Museum (IWM).[9] In all, McEvoy worked on about 19 portraits for this commission. For a successful society painter such as he, the exacting task of depicting sailors who had died serving their country from faded studio photographs was clearly challenging.[10] Indeed, McEvoy's frustration is palpable in his correspondence with the IWM. In March 1919, following enquiries from Alfred Yockney, Secretary of the British War Memorials Commission, about the delay in finishing some of the portraits, he wrote: 'These are all dead and I am only doing heads as I find it almost impossible to do satisfactory works if I try to paint the whole figures without sufficient material'. And then again, six months later: 'I do not know what to think of the dead V.C.s. I find it difficult to finish anything from a photograph.'[11] In the event, the series was left incomplete and Cornwell's portrait was never fully finished, with areas of canvas left bare and the squaring-up still clearly visible – a result of using a photograph as the template. While the effect may seem at odds with McEvoy's reputation as a 'magician of light and colour', the impastoed paint and white highlights suggest that the sepia tones and faded appearance of the unfinished painting were intentional.[12] It is possible that the artist deliberately sought to recall the style and effect of mourning photographs of the previous century, many of which were based on the posed bodies of the dead.[13]

A Naval Valhalla

Representing an ordinary sailor, a working-class boy who could have been anybody's son, brother or nephew, served to bring the human face of war into a familiar and personal, but also democratic, realm. The unusual nature of this focus cannot be overestimated. Traditionally such commemoration would have been the preserve of officers and leaders: indeed, few identifiable portraits of ordinary sailors and soldiers were done before the First World War. That Cornwell was the only rating in McEvoy's group of naval VCs simply serves to underline this point.[14]

In fact, in October 1916, Charles Masterman, head of the British Propaganda Bureau, wrote to General Charteris, Field-Marshal Sir Douglas Haig's Chief of Intelligence at British Expeditionary Force headquarters in France, that 'we regard it as of great importance that we should interest especially neutral nations in the personalities of some of the British leaders. Germany has done any amount of this kind of thing and has hypnotised a great part of the world with the names of Hindenburg and Mackensen and others.' Masterman proposed to commission two series of portraits of generals and admirals from Muirhead Bone (1876–1953), who was then posted on the Western Front as the very first official war artist, and thereby had privileged access to suitable sitters.[15] Acknowledging that this line of art was not his strength, Bone recommended instead his brother-in-law and fellow Glasgow School of Art student Francis Dodd (1874–1949) who, he said, 'has a real genius for portraiture'.[16] Having met his high-ranking sitters at the front, in naval home ports and on board ships of the Grand Fleet in its Scottish bases, Dodd worked rapidly in chalk and watercolour, completing the whole commission within eight months.[17]

Dodd's portraits were meant to communicate to the public the confidence of wartime leadership within the British armed forces. Following the model of Bone's *Western Front* (see Chapter 3: Above and Below Deck), they were widely distributed in newspapers and featured in two publications, *Generals of the British Army* and *Admirals of the British Navy*. These comprised two volumes published by *Country Life* in 1917, each with 12 colour portraits, including Field-Marshal Haig, Admiral Sir Frederick Doveton Sturdee and Vice-Admiral Beatty.[18]

Dodd represented Admiral Sir John Jellicoe (fig.21), the British naval Commander-in-Chief, sitting informally and smiling. His rank and status are indicated by his uniform, campaign ribbons and the papers on his crossed knees, but his relaxed pose expresses the character of a man who, according to his modern *Dictionary of National Biography* entry, had 'earned the lifelong devotion of his officers and men by his thoughtful and humane leadership'.[19] Dodd's portraits were not always well received by either his sitters or commissioners, being sometimes judged as too casual or too uninspiring for propaganda purposes. One critic thought the Jellicoe portrait was 'the most putrid thing [he had] ever seen. No wonder Jellicoe got the sack.'[20] Perhaps it is here worth noting that Jellicoe's handling of the Battle at Jutland (and subsequently his overly cautious approach as First Sea Lord) were matters of controversy.

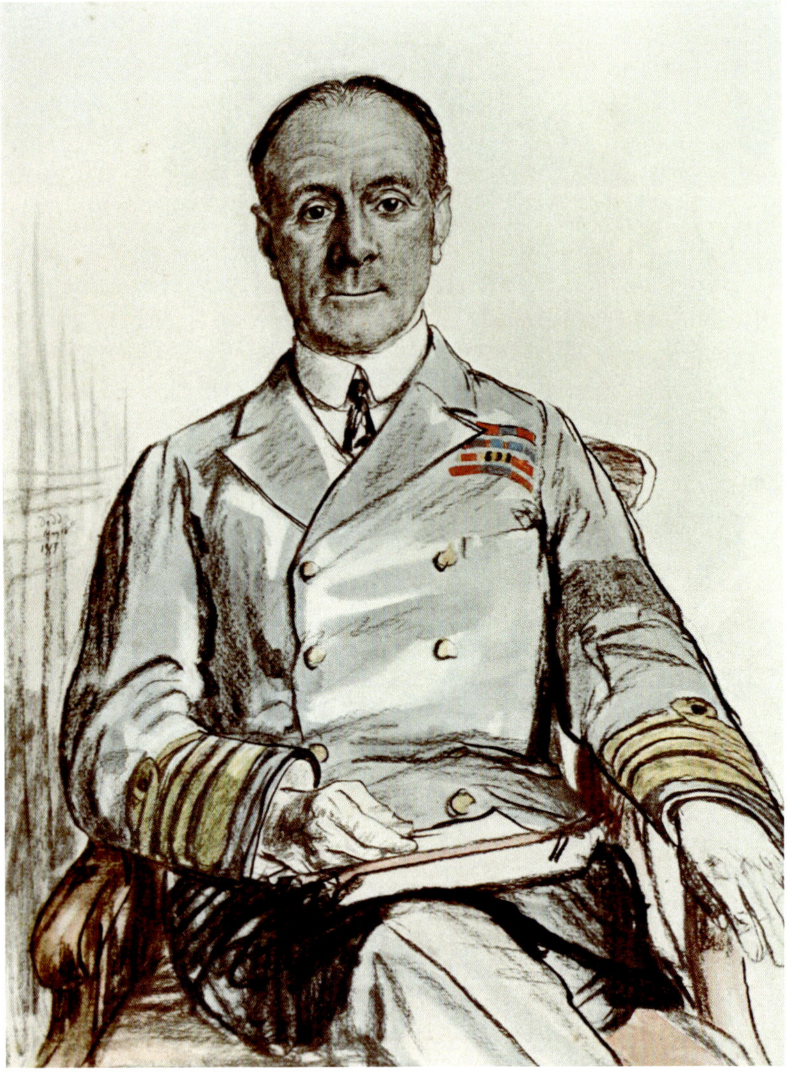

Fig.21
Francis Dodd
Admiral Sir John Jellicoe, GCB, OM, GCVO, 1917
Photogravure
45 x 27.4 cm (17 ¾ x 10 ¾ in)
PAF3622

Fig.22 (opposite)
Thomas Monnington
Admiral of the Fleet John Jellicoe, 1st Earl Jellicoe, 1933
Oil on canvas
127 x 101.5 cm (50 x 40 in)
BHC2804

The image of Jellicoe makes quite a contrast with a later portrait of 1933, by Thomas Monnington (1902–76, fig.22). Here, shortly before his death, we find Jellicoe a stiffer, more sober and time-ravaged figure (he was by then very deaf, partially blind and in ill-health), the sense of isolation that he transmits accentuated by the strange, elongated perspective and the sparseness of the background. The portrait, which was exhibited at the Royal Academy in 1934, had been commissioned by HMS *Excellent*, the Royal Naval Gunnery School at Portsmouth, to commemorate its centenary but was rejected after objections from Lady Jellicoe, who disliked it because the artist did not attempt to disguise her husband's age and infirmity.[21] That she was highly sensitive to the manner and context in which he was portrayed is clear from the preparations for his memorial in Trafalgar Square, after his death in November 1935. In his memoirs, *High Relief*, the sculptor Charles Wheeler describes how he was warned by Sir Edwin Lutyens of the need to show Lady Jellicoe his portrait bust of the Admiral in progress, in his studio, and to 'prepare for a violently prejudiced visitor when she came'. Wheeler carefully stage-managed the whole visit, to the extent that Lady Jellicoe arrived 'in a very good mood'. 'Catching a glimpse of the clay model in the room beyond,' Wheeler recalls, 'she exclaimed, "How wonderful – it's exactly like him," and sending for her chauffeur asked him if he did not think so too.'[22]

Many of the artists discussed here evolved in the same circles and were intimately connected, whether through shared training at the Slade, or through the support of Muirhead Bone, who championed younger artists, notably with the Ministry of Information. Among them was McEvoy's and Dodd's friend, the sculptor Jacob Epstein (1880–1959), who failed to become an official war artist, despite his and Bone's best efforts. At odds with the harsh, menacing angularity of his dehumanised *Rock Drill* (1913–17, Tate), a modernist harbinger of industrial doom, Epstein's portrait bust of Admiral Lord Fisher (plate 14) sensitively evokes the sitter's personality.[23] Fisher was known as a great strategist and reformer (he helped develop cutting-edge weaponry, introduced 'dreadnought' battleships and was in favour of the development of submarines), and for being argumentative and strong-minded. Seventy-three years old at the outbreak of the war, he had come out of retirement to resume his post as First Sea Lord but resigned again on 15 May 1915 following well-founded disagreement with Churchill's plan to invade Gallipoli. By the time he sat for this portrait, in June 1916, Fisher was chairman of the Board of Invention and Research, 'an entity supposed to encourage scientific work for the Navy' but in some quarters known as the 'board of intrigue and revenge'.[24]

Introduced to Fisher at a party hosted by the Duchess of Hamilton (who commissioned the bust, at Dodd's suggestion), Epstein had declared that he was 'of all the living men [the one of whom] I should like to do a bust', and he regarded it as 'the most powerful I have ever done'.[25] It emanates a pugnacious

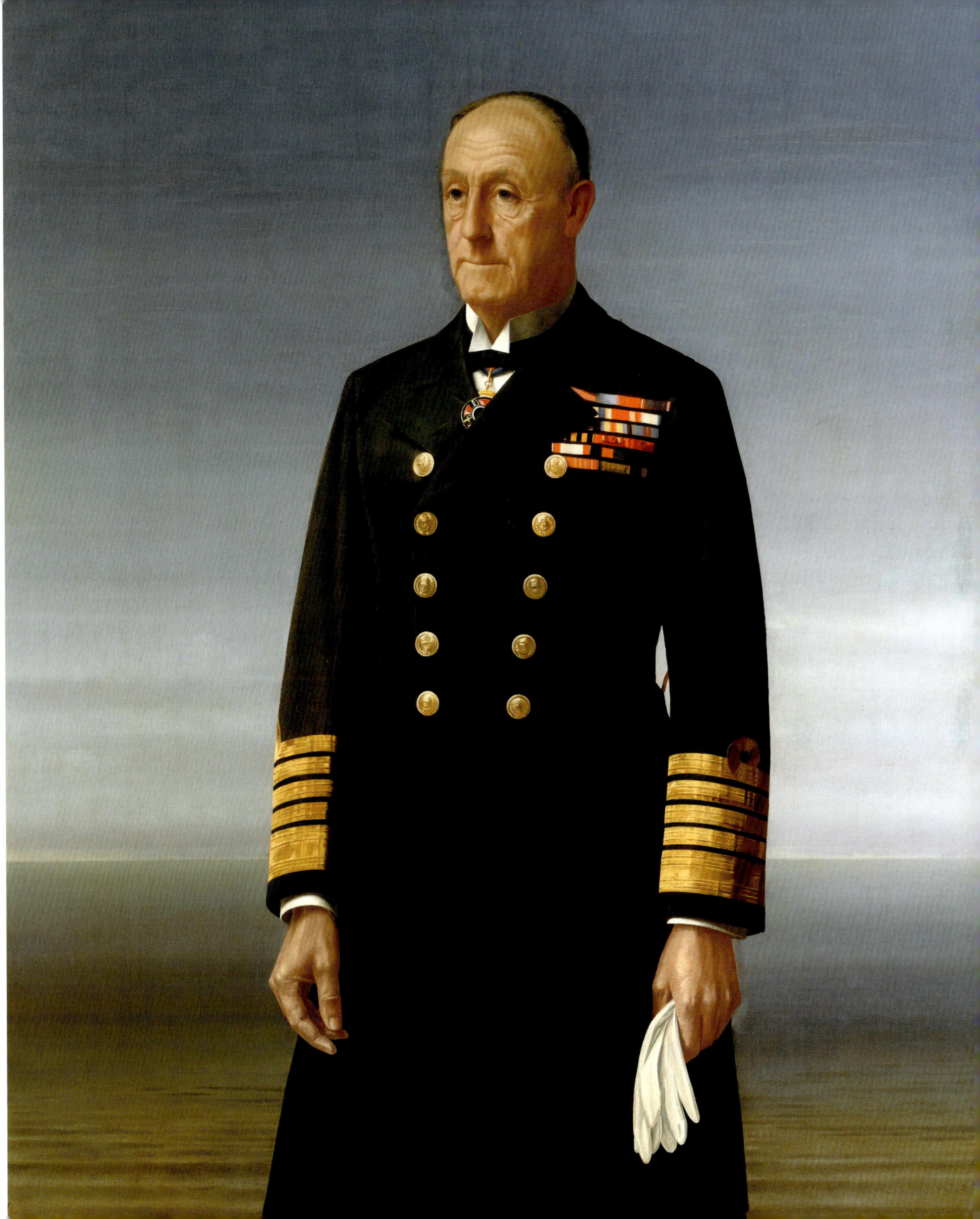

Fig.23
Frank Dobson
Admiral Sir William Milbourne James, 1941
Cast bronze
59 x 47 x 29 cm (23 1/4 x 18 1/2 x 11 3/8 in)
SCU0029

determination befitting its model. With his clamped mouth, chin held high and shoulders thrust back, Fisher seems ready for argument. The determined pose is enhanced by the vigorous modelling, built-up features and rough surface. When the bust was exhibited in Epstein's first one-man show at the Leicester Galleries in 1917, the critics were divided.[26] *The Sunday Times* admired the 'rugged strength' while the *New Statesman* deplored 'the modern tendency to leave clay dabs, etc., directly showing in the bronze'.[27] Most perceptively perhaps, *The Times* recognised in Epstein a 'master of portraiture' because 'the likeness is striking, but it is not the likeness of a moment, not a snapshot; it is the likeness of a whole character. We see Lord Fisher as a public man, one used to express himself to other men, and he seems to be ... thinking in opposition, as if he imagined an enemy before him.'[28] Fisher loved his portrait, appreciating the expressive distortion the sculptor had lent his features.[29]

Like Epstein, Frank Dobson (1886–1963) was a member of the avant-garde London Group. He enlisted in the Artists Rifles in the First World War and – though now best known as a sculptor – was employed as a painter by the Ministry of Information. In between wars, his sculpted figures tended towards abstracted forms, but the propaganda needs of the Second World War led him back to more figurative work. He submitted mainly drawings to the War Artists Advisory Committee (WAAC), as well as two bronze busts. By then, the clay dabs decried in Epstein's portrait of Fisher were no longer controversial, and Dobson used a similarly tactile treatment for his bust of Admiral Sir William James (1881–1973), naval Commander-in-Chief at Portsmouth, 1939–42 (fig.23). James was widely known as 'Bubbles', in reference to a subject painting by his grandfather, Sir John Everett Millais, for which he sat as a child and which became famous when used as an advertisement for Pears soap.[30] As such, the raised 'blobs' and rounded features of Dobson's bronze seem particularly apposite.

By way of contrast, Charles Wheeler (1892–1974) applied smooth, almost stylised facial features to the figures he commemorated. Unfit for active service, Wheeler's involvement in the First World War was on the home front, designing medals and, according to family legend, modelling artificial limbs for amputees.[31] Between the wars, he established himself as one of the leading sculptors of his generation, notably with the architectural sculptures on the façade of the Bank of England (1931) and the Jellicoe memorial in Trafalgar Square, mentioned above. His portrait of Captain George Creasy (1895–1972; plate 15), who became the Navy's Director of Anti-Submarine Warfare in September 1940, is striking both for its sitter's authoritative features and for the tattoo incised on the back of his neck. Neptune, god of the sea, is shown fighting a sea-serpent inscribed with Nazi swastikas, and alludes to Britain's naval aspirations against Germany. Soon after Creasy's portrait was completed, Wheeler was appointed an official war artist, the only instance of a sculptor obtaining a full-time contract with the WAAC. Few bronze portraits were executed during the war, however, presumably from the need to reserve metal for weaponry but also because of their high costs, the relative slowness of execution and the difficulty of disseminating them widely, compared to paintings and drawings.[32] Likewise, none depict individual ratings, for at that time portrait sculpture hardly ever represented ordinary people. From Epstein's *Tin Hat* of 1916 (purchased by Bone, who donated it to the IWM) to Alan Durst's 1944 wood carvings of a *Sailor* and a *Marine*,[33] these are portrayals of a type, 'the everyman' akin to those that populate the many thousands of private and publicly funded war memorials of the 1920s and early 1930s. A striking exception to this rule is Elsie March's plaster bust of the Women's Auxiliary Air Force (WAAF) member, Louise Turner (1940, IWM).[34]

Another medium that produced remarkable results, and included examples of individual ratings, was pastel: unlike costly and time-consuming bronze, its silky effect and fluid handling was suited to lifelike portraits that could be achieved relatively fast. Indeed, Eric Kennington (1888–1960) claimed he only required three hours of sitting, as opposed to the six days that Fisher sat for Epstein, while

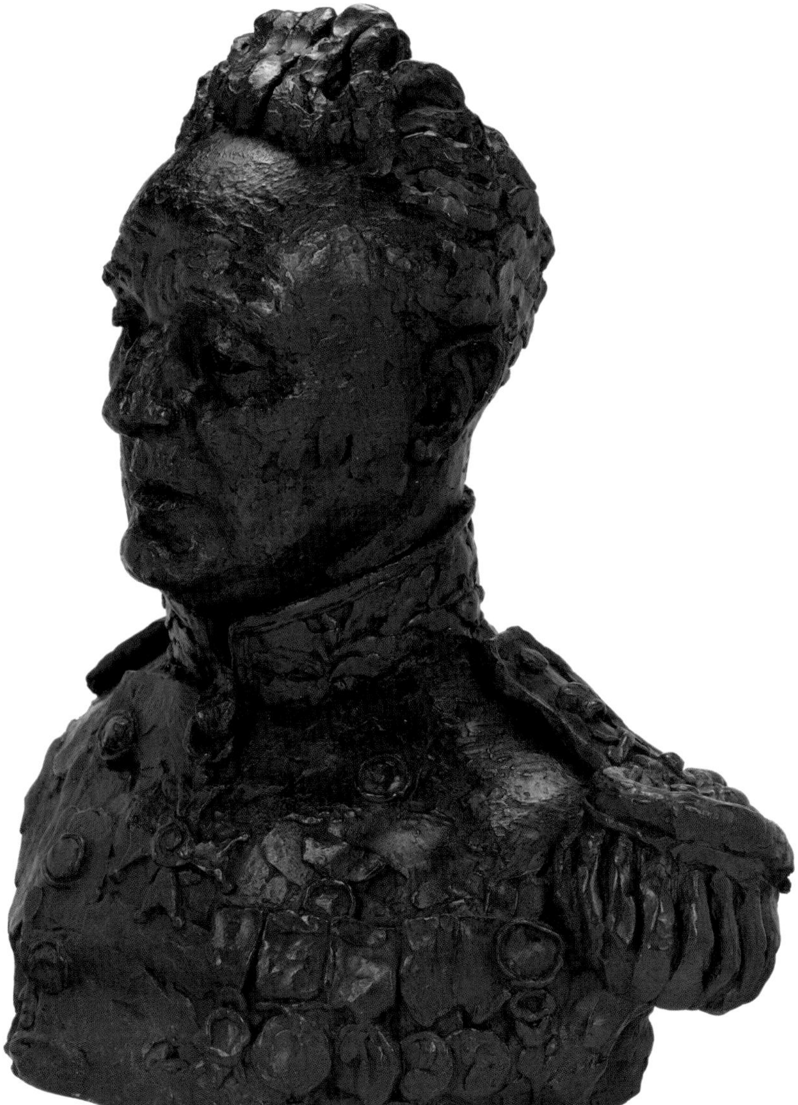

William Dring wrote to Edward Montgomery O'Rorke Dickey, Secretary of the WAAC, saying 'I am a rapid worker and rarely take more than an hour or so over a pastel portrait.'[35]

Kennington was among the few artists who served in the First World War to be approached by the WAAC in the Second. He had shot to fame with *The Kensingtons at Laventie, Winter 1914* (1915, IWM), a stirring tribute to his infantry platoon. Painted while he was convalescing from a war injury, this group portrait struck commentators with its technical virtuosity as well as its 'stately representation of the quiet heroism of the rank and file', and its unemotional depiction of the hardship endured by the exhausted, weary men.[36] Discharged from the Army, Kennington spent the rest of the First World War as an official war artist on the Western Front. At the outbreak of war in 1939, Sir Kenneth Clark identified him as a good recruit for the WAAC, 'not only by reason of his merit as an artist but also because it was thought that his style of drawings readily lent itself to reproduction in the form of picture postcards'.[37] These reproduced particularly well in black and white, as can be seen in *Pilots, Workers, Machine*, a collection of 17 plates of his wartime portraits, published in 1941.[38]

Not only did Kennington have an extraordinary grasp of pastel, his portraits show psychological depth as well as a naturalism that suited the representational and inspirational needs of propaganda. By the time of the Second World War, the genre of state-sanctioned portraiture had become more democratic. After being commissioned to draw high-ranking officers, he pleaded to draw younger servicemen, and was sent to Portsmouth and Devonport, the Royal Navy base up-river from Plymouth, to portray sailors.[39] His *Leading Seaman A.L. Vearncombe DSM, HMS 'Vernon'* (plate 16) is characteristic of the pastels he produced in this period, with its strong focus and tight composition around the face of the sitter, and dramatic chiaroscuro creating an almost photograph-like effect. Kennington's sailors stoically face their uncertain future. In December 1939, Vearncombe had, in the artist's words, defused the first magnetic mine

Fig.24 (opposite, left)
William Dring
Boy First Class Austin, sight-setter, 1942
Pastel on paper
45.2 x 31.5 cm (17 3/4 x 12 3/8 in)
PAJ2985

Fig.25 (opposite, right)
William Dring
Warrant-Engineer Stanley Ball, MBE, BEM, RN, 1943
Pastel on paper
47.6 x 33 cm (18 3/4 x 13 in)
PAJ3020

'with brass tools and great courage [...] whilst, through a microphone he told dispassionately the secrets of its construction'.[40] His self-reflective look equally evokes his modesty and steadfast heroism.

No less impressive is *Stoker A. Martin of HMS 'Exeter'* (plate 17), which was displayed to great acclaim in the WAAC's first exhibition in July 1940. Martin was in HMS *Exeter* during the Battle of the River Plate on 13 December 1939, the first naval action of the war, against the German heavy cruiser *Admiral Graf Spee*, which inflicted heavy losses: 61 on *Exeter* were killed, 23 wounded, and the ship suffered significant damage. In this portrait, Kennington encapsulated the crew's sacrifice and valour. The editor of the *Studio*, Charles Holme, praised it for 'magnificently expressing courage, hardihood and dog-like devotion to duty', showing that 'it is possible to convey through portraiture the strength, determination, courage as well as the individual character of the British sailor.'[41] H. Granville Fell admired 'Kennington's harsh, iron technique [which] has a force admirably suited to convey the unflinching resolution in the faces of his seamen and soldiers.'[42] One onlooker was moved to tears, and declared that 'No picture has ever done that to me before'.[43] Kennington described Martin as a 'Man of Action: instantaneous: 100 per cent reliable: expert technician. Much humour under thorough camouflage. Very gentle, sensitive, and great physical strength.'[44] Stokers were in charge of some of the most physical work on board ship, labouring in the darkness, noise, smell and fumes of the engine rooms. But Martin's presence is more psychological than physical. His erect pose is both intense and formal, his gaze at once remote and penetrating. The undefined background, with the paper left bare, emphasises his chiselled features, and the calculated luminosity of the white uniform gives arresting depth to the portrait.

A Naval Community

If pastels by William Dring (1904–90) do not have the startling presence of those of Kennington, what sets them apart is their informality and human concern. His prolific correspondence with the WAAC reveals how Dring, like many other artists, was eager to earn official commissions. Too old for conscription in 1939, Dring was worried he would have to enlist sooner or later as the conflict intensified. Likewise anxious that his income had diminished since the beginning of the war and that his part-time teaching position at the Southampton School of Art would not be sufficient to scrape a living, he first contacted E.M.O'R. Dickey of the WAAC in September 1940 to offer his services as a landscape and portrait artist.[45] He was at first unsuccessful but persistence paid off: he secured his first commission of two portraits in May 1941, thanks to the support of Lutyens, then President of the Royal Academy, and of Reginald Gleadowe, who was both the Admiralty's representative on the WAAC and a fellow artist who had been Slade Professor of Fine Art at Oxford.[46] Emboldened by the WAAC's response, Dring did not hesitate to send more portraits their way unprompted. Several of these were acquired, for 10 to 15 guineas each.[47]

By May 1942, following a quarrel with his superiors at Southampton School of Art, the Committee's satisfaction with his work and Dickey's sympathy for his untenable position, Dring became a full-time official artist, a post he filled until the end of the war.[48] During that time he travelled around the harbours of Britain, to Portsmouth, the Orkney Islands, Northern Ireland and the Western Approaches to meet his sitters. Chosen by Gleadowe or drawn on Dring's initiative, they were naval personnel of all ranks who had distinguished themselves by their gallantry. The public liked Dring's 'thoroughly convincing pastel portraits'.[49] The critic from *Time and Tide* declared that 'his sitters have a more quiet breathing look than have Kennington's, being not heroic types but plain men and women in uniforms', and it is Dring's compassion and

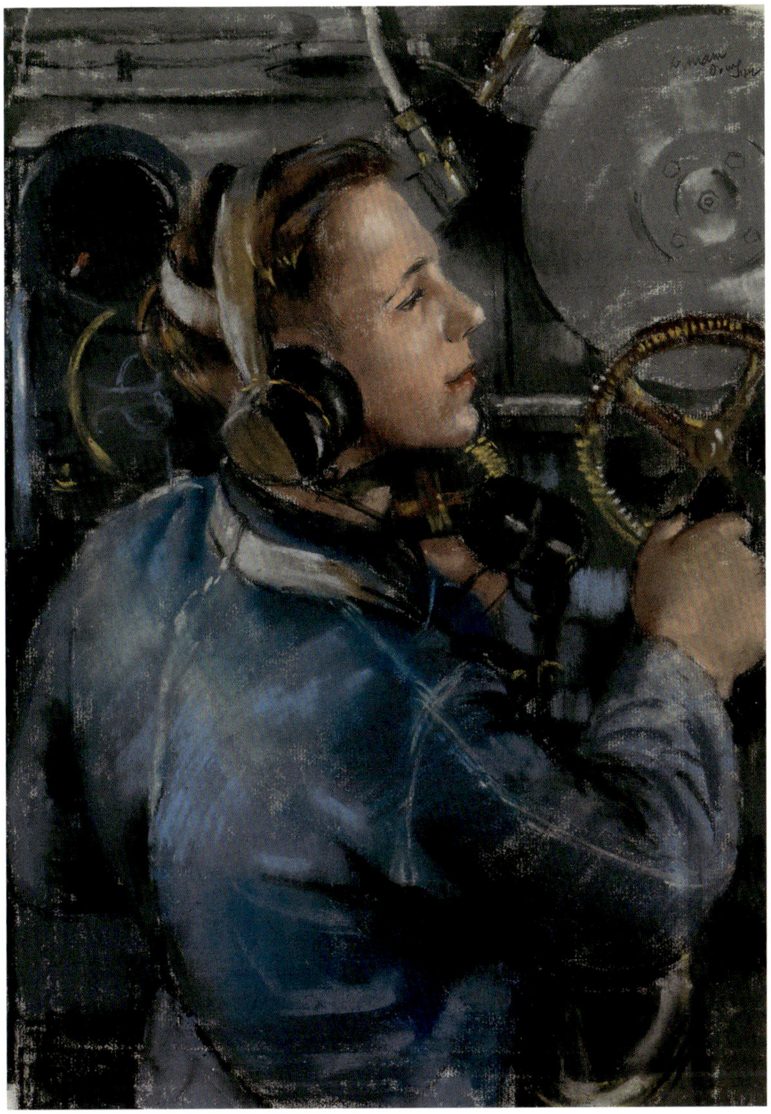

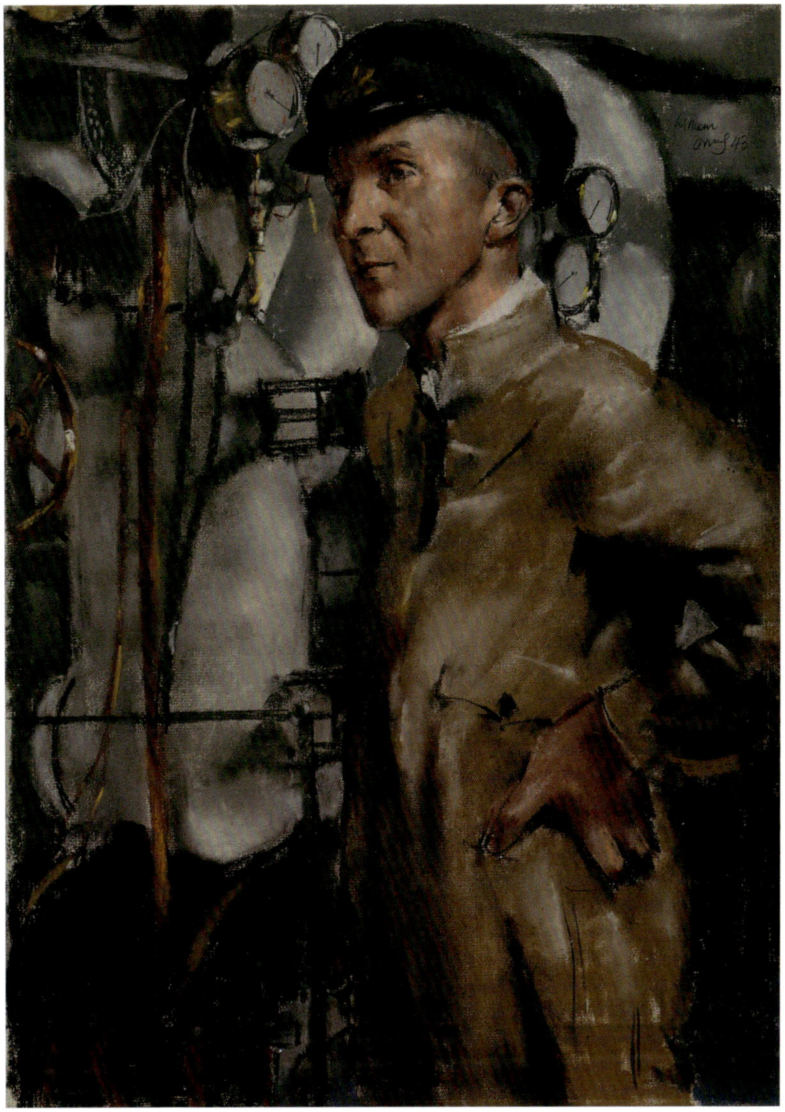

sensitivity to their character that gives his portraits a distinctively personal and genuine aura.[50]

Dring had studied under Henry Tonks at the Slade School of Art, and one may wonder whether he knew Tonks' harrowing pastels of soldiers with facial wounds (1916–18, Royal College of Surgeons of England), which show their disfigurement with uncompromising truth. Dring's portrait of Surgeon Lieutenant Evans (plate 19) allies a perceptive rendering of the sitter's benevolence to the dignity of his suffering. Evans had been involved in a rescue operation, during which his own ship had been damaged, while he had both ankles broken. Despite the gravity of his injuries, Evans tended to the wounded for hours. He earned a George Medal for his selfless conduct but the consequences of this accident affected him for the rest of his life.[51] Choosing to represent him bedridden, turning his head towards the viewer as if just interrupted in his rest, Dring conveys a vulnerability, intimacy and immediacy at odds with the more conventional representation of heroes standing upright, aloof and determined.

While Dring mastered quiet heroism, he also lent a more glamorous mood to some portraits. Commander William (Bill) King (1910–2012; plate 20) was as charismatic as he was audacious, and his swift responses to critical circumstances had on several occasions saved his vessels and crews from fatal difficulties. For one such action, in 1939, he had been rewarded by an invitation for brandy and cigars with Churchill, then First Lord of the Admiralty.[52] Dring's portrait positions him on board his submarine, gazing pensively out of the picture plane. King would distinguish himself further throughout the war and lived an eventful life to the extraordinary age of 102.

No such happy fate awaited Lieutenant-Commander Bridgman (1906–43; plate 21), whom Dring portrayed on a visit to Londonderry

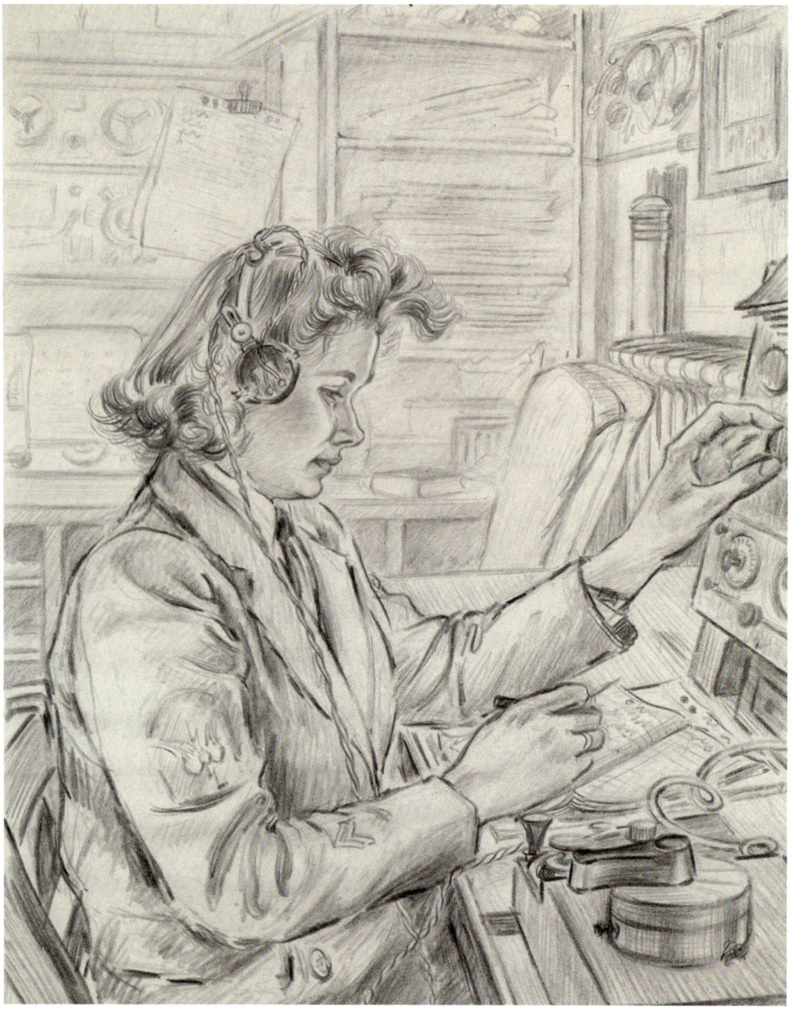

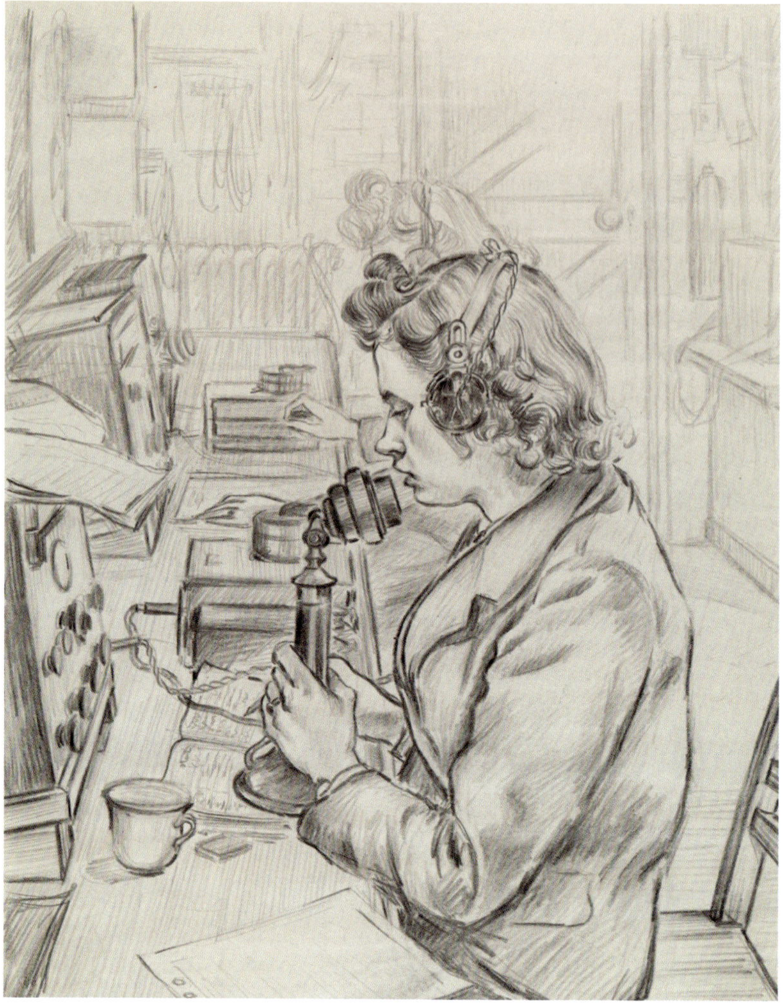

in May or June 1943. Bridgman is shown leaning forward in an amicable way, pipe in mouth and with a twinkle in his eye. Within five months of this portrait being completed, he would be one of 224 men lost when his ship, HMS *Itchen*, was hit by a torpedo in the North Atlantic. Only three men survived.[53]

Dring endeavoured to depict the variety of crew on board vessels, from stokers to commanding officers. Seen together, his portraits *Boy First Class Austin, sight-setter* (fig.24) and *Warrant-Engineer Stanley Ball, MBE, BEM, RN* (fig.25) contrast the energy of youth to the experience of age. Making sure the guns were accurately aimed at their target, sight-setters were among the youngest members of the ship's company, and Dring's dynamic composition evokes Austin's enthusiasm despite the responsibility of his job. Ball was portrayed after he had been awarded an MBE for 'bravery and skill in fighting fires' while serving on the convoy escort HMS *Black Swan*. To become Warrant Engineer required a high standard of education, professionalism and skill in order to supervise the operation and repair of mechanical and electrical equipment. Dring represented Ball standing with his hands on his hips, as though weary from hard work, but with a wise expression on his face.

By the time his portrait was completed, in 1943, the submariner Augustus William Armishaw (1908–79; plate 22) had, in the space of three years, risen from Able to Leading Seaman and then been made Petty Officer (a supervisory warrant rank, between commissioned officers and enlisted sailors). Dring evoked Armishaw's spirit in a full-length portrait, depicting him letting go the anchor of HMS *Torbay*, standing tall and boldly facing the viewer, proud to represent the Navy. Uniform and deck are seen almost blending into each other, emphasising the symbiotic relationship between man and machine.

While both Kennington and Dring's vibrant pastels show an ability to capture the individuals' interior world, neither artist knew their sitters as intimately as someone who had served with them, like John Worsley, John Kingsley Cook (see Chapter 4: From Service to Captivity) or the Wren, Gladys E. Reed (possibly born 1917).[54] Her contribution to our idea of women and the home front is

Fig.26 (opposite, left)
Gladys E. Reed
Wren Wireless Telegraphist receiving a Message, 1944
Graphite on paper
27.8 x 21.4 cm (11 x 8 3/8 in)
PAH0094

Fig.27 (opposite, right)
Gladys E. Reed
Wren Wireless Telegraphist transmitting a Message by Radio-telephony, 1944
Graphite on paper
27.8 x 21.4 cm (11 x 8 3/8 in)
PAH0095

discussed in Chapter 5. It is worth mentioning here, however, given that her detailed drawings are highly expressive and informal pictorial insights into the close-knit community the Wrens formed, as well as being a social document about how the war disrupted established gender roles. Two drawings (figs 26 and 27) show the same person in the wireless room, doing work that Reed performed herself: indeed, the sitter is perhaps her relief. This 'diptych' gives a sense of the intense concentration and strain of long hours on watch. Depicted receiving a message, the Wren is fresh-faced at first, her notebook barely filled. The second drawing shows her transmitting, the passage of time and strenuous work represented by the fuller notebook, cup of tea and bags under her eyes. While one might argue that a 'portrait', as a genre, should claim that status when the sitter is identified, this Wren is clearly individualised even though unnamed. In fact, her anonymity seems to reflect Reed's own desire to remain in the shadows (none of her drawings were signed).[55] Depicted without the pomp of official portraiture, this Wren represents wartime community spirit, the 'all-in-it-together' idea that would be so essential to keeping the nation's spirits up during six long years.

A more emphatic idea of the naval community is represented by the extraordinary composite works of Barnett Freedman (1901–58): *The Captain of HMS 'Repulse' and some of his Officers and Ship's Company. Drawn in the Ship July – August 1941*,[56] and the later *HM Submarine 'Tribune', the Commanding Officer and his Company Drawn on board and in Fort Block House June–August 1943* (plate 23). A fine draughtsman, Freedman was best known as an illustrator, and was appreciated for his distinctive, legible style. The artist himself proposed to the WAAC the creation of what he called 'albums' of portraits. They were enthusiastically received by the commissioners. Rather than bound portfolios, as the term 'album' implies, Freedman's works are large-scale compositions of 38 and 60 small portraits respectively, ranging from stokers and signalmen, gunners, the quartermaster, engineers and surgeons, to the chaplain and the captain. The 'albums' concentrate on the crew as series of individuals who collectively make up a single entity – the ship's company. Each man is portrayed in a single vignette, or in groups of two to four, with their names spelt out and details of their uniform, insignia or tattoos included. However, repeated as part of a wider, complex and rhythmic composition, with loosely defined features and almost mechanical stylisation, one might also suggest that these seamen, of all ranks and roles, seem to morph before our eyes into so many cogs in the machine of naval warfare.[57]

‘Something wrong with our bloody ships today’: The Battle of Jutland

Andrew Choong

The Battle of Jutland, 31 May–1 June 1916, was the culmination of a naval arms race between Britain and Germany. The end of the Napoleonic War a century earlier had left Britain in a position of supremacy at sea, symbolically cemented in popular imagination by Nelson's victory at Trafalgar on 21 October 1805. The Royal Navy had emerged from that conflict with a very high reputation at home and abroad, which it maintained as the century progressed, despite rapid changes in technology and constant challenges from rivals such as France and Russia. With the introduction of the Two-Power Standard in 1889, the *de facto* practice of maintaining the Royal Navy's strength at more than twice that of the next two greatest naval powers combined gained the force of official policy. In 1891 the *Royal Naval Exhibition* at Chelsea attracted huge numbers of visitors, and within four years the Navy's popularity found further expression in the creation of the politically influential Navy League.

British naval dominance was challenged when Germany embarked on the first of a series of large naval expansion programmes in 1898. Britain's status as a great power depended on the maintenance of overwhelming naval strength and the government had little option but to respond in kind. The completion of HMS *Dreadnought* in 1906 gave the world a new kind of warship and a rush ensued to build more vessels of this type. Faster and much more heavily armed than existing battleships, *Dreadnought* and her descendants would come to be regarded as the backbone of any navy that possessed them, and the yardstick by which relative naval power was measured. They were also powerful symbols of national pride and the public was particularly taken with the glamorous battle-cruisers, described by Churchill as 'that supreme combination of speed and power' (fig.28).[58]

Public expectations were for a decisive naval action within days of war being declared in August 1914. That the opposing battle fleets did not meet each other until the end of May 1916 was due to the cautious strategies adopted by both sides.[59] The inactivity was keenly felt by the men of the Navy and their frustrations were summed up

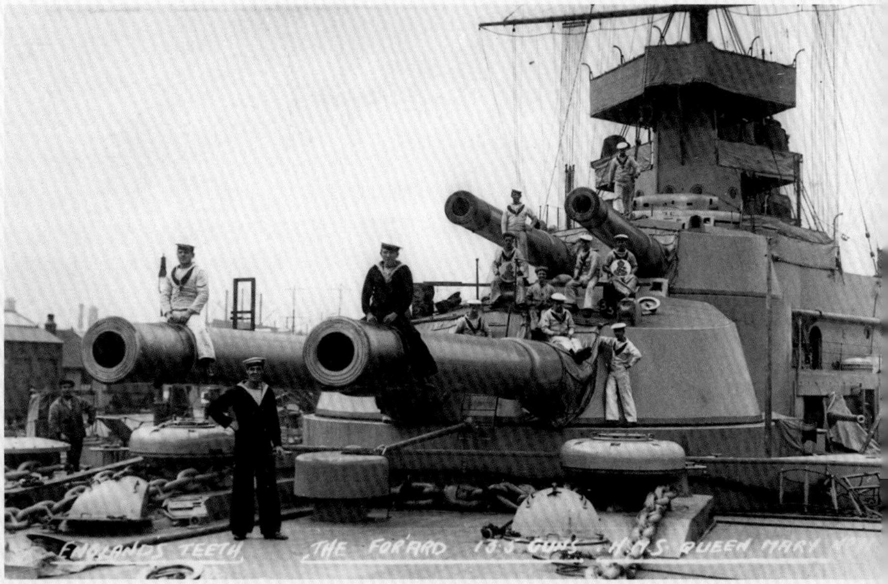

Fig.28
Forecastle of HMS *Queen Mary*, c.1913
Photographic negative
10 x 12.5 cm (4 x 5 in)
C9865

Sailors pose by the forward 13.5-inch guns of HMS *Queen Mary*, the most modern of the three British battle-cruisers sunk at Jutland. Her loss accounted for 1,274 of the British battle casualties.

by Admiral Sir David Beatty, who wrote that 'we are not doing our share and bearing our portion of the burden laid upon the nation [...] We spend days doing nothing when so many are doing so much.'[60]

The outnumbered Germans sought to provoke action with a small part of Britain's Grand Fleet which (it was hoped) they would defeat with their full strength. From November 1914, German ships occasionally raided the English coastline. Their bombardment of coastal towns was carried out by battle-cruisers whose task if engaged by British forces was to draw their pursuers within range of the High Seas Fleet's dreadnoughts. The British responded by creating two rapid-reaction forces based in Scotland. The first of these comprised Beatty's battle-cruisers at Rosyth, in the Firth of Forth, and the second a squadron of Grand Fleet dreadnoughts further north, in the Cromarty Firth. When these forces intercepted a raid they would be supported by the rest of the Grand Fleet sailing from Scapa Flow. These arrangements resulted in only one action between the rival battle-cruisers – the Battle of Dogger Bank in January 1915 – but the likelihood of a fleet action in the North Sea was increased.[61]

The long-awaited encounter took place on 31 May 1916. Alerted by wireless intelligence that the Germans were preparing another raid,

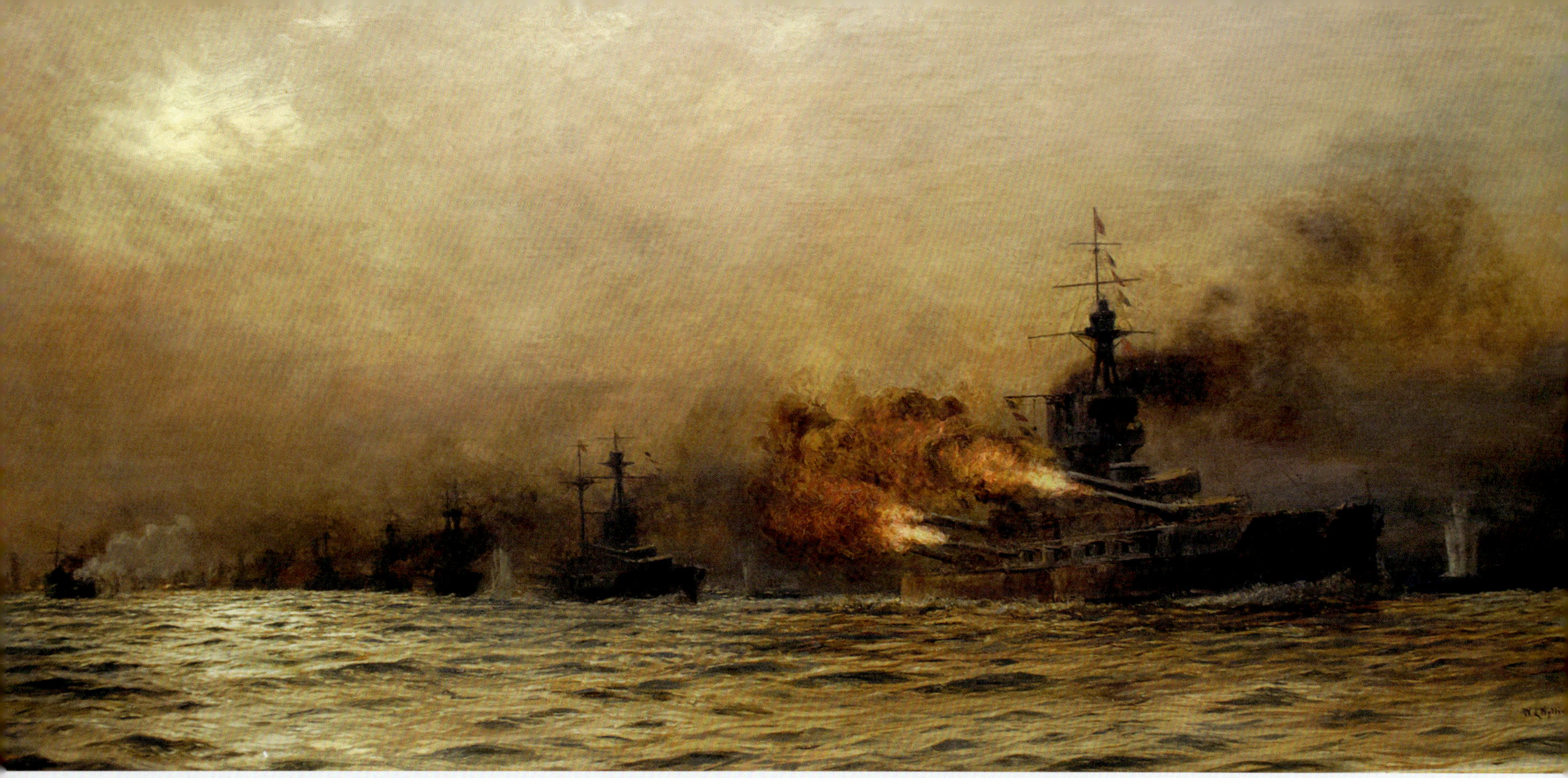

the British put to sea. A few hours later, the High Seas Fleet left Wilhelmshaven. The battle was a complicated affair and for ease of narrative is often described in terms of four phases: the 'Run to the South' (approximately 3.30 to 4.40 PM); the 'Run to the North' (approximately 4.40 to 6 PM); the main fleet action (approximately 6 to 8 PM); and finally the night action (approximately 8 PM to 3 AM on 1 June).

A chance encounter between both sides' smaller warships brought the British and German battle-cruisers into contact and the 'Run to the South' began. Admiral Franz Hipper accepted battle with Beatty but steered his ships southwards, intending to lure the British towards the German battleships. Beatty gave chase but within half an hour lost two of his ships to catastrophic explosions. The destruction of the first, the older *Indefatigable*, and the loss of 1,017 men, was described cold-bloodedly by Captain Chatfield of Beatty's flagship, *Lion*, as 'just a disappointment'.[62] The subsequent loss of the *Queen Mary* prompted Beatty's less controlled 'there seems to be something wrong with our bloody ships today'. Whatever the truth of Beatty's comment, testaments from the small number of *Queen Mary*'s survivors demonstrates there was little wrong with the human element. According to Jocelyn Storey, 'There was no panic or shouting at all, the men were splendid heroes.'[63] Worse for Beatty and his surviving ships, by 4.40 PM the leading German battleships were in sight and rapidly closing.

Thus far, the German plan had succeeded brilliantly. Not only had Beatty's battle-cruisers been lured into a trap but so had four British dreadnoughts temporarily attached to his force. These ships were the most powerful type then in existence and the Germans had a perfect opportunity to destroy them. Despite his losses and serious tactical predicament, however, Beatty perceived an opportunity to reverse the situation by luring the Germans towards the Grand Fleet: thus began the 'Run to the North'.

By now, medical personnel were dealing with a steady stream of wounded men. For the uninitiated, the effects of modern naval warfare on the human body were horrific.[64] Severe lacerations and crushed limbs had been anticipated before the war but nothing had prepared anyone for the effects of cordite-flash burns. The suffering of victims and those tending them was worsened by the fact that standard-issue picric-acid dressings appeared to do more harm than good.[65] A helpless surgeon remembered of his patients, 'The great cry is water [...] They die and die very rapidly.'[66]

Over the next hour and a half, the initial German success began to unravel. As Beatty's squadron headed northwards they were hotly pursued by the entire High Seas Fleet. However, despite intense German fire none of his remaining warships was sunk or crippled, and some scored damaging hits on their pursuers.[67] Eighteen-year-old Harold Dawson, on board the *Valiant*, recalled the mesmerising

Fig.29
William Lionel Wyllie
HMS 'Iron Duke' at the Battle of Jutland, c.1919
Oil on canvas
61 x 123 cm (24 x 48 ⅖ in)
Private collection

effect of being under fire, helpless to respond: 'I could not stop looking out of the aperture, watching the gun flashes of the Germans and then the splashes of their shells as they dropped within yards of us.'[68] Most significantly at this stage in the battle, the Germans had no inkling of the threat that lay ahead of them. Shortly after 6 pm, Beatty sighted the leading British dreadnoughts.

What followed represented the critical point in the battle. Despite very limited information and poor visibility, Admiral Sir John Jellicoe positioned his ships with great skill. When the Germans appeared at 6.17 PM they were subjected to fire from the leading ships of the Grand Fleet, including Jellicoe's *Iron Duke* (fig.29). The immense power unleashed by so many battleships firing in unison was, by many accounts, terrible to behold. Watching the salvos from on board *Colossus*, Harold Foot remarked that 'the concussion of five 12[-inch] guns going off absolutely together is [...] pretty considerable'.[69] On at least one occasion, however, the effect was comical. Francis Burkitt of the *Superb* remembered: 'I went on deck to see what was going on. Just as I did so I was met by a terrific blast which knocked me over, but I was helped up by a sailor who said "It's all right, Sir, it's only one of our own guns."'[70]

Unable to retaliate effectively the Germans turned away, sinking another British battle-cruiser (*Invincible*) as they did so. Believing he had shaken off the British, Admiral Reinhard Scheer tried to re-engage on more favourable terms at about 7 PM, only to discover the British dreadnoughts again deployed across his path. Facing the massed guns of the Grand Fleet for a second time proved too much and Scheer again withdrew – this time for good. Wary of exposing his ships to mine and torpedo attacks in poor visibility, Jellicoe declined to pursue. By 8.45 PM he had grouped his fleet into night-cruising formation with the intention of resuming the battle the next day, as he was still between the Germans and their base.

Despite Jellicoe's precautions, brushes continued during the night between the smaller warships of both fleets. Lieutenant Stephen King-Hall on the *Southampton* recalled the deadly nature of close-quarter fighting in the dark. His ship torpedoed and sank the German cruiser *Frauenlob* but at heavy cost: 'In those 3 ½ minutes we had 89 casualties, and 75 per cent of the personnel on the upper deck were killed or wounded.'[71] Scheer decided to risk a night encounter in order to get his battleships back to Wilhelmshaven. His route took the German fleet through the British destroyer flotillas guarding the rear of the Grand Fleet. British resistance was determined but ineffective. The Germans lost the *Pommern*, an old pre-dreadnought battleship, but by 3 AM had escaped: the Battle of Jutland was over.

Jutland was the costliest naval action of the war and its only full fleet encounter. In terms of losses, the Germans could claim a tactical victory. Fourteen British ships had been sunk and 26 damaged (fig.30), as opposed to German losses of 11 sunk and 30 damaged. British casualties (including prisoners) came to 6,945 compared to 3,058 German.[72] Balanced against this the Germans had retreated, effectively conceding the field to the British. On 1 June, 105 undamaged British warships were ready to renew the fight but, with only 40 combat-ready ships, the Germans did not re-emerge that day or, convincingly, again. Their High Seas Fleet had failed to weaken the Grand Fleet in a critical way and the disparity in fighting power would widen in the Royal Navy's favour as the war continued. Strategically, the battle had little long-term effect other than sowing the seeds of an intensified German U-boat campaign as the only viable alternative to challenging the Grand Fleet.[73] The Royal Navy maintained its dominant position at sea and, most importantly, was able to continue the North Sea blockade that steadily eroded the German war effort.

All this, however, was unpalatable to the British public. Culturally conditioned by a century of supremacy and propaganda to believe in the Royal Navy's invincibility, many found it difficult to accept anything less than an annihilating victory. The contrast of British losses to German made it even harder, particularly for the families of the killed and injured. The Admiralty compounded the problem

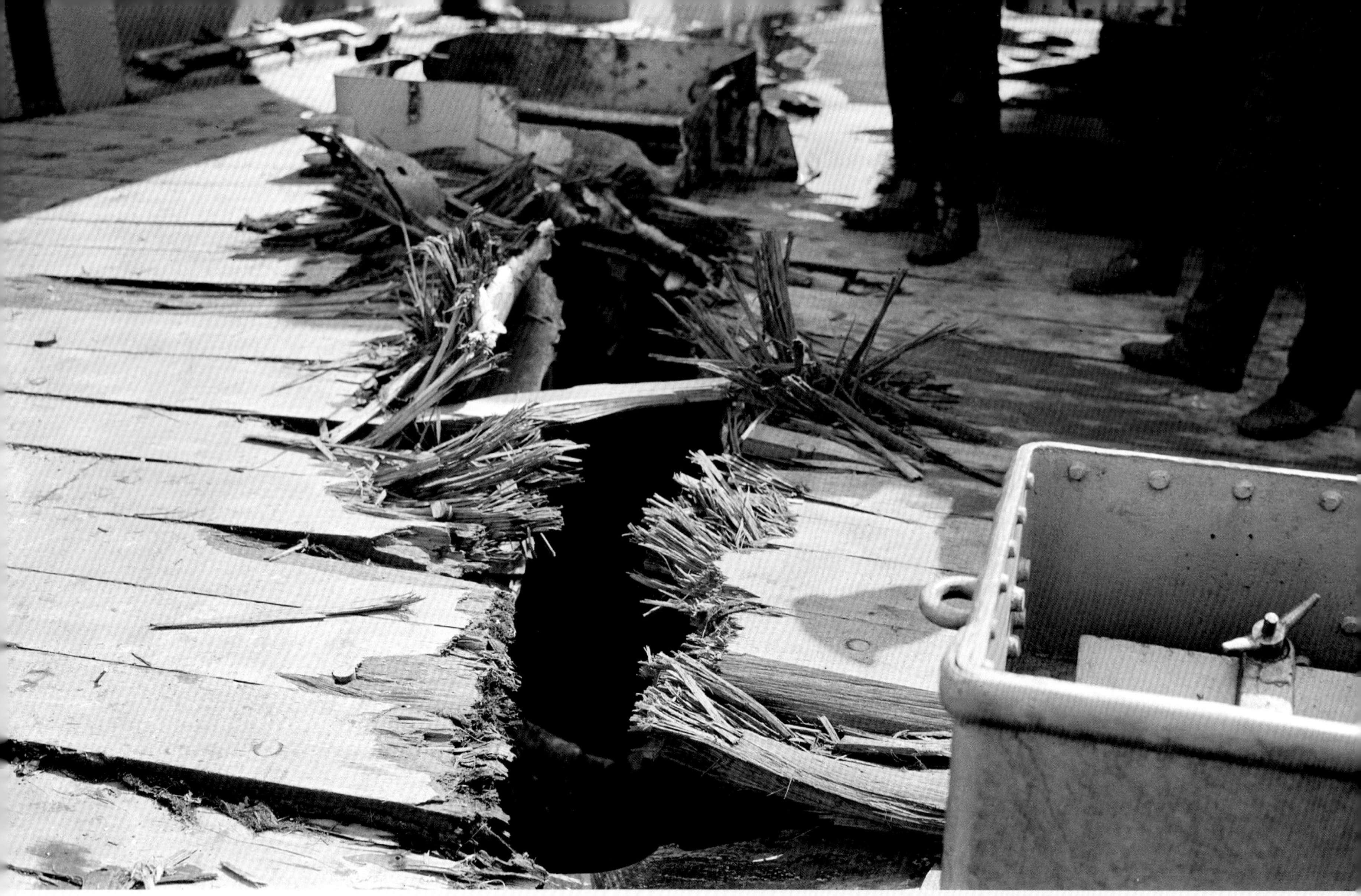

by failing to accompany the announcement of British losses with an explanation of the outcome as a strategic success, and it was not until the neutral press began to print their own assessments of the battle that public opinion in Britain began to change.[74]

The shadow cast by Trafalgar was long and exercised a malign influence on public expectations of the vaunted and expensive British fleet. Nelson's brilliance there, coupled with the pathos of his 'death in victory', obscured the inconvenient fact that it was but a single engagement in a protracted conflict and credited with much more strategic value than it deserved.[75] Ironically, the Royal Navy's study of the Russo-Japanese War of 1904–5 had much the same effect on naval officers. Useful lessons from that conflict had been overshadowed by the comprehensive Japanese victory at Tsushima in May 1905, which reinforced the erroneous view that winning a battle could substitute for winning a war.[76] In the absence of a clear-cut victory and obvious scapegoats for a 'defeat', the public fixated upon a search for heroes. This manifested itself most spectacularly in the case of 16-year-old Jack Cornwell (fig.20 and plate 13) of HMS *Chester*, who was awarded a posthumous VC, and of whom intense public idolisation became a phenomenon (see Chapter 2: The Face of War).[77] This was all the more remarkable in comparison to the relatively muted response to other posthumous Jutland VC winners such as Loftus Jones and Francis Harvey, whose contributions to the battle were far greater. The explanation lies, perhaps, in the authorities' urgent need for an 'ideal' exemplar with whom most of the British public could identify: hence the promotion of a young man of working-class stock (as opposed to officers such as Jones and Harvey) who, by his heroic death, epitomised the desirable virtues of loyalty, courage and obedience (fig.31).

Fig.30 (opposite)
Shell damage suffered by HMS *Warspite* at the Battle of Jutland, June 1916
Photographic negative
11 x 16 cm (4 ⅜ x 6 ¼ in)
NMM, Earl Howe Collection
N16510

Torn decking marks the passage of a 12-inch shell which struck HMS *Warspite* during the Battle of Jutland, one of 13 such projectiles to hit the ship. This one carried on to explode inside the *Warspite*'s shelter deck.

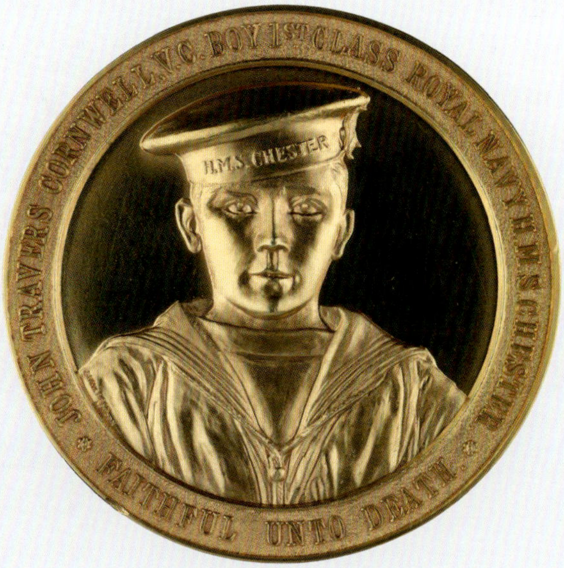

While Jutland caused much soul-searching among the Royal Navy's leadership, it affected the morale of the service considerably less than that of the British people. There was certainly grief for lost comrades but it was matched by a determination that, in future, the German fleet would not be allowed to escape without accounts being settled. William Jameson wrote years later: 'For the men of the Grand Fleet Jutland was a bitter disappointment, though their faith in themselves and in their Commander-in-Chief was unshaken. I speak knowingly for I was there, a sixteen-year-old midshipman, quite ignorant of most of the great matters involved, but closer than the mighty to the men of the lower deck.'[78]

In the meantime, the Grand Fleet continued to train and iron out the deficiencies that the battle had revealed. As commanders, Jellicoe and Beatty were deemed to have performed creditably, although criticism was naturally levelled at them both. Jellicoe remained Commander-in-Chief until November 1916 when Beatty succeeded him for the rest of the war. Neither participated directly in the subsequent Jutland controversies, although Beatty's tampering with the official record, and the resultant backlash, did not reflect well on him.[79]

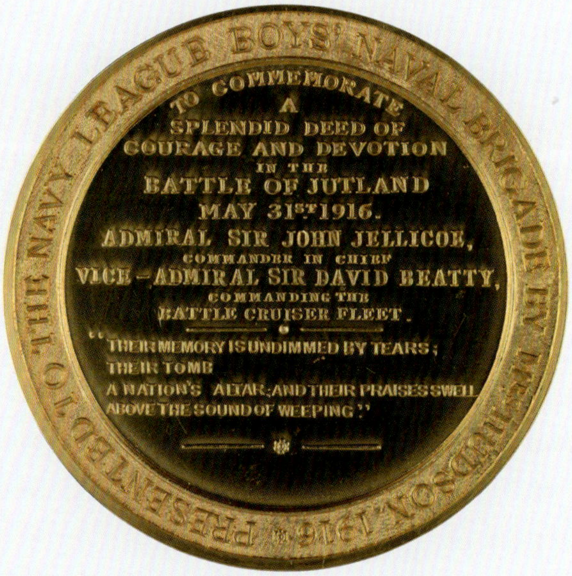

Jutland was the largest naval battle in modern history until the American action with the Japanese at the Leyte Gulf in 1944, and remains the largest involving battleships. It exercises a fascination to this day and, like many incomplete victories, will continue to generate controversy and debate. What is beyond doubt is the bravery of the British and German sailors involved. The normally reserved Jellicoe was effusive in praise when he wrote that 'wherever there was opportunity, officers and men displayed courage and self-sacrifice of the highest order. There were innumerable instances which proved that the personnel of the present Navy has nothing to learn in this respect from its forefathers.'[80]

Fig.31
Spinks and Sons
Medal commemorating John Travers Cornwell VC, 1916
Gold
6.4 cm (2 ½ in) diam.
MEC2775

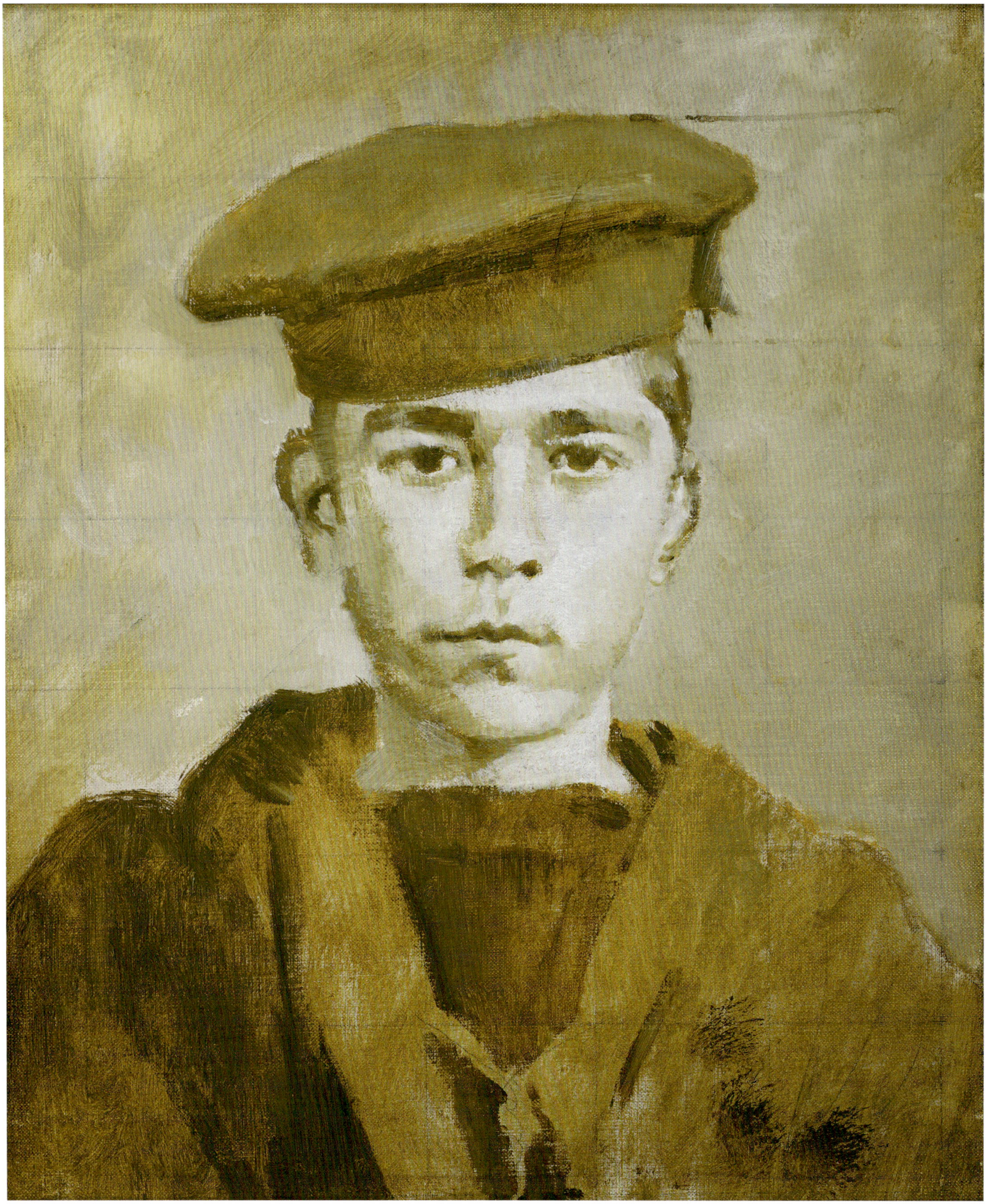

Plate 13 (opposite)
Ambrose McEvoy
John Travers Cornwell, Boy First Class, VC (1900–1916), 1918
Oil on canvas
50.8 x 40.6 cm (20 x 16 in)
Kindly lent by Mrs Mona McEvoy
to the National Maritime Museum,
Greenwich, London
BHC2635

Plate 14 (right)
Jacob Epstein
Admiral of the Fleet Sir John Arbuthnot Fisher, 1st Baron Fisher of Kilverstone, 1916
Patinated plaster
68.6 x 58.4 x 38.1 cm (27 x 23 x 15 in)
SCU0018

'Fisher had an extraordinary appearance [...] Here [...] is one of the greatest men of this age, one of the greatest figures of this war, and the head and features are a wonderful expression of this tremendous personality [...] His light eyes, with strange colours, were set in a face like parchment ivory, and his iron-grey hair was cut short and bristled on his head. He was short, but had the appearance of combative sturdiness [...] He was the typical man of war. He made no bones about it. War was terrible, and should be terrible.'

Jacob Epstein, 'How I sculptured Lord Fisher', *Weekly Dispatch*, 24 December 1916

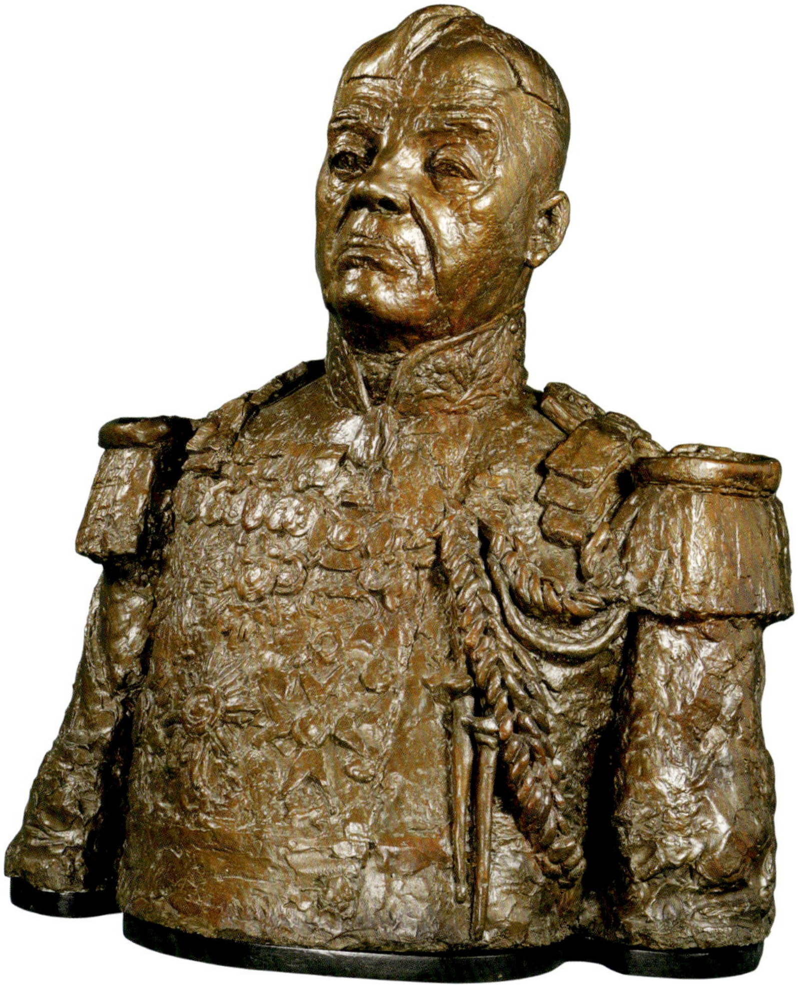

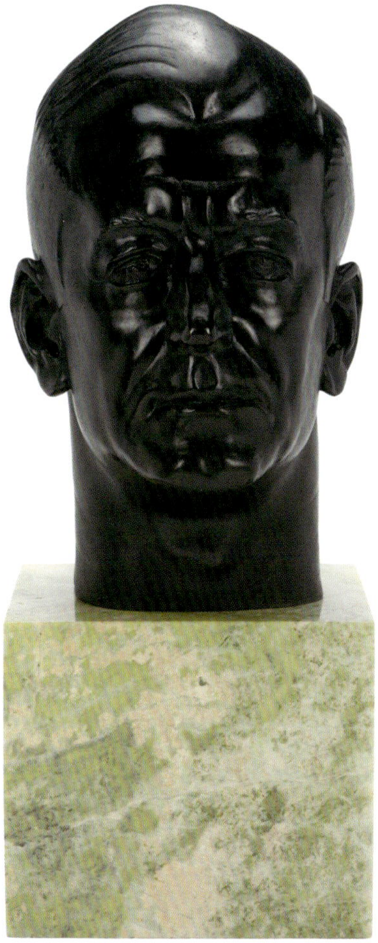

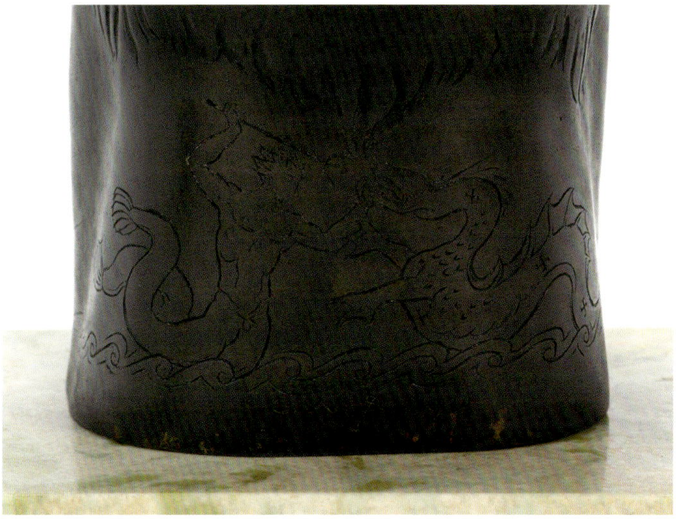

Plate 15 (far left and detail, left)
Charles Wheeler
Captain George Elvey Creasy, 1941
Cast bronze
49 x 20 x 26 cm (19 ¼ x 7 ⅞ x 10 ¼ in)
SCU0013

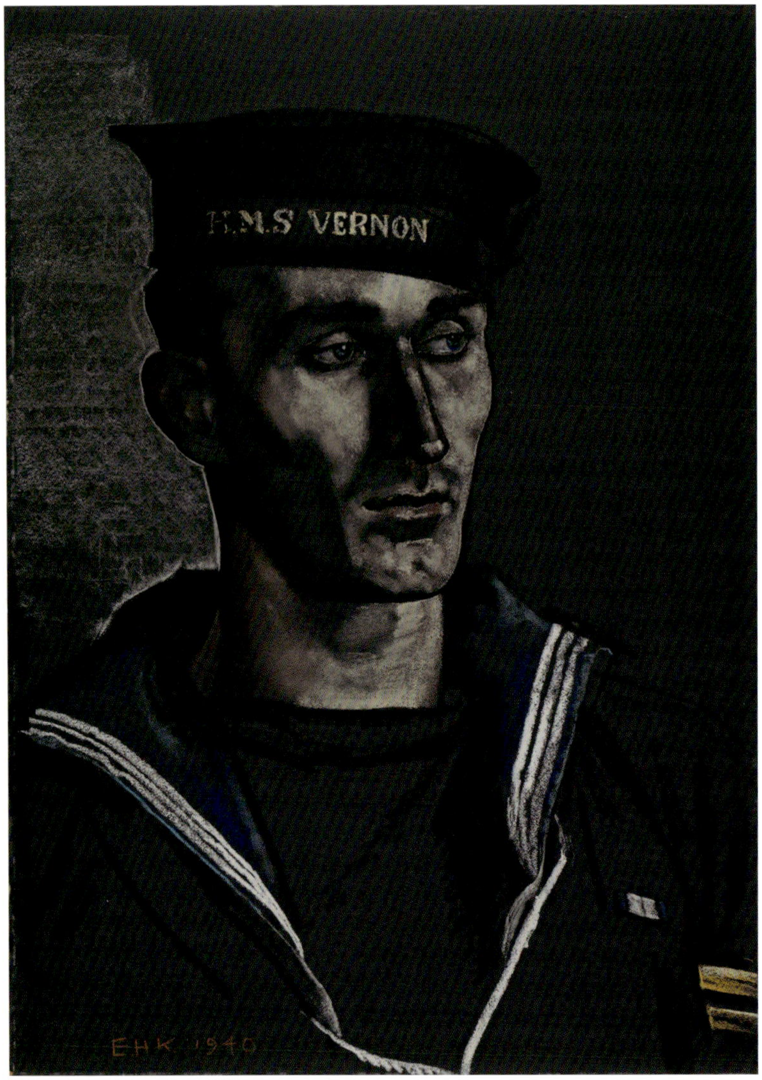

Plate 16
Eric Kennington
Leading Seaman A.L. Vearncombe DSM, HMS 'Vernon', 1940
Pastel on paper
74.6 x 52.4 cm (29 3/8 x 20 5/8 in)
ZBA4943

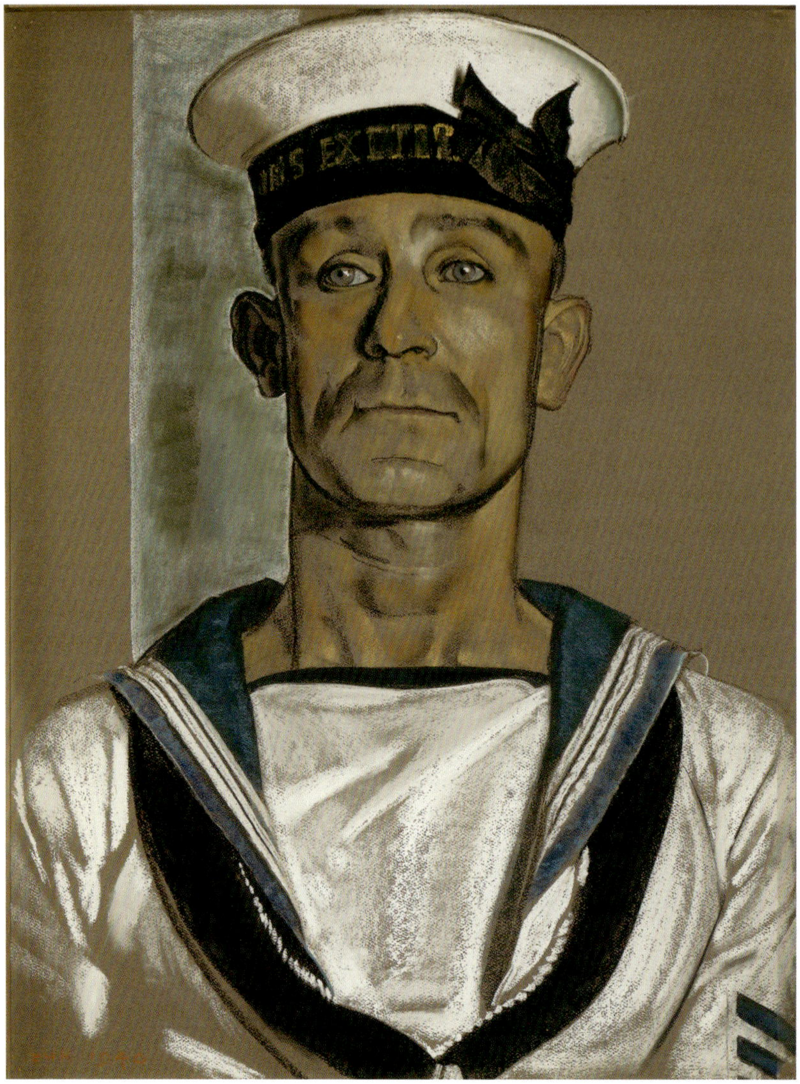

Plate 17
Eric Kennington
Stoker A. Martin of HMS 'Exeter', 1940
Pastel on paper
73.5 x 53 cm (28 7/8 x 20 7/8 in)
PAJ2894

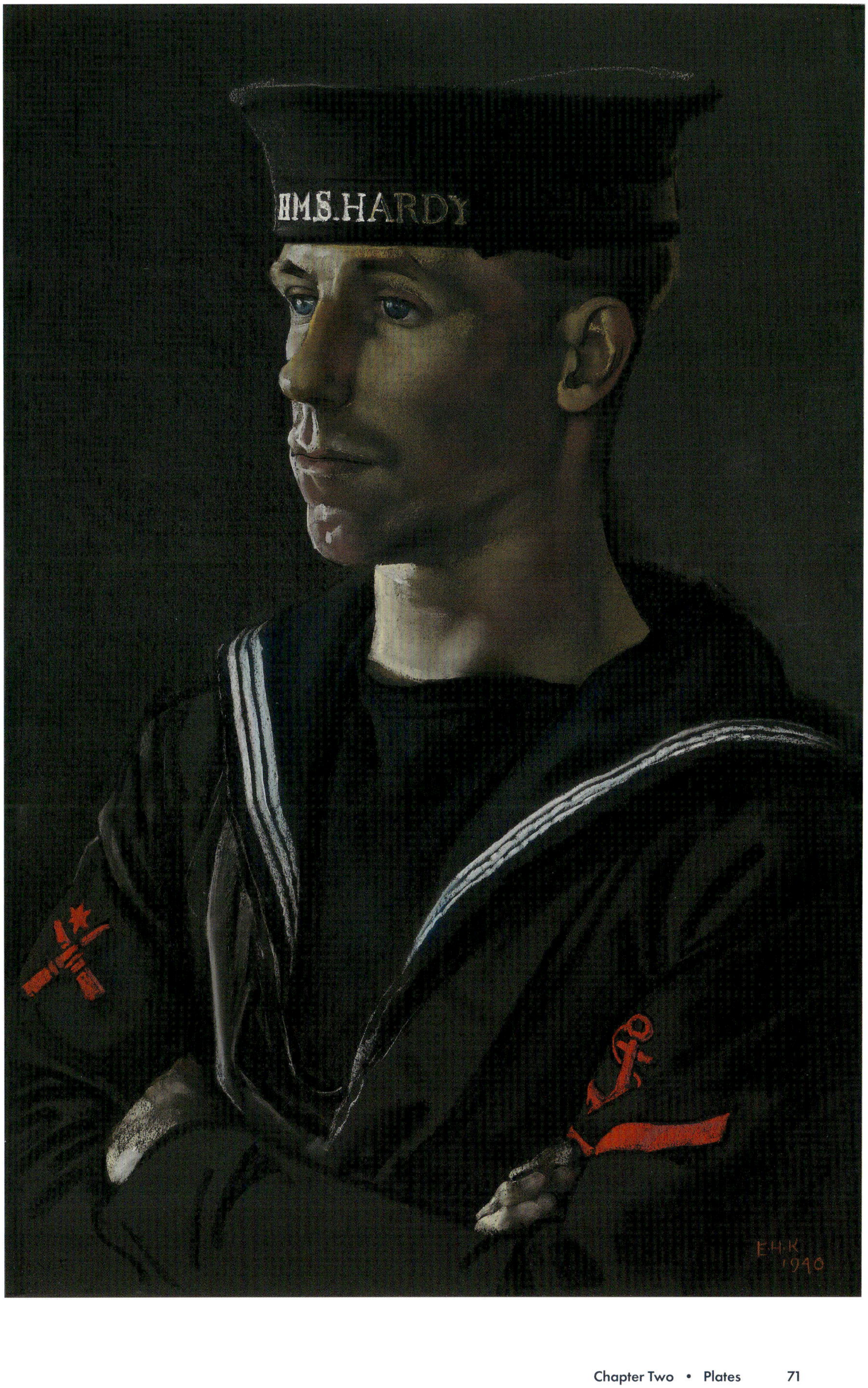

Plate 18
Eric Kennington
Leading Seaman Dove of HMS 'Hardy',
1940
Pastel on paper
94.5 x 69 cm (37 ¼ x 27 ⅛ in)
PAJ3022

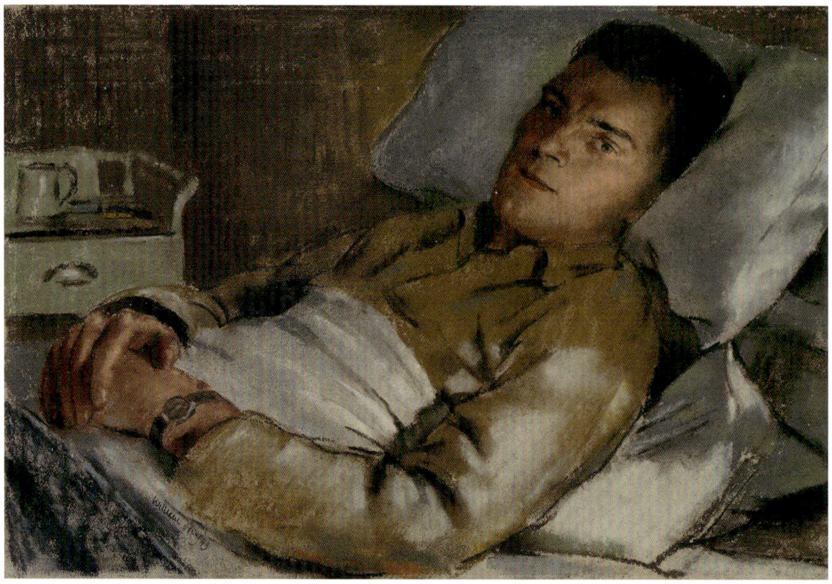

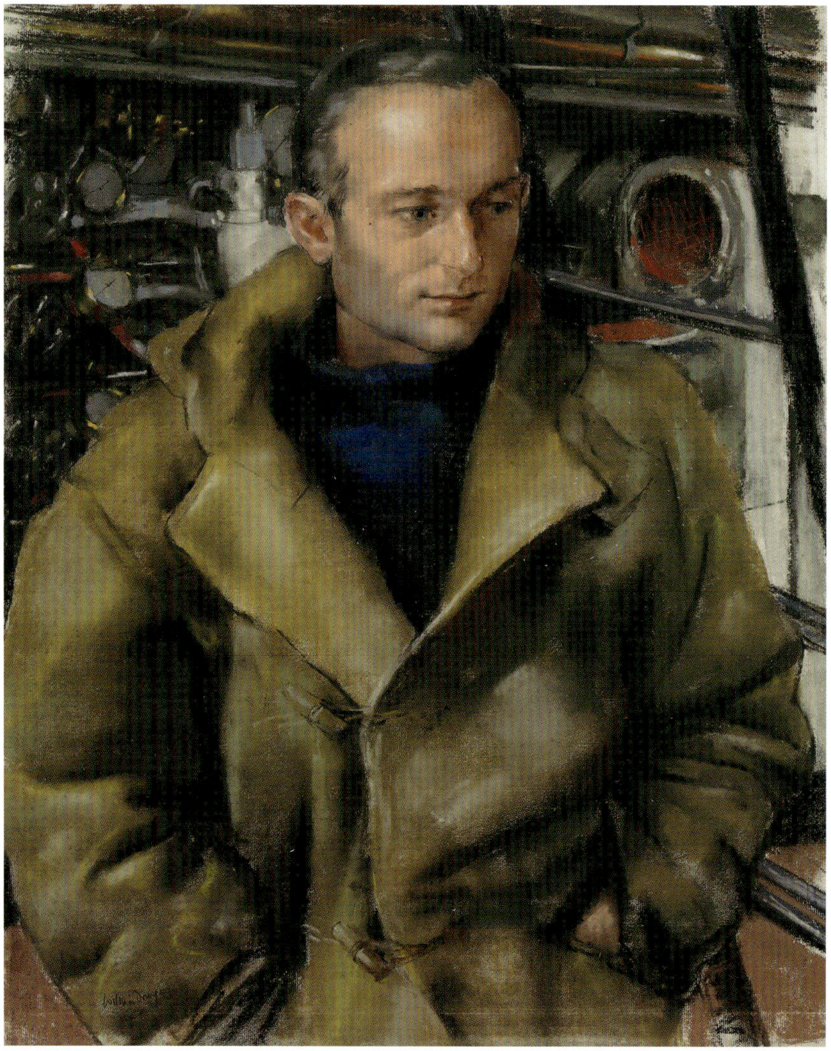

Plate 19 (above)
William Dring
Lieutenant-Surgeon Philip R.C. Evans, GC [GM] RNVR, 1943
Pastel on paper
33.5 x 48 cm (13 ¼ x 18 ⅞ in)
PAJ2986

Plate 20 (below)
William Dring
Commander William D. King, 1943
Pastel on paper
77.1 x 64.6 cm (13 ⅜ x 25 ⅜ in)
PAJ3017

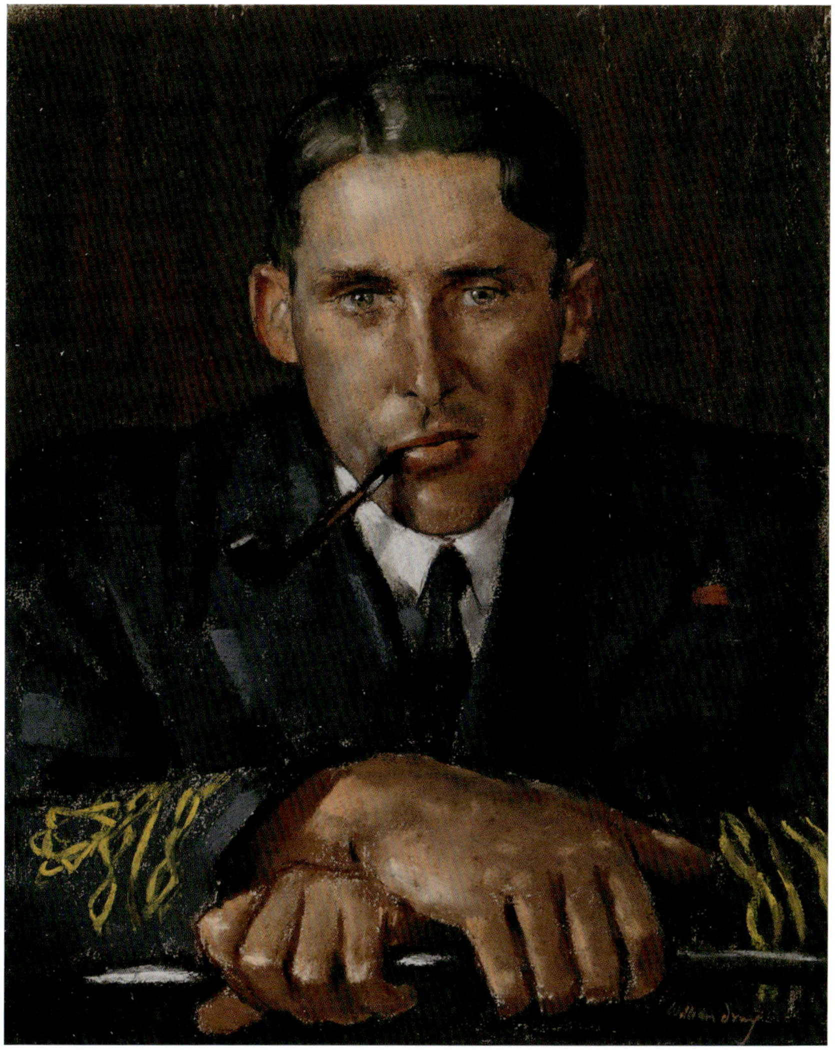

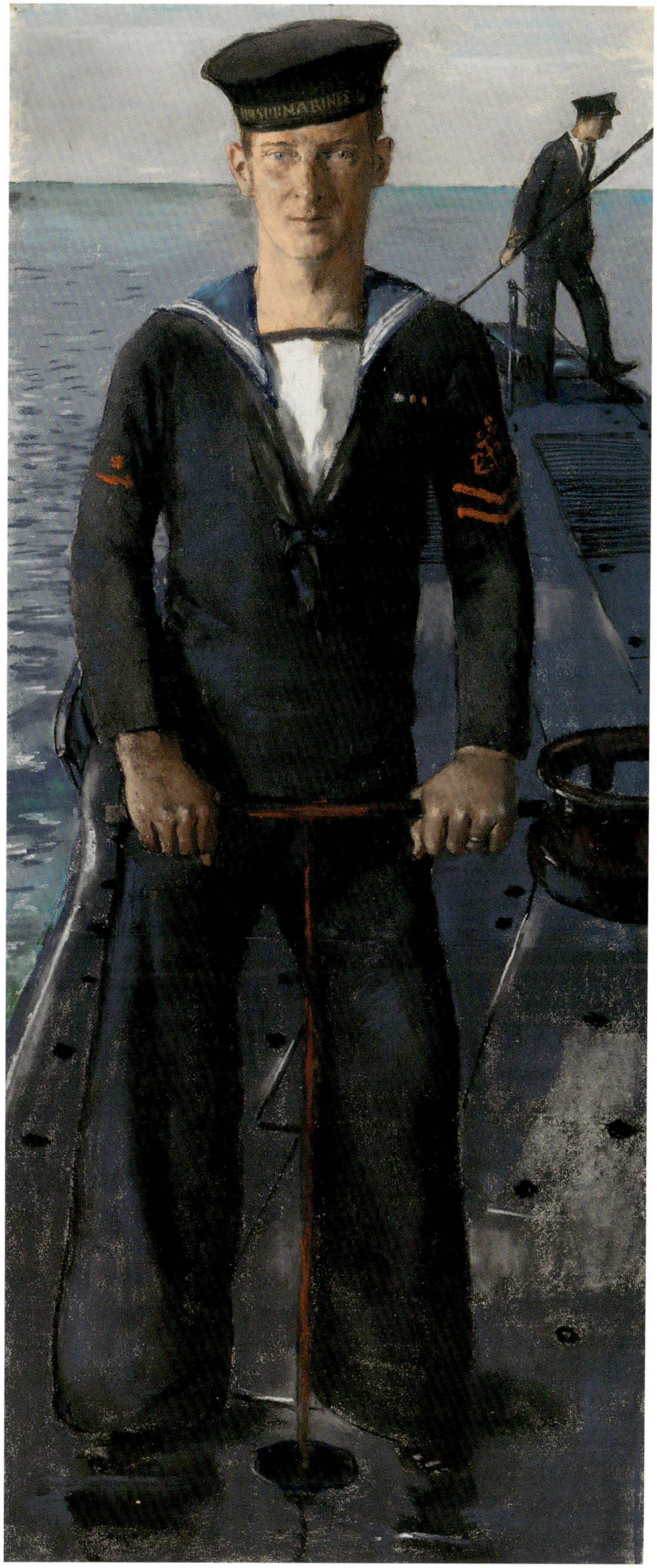

Plate 21 (above)
William Dring
Lieutenant-Commander C.E. Bridgman, DSO, 1943
Pastel on paper
40 x 31 cm (15 3/4 x 12 1/4 in)
PAJ2987

Plate 22 (right)
William Dring
Petty Officer Augustus William Armishaw, DSM and Bar, 1943
Pastel on paper
98.5 x 50.6 cm (38 3/4 x 19 7/8 in)
PAJ2889

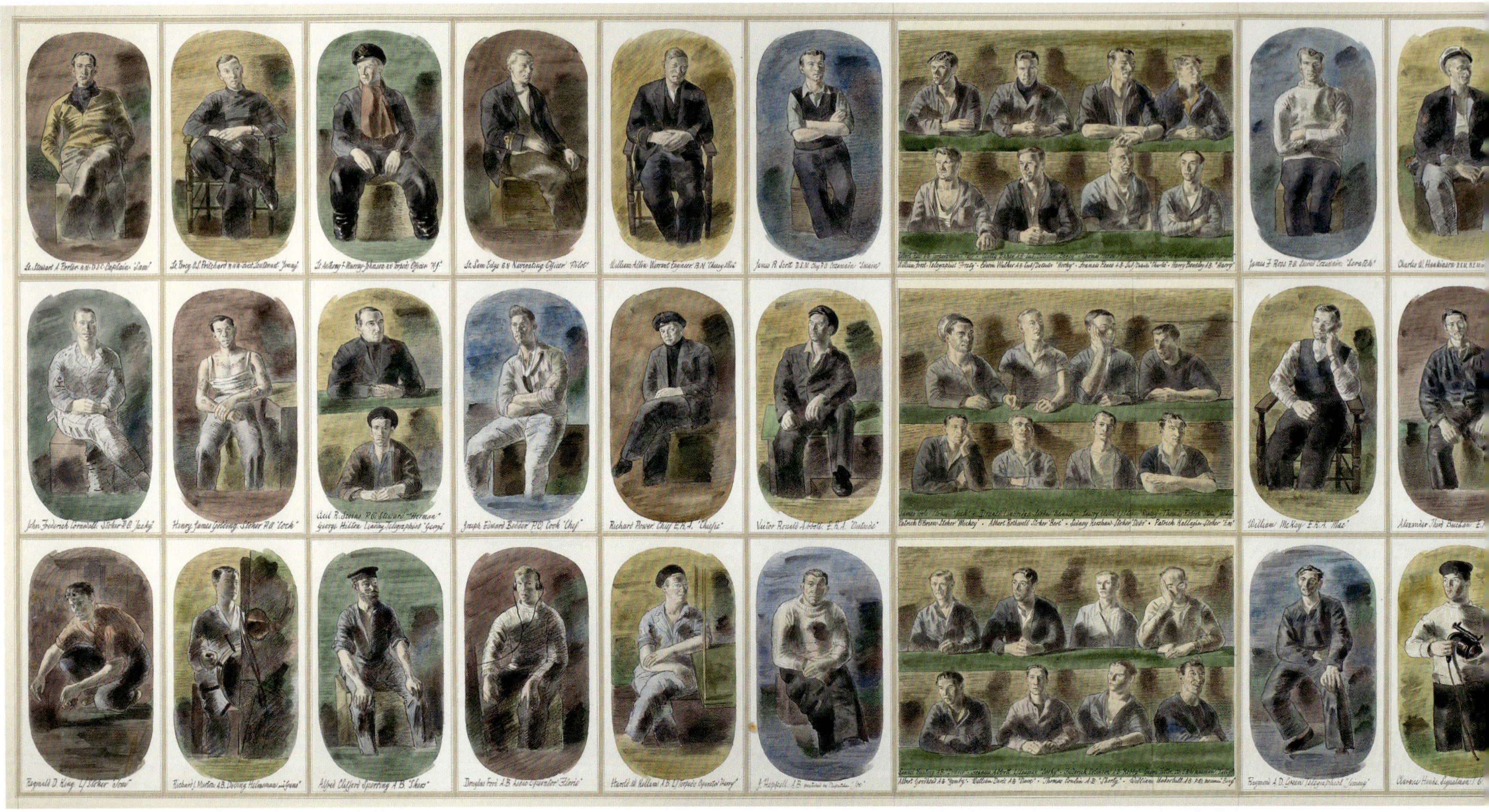

Plate 23 (above and detail, right)
Barnett Freedman
HM Submarine 'Tribune', the Commanding Officer and his Company Drawn on board and in Fort Block House June – August 1943, 1943
Watercolour, pen and ink on paper
104 x 200 cm (41 x 78 3/4 in)
ZBA4343

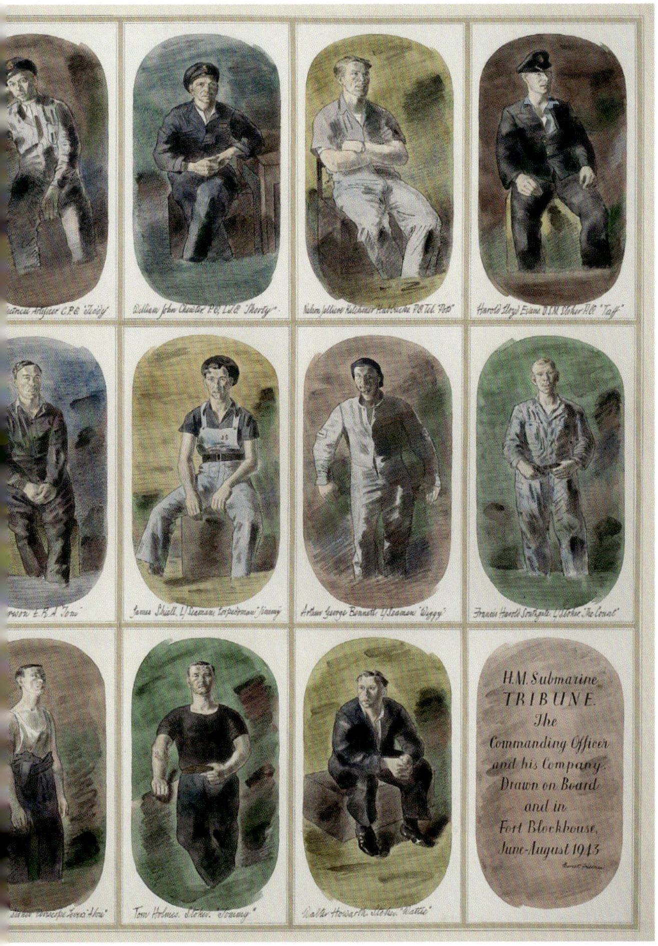
H.M. Submarine
TRIBUNE
The
Commanding Officer
and his Company
Drawn on Board
and in
Fort Blockhouse,
June-August 1943

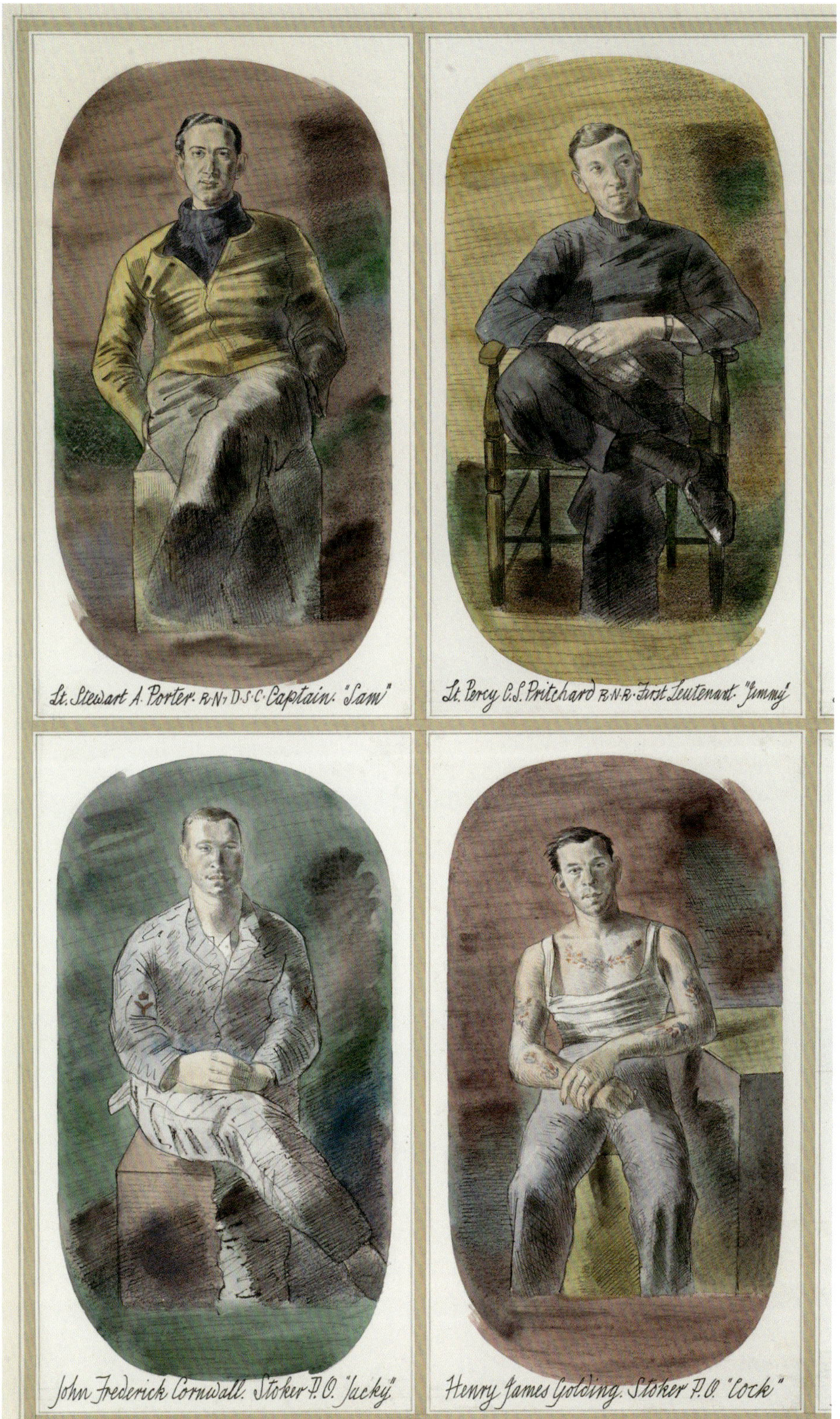
Lt. Stewart A. Porter. R.N. D.S.C. Captain: "Sam"
Lt. Percy C.S. Pritchard R.N.R. First Lieutenant. "Jimmy"
John Frederick Cornwall. Stoker P.O. "Jacky"
Henry James Golding. Stoker P.O. "Cock"

3

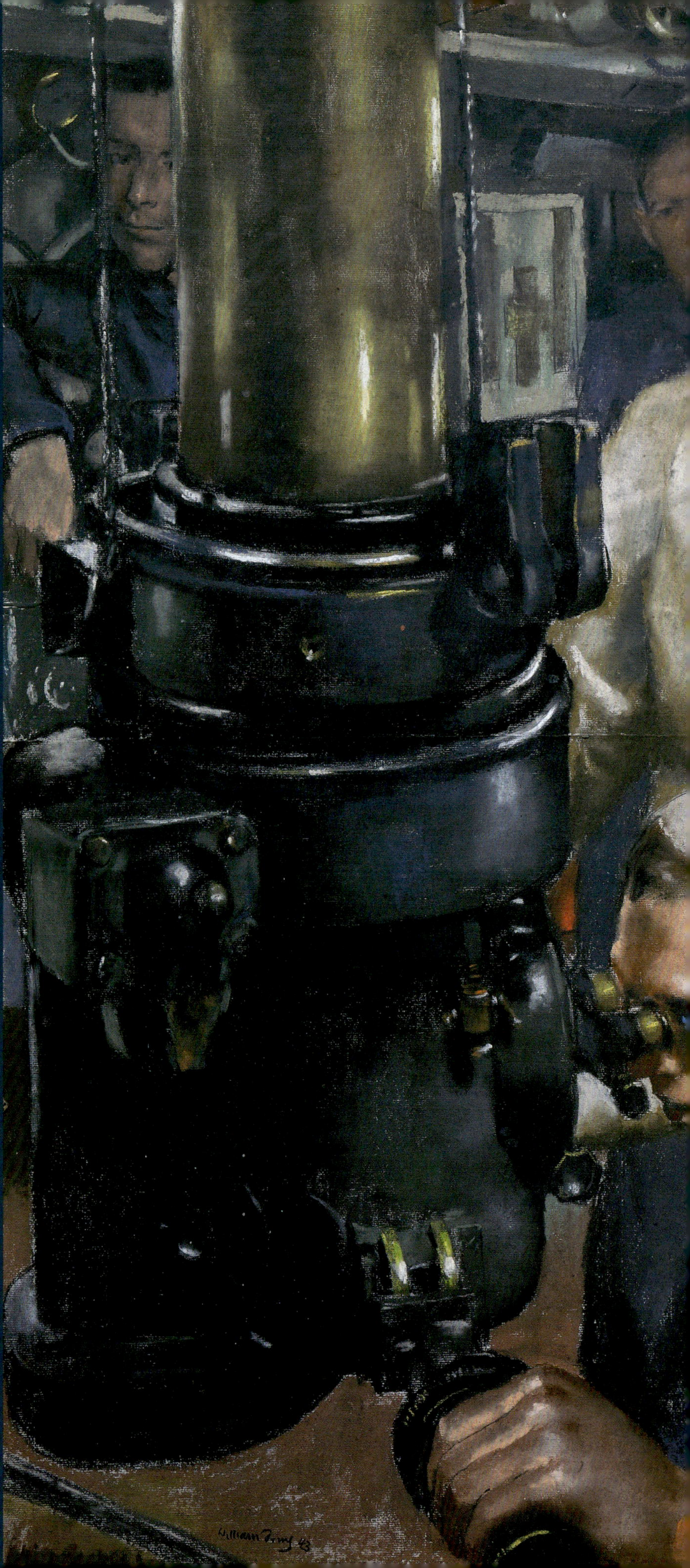

William Dring
Stand by Tubes. The Control Room of HMS 'Stubborn', 1943
Pastel on paper
96 x 119 cm (37 3/4 x 46 7/8 in)
PAJ2897

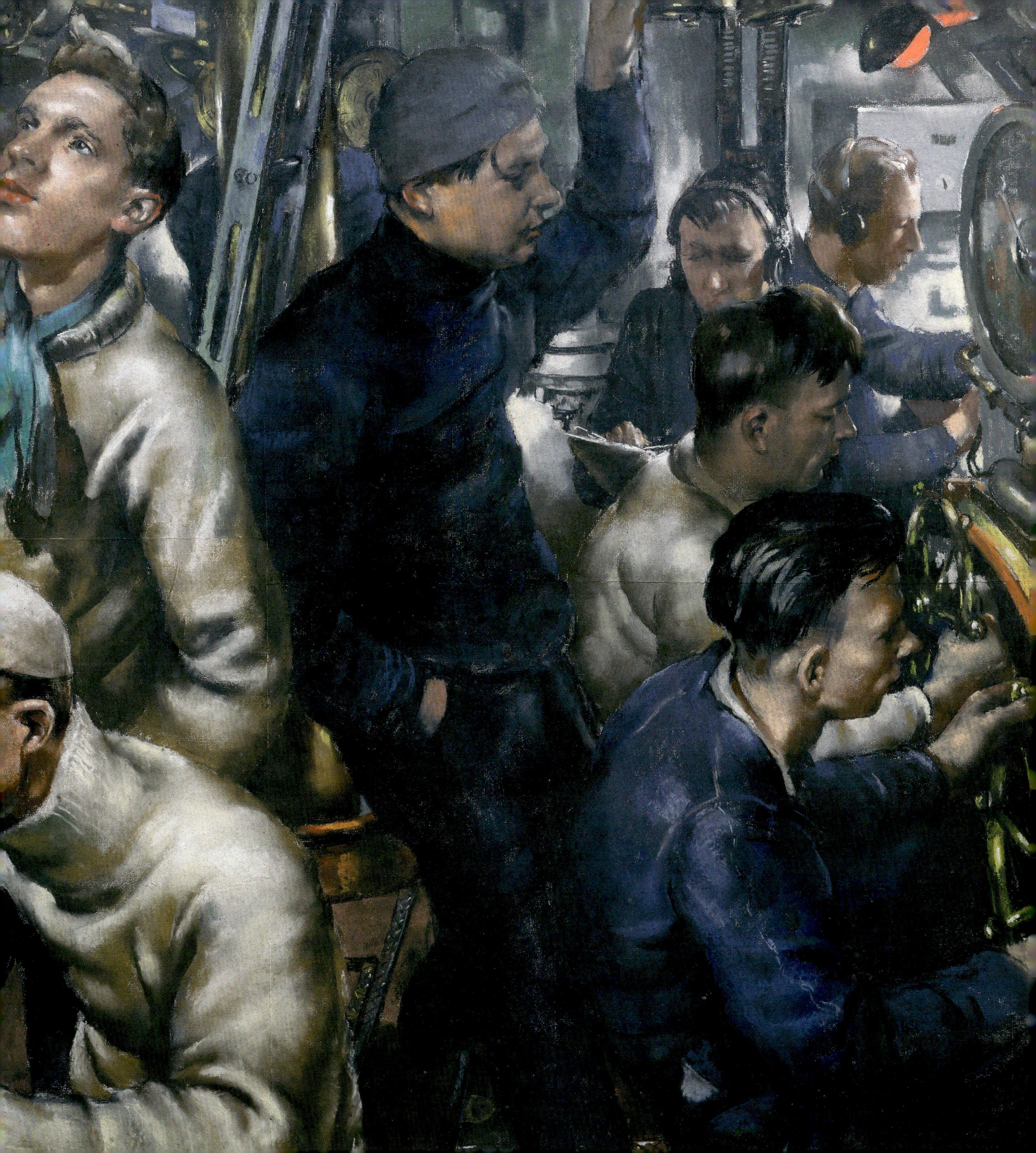

3

Above and Below Deck

Melanie Vandenbrouck

In addition to recording engagements and individuals at all levels in the conflict, a strong motive in official war art of both World Wars was to represent scenes of everyday life. This was, perhaps, what most fascinated the public, since everyone had family, friends and acquaintances serving in the forces, while many civilians were also engaged in war work of all sorts. As regards those afloat, above- and below-deck views offered a glimpse of the roles of seafarers in the war, and the camaraderie and social life that existed on board ship. Furthermore, such artistic representations were intended to promote, to both British and international audiences, the idea of the ship's company as a loyal and dutiful community.

Muirhead Bone: Official War Artist

First-hand observation was key to the perceived truthfulness and thus authority of such visual accounts. While, in the First World War, few artists were granted privileged access to naval environments, during the Second, arrangements were made to ensure this was possible. As discussed in the previous chapter, Muirhead Bone (1876–1953) was a key artistic figure in both wars. A renowned draughtsman, he was appointed Britain's first official war artist in May 1916 by the War Propaganda Bureau at Wellington House. An ideal candidate for the job, he was known for his rapid production of high-quality, accurate drawings that could be easily reproduced, including through his own output as a printmaker.[1]

Bone was first sent to the Western Front in France in August 1916, in the honorary rank and uniform of an Army Second Lieutenant, which provided him with the security clearance needed to travel with ease.[2] He worked quickly, often in pencil, pen, charcoal and chalk, and had completed some 150 drawings by October. He suggested the idea of publishing them in aid of the war effort and for propaganda purposes, including abroad, with brief descriptive texts. Bone himself identified an author for these in C.E. Montague, a respected pre-war journalist on the *Manchester Guardian* (for which his brother, James Bone, also worked), then serving on headquarters intelligence staff at the Front. The idea was swiftly embraced both by the Army (Field-Marshal Sir Douglas Haig, the Commander-in-Chief in France, supplied a preface) and by Wellington House. The drawings were to be selected by Bone's friend, Campbell Dodgson, Keeper of Prints and Drawings at the British Museum, where the original works would find a permanent home. *Country Life* agreed to act as publisher, giving civilian cover to the propaganda aspect, and 200 were reproduced as a collection of lithographs entitled *The Western Front*, issued in ten monthly parts from January 1917. The first issue was, in fact, available in December 1916, ready to accompany a general and promotional exhibition of some of the drawings at Colnaghi & Obach's New Bond Street gallery, London, in January, with subsequent display elsewhere. Each issue was printed in 30,000 copies, of which 12,000 were for sale at 2 shillings, 12,000 were for use as propaganda and 6,000 were for distribution in the United States, where Wellington House was keen to promote the British war effort.[3]

Commenting on the Colnaghi exhibition, the art critic of *The Times* explained that Bone had been expected to depict mostly ruins but was reported as saying, 'How could I think of ruined buildings [...] when I had the opportunity of drawing these splendid men'.[4] The lithographs thus showed not just scenes of destruction but covered a wider range, including portraits and behind-the-lines activities, such as the daily life of off-duty soldiers, the work of the medical services and the maintenance of weaponry, as well as maritime subjects. In 1918, the War Office also separately republished 60 of the lithographs as a portfolio entitled *War Drawings*. While some are in a highly descriptive style, others, like *Off Havre – Taking the Pilot aboard a Hospital Ship* (plate 24) have an evocative, sombre mood, befitting the seriousness of war. The sketchiness of this image transmits the feel of an on-the-spot record. The figures leaning on the deck express anticipation,

Fig.32
Stephen Bone
The Galley, HMS 'Norfolk', 1945
Crayon and graphite on paper
39.1 x 54.7 cm (15 3/8 x 21 1/2 in)
PAI0526

and the pilot's glance backward as he steps aboard adds to the sense of immediacy. Displayed in Bond Street in June 1917, the 'fine, dramatic charcoal sketch' from which this lithograph was taken was described in the *Manchester Guardian* as 'more expressive and at the same time more astonishing in ease and daring execution than similar drawings before'.[5]

While Francis Dodd replaced him at the Western Front to execute portraits of British leaders (see Chapter 2: The Face of War), Bone returned to Britain to depict munitions works and shipyards. In March 1917, he was sent to the Grand Fleet in Scotland (at Rosyth, in the Firth of Forth and Scapa Flow, Orkney), where he spent three weeks recording daily life on board. As Meirion and Susie Harries note, Bone's access was unique for, other than him – and although W.L. Wyllie had already privately done the same thing by officially sanctioned invitation – 'no official artist was able to live and work successfully on board the battleships. Suspicion of civilians, especially artists, was particularly acute in the Navy.'[6]

The Bridge of HMS 'Princess Royal', Scapa 1918 (plate 26) concentrates on the brass, iron and wood environment of the vessel, while conveying the cool light and chilly atmosphere of the Orkney Islands, in which a strong element of 'here and now' is added by the lone figure of an officer looking out to sea. In May 1917, scenes from this trip were published as part five of Bone's *Western Front* under the title *With the Grand Fleet*, with six of these issued as a deluxe portfolio.[7] Although the prints may each be viewed as works of art in their own right, they were clearly intended as propaganda and Montague's descriptions overlaid on them an idea of British superiority, pride and power. To give just one example, a print from that portfolio (plate 25), depicting stokers at work in the bowels of a ship, was accompanied by the caption: 'The vessel is oil driven, so the stoke-hold is robbed of its old terrors, and is remarkably cool. The stokers seem few in proportion to the size of the place, but they are experts of a higher class than the coal furnaces required.'

Bone's work was appreciated for its 'journalistic language' and 'realistic intensity'.[8] Its perceived 'photographic' accuracy made it an important record of activity below deck that could not have been achieved with contemporary photography (the dark environment and constant vibrations of the engines would have rendered any shot blurry and indistinct). Having originally trained as an architect, Bone had 'established a reputation as a London Piranesi' with his early drypoint views of scaffolding and monumental demolition of buildings, a comparison that still had currency during the war.[9] His boiler-room scene gives a sense of the cathedral-like internal scale of engineering space in large ships, which would have been unfamiliar to the general public. Likewise, *Inside the Turret* is painstakingly detailed and shows an officer visiting the gunnery specialists at work in the glowing light of that confined space.[10] Representations of the impressive machinery of conflict would become a recurring theme in both World Wars: indeed, Barnett Freedman's *15" Gun Turret, HMS 'Repulse', August 1941* (plate 27) is almost identical to Bone's print, in subject, angle and composition.

Thanks to his role in the First World War, both as official artist and for recommending others he thought suited to the task, Bone became the first and most senior of all Admiralty artists during the 1939–45 conflict, as well as being a member of the War Artists Advisory Committee (WAAC).[11] This time it was arranged for the *Illustrated London News* to have first option on publication of his drawings, giving them wide currency.[12] He was noted in the press for the 'realism' with which he documented official gatherings and depicted various vessels. He also made atmospheric scenes, such as the series of drawings of mine-laying operations made aboard HMS *Southern Prince*,[13] which also prompted a rare oil painting by him (*Winter Minelaying off Iceland*, IWM) exhibited to critical acclaim at the National Gallery in 1942.

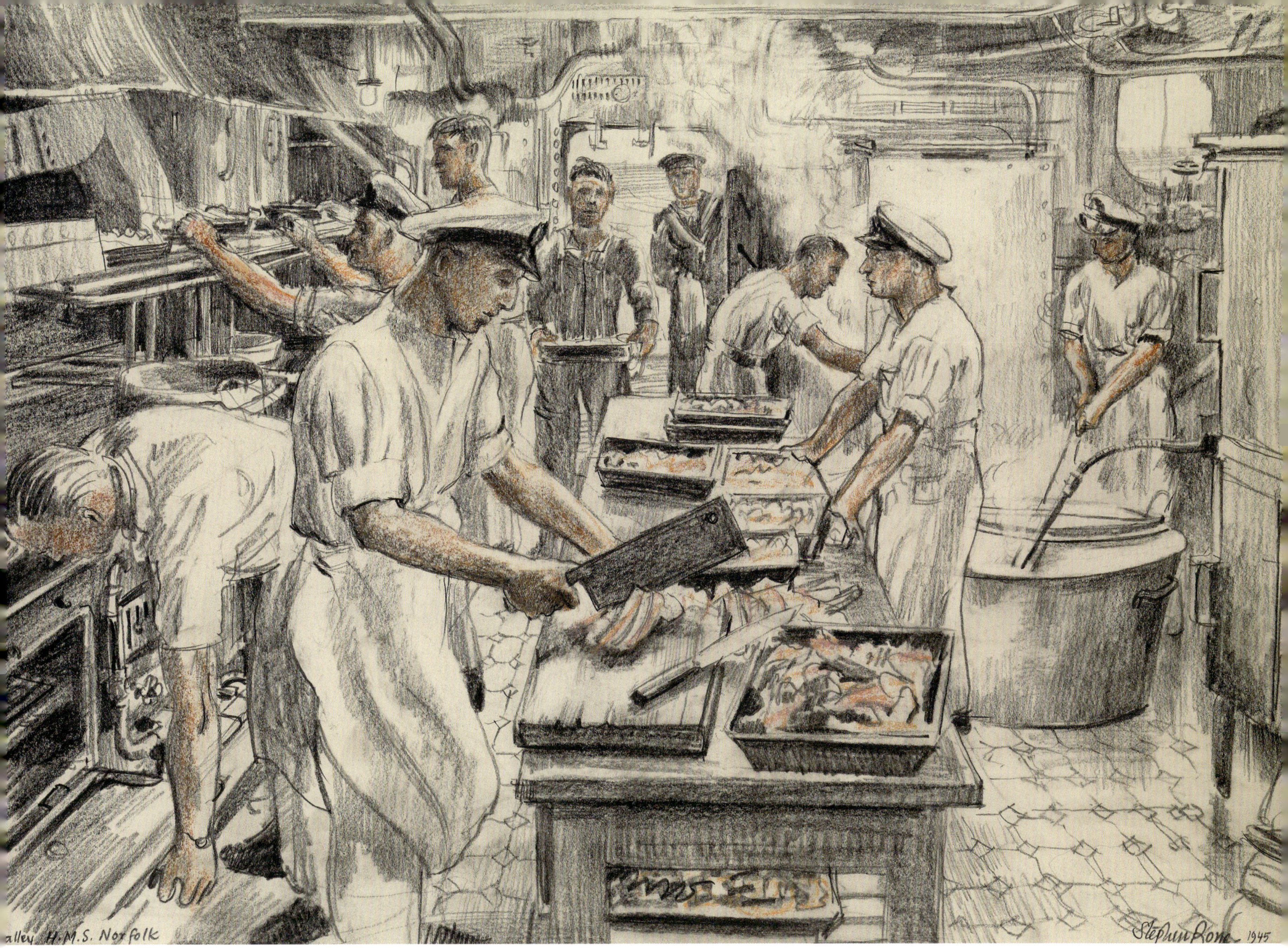

Stephen Bone: Like Father, Like Son

Wartime tragedies not only resulted from active service or enemy attack: natural causes also took their toll and, in 1943, Muirhead Bone's second son, Gavin, died of tuberculosis. Grieving for his son, Bone gave up his official work as an Admiralty artist, although he remained a member of the WAAC until 1946, but with a lesser involvement. He was replaced, if not formally at least effectively, by his other son Stephen (1904–58), who was appointed an official war artist in June 1943.

Trained as a painter at the Slade School of Art, Stephen Bone started the war as a camouflage officer, based at Leamington Spa, Warwickshire, with some 200 other artists.[14] He had occasionally submitted works to the WAAC, such as *Railway Men* (1942, Rugby Art Gallery and Museum), or sent lists of possible subjects, which were often turned down on censorship grounds.[15] As the son of one of the most influential figures on the Committee, it would perhaps have been seen as improper to appoint him while his father was an official salaried war artist.[16] Following in his footsteps was no easy matter and Stephen's name usually appeared in the press linked to that of Muirhead: 'Stephen Bone, like his father, has the same call of the sea in his blood.'[17] First sent to record wartime activities in the Scottish port of Greenock, Stephen was subsequently given the rank

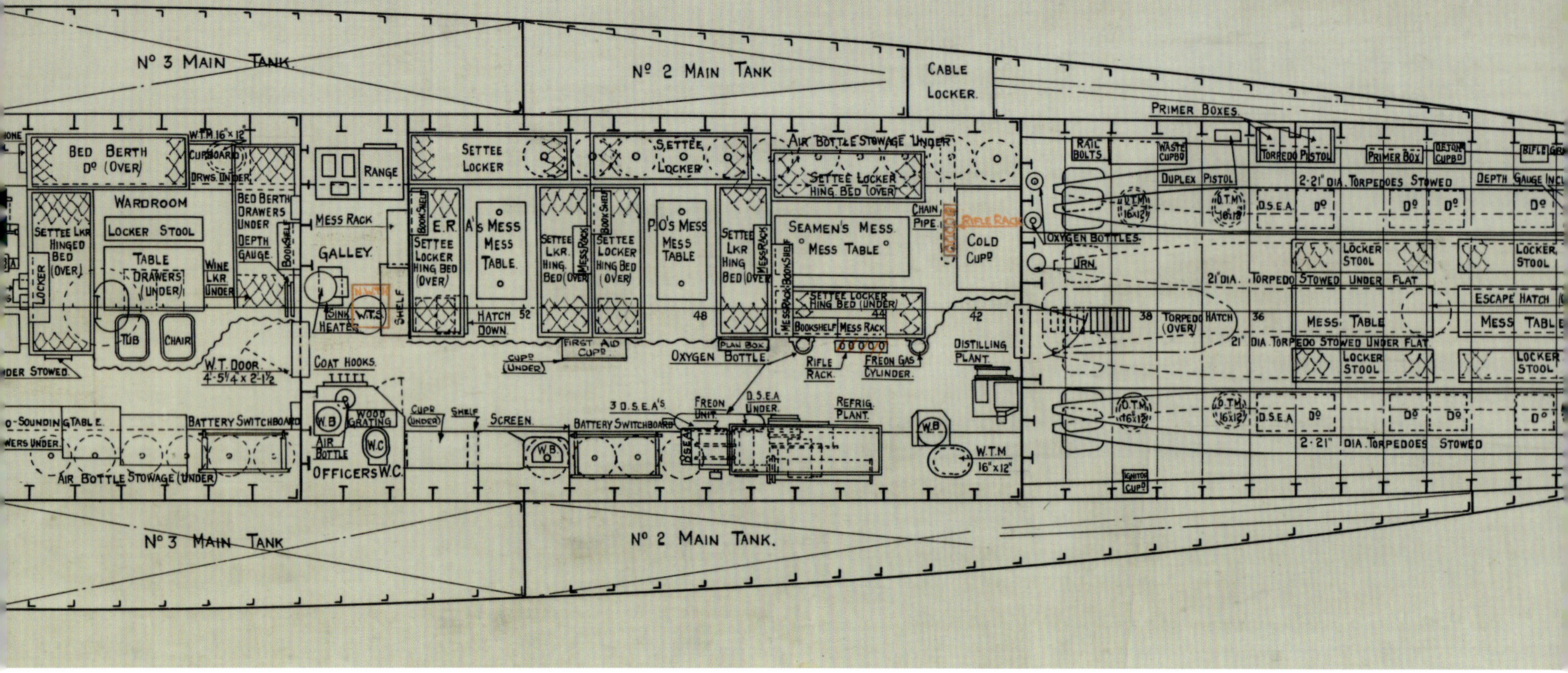

of Lieutenant RNVR and sent out to draw and paint the war at sea on board a variety of vessels until the end of the conflict. 'Once in Naval Lieutenant's uniform,' his son Sylvester Bone later wrote, '[he] felt he had a more worthwhile place within the war effort.'[18]

Stephen submitted his resulting works to the WAAC with descriptions in neat handwriting, providing details of what was shown and its significance.[19] Like those of his father, many of his drawings were reproduced in the *Illustrated London News*. *HMS 'Mauritius', The Engine Room* (plate 28) is characteristic of his output in the painstaking detail and the close association of machine and man. The image's wide-angle view and the small figures lost in an environment of pipes, valves and pressure gauges suggest the modernity and vastness of this light cruiser while, at the same time, making the crowded space look remarkably empty given that there were about 920 crew on board. By way of contrast, *The Galley* in the heavy-cruiser *Norfolk* (fig.32) is heaving with activity, as the cooks prepare a hearty meal for the 700-strong company. It is not difficult to see here how 'he felt like his pencil drawings were too like his father's', both in terms of style and technique.[20]

Among Stephen's drawings were many recording his time on the aircraft carrier *Pursuer*. Below deck, he turned his attention to the Air Staff and Fighter Direction offices and the Pilots' Ready Room, where lectures and briefings took place. Above deck, he recorded Lieutenant Commander (Flying) 'Wings' Oliphant (plate 29) observing the deck crew refuelling aircraft from the bridge, or a Grumman Martlet taking off (plate 30) under the watchful eye of gunners. The latter shows Stephen experimenting with green and orange washes and cross-hatchings of ink, in a manner perhaps inspired by Eric Ravilious.

In the way that submarines had been a new type of vessel in the First World War, so were aircraft carriers in the Second. They soon demonstrated their effectiveness both in crippling the *Bismarck* and, later and more strategically in 1941, in Japan's use of them against the US fleet at Pearl Harbour (see Chapter 1: Pictorial Narratives of the War at Sea). They also performed essential merchant convoy protection duties and the exploits of the fighter planes they carried were regularly reported in the press. Another war artist, Vivian Pitchforth (1895–1982), recorded the deck scenes on board such ships in large watercolours. One of them (plate 31) evokes the heat of warmer waters, as the half-dressed deck crew tend to aircraft.

Fig.33 (above)
Detail of plan of S-Class submarine (HM Submarine *Sturdy* and *Stygian*, 1943), 1945 (detail)
Ink on waxed linen
87.5 x 228.8 cm (34 ½ x 90 in)
NPC2285

The wardroom can be seen on the extreme left of the image, while the forward mess deck is to the extreme right.

Fig.34 (below)
Stephen Bone
S-Class Submarine: The Wardroom and Forward Mess Deck, 1945
Oil on canvas
76 x 76 cm (29 7/8 x 29 7/8 in)
BHC1555

Oil painting, however, was Stephen Bone's preferred medium and much of his wartime output comprises small, impressionistic coastal scenes and paintings of ships at sea, executed on panel. In addition to these mostly unpopulated scenes, there are more detailed representations of ship-board life, full of narrative incident. Perhaps the most remarkable aspect of these compositions is the emphasis on an inclusive viewpoint, calculated to draw the spectator into the picture, as if he or she were participants in the action. In one such painting (plate 32), the vantage point is that of the Flight Commander of HMS *Pursuer*, standing on the bridge, ordering the men to clear the Flight Deck as three aircrafts are about to take off.

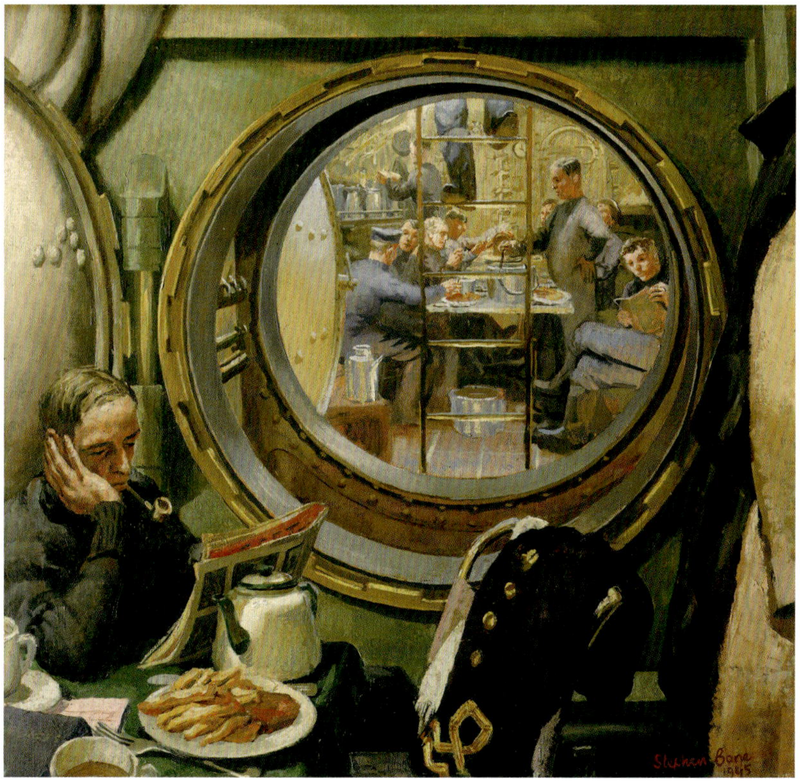

The deck crew hurries to the walkways, mechanics in white sweaters, seamen and petty officers wearing yellow, port and starboard watches wearing red and green respectively. In the starboard walkway, pilots, gunners, the surgeon and a firefighter stand by.

Bone also included the audience in his submarine scenes. Submarines in the First World War, partly because of their novelty and for being an invisible threat lurking beneath the surface, were often considered ominous machines, sometimes depicted as artificial monsters.[21] Greater familiarity by the Second World War shifted artistic attention towards everyday life and work on board them. In *On Board an S-Class Submarine: Up the Conning Tower* (plate 33), the position of the viewer is implied by the hand on the lower ladder at the bottom of the composition, while the figure climbing toward the daylight and a third man at the very top lead us (as viewers) from the depths of the vessel to the open air above. Subtly contrasting artificial and natural light, Bone represents this vertical passageway as the submarine's link to the outside world, both literally and metaphorically connecting the crew in the painting with the viewer in the picture gallery. Here, the artist accurately conveys the inner structure, perspective and depth of the conning tower. However, comparison of the plan of an S-class submarine to another scene (figs 33 and 34) reveals how he modified the real spatial organisation in order to contrast, in one composition, rank-and-file living conditions on a submarine. In the foreground, an officer smokes a pipe and reads at the wardroom table, on which a breakfast plate is awaiting the arrival of the viewer to join him. The single relaxed figure in relatively comfortable quarters, the fact that the place-setting is properly laid over a green cloth and an RNVR lieutenant's uniform jacket (possibly Bone's) is draped over the waiting empty chair, imply a space designated for officers. In the background, eight sailors crowd round a bare forward-mess-deck table. Most of the tableware is metalwork and a standing figure doles out indeterminate 'gloop' with a ladle from the large mess can in which it was cooked.

In a related drawing (plate 34), possibly a study for the painting, Bone made acute observations of the men socialising or sharing a meal in their mess. They are seen through a similar circular bulkhead door, left ajar, like a porthole between the worlds occupied by the viewer and the subjects. While the community of all those shown in the painting is clear from the overall restriction of the space and the similar jersey working dress, Bone clearly separates the realms of 'wardroom' and 'mess' by what looks like a Davis escape chamber but which should, in fact, be a long corridor interspersed with other segregated sections. As a whole, the image is one of brief rest and recuperation, in which everyone is dedicated to a common purpose within the shared experience of an unnaturally confined environment; yet the differences of rank and class separating 'officers and gentlemen' from 'ratings' are suggested by the differences between their respective accommodation. A viewer (British, in particular) who has never been in a submarine therefore gains a fair impression of what that alien environment is like, while also recognising familiar social markers carried into it from the normal outside world.

If the likes of Muirhead and Stephen Bone made a speciality of scenes of everyday life on board ship, other artists did so more episodically as part of their wider projects for the WAAC. An important figure in the London art world, Henry Lamb (1883–1960) saw active service as a doctor in 1914–18, for which he won the Military Cross; he only painted one official war work, in 1919, but was a more regular official war artist in 1939–45.[22] For the WAAC, he predominantly produced portraits, though *Eleven o'Clock in the Forecastle* (plate 35) shows a group of peacetime fishermen, now working as minesweepers, enjoying mugs of tea below deck. Although, as in Bone's *S-Class Submarine* mess-deck, the men are represented in positions of repose, they here manifest an underlying tension. The figure in the hammock, top right, the stove in the background and the sharp narrowing of the space towards the bow indicate their cramped living accommodation and that its discomforts are increased by challenging weather conditions at sea. The muted tones, stylised features and loose handling of the paint, are characteristic of Lamb's restrained, modernist style.

Eric Ravilious: 'modernity free from eccentricity'

Very different from Stephen Bone's descriptive approach, *The Submarine Series* is perhaps the most coherent group of wartime works by Eric Ravilious (1903–42). Ravilious was, with John Nash (1893–1977), one of the first artists to be given an official contract by the WAAC. Having spent his first, restless, months of the war in the Observation Corps, in December 1939 he wrote to his father-in-law about Reginald Gleadowe's invitation to join the WAAC's ranks as 'a sort of Christmas present from the Admiralty'.[23] Appointed a captain in the Royal Marines on 10 February, his first assignment was in the Royal Naval Barracks in Chatham, where he learnt naval and mess etiquette, explored the dockyard area and, though finding that there was not a 'great deal in the way of war activity', made drawings of camouflaged ships, suited to his graphic style and interest in patterns. From there he went to Sheerness, Grimsby and Scapa Flow, sailing on to the Arctic Circle in the destroyer *Highlander*. A group of 17 of his watercolours were in the first War Artists exhibition at the National Gallery in July 1940 and, in characteristically humble fashion, Ravilious wrote to Dickey, the WAAC secretary, of his embarrassment at seeing so many of his drawings on display.[24]

Ravilious moved on to Portsmouth, which he found 'almost overwhelming in size and variety', and, in August, to HMS *Dolphin*, the 'stone frigate' shore-base of the Royal Navy submarine service at Gosport. There he spent time on board L-class submarines which, by the time of the Second World War, were used for training but no longer for general active service. Ravilious wrote to Dickey about drawing interiors of these, to him, extraordinary environments:

> Some of them may be successful I hope, but conditions are difficult for work. It is awfully hot below when they dive and every compartment small and full of people at work. However this is a change from destroyers and I enjoy the state of complete calm after the North Sea – there is no roll or movement at all in submarines, which is one condition in their favour apart from the smell, the heat and noise. The scene is extraordinarily good in a gloomy way. There are small coloured lights about the place and the complexity of a Swiss clock.

Applied to this subject, Ravilious' unique formal language and design focus conjured a dreamlike atmosphere. His imagination was fired: 'Naval interiors are special things in themselves, quite different from everything else,' he wrote to Dickey.[25] He set to work quickly. By 2 August, he wrote to his friend Helen Binyon that 'the submarine has taken a lot of doing, but now there are half a dozen drawings on the way, of interiors (with people!). [...] There is something jolly good about them, if only I can manage it. Blue gloom with coloured lights and everyone in shirts and braces. People go to sleep in odd positions across tables' (fig.35 and plate 38). The cramped conditions made drawing difficult and hasty or, as he told Binyon, 'submarine drawing is uphill work; however there is enough material for about six or seven lithographs. Don't you think that might be a good idea?'[26]

While his favoured medium was watercolour, even prior to confirmation of his WAAC appointment, Ravilious had intended to produce lithographs and supplied Dickey with an estimate of printing costs from the Curwen Press.[27] Asked to comment on the suitability of submarine subjects for publication, the Committee at first suggested a children's book, 'to sell at a shilling, and print 10.000, so the rising generation will clamour to go to the Navy', an idea not entirely to Ravilious' liking.[28] In the end, the WAAC told him to pursue the lithographs as a private venture, in between periods of official employment, with the possibility that the Committee

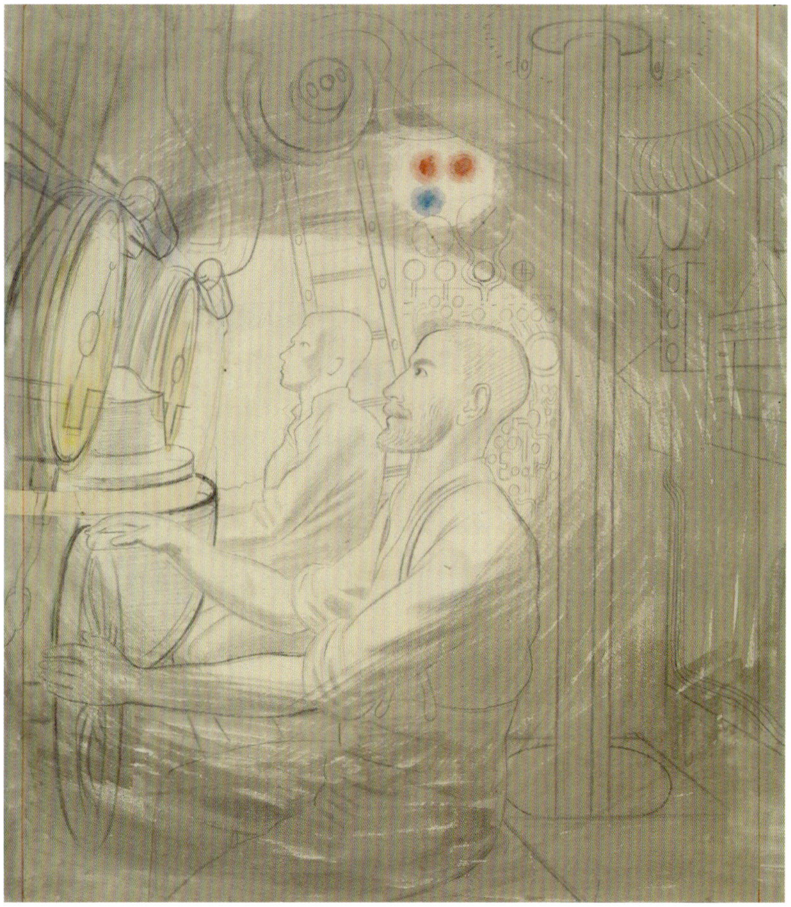

Fig.35
Eric Ravilious
The Submarine Series. Diving controls, 1940
Graphite and watercolour on paper
29.1 x 34.5 cm (11 ½ x 13 ⅝ in)
PAJ0750

Fig.36
Eric Ravilious
The Submarine Series.
Testing Davis Apparatus, 1941
Lithograph
30.3 x 33.7 cm (11 7/8 x 13 1/4 in)
PAD8077

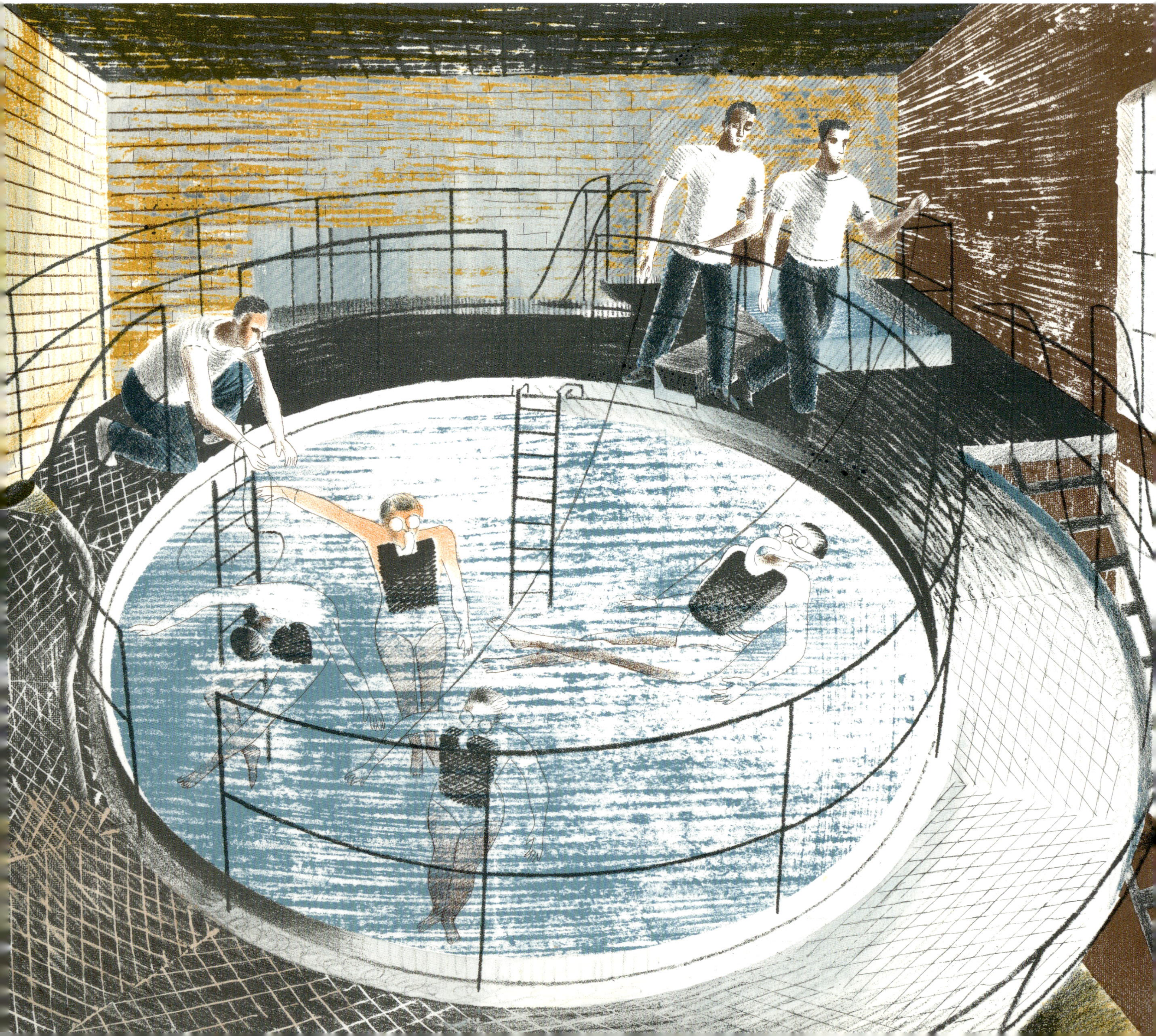

might purchase a set in due course. The prints were giving Ravilious trouble, however, notably in finding a publisher up to the task. Frustrated, on 12 November he wrote to Dickey, 'I wish I could tell you when [their completion] will be. The more I burn to begin the job the further it seems to recede.'[29] Eventually Ravilious found a printer in Ipswich, with whom he was able to experiment on different finishes, but lamented to his friend Diana Tuely: 'It is fairly difficult and absorbing to work out the superimpositions of five colours in all sorts of tones and textures and the rest. Lithography ink is beastly stuff, greasy and thick.'[30]

In February 1941 the edition of 50 sets of 10 prints was complete, and subsequently shown at the Leicester Galleries, London. Despite his efforts, the artist was still dissatisfied, finding the prints 'overworked, and overdone compared to the first drawings which are much better'.[31] Ravilious had annotated the drawings to indicate the effect, colours and framing he wanted to achieve in lithographic form, which offers an idea of his working practice. The preparatory drawing of a diver and the resulting print (plates 37 and 38) show how denser the cross-hatching and tones became from the former to the latter, the soft washes of the watercolour replaced by the harder, darker colours of the heavy ink.

What harmoniously links all the designs of the series is their dreamy mood, sense of geometric order and formal arrangements of line, colours and light effects. Haloes of light and windows into other spaces recur, lending a remarkable clarity to the series as a whole. They show the various activities undertaken by the submariners, from the commanding officer observing an enemy vessel through the periscope, to men playing cards, resting at tables or exercising in the escape-training tank at HMS *Dolphi*n (fig.36). In both drawings and prints, the sense of stillness, space and light in the interiors contrasts with Ravilious' complaints of overbearing heat, confinement and noise. The men, often featureless silhouettes, add to the eerie atmosphere of the scenes.

Interestingly, two of the drawings from the series were censored. It was specified in handwriting on the back of the introductory drawing (plate 40), with a censorship stamp dated 19 May 1941, that it was 'not to be used in its present form until after the war and then only with Admiralty approval', although the reason remains unclear, since nothing of a sensitive nature seems to be depicted. In a way typical of Ravilious, it is a composite of different elements, associating an inside and an outside underwater world: the artist's hand drawing a hatch, a sailor at the wheel, marine elements – a diving helmet, anchor and compass – and a small amphibious craft pulling away in the dark depths of the sea. By comparison, *The Whitstable Mine* (plate 39) was a more delicate subject, with its list of tools and equipment necessary for defusing a magnetic mine.[32] Showing efforts to keep submarines safe in waters plagued by enemy mines, it would have been the design for the last sheet in the series. Despite the hazardous nature of mine disposal, the drawing has a certain humour and almost child-like naivety. In contrast, Leslie Cole's approach to a similar subject, *Minesweeping in the Straits of Gibraltar, swinging out an Oropesa*,[33] is perhaps more descriptive but contains stylistic similarities to that by Ravilious, in the simplified, linear forms, and cross-hatchings of the watercolour.

Although Ravilious went out to sea in submarines and was given official photographs as reference for his work, his graphic and otherworldly style was perhaps not the sort of accurate representation favoured for propaganda purposes. With their simplified designs and uncluttered environments, his *Commander looking through the periscope*,[34] and sailors at the diving controls widely differ in mood and execution from William Dring's *Stand by Tubes. The Control Room of HMS 'Stubborn'* (plate 41), which painstakingly reproduces the interior of the submarine, diligently placing each man at his post as they prepare to launch an attack. Dring rarely went on board vessels – although a letter recalls the momentous occasion of his first sight of the control room of a submarine as 'a gorgeous place, an Alladin's [*sic*] cave of glistening machinery, wheels and dials' – and would reconstruct interiors from photographs.[35] Nevertheless, his large pastel vividly renders textures

– from hard machinery to the soft skins of the sailors or the fluffy wool of their jumpers – as well as space, anticipation and protocol.

Having taken several months' break from official work to complete his *Submarine Series*, Ravilious resumed his service for the WAAC by drawing coastal defences in Dover, convoy subjects in the Dunfermline area and Walrus flying boats in Dundee, before being reassigned to the RAF. In the summer of 1942, he went to Iceland, never to return: his aircraft was lost during a rescue operation on 2 September.[36] At the War Artists exhibition that followed his death, critics lamented the untimely disappearance of one of Britain's leading artists. He was hailed as a 'singularly versatile' artist with his 'own particular style', 'a gifted artist, whose modernity is free from eccentricity', whose 'formal and detached recordings have remarkably vivid personality', 'a painter of charming fantasy [who] had most successfully come to grips with reality' and was 'steadily progressing towards greater clarity and crisper draughtsmanship'.[37] Ravilious was to be the first of three official war artists killed on active duty. His friend Thomas Hennell (1903–45), who immediately volunteered to replace him in Iceland, disappeared in Indonesia in November 1945. The youngest, Albert Richards (1919–45), had insisted on taking a fighting role while being an official war artist, and was killed by a landmine in the Netherlands in March 1945.[38] For those enrolled in the Royal and Merchant navies, dangers abounded, as will be seen in Chapter 4.

The Cruel Sea

Tragedies at sea and at the Front were, of course, also the subject of paintings produced during the war. While Richard Eurich mostly painted coastal and battle scenes, he was fascinated by stories of survival at sea. One of his paintings, with the crew of a torpedoed merchantman huddled together in a ship's boat, was first exhibited at the National Gallery in 1943 (fig.37). With Eurich's characteristic predilection for anecdotal detail, it shows remarkable inventiveness in literally merging above- and below-deck activities, both navigating and killing time: a boy holds the ship's cat, one man plays the harmonica, another stretches out with a photo of his sweetheart, others play cards. While it shows the British 'stiff upper lip' in the face of adversity, the survivors have clearly been drifting for some time and their fate remains uncertain: some of the sailors look ill or in despondent mood, and one sticks his tongue out, expressing thirst.

Such depictions of struggle and death at sea were not always welcome. At the same exhibition, a critic of the *Yorkshire Observer* had commented on 'Two "horror" paintings [that] stand out conspicuously [for being] tough and realistic.'[39] One was Sub-Lieutenant Garth Weston's *The Admiralty Regrets* (1942, IWM), which recalls the sinking of Weston's ship by Focke-Wulf aircraft in the North Atlantic. As Weston wrote to the WAAC, of the 170 men on board only about 40 survived, and, clearly shocked by the incident, he chose to depict sailors bleeding and dying on the deck of a ship – the first time that a subject with blood in it had appeared in a War Artists exhibition.[40] The other was Raymond Coxon's *Shipwrecked* (1942, National Gallery, Cape Town, South Africa), which the critic termed 'no less harrowing', 'the subject ghastly and the treatment unsparingly vivid'.[41] In fact, after its first showing at the National Gallery, one of Eurich's castaway pictures, *Survivors from a Torpedoed Ship* (1942, Tate), was rejected by the censors who feared it would have a negative effect on morale.[42]

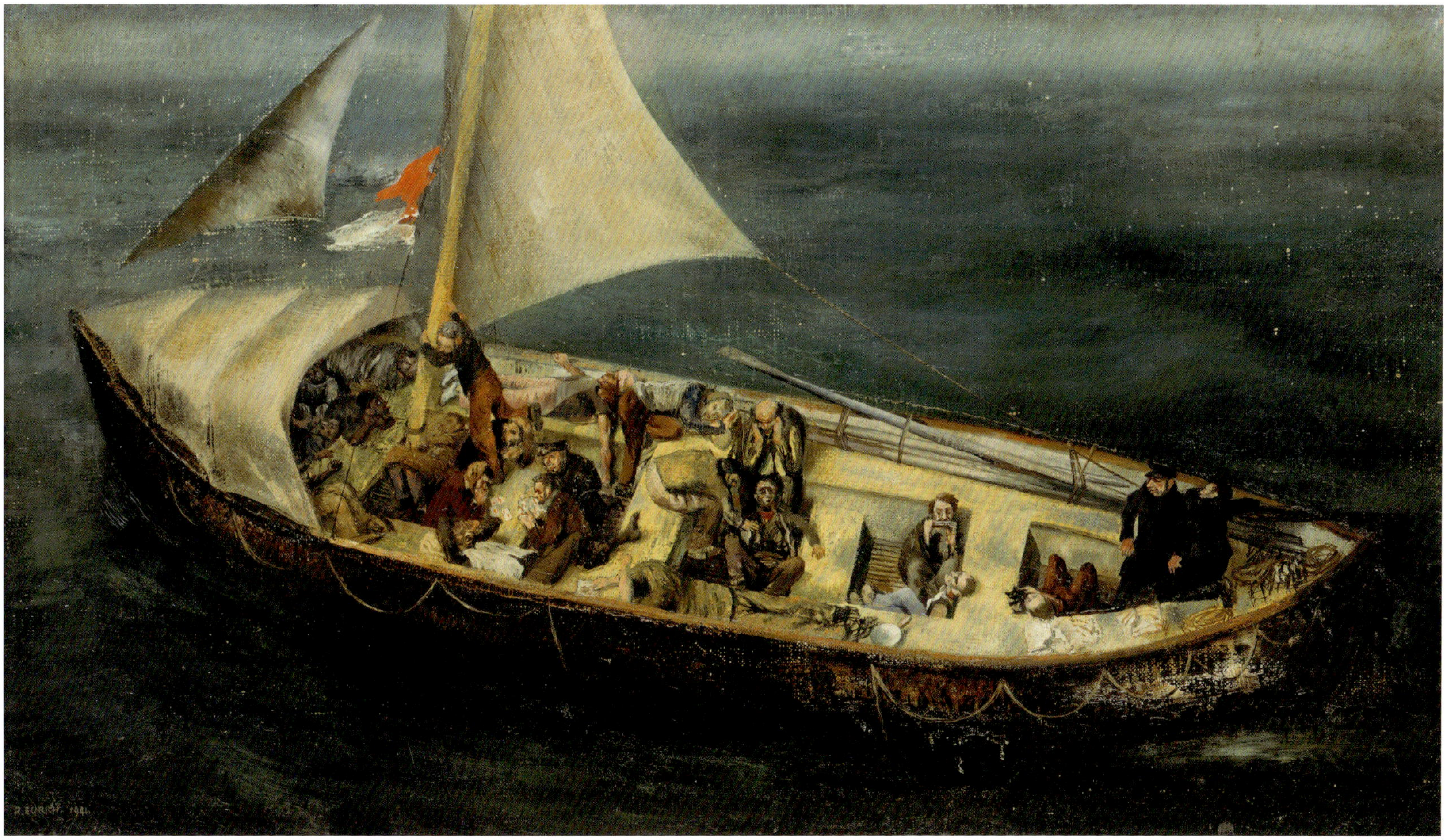

Fig.37
Richard Eurich
A Ship's Boat at Sea, 1941
Oil on canvas
35.6 x 62.2 cm (14 x 24 ½ in)
BHC1569

Weary Watching and Waiting: Daily Life in the Battle Fleets of the First World War

Jeremy Michell

The Royal Navy has always been important for supporting Britain's interests at home and abroad. It played a part in diplomatic negotiations, using its presence across the world as a tool of power projection. If this failed, it had to be an effective multi-faceted weapon; one that could defeat an enemy fleet, blockade coastlines, protect British merchant shipping and cooperate with the Army. The significant technological developments of the late nineteenth and early twentieth centuries, including the submarine, long-range gunnery and powered flight, forced governments to rethink how they would achieve their war aims using this technology.[43]

However, even in wartime, combat itself was only occasional and most sailors experienced an ordinary, unremarkable world in which the traditions and recreations of peace were recognisably present (fig.38). The ships were not just fighting platforms: they were home to those expected to command and operate them. Although the early twentieth-century Navy stood at the cutting edge of many technological developments, these everyday customs still contained more than a hint of the institution's Nelsonic past.[44] The wooden-slab tables around which seamen gathered for their meals were little different from those in eighteenth-century warships; the same applied to the canvas and rope hammocks in which they slept, though now suspended from steel deckheads. Barefoot, and with their trousers rolled up, men still scrubbed the decks with holystones; they still lined up for their daily issue of rum; and the letters they wrote to sweethearts at home, and the bantering camaraderie of the mess, only gradually changed. In Nelson's day, this shipboard environment was also shaped by rank and status, with officers and men inhabiting very different worlds within the same ship. By the First World War these boundaries had become sharper (a development mirrored on land, as society industrialised through the nineteenth century), with the nature of daily life in the service depending greatly on one's place within its much more complex professional and cultural hierarchy.

Fig.38
G.W.W. Hooper
R.R. Wallace Clerk, asleep on the quarterdeck of the light cruiser HMS *Aurora*, May 1916
Photographic negative
6.1 x 9.4 cm (2 3/8 x 3 3/4 in)
NMM, Captain Gunn Collection
N22880

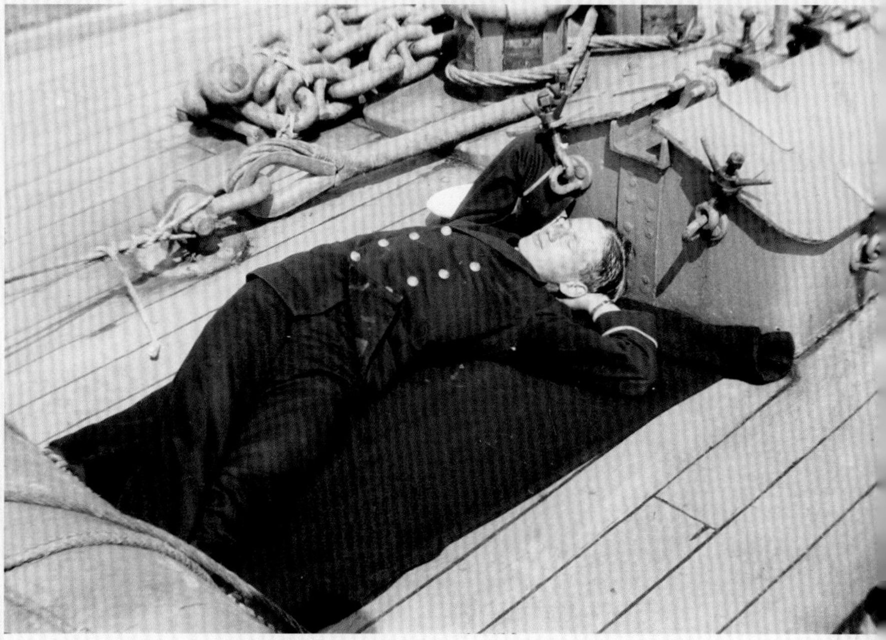

Wartime in the Royal Navy was hard for every member of a crew. The ships themselves had to be in a near-constant state of readiness, resulting in shore leave being sporadic or curtailed. This was a particular problem if home and loved ones were hundreds of miles from the remoteness of Scapa Flow, the main base of the Grand Fleet in the Orkney Islands. Officers and men had their daily lives dictated by strict naval routine. Each ship had its day divided into seven 'watches', which placed the crew in a 24-hour duty rota. This watch-keeping worked independently from the daily routine on board, which started at 5.30 AM when the men got up and stowed their hammocks away for the day. At 5.40 AM they had hot cocoa and time for a smoke and wash before they spent the next hour cleaning the ship. Breakfast was served at 7 AM and an hour later they began their duties according to respective specialisations. A parade called Divisions was held at 9.50 AM, and a roll-call taken

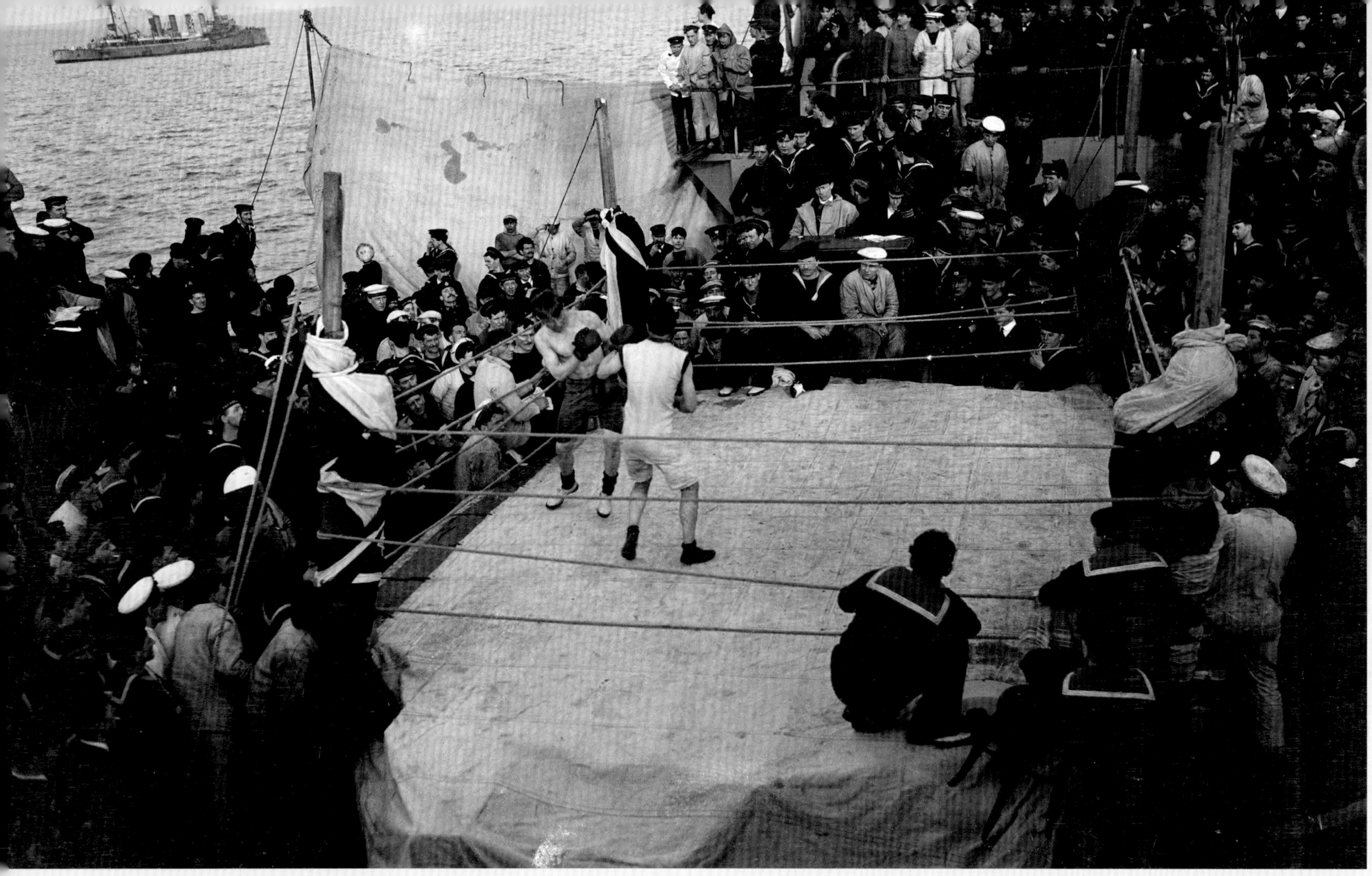

before the men went aft (towards the stern) for prayers, followed by drill or physical training and further specialised work. Dinner was from noon to 1.15 PM after which work resumed. From 4 PM the crew had leisure time that might include shore-leave, returning for supper at 7 PM. 'Pipe Down' was sounded at 10 PM and all sailors had to turn in unless they were on special duties.[45]

The Commander-in-Chief, Admiral Sir John Jellicoe, frequently led the Grand Fleet into the North Sea for patrol, fleet and gunnery exercises. In fact, on the day of the Battle of Jutland on 31 May 1916, a number of ships assumed that they were on another routine sweep. Lieutenant-Commander Henry Hitchins commented in a letter to his mother after the battle: 'We were on one of our frequent cruises off the other side & no one expected anything more than usual.'[46] On returning from fleet exercises the ships had to be refuelled, cleaned and readied for action. However, when they were not at sea, the men had time for recreational activities. It was important for captains and admirals to ensure that they were kept mentally and physically occupied, especially in larger warships, which had longer periods of operational inactivity. This was partly to ensure they were fit and alert, but was also to prevent the crew from the effects of boredom that could lead to ill-discipline. While the daily routine and the frequent exercises helped with the fighting aspect of naval life, they could not afford to neglect the need to provide some form of distraction when at anchor in the various bases. These recreational activities were an important physical release from the differing mental pressures of tedium and terror that built up after long spells of routine work interspersed with the intensity and horror of close engagement with the enemy.[47]

Opportunities for recreation also depended on where ships were based. In this regard, Scapa Flow presented a particular challenge for the large number of ships in the Grand Fleet and their crews. North of mainland Scotland, the Orkney Islands were sparsely populated, with very little in the way of public entertainment facilities for large numbers of men. The weather could also be particularly unpredictable and often inhospitable. In spite of this, commanders were keen to keep everyone entertained: in 1915,

Fig.39
Viscount Curzon
A boxing contest aboard the battleship HMS *Queen Elizabeth*, January 1915–May 1916
Photographic negative
11 x 16 cm (4 3/8 x 6 1/4 in)
NMM, Earl Howe Collection
N16605

for example, Captain William Fisher of HMS *St Vincent*, a battleship in the Grand Fleet at Scapa, devised a seven-mile treasure hunt for his midshipmen and seamen, which involved them visiting numerous Orkney crofts to find a tin with ten shillings (50 pence) inside. About 60 sailors set off to search for the prize and Fisher regarded the event as a success: 'They have a lot to talk about in their messes tonight – the whole thing was a rare lark.'[48]

Officers were less constrained in their recreational activities and some found time to get ashore for shooting, later sharing their successes with other ships. Commodore Charles Le Mesurier wrote to his wife that 'The hills and vales surrounding this big sheet of water [Scapa Flow] have advantages: yesterday evening, to my great surprise, a picquet-boat from one of the big ships came alongside, containing a shooting party, and disgorged half a dozen brace of grouse, shot that very day! Quite reminded one of old Mediterranean days up the Levant.'[49] The officers from the battleship *Hercules* indulged their gardening interests by setting up allotments on Flotta, one of the islands round Scapa. Officers also had the chance to play golf on the links of the newly created Grand Fleet Golf Club.[50]

In sharp contrast, when the battle-cruiser squadron moved to the Firth of Forth, they were within easy reach of Edinburgh and its diverse amusements. Filson Young, a journalist allowed access to the squadron in the early part of the war, records that the officers had time to go ashore, lunch in Edinburgh, go to a cinema or walk down Princes Street and still be back at nightfall. As with the main fleet at Scapa, officers in the ships based at Invergordon, on the Cromarty Firth north of Inverness, found time for Highland walking. Young recalled: 'It was pleasant up there among the hills, walking over the hard frosty roads or beside the bed of a burn, brown and swollen, whose music was refreshing after the clangour of the ship.'[51] Men, too, were granted unsupervised shore leave. Like officers, their activities were determined by location and the length of time available, but age, marital status and money also influenced 'runs ashore'. Long leave could include visiting home using railway warrants to the closest station. However, these occasions were infrequent, especially considering the distances required from the north of Scotland.[52]

More organised physical recreation was also important. Boxing matches were great spectator events (fig.39) as well as a staple part of keeping the men fit and occupied. Perhaps unsurprisingly, there were experienced fighters among the crews. As Walter Cowen, captain of the battlecruiser *Princess Royal*, recalled of his wartime service: 'We used to have Boxing tournaments every few months and very good ones. [Admiral] David Beatty greatly encouraged it and every one of our ships had good entries and quite often [there] would be found [among them] well known high class professional boxers from the outside world, disguised generally as stokers.'[53] However, the war was never far away. HMS *Defence*, the ship referred to in the following quotation, was sunk at the Battle of Jutland: 'The Boxing was quite a show: must have been over ten thousand spectators. All the [trophy] cups went down in *Defence*. Poor Robert Arbuthnot had got 'em all on board, so the winners got medals instead.'[54]

Of course, more sea-focused sports were also organised. These included the fleet regatta (fig.40), which usually involved crews in ships' cutters and whalers training and then racing against the crews of other ships in the fleet for trophies. Here useful physical exercise was combined with activity to develop crew morale and camaraderie, and instil a friendly rivalry between the ships. Commodore Le Mesurier noted, 'we hope to bring our regatta off early next month – and the sailors go away fairly often boat-pulling [i.e. rowing]'.[55] As the war progressed the main Scottish bases improved their leisure facilities for men and officers, constructing cinemas, football pitches and canteens.[56] Ensuring that ships' companies were kept occupied and engaged in naval life was to become ever more critical as the battleships and battle-cruisers were less frequently used, which particularly became the case after Jutland.

A variety of activities could take place in the evenings on board ship. Filson Young records how, in the winter of 1914–15, 'Every kind

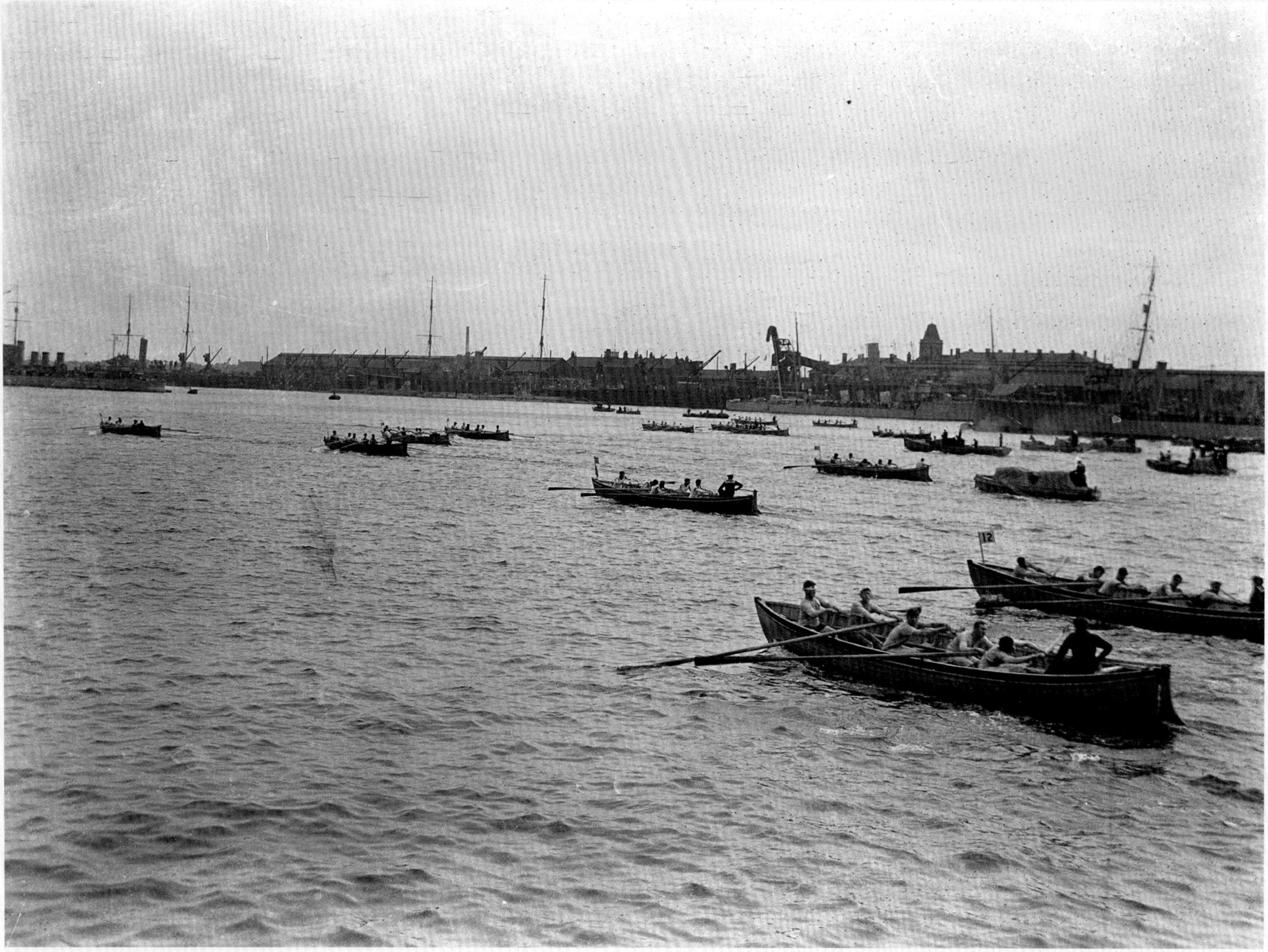

Fig.40
G.W.W. Hooper
Whalers crewed by stokers racing on the river Stour on Regatta Day, September 1916
Photographic negative
8.5 x 11.4 cm (3 3/8 x 4 1/2 in)
NMM, Captain Gunn Collection
N22685

Fig.41 (opposite)
Viscount Curzon
The 'Gunroom Glee Club' concert party in costume on the battleship HMS *Queen Elizabeth*, January–August 1916
Photographic negative
11 x 16 cm (4 3/8 x 6 1/4 in)
NMM, Earl Howe Collection
N16515

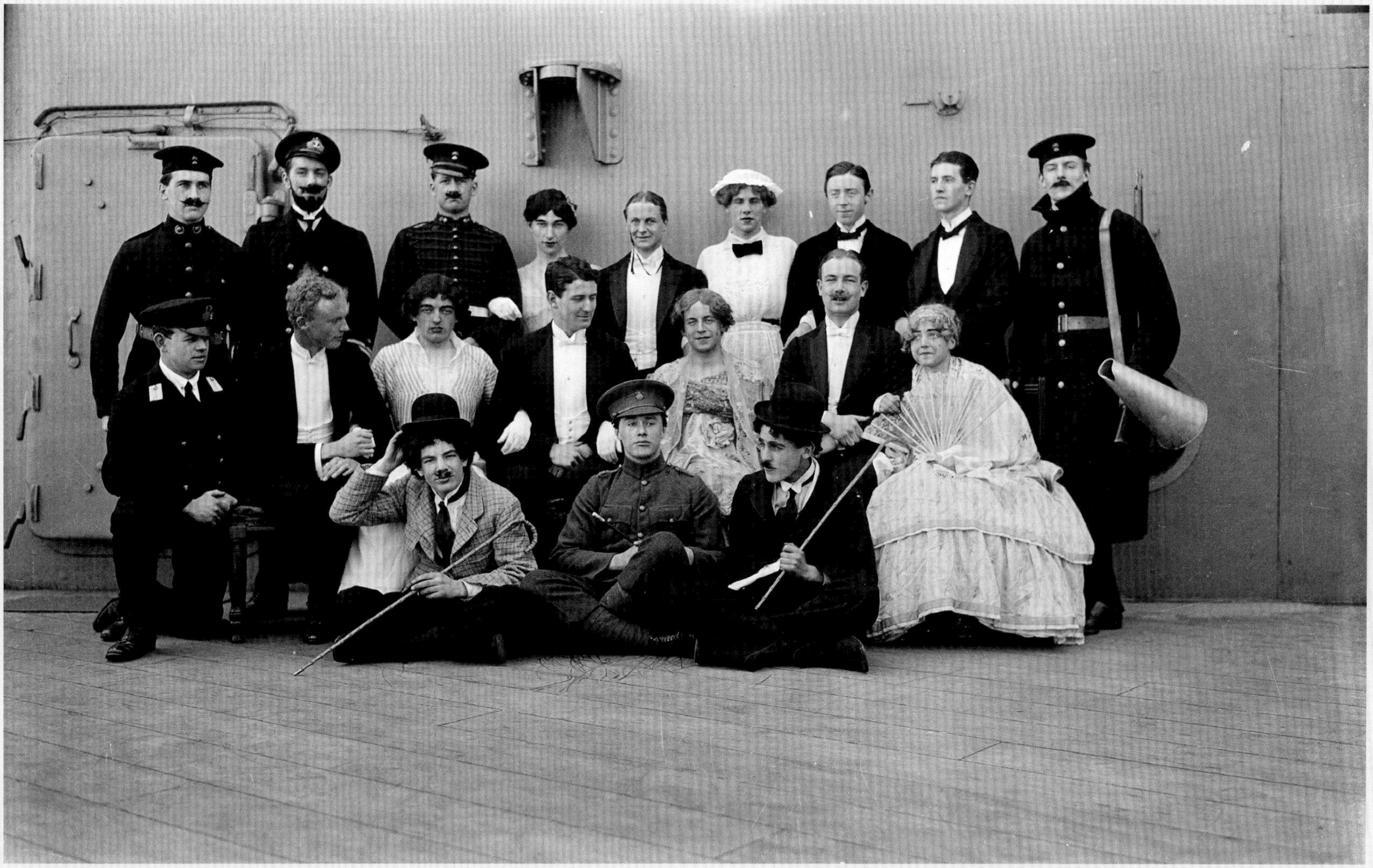

of game and puzzle would be produced, from jig-saws to attaque [a military board game]; and often the long wardroom table after tea would look like nothing so much as a kindergarten, littered with apparatus of recreation.'[57] Victor Hayward, Able Seaman from the battle-cruiser *Tiger*, recalls the illegal gambling in a dice game called 'Crown and Anchor', sometimes for large sums of money. The men had few opportunities to spend their pay and some had a fatalistic view that they lived dangerous lives and did not expect to survive. A lookout was posted on the door to warn against unwanted visitors.[58] In less clandestine activities, officers and men also spent time reading, writing and darning their socks, among a host of other quiet pastimes.

As this begins to reveal, the Navy's worlds of class and rank were often reflected in the recreations of its personnel. The different social and cultural positions occupied by officers and lower-deck sailors meant that their moments of relaxation usually reflected separate priorities. The limited personal space afforded to an ordinary seaman meant that the shotguns, fishing rods and boxes of flies stowed in the corner of an officer's cabin would never make an appearance on the open mess deck of a battleship. At the same time, though, the expense of these items, and the foreignness of such pursuits to working-class people, would have made their absence irrelevant.

Communal sports and regattas brought the warship's various social worlds into closer communication, and there were also a number of occasions in the naval calendar when the boundaries of discipline and authority were thoroughly subverted in the name of entertainment. Concert parties can certainly be included under this heading (fig.41), with their liberating influence of humour, costume and cross-dressing blurring the formalities of everyday life. Christmas festivities and crossing-the-line ceremonies were also moments when gold lace and dignity were often turned on their heads, and men saw each other temporarily disassociated from the hierarchy that usually held them firmly in place. If only briefly, such occasions also sweetened the bitter realities of war.

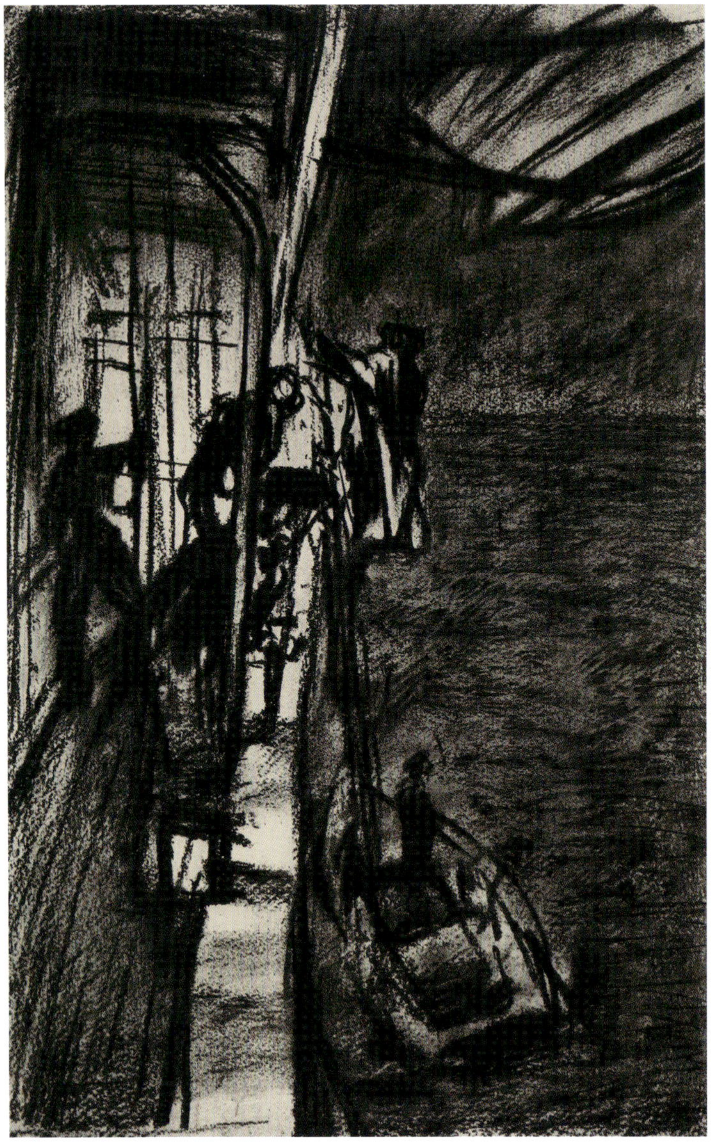

Plate 24 (left)
Muirhead Bone
Off Havre – Taking the Pilot aboard a Hospital Ship, 1918
Lithograph
50.6 x 38.1 cm (19 ⅞ x 15 in)
PAI0642

Plate 25 (below)
Muirhead Bone
The Boiler Room of a Battleship, 1917
Lithograph
79.6 x 55.4 cm (31 ⅜ x 21 ¾ in)
PAI0685

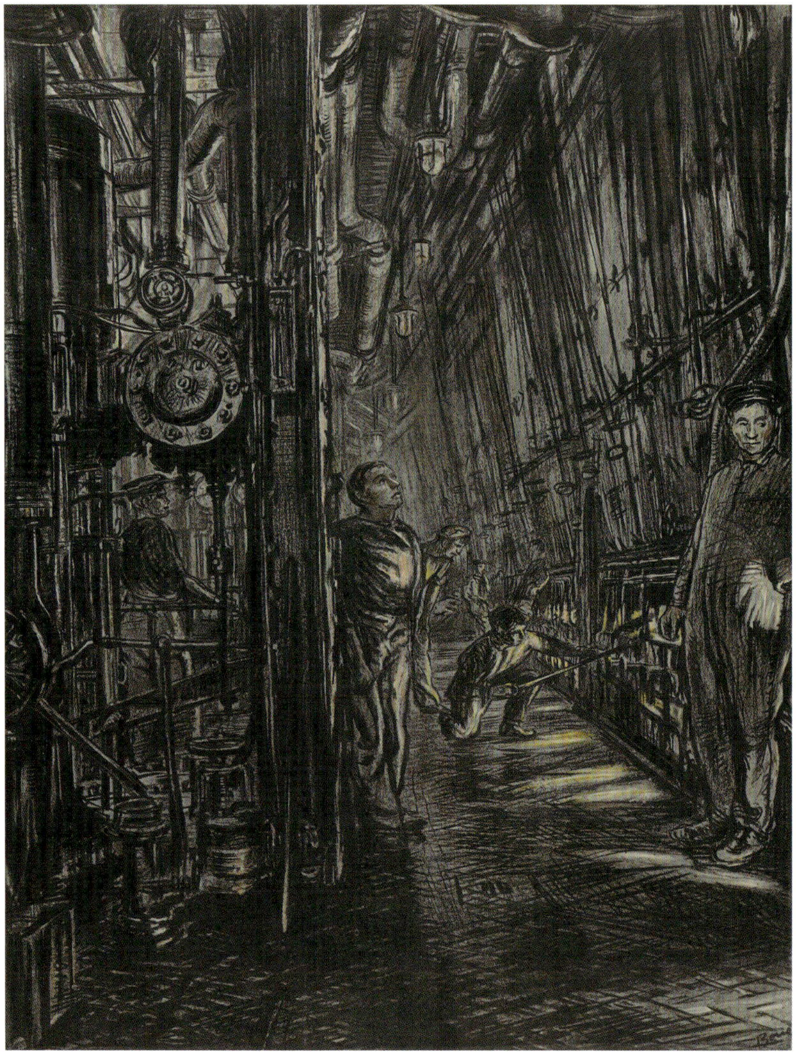

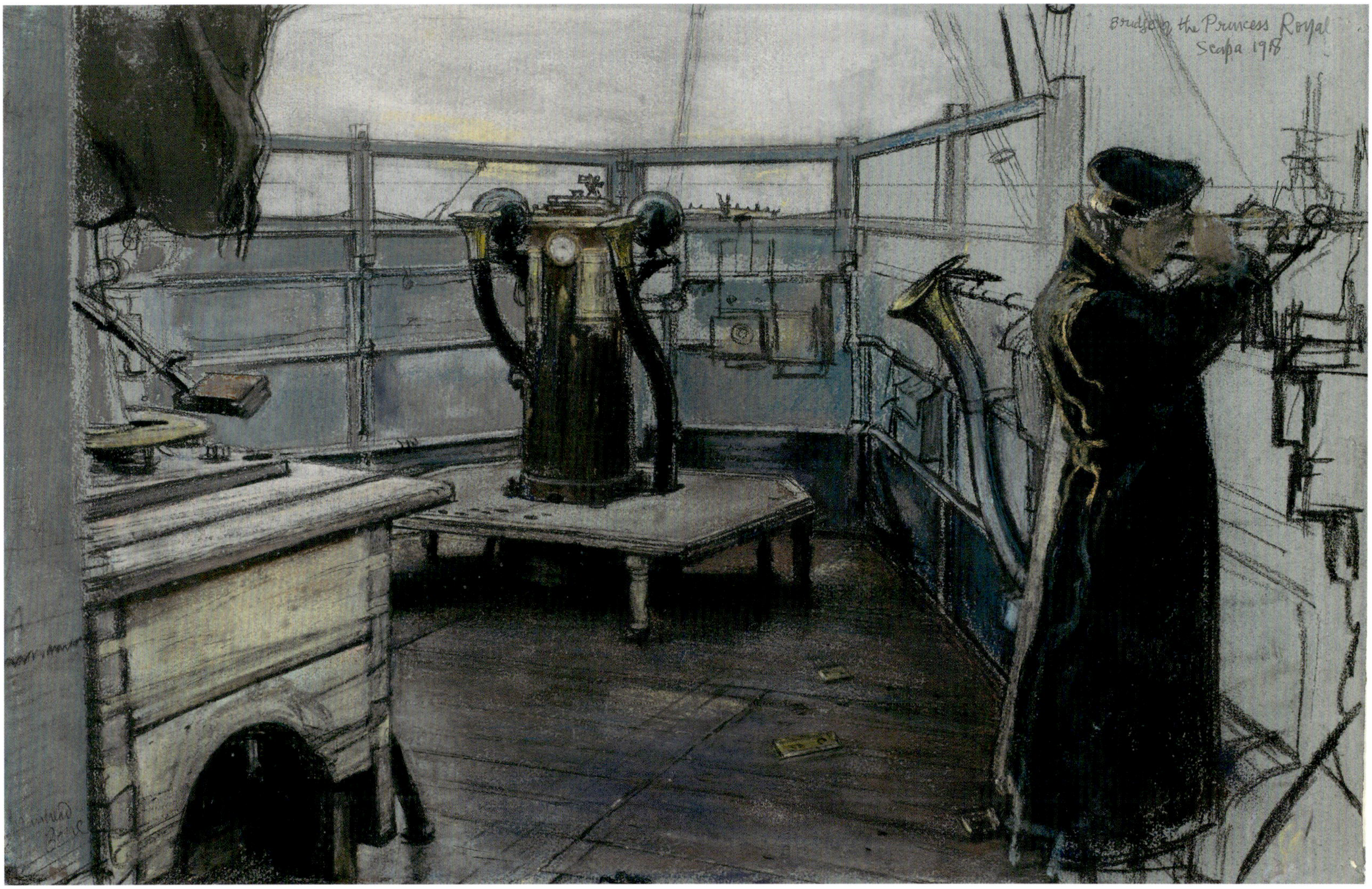

Plate 26
Muirhead Bone
The Bridge of HMS 'Princess Royal', Scapa 1918, 1918
Crayon on paper
34 x 52 cm (13 3/8 x 20 1/2 in)
PAJ3142

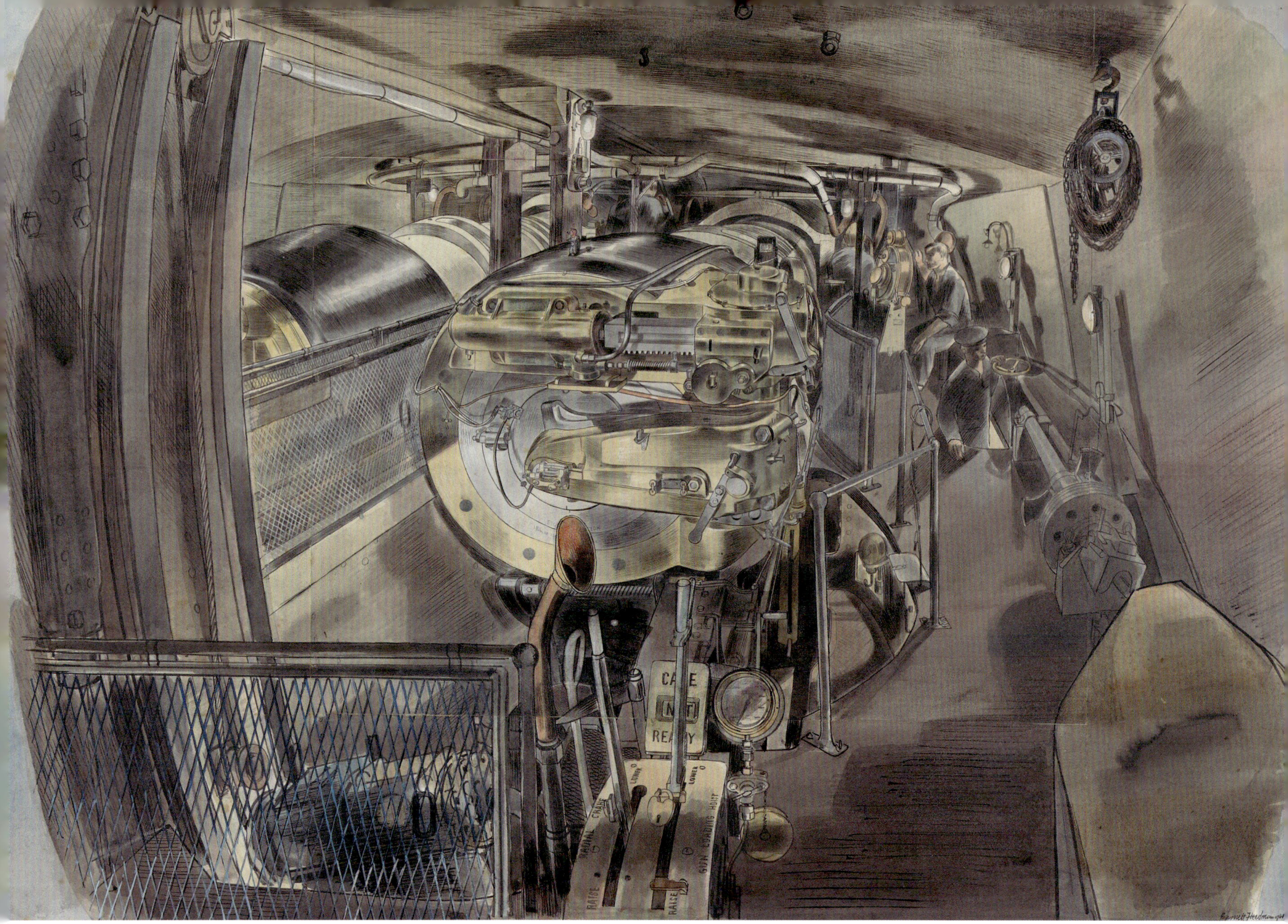

Plate 27
Barnett Freedman
15" Gun Turret, HMS 'Repulse', August 1941, 1941
Watercolour, pen and ink on paper
62.5 x 90 cm (24 $^{5}/_{8}$ x 35 $^{3}/_{8}$ in)
PAJ2870

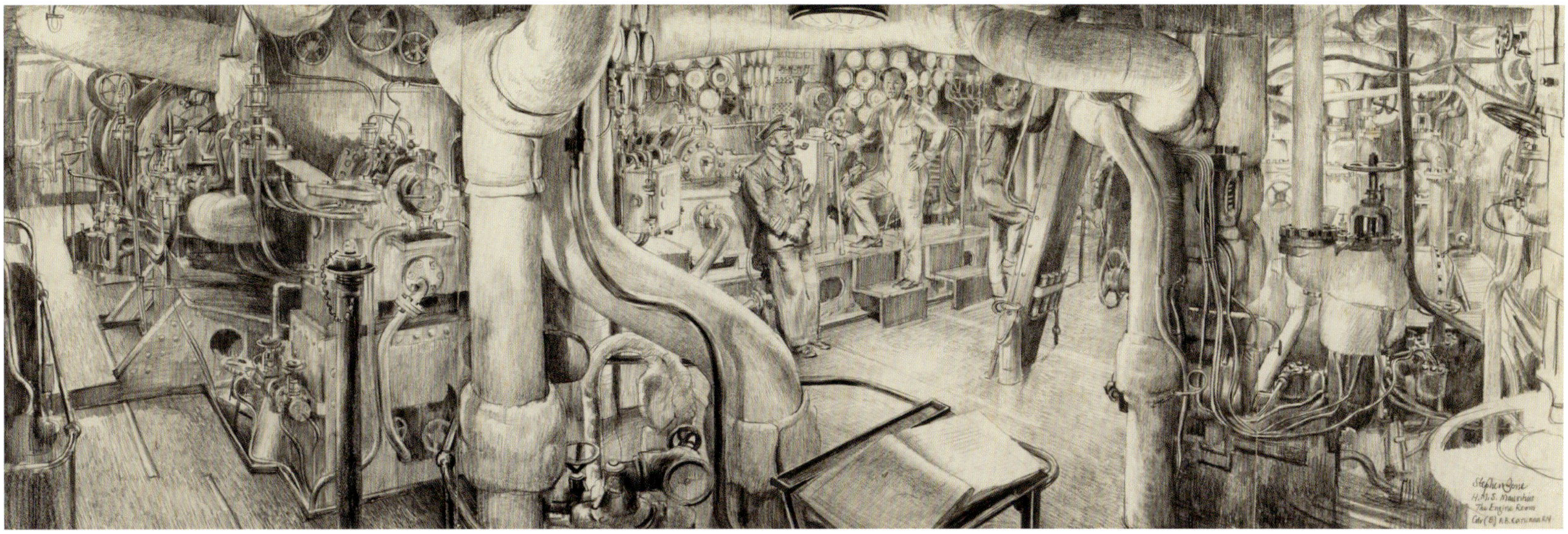

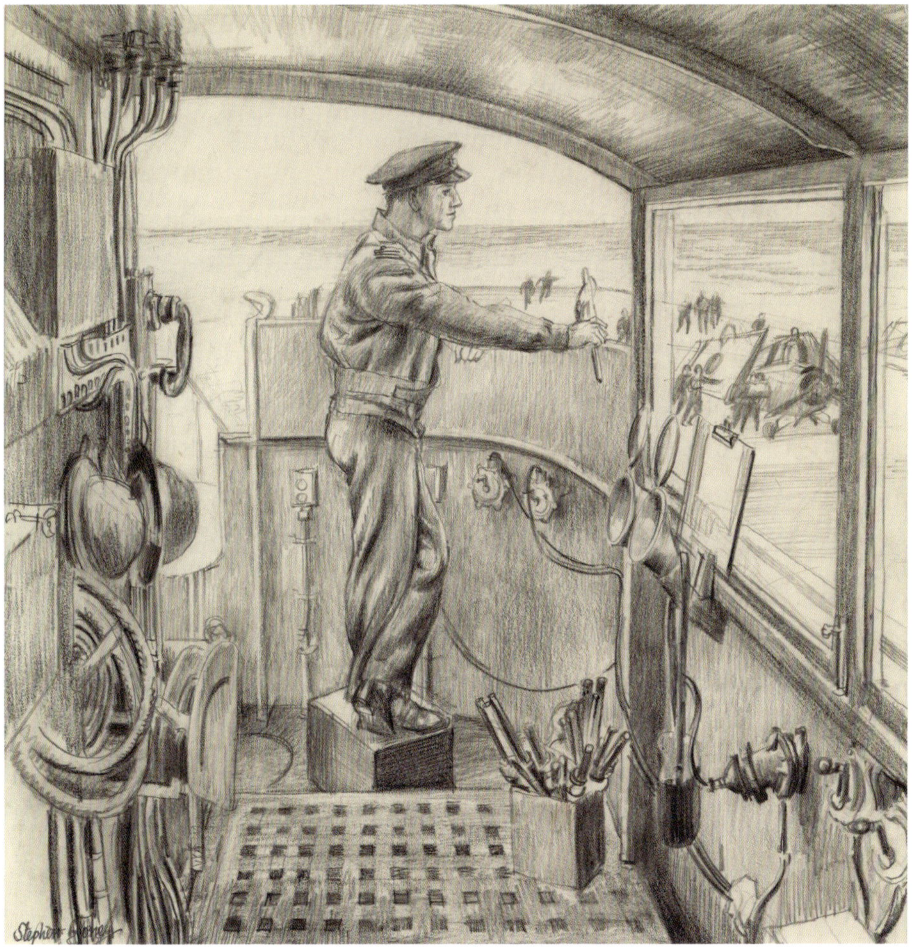

Plate 28 (above)
Stephen Bone
HMS 'Mauritius', The Engine Room, c.1944
Crayon on paper
35 x 103 cm (13 3/4 x 40 1/2 in)
PAJ3023

Plate 29 (below)
Stephen Bone
Lieutenant Commander (Flying) 'Wings' Oliphant, c.1944–5
Crayon and graphite on paper
40.5 x 38.4 cm (16 x 15 1/8 in)
PAI0551

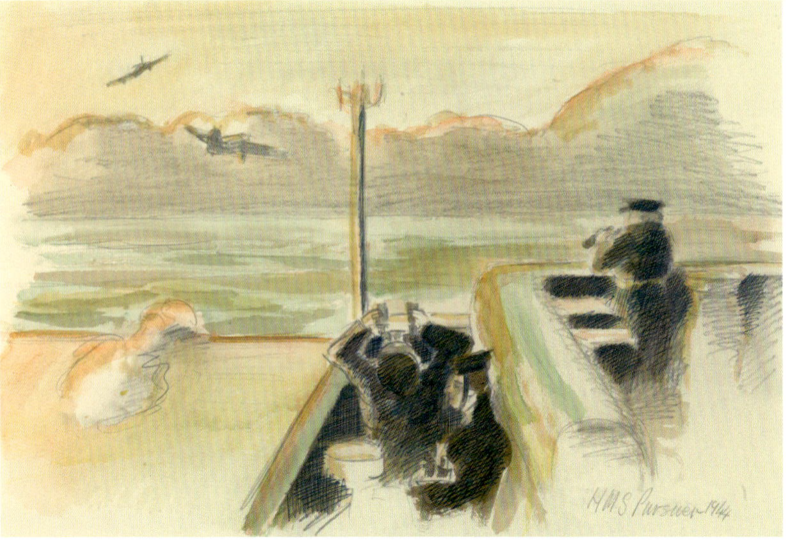

Plate 30 (left)
Stephen Bone
Grumman Martlet taking off, 1944
Graphite, watercolour, pen and blue ink on board
32.1 x 46.1 cm (12 ⅝ x 18 ⅛ in)
PAH0025

Plate 32 (opposite)
Stephen Bone
Clear Flight Deck: On Board an Aircraft Carrier, 1944
Oil on canvas
102.2 x 76.5 cm (40 ¼ x 30 ⅛ in)
BHC1550

Plate 31 (below)
Vivian Pitchforth
Tethered Aircraft on Carrier Escort, 1945
Graphite and watercolour on paper
45.3 x 78.6 cm (17 ⅞ x 31 in)
PAI0556

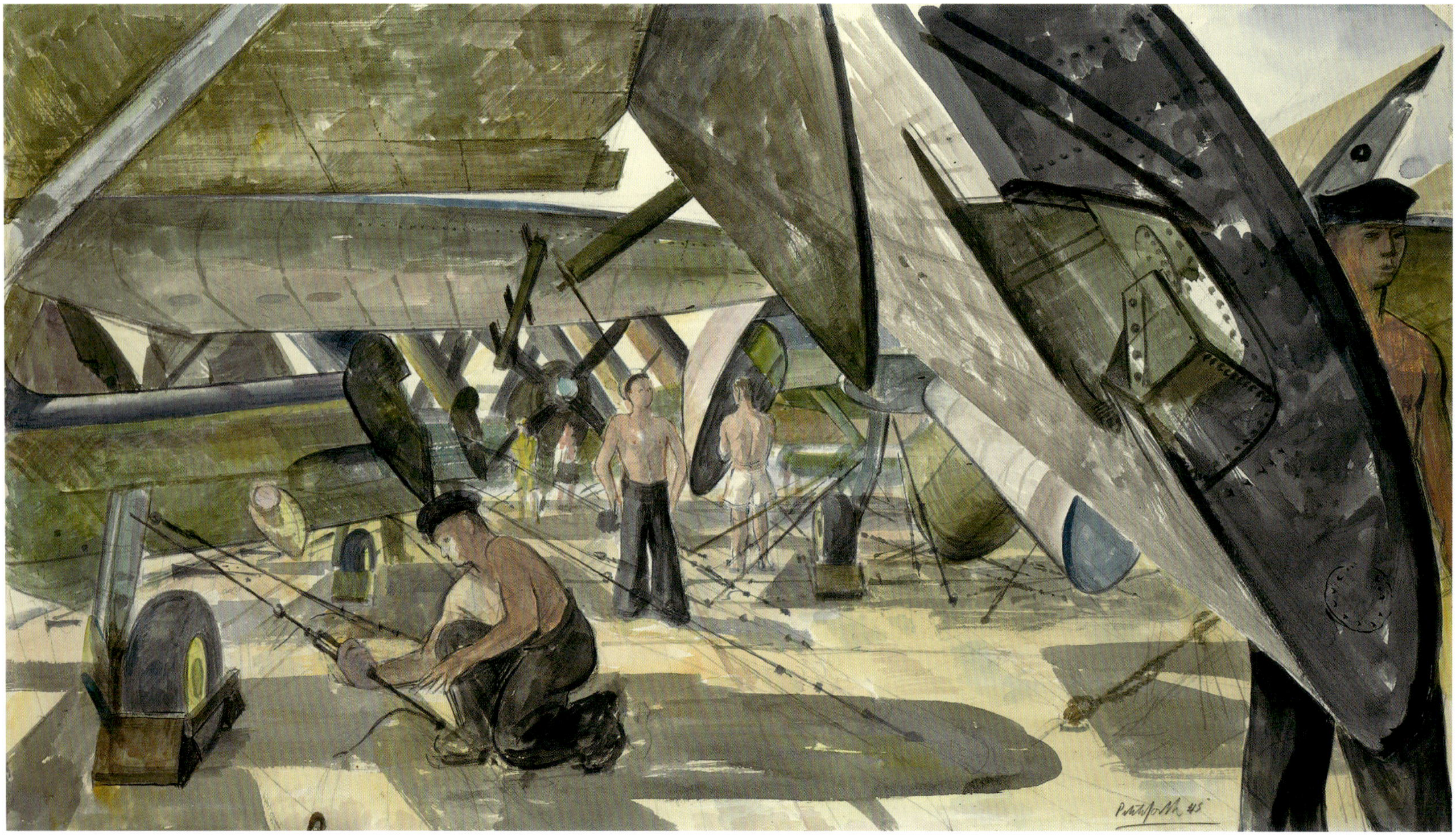

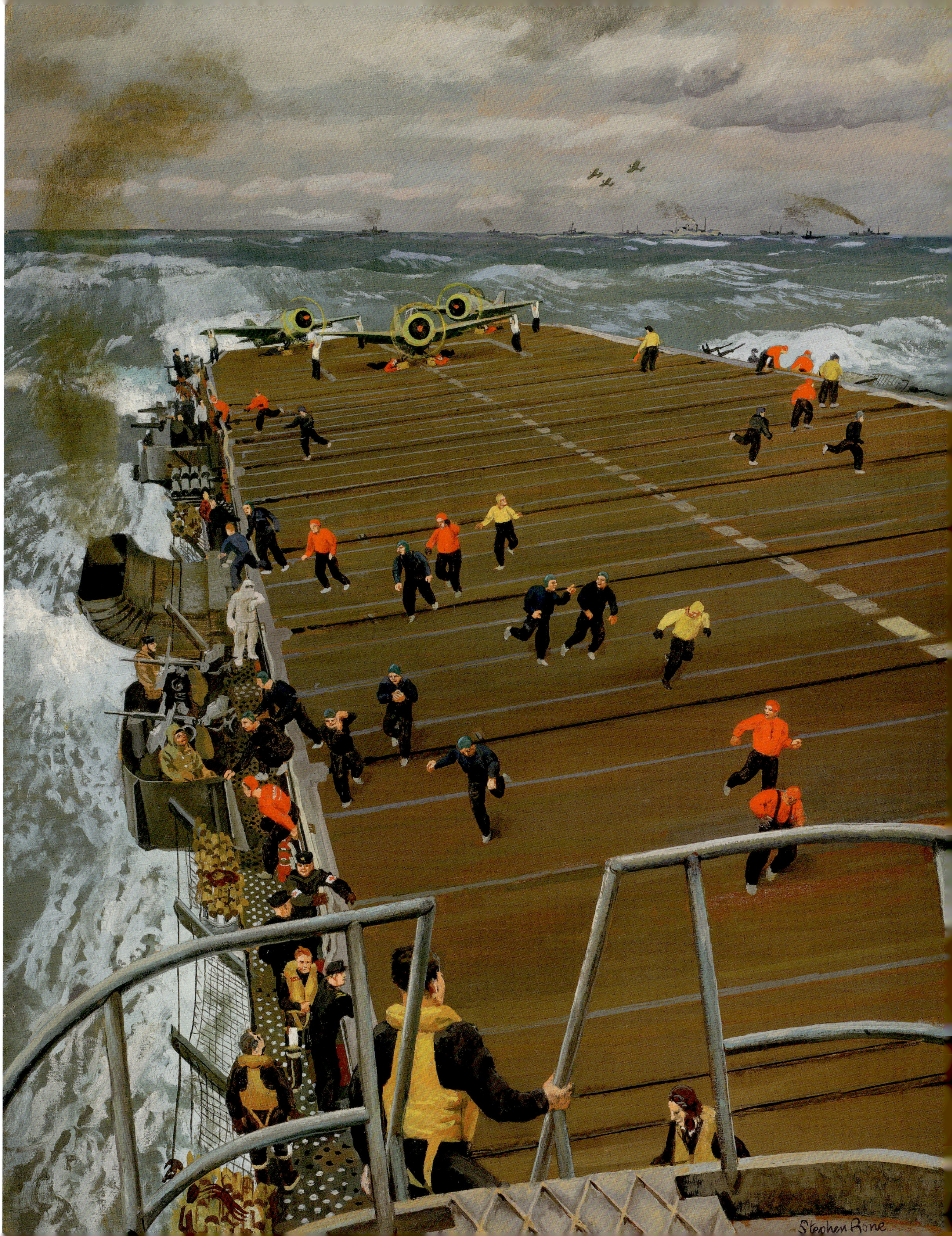
Stephen Bone

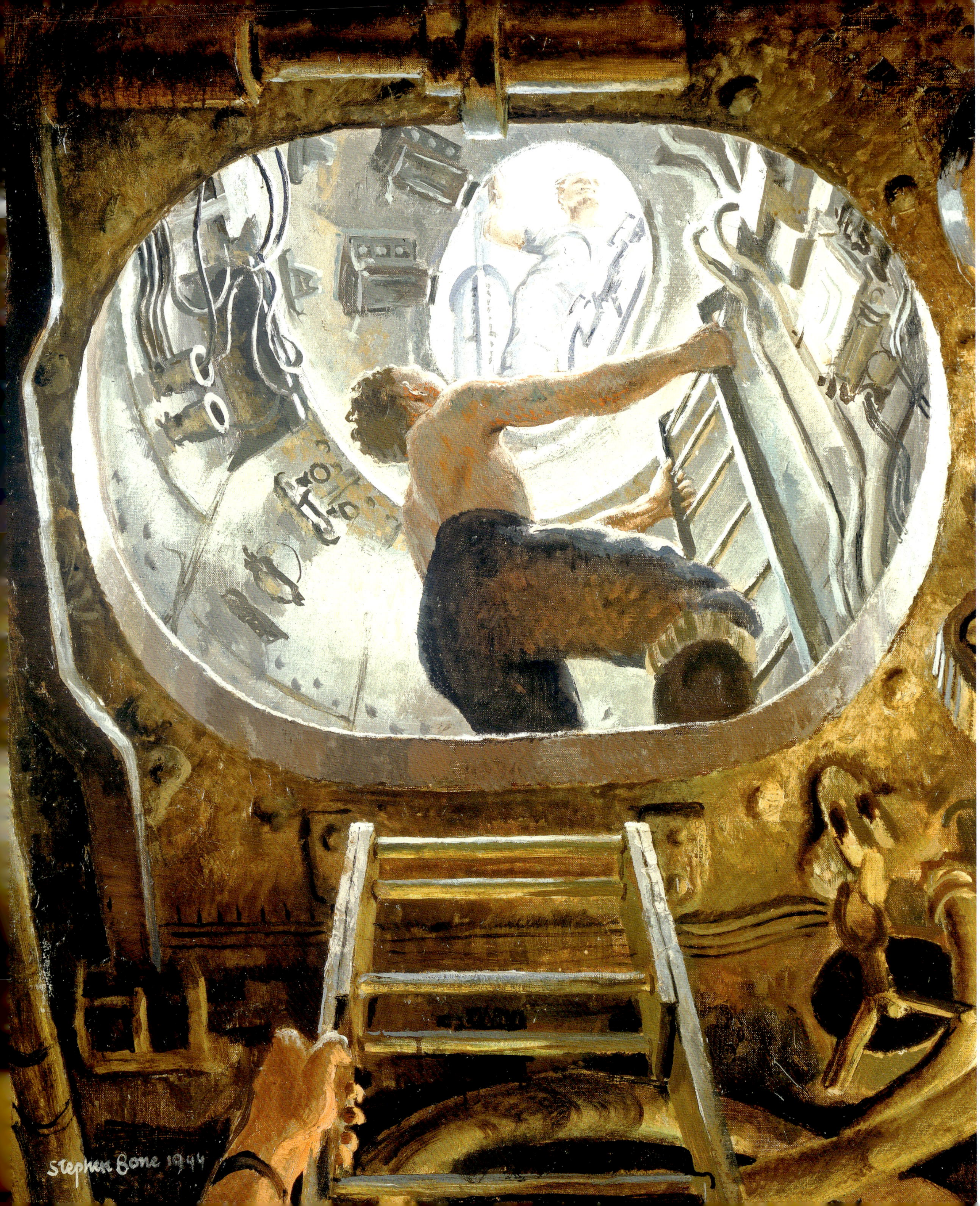
Stephen Bone 1944

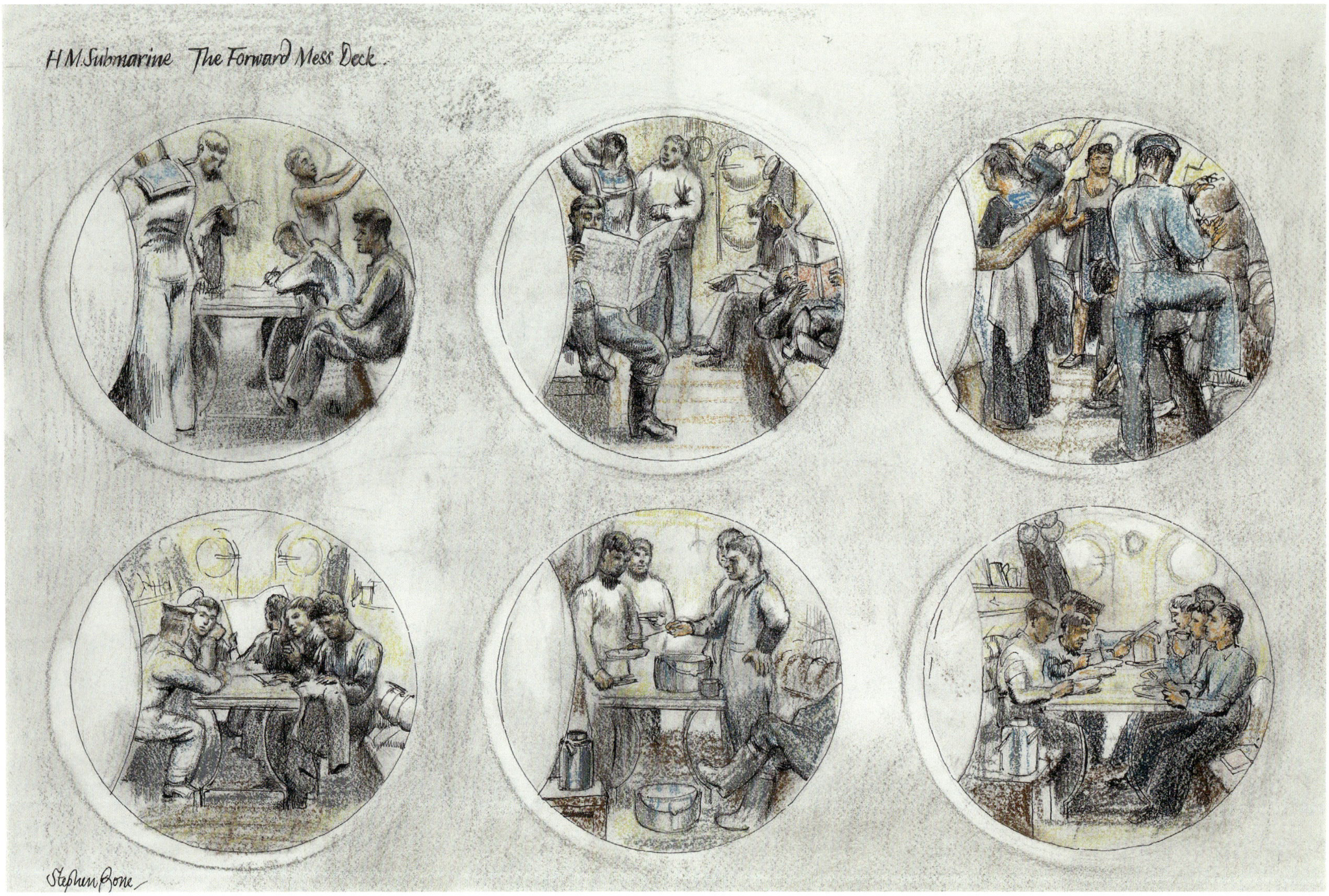

Plate 33 (opposite)
Stephen Bone
On Board an S-Class Submarine: Up the Conning Tower, 1944
Oil canvas
77.5 x 64.8 cm (30 ½ x 25 ½ in)
BHC1553

Plate 34 (above)
Stephen Bone
HM Submarine. The Forward Mess Deck, c.1944–5
Crayon, pen and ink on paper
46.2 x 59.9 cm (18 ⅛ x 23 ⅝ in)
PAI0525

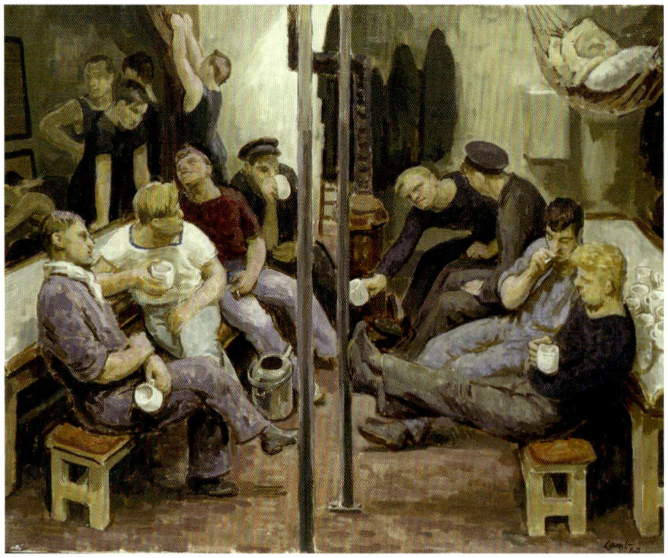

Plate 35 (right)
Henry Lamb
Eleven o'Clock in the Forecastle, 1940
Oil on canvas
50.8 x 60.9 cm (20 x 24 in)
BHC1660

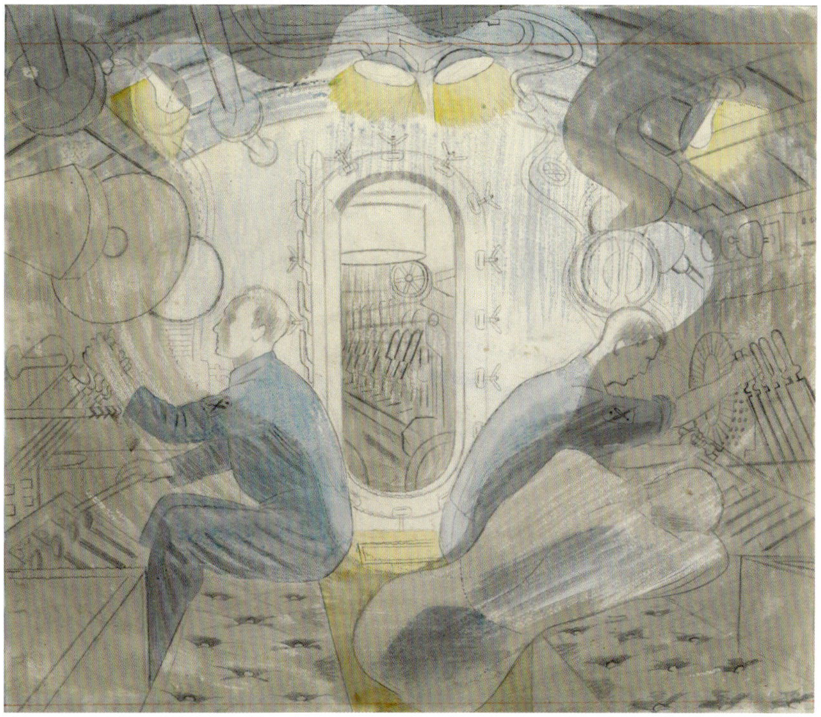

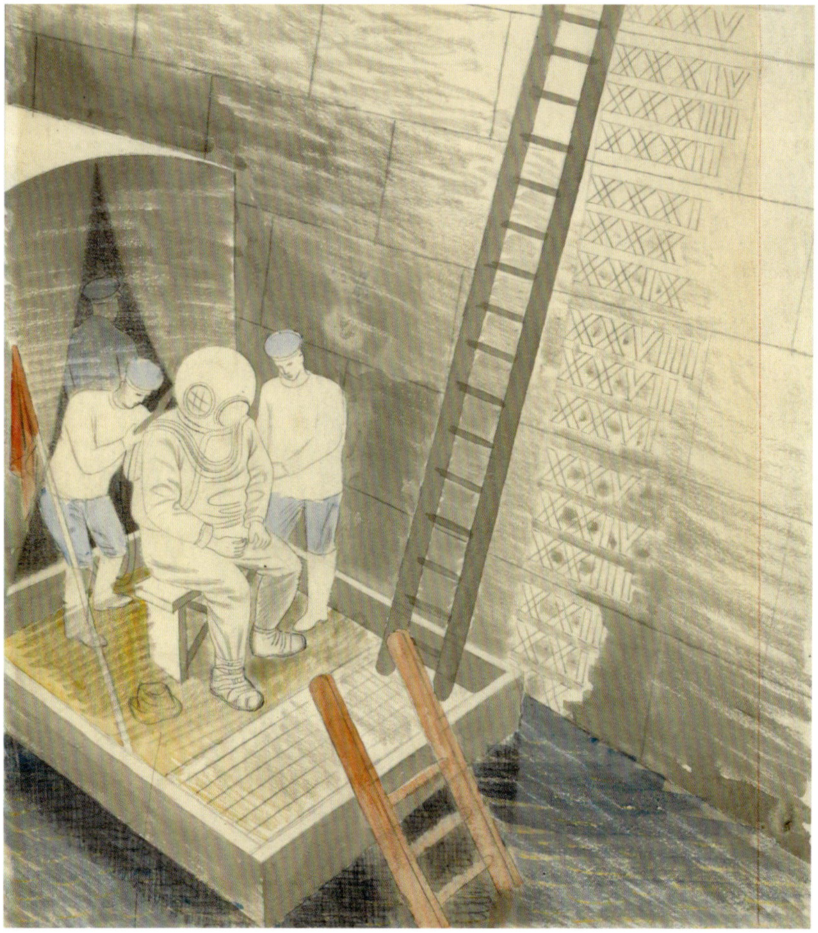

Plate 36 (above)
Eric Ravilious
The Submarine Series. Diving controls when submerged, 1940
Graphite and watercolour on paper
29 x 41.9 cm (11 3/8 x 16 1/2 in)
PAJ0749

Plate 37 (below)
Eric Ravilious
The Submarine Series. Diver, 1940
Graphite and watercolour on paper
42.2 x 29 cm (16 5/8 x 11 3/8 in)
PAJ0748

Plate 38 (opposite)
Eric Ravilious
The Submarine Series. Diver, 1941
Lithograph
34.3 x 30.5 cm (13 1/2 x 12 in)
PAD8073

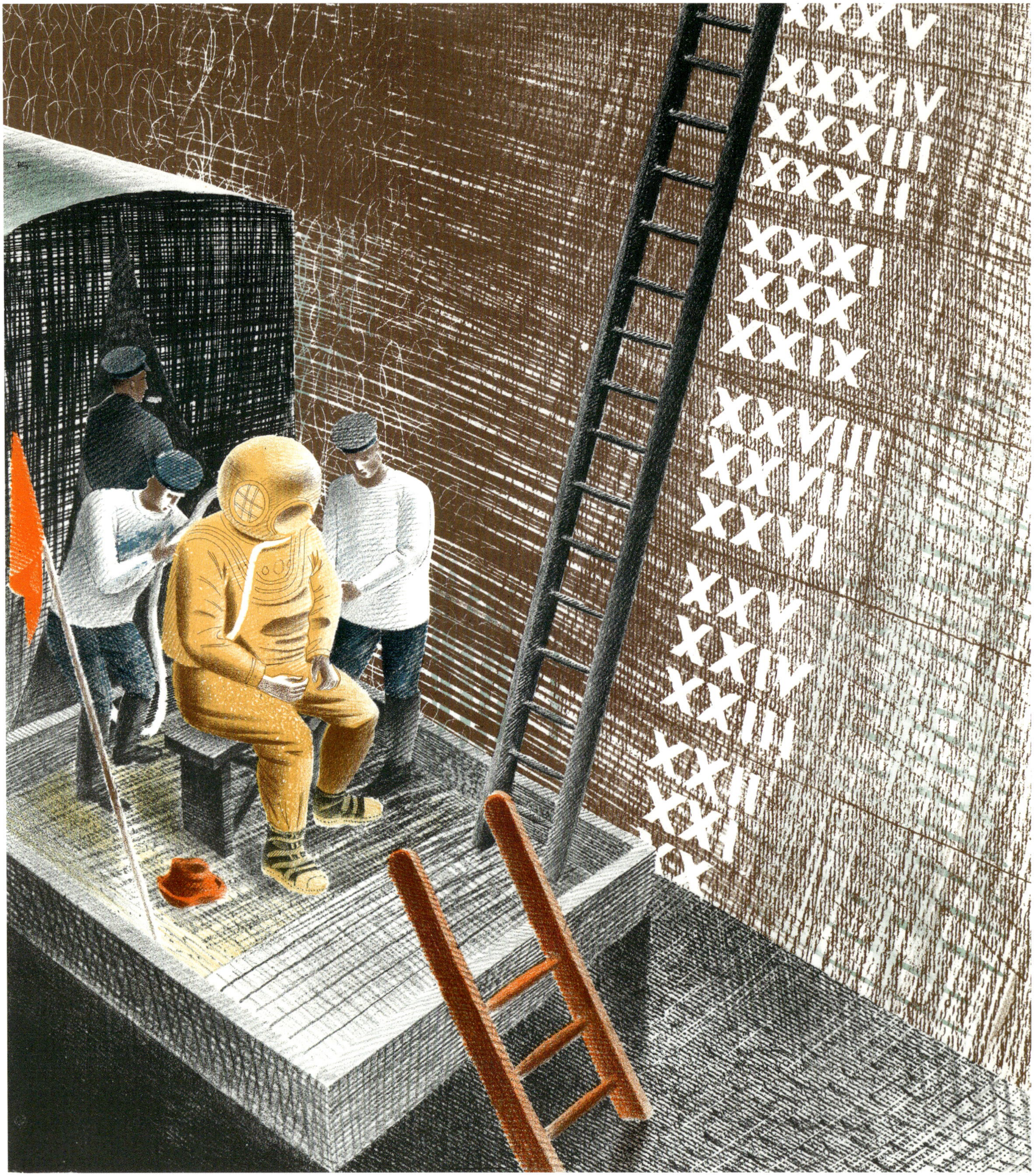
XXXV
XXXIV
XXXIII
XXXII
XXXI
XXX
XXIX
XXVIII
XXVII
XXVI
XXV
XXIV
XXIII
XXII
XXI

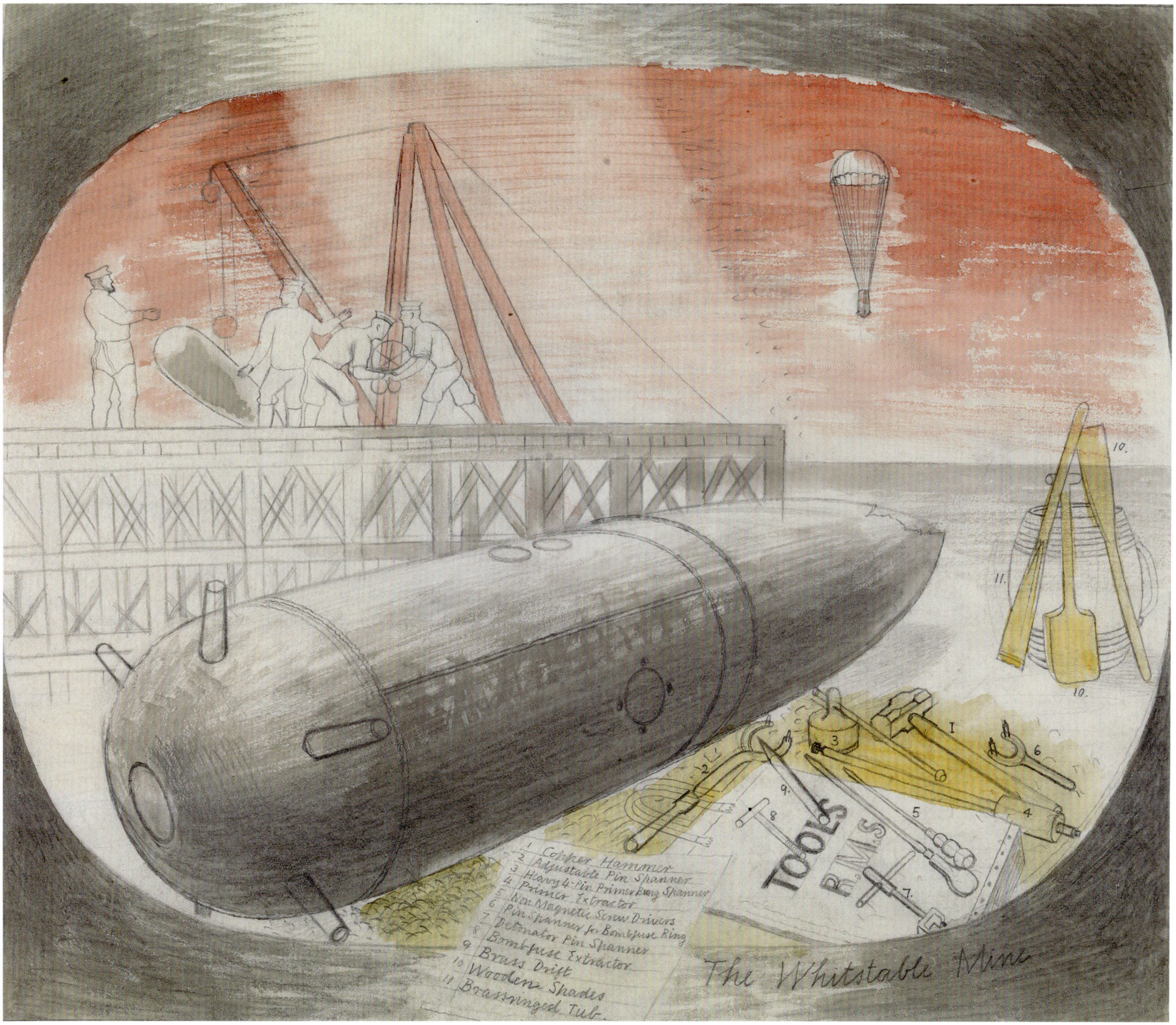

Plate 39
Eric Ravilious
The Submarine Series.
The Whitstable Mine, 1940
Graphite and watercolour on paper
29 x 46 cm (11 3/8 x 18 1/8 in)
PAJ0744

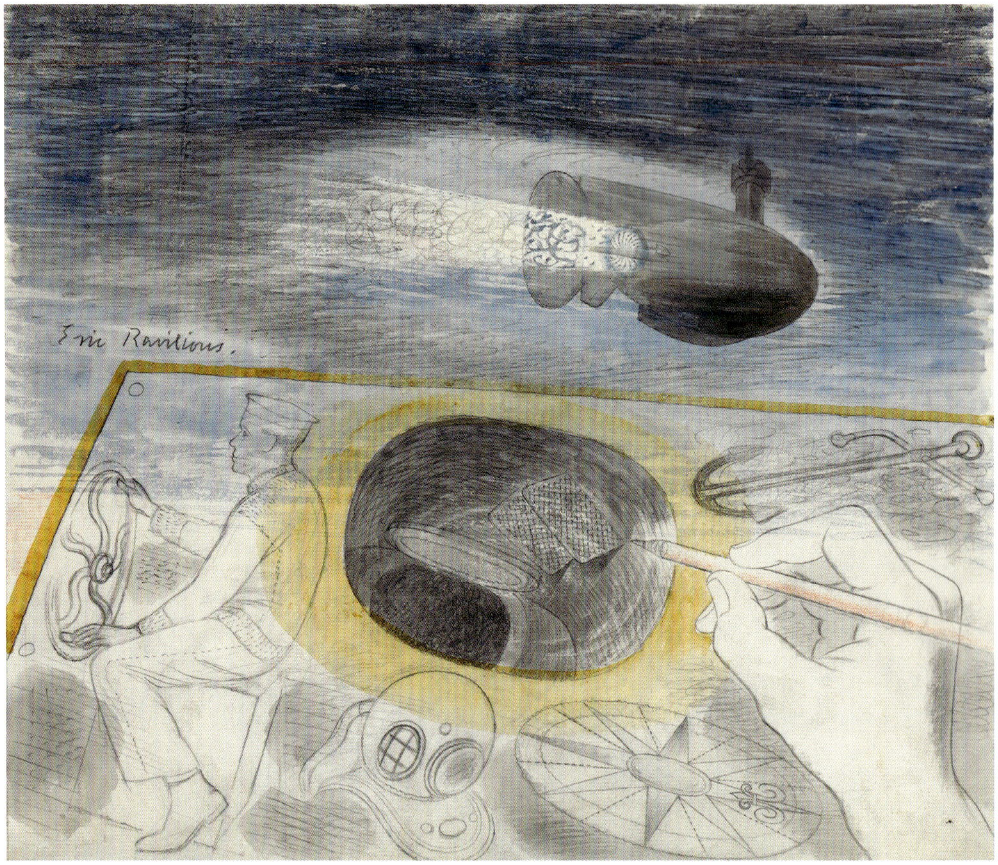

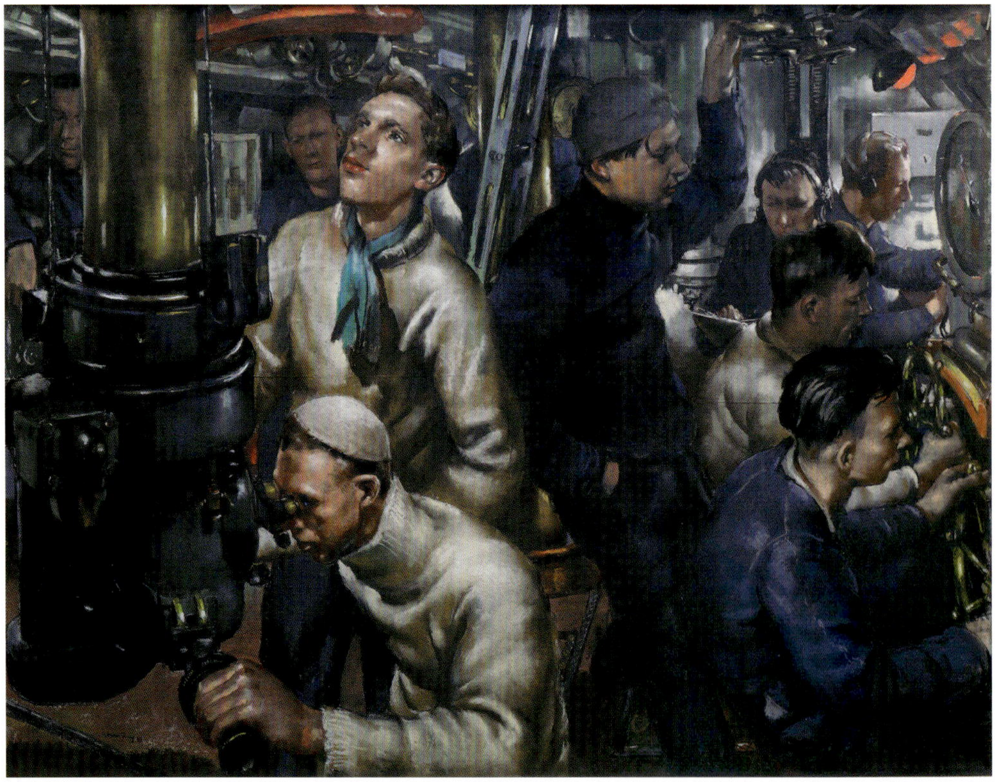

Plate 40 (above)
Eric Ravilious
The Submarine Series.
Submarine Dream, 1940
Graphite and watercolour on paper
28.8 x 46.5 cm (11 3/8 x 18 1/4 in)
PAJ0746

Plate 41 (below)
William Dring
Stand by Tubes. The Control Room of HMS 'Stubborn', 1943
Pastel on paper
96 x 119 cm (37 3/4 x 46 7/8 in)
PAJ2897

4

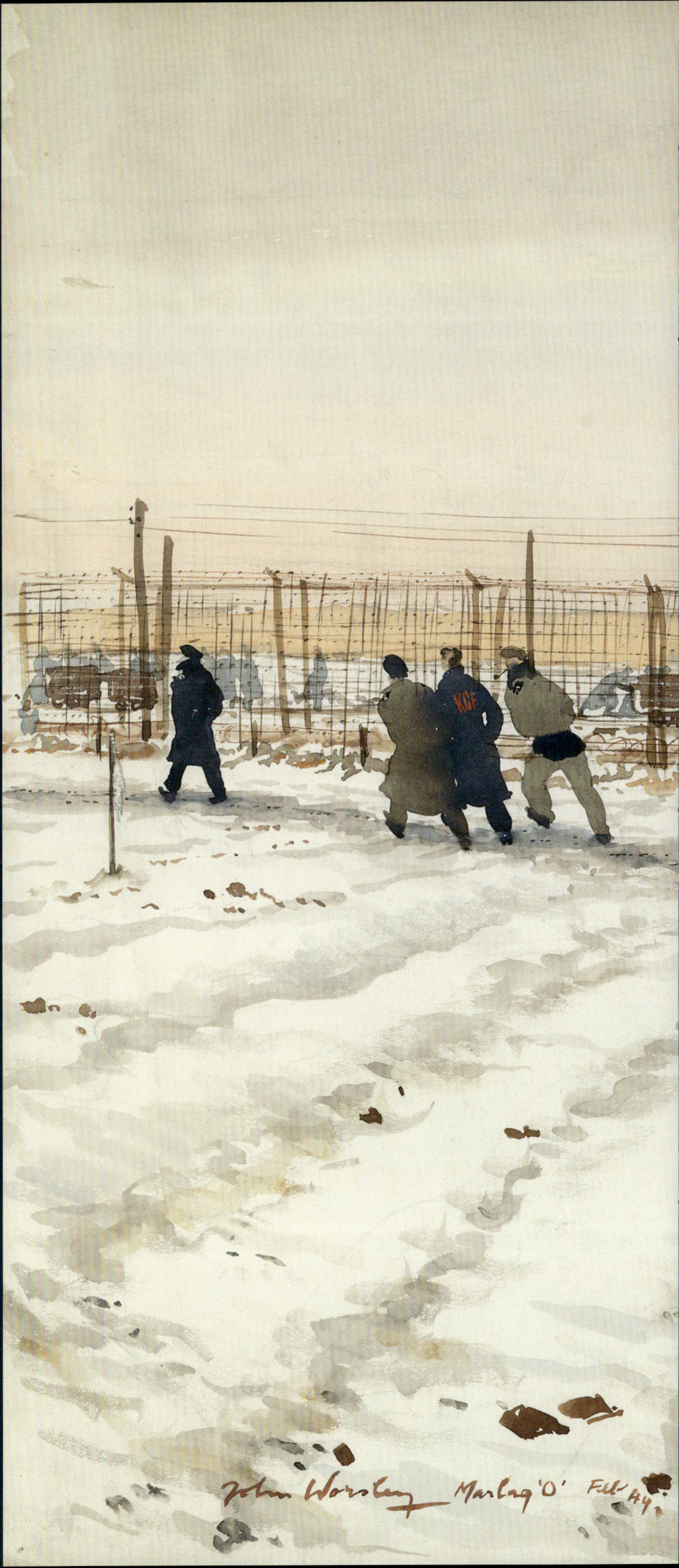

John Worsley
Marlag 'O' Feb '44 S.W. Corner of Naval Officers' Prison Camp, Westertincke, Germany, in winter, 1944
Watercolour on paper
49.8 x 65 cm (19 5/8 x 25 5/8 in)
PAI0527

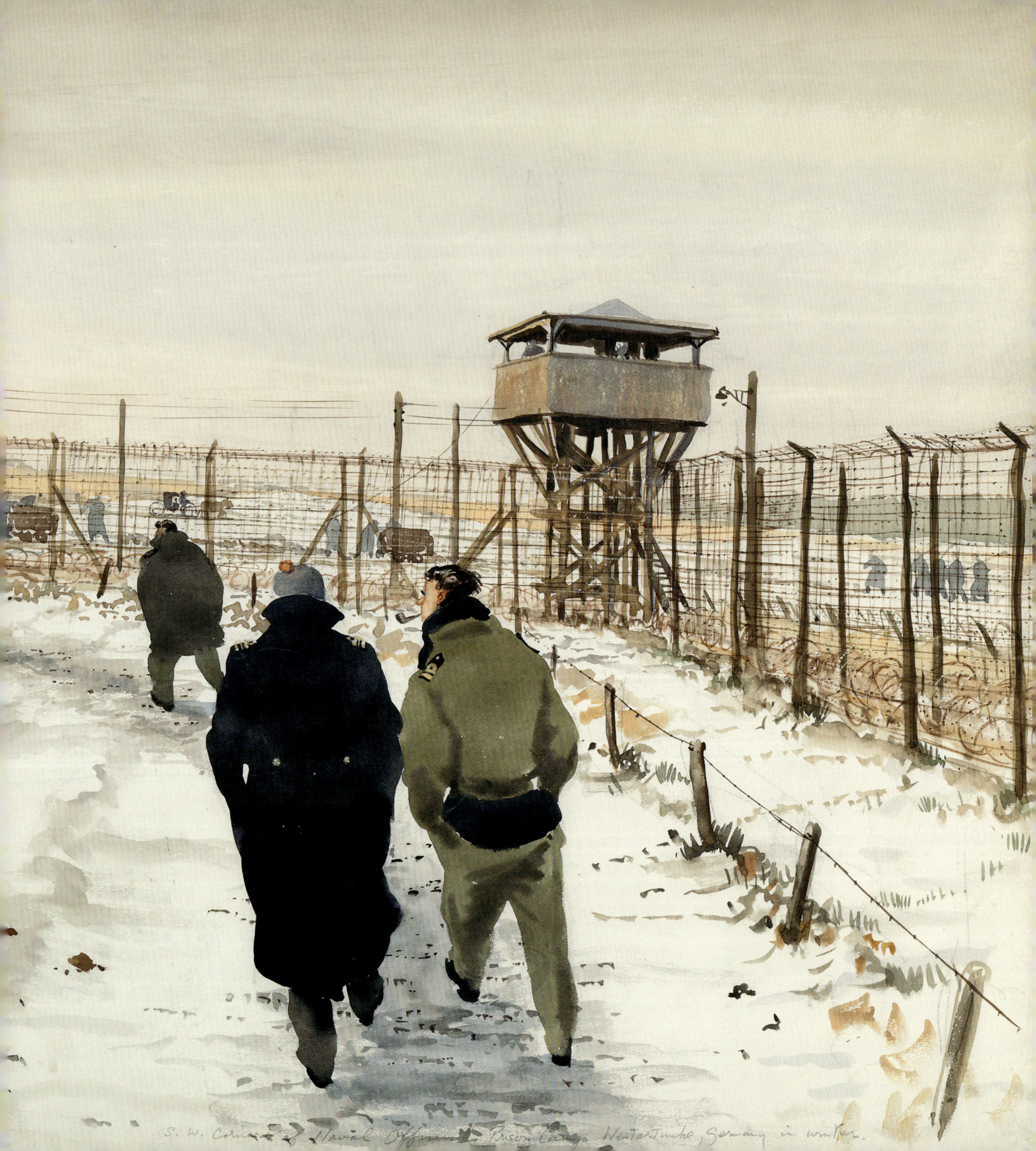
S. W. Corner of Naval Officers' Prison Camp Westertimke, Germany in winter.

4

From Service to Captivity: The Artist as Eyewitness

Melanie Vandenbrouck

John Worsley and John Kingsley Cook were both trained artists who saw active service during the Second World War and shared the daily routines of their fellow seamen. They also experienced the dangers of life at sea, the disaster of losing one's ship, the drama of capture by the enemy and the deprivations of captivity. But these similarities also betray a number of stark distinctions. Worsley was an official war artist, a Royal Naval officer and held in a German prisoner-of-war camp; Cook, on the other hand, had no official commission, was in the Merchant Navy, and interned in rather different conditions in Vichy-held North Africa. These disparities affected the outputs of both men in a number of ways and, seen together, their work reveals highly personal views of the conflict, the difficulties of creating art in exceptional circumstances and the sheer resourcefulness of artists engaged at war.

Lieutenant Worsley, Royal Navy: Artist

John Worsley (1919–2000) was trained at Goldsmiths College in London and, before the war, was employed as a commercial illustrator. In 1939 he enlisted in the Royal Naval Volunteer Reserve, joining the crew of HMS *Laurentic*, an armed merchant cruiser, patrolling the waters around Iceland and Greenland.[1] His drawings record life at sea, with many concentrating on mess-deck scenes, while others give a sense of wartime dangers, however great or small. In one drawing (plate 42), Worsley presents the comical but essential sequence of a seaman dressing up in layers of clothes before going out on watch in the freezing cold. Another (plate 44) highlights the physical toll imposed on the crew by the demanding watch roster. Exhausted, they would fall asleep fully clothed, ready to get up at any alert; the artist's caption, 'Jerrys or no Jerrys!', indicates how sleep became irresistible, despite the need for constant watchfulness. The narrative nature of Worsley's output shows him consciously recording the war for an audience, rather than for his own benefit. He submitted these two drawings, with six others, to the War Artists Advisory Committee (WAAC), which approvingly commented on the 'amusing scribble of dressing for the north sea weather' and acquired the group for 15 guineas.[2]

Worsley wrote to the WAAC about another work, noting 'this is no exaggeration but the results of careful observation, both of form and colour', thereby establishing his artistic credentials and objectivity as an eyewitness.[3] He was thus keenly aware of his unique vantage point as an artist observing from the heart of the conflict. Indeed, in August 1940, he coolly wrote to the WAAC:

> It does seem to me that my drawings, however rough they may appear, are worth more than 5 guineas for 3 sketches; its [*sic*] almost like being rabbits or saucepans or something!! On the spot drawings by Artists taking an active part in this war are not so numerous, and I feel that the Artists Advisory Committee might realize that more than they do.[4]

But in reality, the perceived freshness and spontaneity of these drawings, coupled with his first-hand experience of the war at sea, made him a valued recruit and, consequently, his work was regularly included in War Artists exhibitions.[5] For example, the catalogue for the *Britain at War* exhibition, which opened at the Museum of Modern Art, New York, in May 1941, describes 'Midshipman Worsley' as 'perhaps one of the most startling artistic finds of the war', 'his work […] gives the human side of the British Navy and the war at sea – pictures of sailors by a sailor of unusual gift.'[6]

Having been reassigned to escort duty in a convoy bound for Gibraltar, the *Laurentic* was torpedoed and sunk by a U-boat on 3 November 1940.[7] A hundred men were lost but Worsley survived and was made a lieutenant. Returning to escort duties, he continued to send work to the Committee from HMS *Lancaster* in the Atlantic and then from HMS *Devonshire* in the Indian Ocean and Far East.[8] In July 1943, he was finally appointed an official war artist.[9]

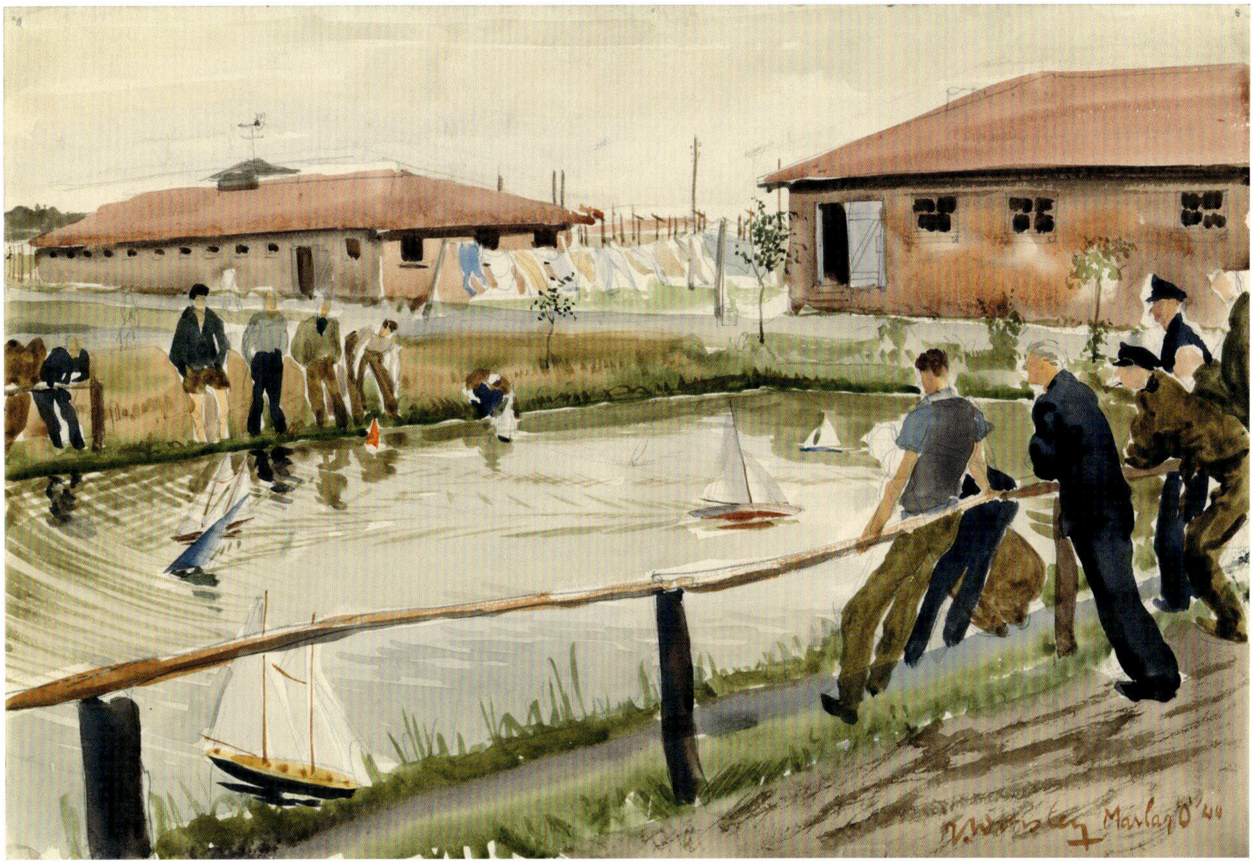

Fig.42
John Worsley
Naval Officer prisoners sailing boats, Marlag 'O', 1944
Watercolour on paper
29. 2 x 41.5 cm (11 ½ x 16 ⅜ in)
PAJ0741

Summoned to Portsmouth by Admiral Sir William James, Worsley was sent off to the Mediterranean with these words: 'My boy, you are the youngest Official War Artist ever [...] but I don't want you sitting on your backside in Malta. Get out, and go where the action is. Get into the lion's mouth';[10] and so he did. The Allies were progressively gaining control of the Italian coast and Worsley's drawings from that period include the sight of Port Augusta, Sicily, littered with the wreckage of enemy seaplanes, and large watercolours of the island's awe-inspiring caves at Melilli, employed by the Axis as mine and torpedo stores. Several of these were reproduced in the *Illustrated London News*.[11] However, depicting war from the thick of the action was clearly challenging. Worsley recorded the preliminary mainland assault on Reggio di Calabria, in September 1943, from a Flak Landing Craft, noting:

> I had felt that as a war artist I was as an onlooker watching, and therefore somehow immune from danger. I set up my board and paints close to two anti-aircraft guns and got a little wash going. Then, of course, we were divebombed by an Italian aeroplane and everything went for six: painting, drawing, board and paints. From then on, I used just a drawing board.[12]

Having witnessed the capitulation of Salerno on HMS *Roberts*, he was involved in covert operations in the Adriatic when the Germans captured his party. After a difficult transit across Yugoslavia and Germany, they were incarcerated in Marlag 'O', the naval officers' camp near Bremen (plate 43). Suspected of being a spy, Worsley (POW no.1182) spent two months in solitary confinement, suffering from cold and hunger but, as he later revealed, 'this is a time when being an artist paid off [...] because I used to do absolutely filthy drawings for the guards and I used to get extra potatoes and things like that'.[13]

Worsley's incarceration was unique: he was the only official war artist held as a prisoner of war.[14] Life inside was far from easy. He wrote to his parents of shortages but Red Cross supplies arrived as some relief. *The Contents of a Red Cross Parcel* (1944, IWM) shows the 'luxuries' that made the privations of camp tolerable: corned beef, chocolate, powdered milk, soap and cigarettes.[15] Some of these were used as currency to bribe German guards, while the cardboard and string from the parcels, and the wood from the crates, were recycled to make furniture or model boats, which the inmates raced in the reservoir (fig.42). Meanwhile, Worsley drew as much as he could, recording daily life in captivity with Winsor & Newton materials

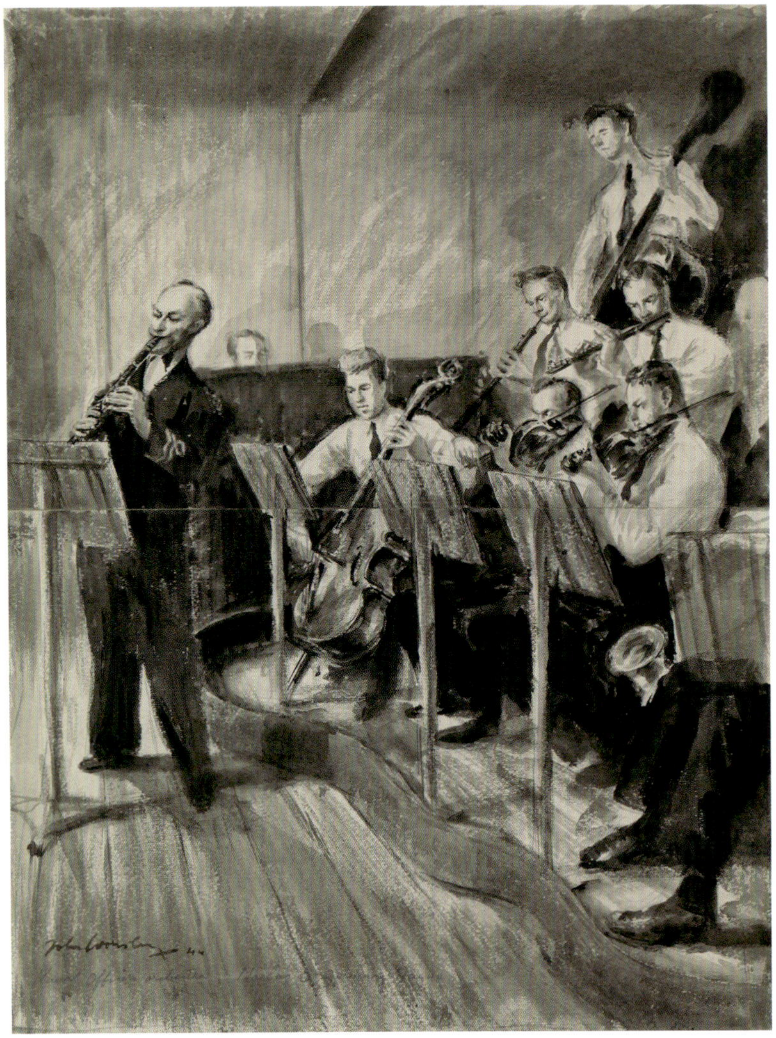

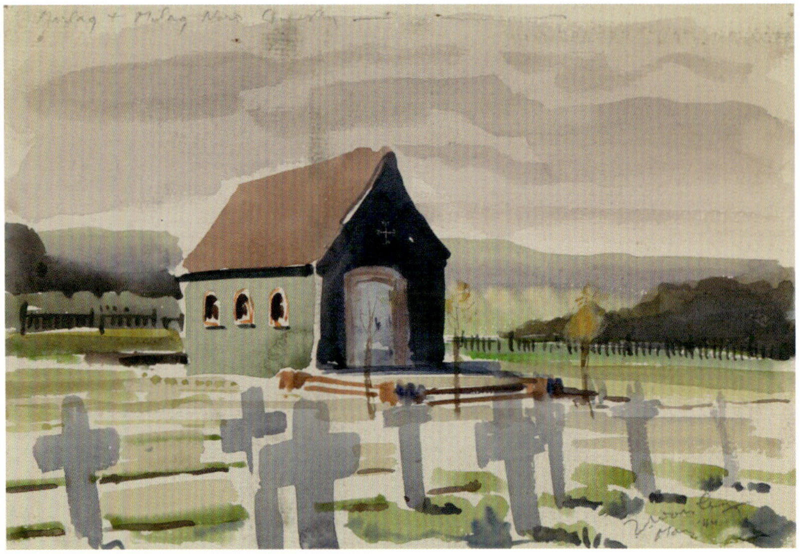

Fig.43 (left)
John Worsley
Naval Officers Orchestra – 1944, Marlag 'O', 1944
Graphite and wash on paper
59.5 x 45.1 cm (23 3/8 x 17 3/4 in)
PAI0518

Fig.44 (right)
John Worsley
Marlag and Milag Nord Cemetery, May 1944, 1944
Watercolour on paper
17.6 x 25.2 cm (6 7/8 x 9 7/8 in)
PAD9701

sent by the WAAC via the Red Cross.[16] Unlike the naval ratings and merchant seamen held in the nearby camps of Marlag 'M' and Milag Nord respectively, the officers were not allowed to work. Worsley's fellow inmates were adept at organising entertainment, staging plays and forming an orchestra to fend off 'boredom and despair, [...] the twin evils of any P.O.W camp' (fig.43).[17]

Living in cramped cells was a strain on morale too. *Naval officers room at Marlag 'O', prisoner of war camp* (plate 45) shows the prisoners gathered around a table spread with books, a gramophone and some records. The muted atmosphere of the scene is rendered in dark browns, ochre and green tones in thick impastos, which suggest confinement, while our eyes are drawn to the two bright red dots of the record labels. These are not only the focal point of the image in formal terms but also in the subject matter, for this scene focuses on the act of listening to music as perhaps a conduit to an inner world. Captivated by their thoughts, the men recapture a sense of privacy, despite the claustrophobic environment.

In contrast, Worsley also made a number of perceptive portraits of the Victoria Cross holders among his fellow prisoners. Far from lost in their own thoughts, the sitters seem keenly aware of being viewed, such as in the portrait of Lieutenant Godfrey Place (plate 46), who was captured in the miniature submarine raid that attempted to sink the German battleship *Tirpitz* in Norway in 1943. Worsley used any available material to keep working and these oil portraits are on bed sheets, which he had previously decorated with floral designs for use as curtains: the lively patterns are still visible at the back of the paintings.[18]

If his depictions remained mostly optimistic and showed the inmates' stoical temperament, Worsley sometimes represented the grim side of life in captivity. As POWs the men were reasonably well-treated, thanks in part to the vigilance of the Red Cross, but wartime privations also resulted in illness and even death, represented by the melancholy watercolour of the camp's cemetery (fig.44).

In captivity (as in service), daily exercise was vital, both in physical and in social terms. This fed into the prisoners' main preoccupation – that of escape. In a large watercolour (plate 48) their hunched postures suggest both winter cold and clandestine plotting. Some of Worsley's drawings show POWs digging tunnels

Fig.45
John Kingsley Cook
Trouble with the Kite, 1941
Pen and wash on paper
19.1 x 13.3 cm (7 ½ x 5 ¼ in)
ZBA5206

or filling in discovered excavations.[19] But his artistic skills were of more practical use to the Escape Committee. He faked passports (imitating photographs in pencil drawings and Nazi stamps in ink) and made a dummy prisoner, named 'Albert RN', used as a stand-in for headcounts to buy time for successful escapees.[20]

It was not only prisoners that Worsley was keen to see leave Marlag 'O': he also went to considerable efforts to send his testimonies of camp life to the WAAC. Some were smuggled out in the plaster-cast set round the broken arm of his friend Guy Morgan, who was repatriated by the Red Cross because of the injury. These drawings were displayed in a War Artists exhibition in 1944.[21] Later, he wrote to the WAAC, voicing discontent at not seeing his POW works at a post-war Royal Academy exhibition:

> Please do not think that I am endeavouring to assert my ego, but I took so much trouble, and underwent such considerable hazard (including hiding much from the Germans) to get them out of Germany and in a small way justify my capture, that the disappointment was extreme. I even constructed a container from Red Cross milk tins, which I carried for an eighty mile march, under strafing from allied fighter planes, to [...] bring back authentic records for the War exhibition.

The WAAC promptly rectified its oversight.[22]

Worsley remained in captivity until his liberation in May 1945 but, even within the camp, the turning tide of the war was visible. With Allied daytime air raids over Germany a regular occurrence, the inmates congregated outdoors to watch the vapour trails left by American Flying Fortress bombers, as seen in one watercolour (plate 49). These were ominous signs for the prison guards, but the sight of B17s overhead in ever-growing numbers and increasing frequency brought hope to the POWs.

Radio Officer Cook, Merchant Navy: Artist

While Worsley was the only official war artist to spend time in captivity, other remarkable eyewitness accounts of wartime imprisonment were made by John Kingsley Cook (1911–94). Trained at the Royal Academy and Central schools in London, Cook was about to take up an appointment as tutor in typography and design at the Edinburgh College of Art when the war intervened. He enrolled in the Merchant Navy as a Wireless Radio Officer, fulfilling a long-held dream of going to sea.

His first transatlantic crossing in December 1940 – which saw him triumph over seasickness and gain his sea-legs, despite the appalling weather – was rewarded with an exciting stopover in the United States (plate 50).[23] As he wrote in his logbook and recalled in his wartime memoirs, however, slow-moving Atlantic convoys were gruelling and nerve-jangling.[24] The enemy threat was constant and long hours of inactivity were punctuated by watches, firing practice, boat drills and flying kites against enemy aircraft (fig.45 and plate 51). Cook found time to draw on the back of obsolete charts which, he noted, 'can take pen and ink beautifully'.[25] Reflecting on the barren ocean and the dangers of boredom, he wrote in his log: 'I can understand how seamen often get "peculiar"'. But looking out to sea also conjured up the work of his artistic forebears. 'Fine effects of black storm clouds and sunlight' made him think of Turner, whereas 'a wonderful golden sunrise [...] with a luminous pathway across the dark water' brought Claude Lorrain to mind.[26]

Cook also dabbled in the art of caricature, which proved very popular with the crew. During a tense eastward journey from the United States, as he recalled later, one of his cartoons helped relieve the general mood of attrition: 'In retrospect, I consider that this was perhaps my most valuable contribution to the war effort!'[27] Another cartoon (fig.46) shows the crew in a flimsy paper boat, passing time away while awaiting rescue.

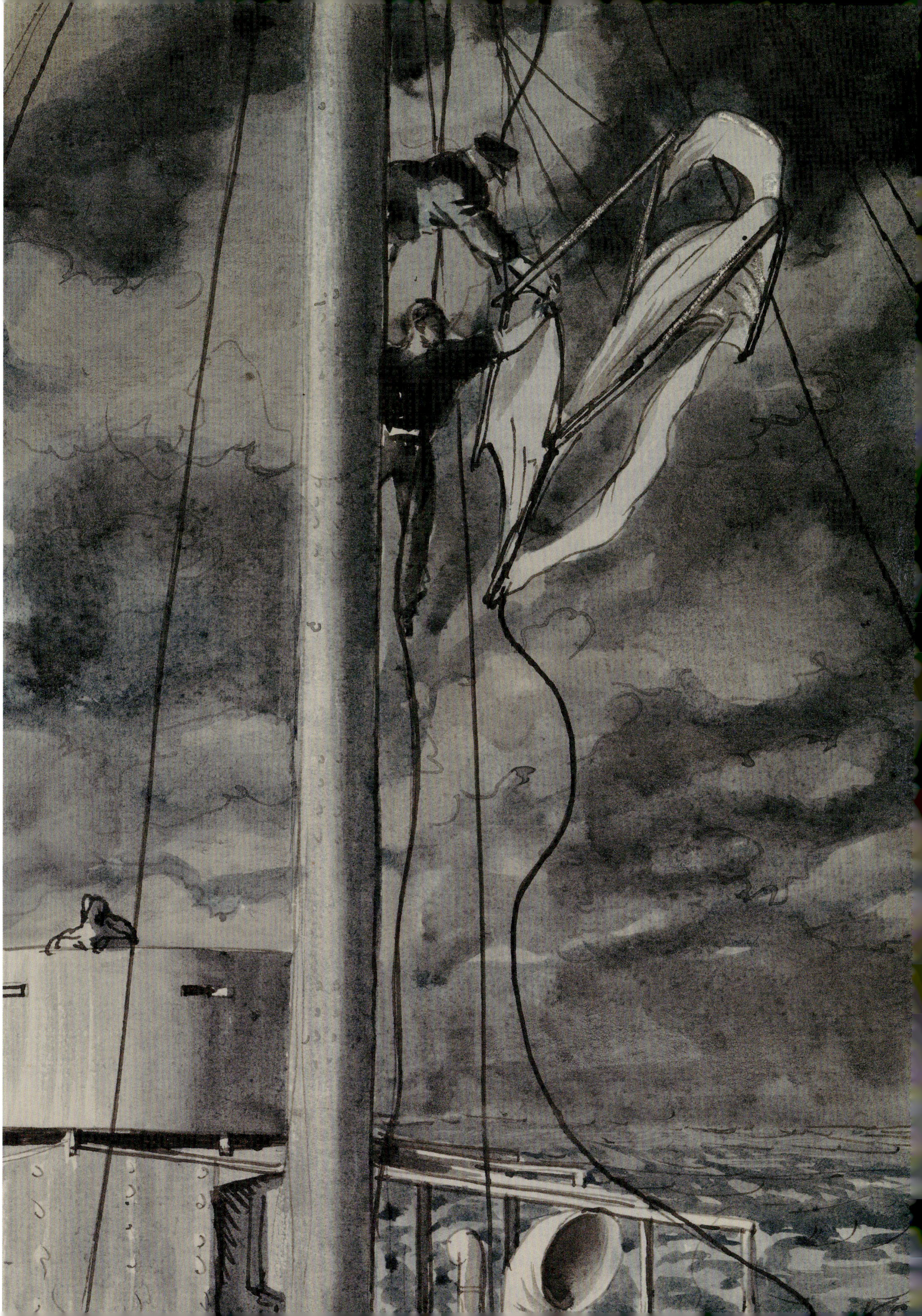

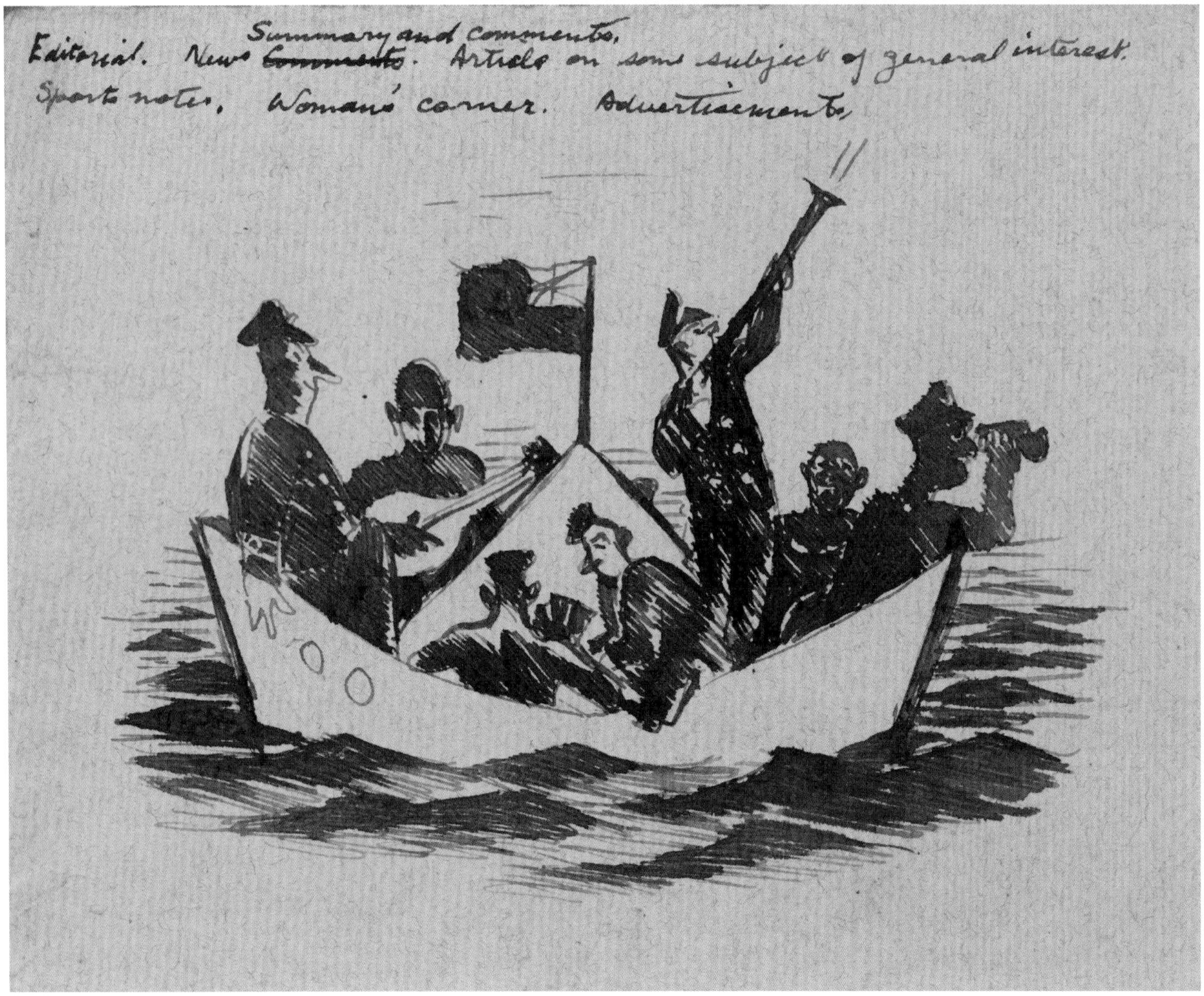

Fig.46
John Kingsley Cook
Untitled cartoon, 1941 (detail)
Pen and wash on paper
15.1 x 23.5 cm (6 x 9 ¼ in)
ZBA5296

With cargo ships a primary U-boat target, the Merchant Navy suffered heavy casualties. For Cook, the danger was heightened when his ship, the *Empire Guillemot*, carried high explosives. His drawings and diary recount the repeated engine failures that often rendered this floating bomb a sitting duck and threatened to separate it from the convoy (plate 52). Wartime depictions of engines usually emphasised reliability and modernity, but Cook exposed their failings with drawings at once humorous and evocative of the seriousness of the situation. His logbook entries speak of the crew's lack of sleep, the sense of doom and depression at having lost the convoy, and the relief of catching sight of it again.[28]

In the summer of 1941, Cook was sent on a covert mission to bring munitions and supplies to blockaded Malta. The *Empire Guillemot* was disguised as a peacetime vessel, successively flying Spanish, French and Italian civilian flags. The mission was a success, despite engine breakdowns and narrowly evading the enemy. After discharging the precious cargo, the crew spent a month resting in Malta.

During this time Cook sketched extensively but only four drawings survive, their faint outlines washed by seawater after the *Empire Guillemot* was sunk by the Italian Air Force during its return trip on 24 October.[29] Separated in two overcrowded lifeboats, the crew spent four days drifting at the mercy of the elements. Apathy, dejection and mutiny spread among the castaways as hope of rescue faded. Cook's lifeboat capsized, leaving no choice but to swim ashore in rough seas: half of the men were lost. Washed up on an Algerian beach, then part of Vichy France, the survivors were taken prisoner and moved into a French Army barracks in Bône. In stark contrast to Worsley's experience, the authorities considered them 'low grade prisoners, neither internees nor prisoners of war'. Their mail was held for several months and Cook's family waited an agonising 48 days to receive news of his survival.[30]

For Cook, art became a lifeline, but it could also be a source of anxiety. In his first letter home from Algeria, he wrote: 'I am particularly sore at losing the drawings I did in Malta, and all my materials. I feel lost without them.' A few days later: 'I have now got a fountain pen, so I am much happier, and I'll be able to write up a log. I've also got a few drawing materials too, but the paper is harder to find'. Then: 'I now have a watercolour paint box. […] Most of them are violent dyes and the least touch stains the paper. […] I can't say I produced anything any good, somehow the materials and the conditions here aren't conducive to artistic production.'[31]

Working was hard, and six weeks after his arrival he wrote despondently: 'I have been meaning for a long time to start a series of portraits of the men, but somehow I can't bring myself to do it. I suppose it is partly a fear of failure that prevents me. Material is so precious that I am loathe to use a good piece of paper'. The same letter contains a drawing of sleeping prisoners wrapped in their blankets, a composition that recalls Henry Moore's famous *Shelter* drawings (plate 53). What he really lacked, in fact, was stimulus: 'I find it very difficult to do anything creative without the motivation of other artists or any works of art.'[32]

In the camp, the men were afflicted by lice, painful boils and dysentery. One young able seaman called Lacey died of typhus six months after their arrival in Algeria. As his memoirs and drawings reveal, Cook and his companions learnt to kill time by cultivating friendships, observing local life, engaging in petty theft, playing chess and music or making model boats, a common pastime for prisoners from a seafaring background. Again Cook's experience contrasts with that of Worsley: the official war artist received art supplies from Winsor & Newton, but Cook received none until his last weeks of captivity.[33] He resorted to being even more resourceful than Worsley, using the back of envelopes or packing paper for drawing, and cardboard and plywood recycled from Red Cross packages for his oil paintings.

In January 1942, the survivors were transferred to Mécheria, a convict camp in the Atlas Mountains (plate 55). While detention with criminals had its dangers, they had more freedom than in Bône and, on parole, explored the nearby village and mountains. In this environment, Cook returned to his art. An early letter reports some difficulties: 'they seem to lack almost everything that is necessary for painting here. Certain raw pigments are procurable, but linseed oils, turps, brushes, panels, white lead, rags, are quite unobtainable.' By 6 March, however, Cook had set up a proper studio in one of the rooms set aside for officers: Tommy, Fifth Engineer, was the studio assistant, priming small panels made out of scraps of wood; Len, Second Steward, enrolled as a pupil; Sydney, Chief Steward, was the business manager, with camp inmates and Vichy officers alike queuing for portraits.[34]

The scarcity of colour, the result being his reliance on earth tones, is evident in one of Cook's rare Algerian paintings, showing the men playing volleyball (plate 54). The handling is free and dynamic but painting proved too challenging, and Cook's favoured support remained paper. In Algeria he predominantly used a thick, handmade packing paper, which may also be a response to his surroundings as it evokes the dry and rugged landscape, while the porous support readily absorbed inks and paints.

He made a number of drawings of inmates walking around the camp, some clearly engaged in intrigues (plate 56). His Arab guards were reluctant to sit for him but he managed to make a few portraits (plate 57).[35] For Cook, Algeria conjured up the great Orientalists, as he related in his drawings and letters home. About an officer visiting the camp, he wrote: 'He has an Arab stallion with long mane and tail and graceful arched neck of the type Delacroix delighted in painting.'[36] The surroundings, on the other hand, reminded him of the 'classical pastorales of Claude or Poussin', and some of his views of the mountains near Mécheria certainly recall Turner's alpine scenes.[37]

Keeping pets helped the inmates deal with the strain of incarceration and provided Cook with another source of inspiration. Some were of an unexpected kind, like 'large fluffy caterpillars', but more popular were chameleons (plate 58), which the inmates found 'a never-failing source of interest and amusement'.[38] Cook's written and drawn descriptions of the life and untimely 'death-by-cat' of his own pet chameleon, Josephine, are at once tender and detailed. He studied almost obsessively her diet, interactions, changes of colour in various environments, mating and nesting.[39] Stray dogs roamed around the camp and the story of 'Lola the mad dog', which forms a whole chapter of Cook's memoirs, combines warmth and weariness. She was put down when the camp's commandant decided to destroy every dog in the place, and from this comes the greatest moment of bitterness in his memoir, and the most poignant of his retrospective drawings.[40]

Cook's time in Algeria ended with the Allied landings in North Africa on 8 November 1942, when a voyage home (of which he remembers little) brings his memoirs to a close. That he chose to stop his account with his liberation perhaps stresses how captivity had affected him. The letters from Algeria were intentionally upbeat: he described his surroundings at length and insisted that he was well, clearly intending to dispel his parents' anxiety. Upsetting events were edited out: neither the tragic end of Lacey, nor the loss of Lola, nor even the treachery of some of the convicts figure in them. Cheerful, the letters home often finished with the words 'Keep smiling',[41] but his health suffered badly and on his release he was invalided for months. During that time, he sent some of his Algerian works for the WAAC's attention and, in March 1943, an oil and three drawings were acquired for 30 guineas.[42]

In July that year, he returned to sea, this time on fuel tankers in the Mediterranean and Atlantic.[43] Perhaps as a result of his experience in Algeria, his subsequent letters home have a different tone and are scarcer. Despite some moments of humour, they betray a new listlessness: war had taken its toll. There are tragic incidents, like the death of his ship's elderly fireman, buried at sea, but Cook clings to happier things, and the antics of the ship's kittens punctuate time on board SS *Esturia*. Keeping active, he practised lettering, designed monograms and continued drawing.[44]

In December 1943, Cook sent a number of portraits of merchant seamen for inspection by the WAAC, 'not in the hope that you will buy them', he wrote, 'but that they may interest you in my work'. While the Committee had purchased his Algerian drawings, they showed no interest in those depicting life in the wartime merchant service. Cook expressed his frustration with the WAAC's inadequate recognition of the subject, noting its conspicuous absence in the War Artists exhibitions:

> One sees heroic portraits of fighter pilots, and of Army and Navy men who have distinguished themselves, but the MN heroes seem to be forgotten. Their achievements are not often spectacular but their work requires a steady courage and endurance of a very high order. Remember that the casualty percentage of the Merchant Navy is heaviest of all four services. They do not seek publicity but of all the services they deserve and need it most.[45]

Cook's letter was uncharacteristically forward but he had a point. The Admiralty had appointed William Dring to immortalise the features of Royal Navy personnel, but wartime portraits of Merchant Navy men, such as those by Bernard Hailstone, are rare. John Platt provided paintings documenting maritime traffic – including some of the merchant convoys – but his tenure as an official artist was brief and his output scant. Cook followed this plea by offering his services as an official war artist for the Merchant Navy, with particular emphasis on portraits. Four of his drawings were purchased in response to this request but no such appointment was made.[46]

A highlight of these times was a chance meeting with the Admiralty artist Vivian Pitchforth, in spring 1944. Cook caught sight of him while the *Esturia* was refuelling another ship: 'there, sure enough was a full sized artist working away like a demon on the gun deck of the frigate', he wrote to his parents. 'He was doing it properly, with easel, oil paints and everything, dashing off one study after another. He didn't look like one of the ship's company, and judging from the way he was working, he was getting paid for it, so I guessed he was an official war artist.' Using Morse code to

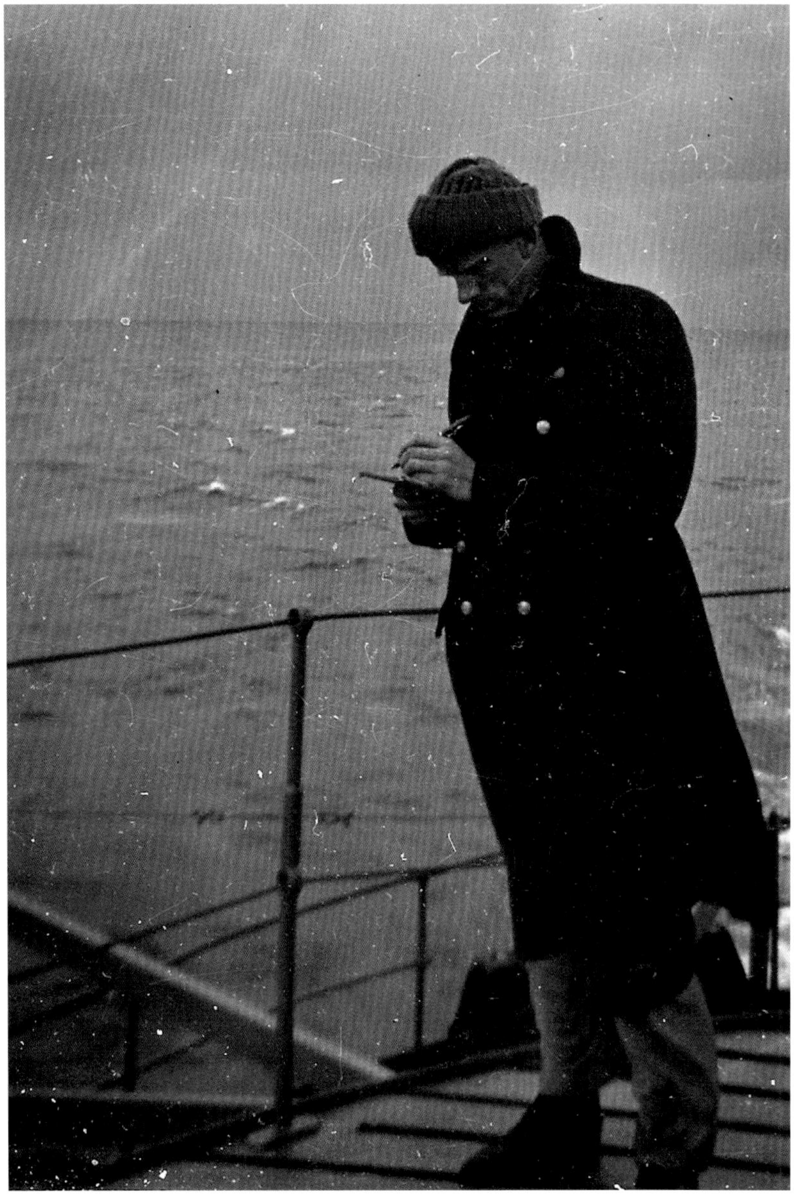

Fig.47
John Kingsley Cook sketching on board ship, 1941
Photograph
14.8 x 10.4 cm (5 ⅞ x 4 ⅛ in)
Private collection, image courtesy of Bridget Cook

exchange a few words, they agreed to meet in Gibraltar: 'I look forward to meeting an artist when we reach port. I realise its [*sic*] years since I spoke to one! Such was the stimulus of seeing him that I worked hard all afternoon doing studies of our end of the oiling operations. I must have something good to show him!'[47] Cook found himself reinvigorated, with a new sense of motivation and purpose.[48] The scale of his drawings increased and, influenced by Pitchforth's style and formal approach, he adopted a more colourful palette, now looking at the vessel's propeller, girdles or metallic structure in greater detail (plate 59). As he wrote in his memoirs, 'for the duration of the war I led another life, much simpler, much more basic, but the artist in me survived and whenever I could in spare moments I would bring out my sketchbooks and paints and become absorbed in my work' (fig.47).[49]

A Shared Experience

There is no doubt that art has a role in dealing with trauma and memory. Cook's and Worsley's artworks were produced in exceptional circumstances. Like other war art, they document extraordinary and often traumatic experiences, and make them intelligible for the public. Worsley strove to show an inspiring view of time in captivity for the benefit of audiences back at home and, as an official war artist, did so for the nation's collective memory. By contrast, Cook's art seems to have been a way of coping with the remarkable circumstances in which he found himself. Wartime memories also must have played on his mind for, late in life, he felt compelled to share his experiences more widely and devoted time to his (unpublished) memoirs. His works at the National Maritime Museum include on-the-spot drawings, contemporary to the events he experienced, as well as retrospective ones, since his intention was to illustrate the memoirs with a selection of both. Executed on the back of charts or on wrapping paper, the former show evidence of their history – censorship stamps, captions and numbers, sometimes crossed over and superseded by later ones. These represent the marks of wartime as well as the artist's continuous engagement with the memory of these events, long after they took place. It is a remarkable archive.

The camaraderie and solidarity of the inmates, how to make do with very little and not to lose courage and hope, are themes that recur in the paintings and drawings by Worsley and Cook, and ones familiar to those living under the Blitz and rationing at home. More than just propaganda pieces or historical records, they communicate the experience of individuals who lived through captivity, with its privations, difficulties and the stresses of life under constant watch. That they often did so showing remarkable fortitude and humour is a poignant testimony to their resilience and sense of artistic purpose.

White Ensigns and Red Dusters: The Royal and Merchant Navies in Wartime

John Graves

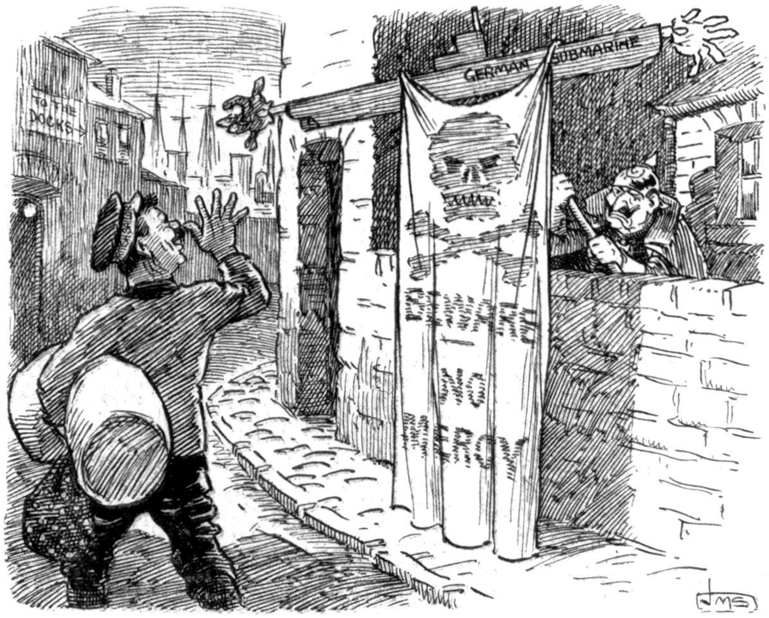

Fig.48
Beware No Mercy
From *The Seaman*, 2 March 1917
Cartoon
L7847

Despite the fact that the German U-boat menace hung like a spectre over all merchant seamen, here a British sailor is shown defiantly cocking a snook at the enemy nearby.

Since the inception of the Royal Navy in the early sixteenth century Britain's merchant and fighting fleets have enjoyed – or endured – an almost symbiotic relationship. A large fleet of merchant ships connecting Britain with world markets was vital to facilitate trade and the movement of people, and for servicing her overseas possessions, while British warships protected those merchantmen, the trade routes and Britain's spheres of influence. In turn, it was the enormous wealth generated by this global trade that for so long enabled Britain to develop and maintain the world's pre-eminent navy. In the 200 years before the great conflicts of the twentieth century, the Royal Navy grew to become technologically, organisationally, strategically and numerically superior to any other fighting fleet.

This interdependency increased during the First and Second World Wars. During both conflicts Britain's island status was both a strength and a weakness. For while the British Isles were a fortress against invasion the country was reliant on essential resources – food, goods and raw materials – imported from overseas, which were in constant danger of running out. Britain was, therefore, critically dependent on the merchant fleet transporting those resources so that she would not be starved into surrender, and also for other important wartime duties like transporting troops and aiding the wounded.

The German U-boat menace in both wars (fig.48), and that country's policy of unrestricted submarine warfare, meant that both Royal Navy and merchant ships, and those of allies, were fair game for attack: Cunard Line's transatlantic express liner, RMS *Lusitania* (see Chapter 1: The Sinking of the *Lusitania*), was an early high-profile casualty. During both wars countless merchant vessels were requisitioned and tens of thousands of merchant seamen were employed in the war effort. In the first decade of the twentieth century, with the Anglo-German naval race in full swing and the threat of war looming, RMS *Mauretania* – like her sister *Lusitania* – was designed from the keel up to be easily converted into an armed merchant cruiser should the need arise. Proving too expensive to operate for this sort of work, *Mauretania* instead served as a troopship in the Gallipoli campaign and, later, as a hospital ship with many of her peacetime crew remaining in post.

It was during the 1914–18 conflict that the merchant-ship convoy system was developed or, rather, revived, since it is a very old trade-defence measure but one often reluctantly readopted, either for commercial reasons or because of the warship commitment it involved, as was the case from 1914. However, by 1917 merchant ships were being sunk at such a rate – almost 700 in the first six

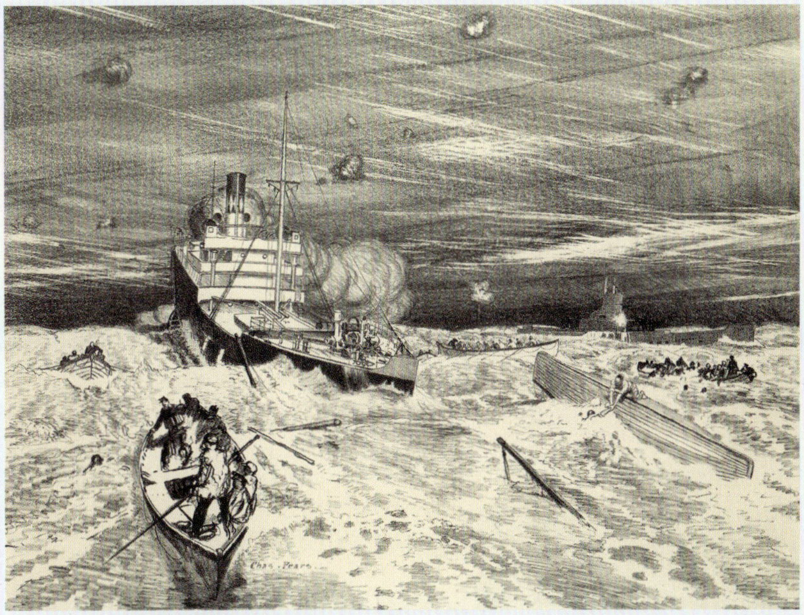

Fig.49
Charles Pears
The Place of Safety (from *Transport by Sea – The Great War, Britain's Efforts and Ideals*), c.1917
Lithograph
38.4 x 50.9 cm (15 1/8 x 20 in)
PAG9452

months of that year alone – that they were defensively armed (though no match for an enemy warship), 'dazzle-camouflaged' and, from 24 May, required to sail in convoy for collective protection by naval escorts and by each other (fig.49) (see Chapter 5: Art, Artists and the Home Front).[50]

The convoy system was even more effectively used during the Second World War, the main theatres being the North Atlantic, Mediterranean and the Arctic Ocean (fig.50). When war was again declared in September 1939 all merchant ships came under government control regardless of age, condition or state of repair. Lessons learned during the 'Great War' brought into sharp focus the fact that Britain had come perilously close to running out of supplies: in the spring of 1917 it had been estimated that grain reserves would last for only another six weeks.

The Second World War was the British merchant service's darkest time. At sea, U-boats were able to operate from the coasts of enemy-occupied France and Norway, as well as Germany; aircraft were now a much greater threat to shipping with their longer range, accuracy and speed; German surface raiders preyed on vessels frequently made more vulnerable by the cargoes they were carrying like aviation spirit or munitions; and the Royal Navy's escorts were being stretched ever more thinly across the world's vast oceans and seas covering tens – if not hundreds – of thousands of miles as their areas of operation changed from the Mediterranean to the Pacific rim, to the Arctic, or wherever they were required.

Although the merchant navy has been with us for centuries, 'Merchant Navy' as a formal title dates only to 1928, when King George V made the Prince of Wales (later Edward VIII) 'Master of the Merchant Navy and Fishing Fleets [...] in recognition of the splendid services which [they] have rendered to the Empire for many centuries both in peace and war.'[51] From 1914 to 1918 around 7,760,000 tons of merchant shipping had been lost and almost 15,000 seafarers had perished. Later on, in the Second World War, German U-boats sank a staggering 11,700,000 tons of British merchant shipping, amounting to 2,714 ships, 54 per cent of the total British merchant fleet at the outbreak of the war.[52] On board convoy vessels, some 32,000 merchant seafarers were killed, many of whom were teenagers or – at the other end of the scale – veterans brought out of retirement to help fill the losses sustained. In a debate in the House of Commons after the war, Douglas Marshall, MP for Bodmin, said 'it is true that the Merchant Navy gets through, but they get through only at a terrible self-sacrifice and a terrible loss of life'.[53] Similarly the Royal Navy had its fair share of calamities in both wars, from the bloody nose it received at Jutland in 1916 to the loss of HMS *Hood* on 24 May 1941, which sank in only three minutes with the loss of all but three of 1,418 men, in action with the *Bismarck* and *Prinz Eugen*.

The *esprit de corps* of the men of the 'Senior Service', which had welded them into a united fighting force through centuries of battle honours, was not present in the mercantile marine, with its absence of heroic tradition, self-sacrifice, sense of purpose, clear command structure and strict discipline. The losses incurred by the Royal Navy in both wars undoubtedly tested its confidence to the limit, but 400 years of fighting spirit, stretching back to its foundation by Henry VIII, fortified it during testing times. The Merchant Navy by contrast, always dependent on the vagaries of the British economy, had to weather its ups and downs and fared particularly badly during the Depression of the inter-war period. In 1939 the merchant seaman was feeling underpaid and undervalued, with generally low morale, and, until the matter was rectified in May 1941, living with the thought that his pay stopped if his ship was sunk beneath him. The ships, too, were markedly different in that a warship might be

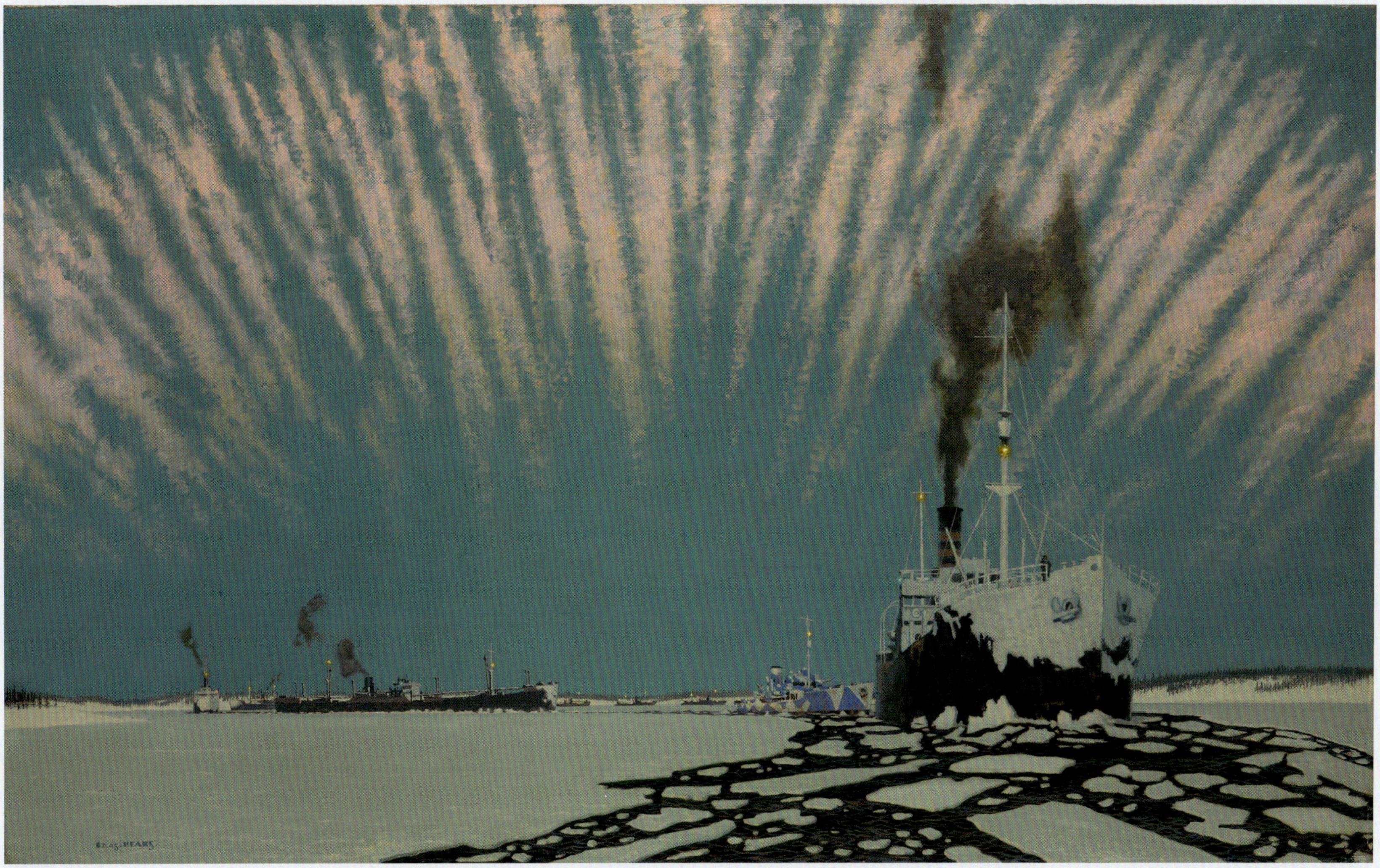

Fig.50
Charles Pears
Convoy to Russia, 1942
Oil on canvas
81.2 x 127 cm (32 x 50 in)
BHC1576

Allied merchant ships are approaching the north Russian port of Murmansk, comprising one of the Arctic convoys that supplied materiel to the USSR. The surreal quality of the picture, with the *Aurora Borealis* celebrating the vessels' arrival like a meteorological firework display, belies the appalling conditions suffered by Merchant and Royal Navy crews alike. The intense cold and incredibly violent seas are indicated by the encrustation of ice that has formed on the ship's bow and superstructure.

old but was at least well maintained, whereas many requisitioned merchant ships were in a sorry state. Such was the difference between sailing under the 'red duster' as opposed to the Royal Naval white ensign.[54]

One might assume that given the vital and interconnecting – albeit very different – roles of the Royal and Merchant Navies in wartime, their perception of each other would be one of comrades and brothers-in-arms, together facing a common foe. Certainly a shared, potent and all too tangible enemy was effective in ensuring close cooperation and mutual support, but it was not a case of comparing like with like. The idea of a 'Merchant Navy' to mirror that of the Royal Navy may be convenient for parcelling together myriad different types of vessels from tugboats to trawlers but it has never actually existed as a single, coherent force.

For a start, the merchant ships requisitioned for war duties in both World Wars were owned by countless different companies and organisations, representing the entire spectrum of corporate

Fig.51
A Second World War convoy at sea under the watchful eye of an officer and protective guns of a King George V-class battleship. The vessel on the left is a tanker, the one in the centre, an intermediate-sized liner.
L7845

management and responsibility. Government control of shipping in both conflicts, particularly under the overall direction of the Ministry of War Transport from May 1941, went some way to harmonise disparities, but crews continued to feel the dislocation of working directly for the war effort, often in dangerous situations for long periods, unlike their Royal Navy comrades whose very *raison d'être* was war and all its implications. Perhaps the closest merchant vessels came to the concept of a 'Merchant Navy' was at Dunkirk from 27 May to 4 June 1940, when Operation Dynamo, the evacuation of Allied troops, mobilised an extraordinarily diverse flotilla of vessels – the famous 'little ships' of Dunkirk – to effect the rescue operation.

The arming of merchant vessels from June 1939 blurred things somewhat. The crews that manned the guns, known as DEMS ratings (from Defensively Equipped Merchant Ships, the programme for arming merchantmen), were mainly naval seamen or soldiers from the Maritime Royal Artillery, with merchant officers being trained as and when necessary. The presence on board merchantmen of armed and uniformed personnel could lead to friction and resentment, as they sometimes felt themselves to be superior to ordinary sailors and would say so.[55] Conversely, a merchant sailor finding himself on board a Royal Naval vessel would, it was frequently noted, extend no obedience or deference to the host naval officers. Ranks in the Royal Navy have their equivalent rank in the Merchant Navy: for instance, a Lieutenant in the Royal Navy would be equivalent to a Master or Chief Engineer of a small merchant ship of up to 2,500 tons,[56] and officers' uniform of some shipping lines emulated those of their Royal Navy counterparts.[57] Merchant crews, however, could be a tough, hard-bitten bunch and many companies employed international crewmen who occupied a lowly status on their ship. The nature of discipline was also different for the merchant sailor as it was contractual rather than deferential. Moreover, his uncertain economic conditions, employment and future could easily induce in him a feeling of poor morale rather than the fighting flair of his Royal Naval kinsmen.

The differences that existed between the Merchant and Royal Navies at times surfaced during the crises of war, but the perception that the former was inferior to the latter is steeped in the traditions of both services. Rear-Admiral Sir Kenelm Creighton notes in his memoirs, *Convoy Commodore*, that 'The men sailing under the Red Duster felt that they were the only real sailors and the sailors who manned our warships were a bunch of softies.'[58] The means provided for merchantmen to arm and protect themselves was certainly sometimes construed as a token gesture. In the First World War, they were armed with a single gun, similar to that carried by a U-boat, and captains were encouraged to flee before firing from a safe distance. Artistically inspired and gaudily painted dazzle 'camouflage' was believed by some crews to attract enemy targeting rather than dupe it. In the Second World War, the Merchant Navy's anti-aircraft PAC (parachute and cable) rockets never worked properly and there is no record of one ever bringing down an attacking aeroplane, for which the device was intended. Fuelled by rumour, always rife in wartime, with a frequent lack of direct communication and hard information, and often saddled with dangerous cargoes, merchant crews sometimes felt that they had been abandoned to the sea, the elements and the enemy, as their naval protection was deflected to other tasks.[59]

Perhaps the one event that crystallised merchant seafarers' feelings of inferiority, vulnerability and insignificance was the tragedy of the Arctic Convoy PQ17 in the summer of 1942. The order for this convoy to scatter, and for the protecting Royal Naval escort immediately to leave the area, was made by the First Sea Lord himself, Admiral of the Fleet Sir Dudley Pound, because of a perceived imminent attack by a vastly superior German force. From the merchant seamen's point of view, it was a betrayal made all the more incredible as it flew in the face of the notion that convoys – and indeed their crews – needed always to stick together. In the event 22 merchant ships and their valuable cargoes were destroyed and 153 of their men died. Despite the bald statistics that in the

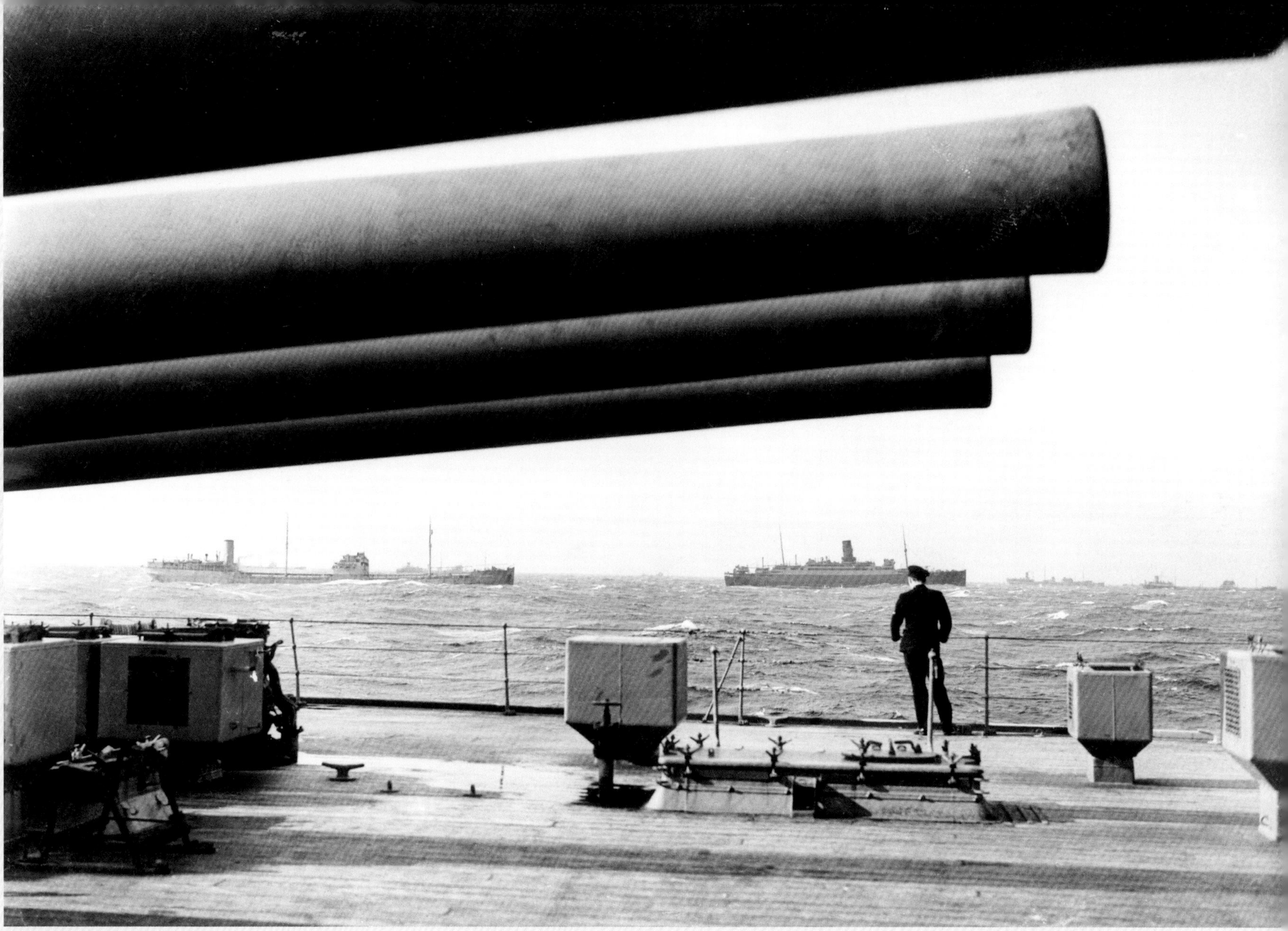

months leading up to PQ17, 4,000 Royal Navy servicemen had perished at sea and a comparable number of Navy ships had been sunk, merchant seafarers later remembered events that summer in terms of not a single Royal Naval crewman being lost. The episode caused much bitterness for the remainder of the war, and was the cause of innumerable pub brawls between Royal and Merchant Navy sailors.[60]

The World Wars did, however, help to open the eyes of Royal and Merchant Navy seamen to one another's mutual strengths. There are countless stories from both conflicts of when the Navy was in the right place at the right time, doing its job in the defence of merchantmen, of its ships lying stationary and vulnerable in U-boat-infested waters as they picked up merchant survivors, or protectively placing themselves between merchant convoy and foe (fig.51).

Such actions prompted many a merchant sailor's heart to lift at the sight of the white ensign, while PQ17 was regarded with shame by many in the Navy. Captain L.S. Saunders in HMS *Trinidad*, while protecting an earlier convoy, PQ13, noted afterwards:

> My admiration for the sheer guts of these merchant seamen defies description. We in the Navy were trained for war; we were provided with the offensive and defensive means of waging it. They were trained for peace; their ships so vulnerable that a single shell, bomb or torpedo would sink them, or set them on fire. They could not hit back, but no Hun was going to stop them sailing the seas. I felt uncomfortable when I allowed myself to think of it – I so well equipped for, and they so exposed to, the horrors of war.[61]

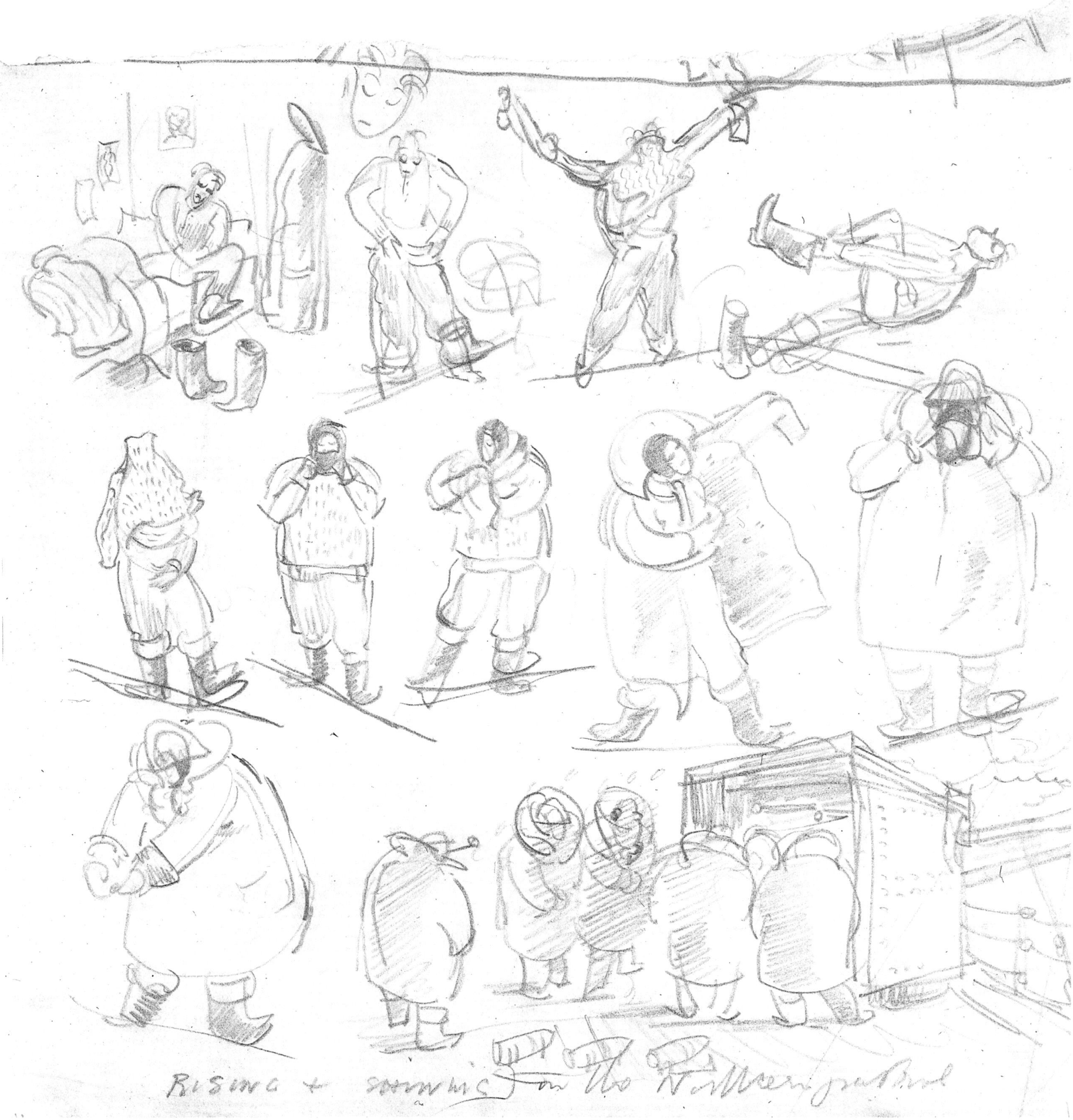
RISING +

Plate 42 (opposite)
John Worsley
Dressing on Northern Patrol, 1939–40
Graphite on paper
26.2 x 25.4 cm (10 ⅜ x 10 in)
PAJ0742

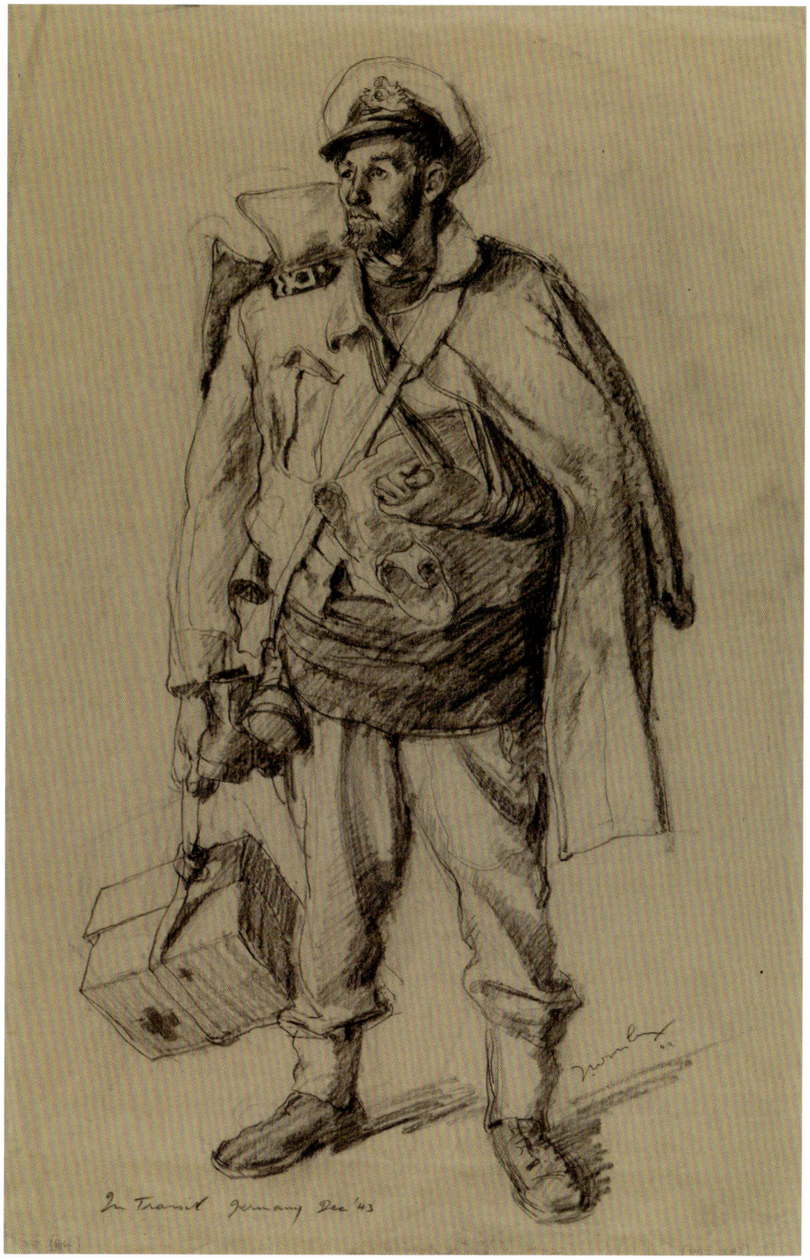

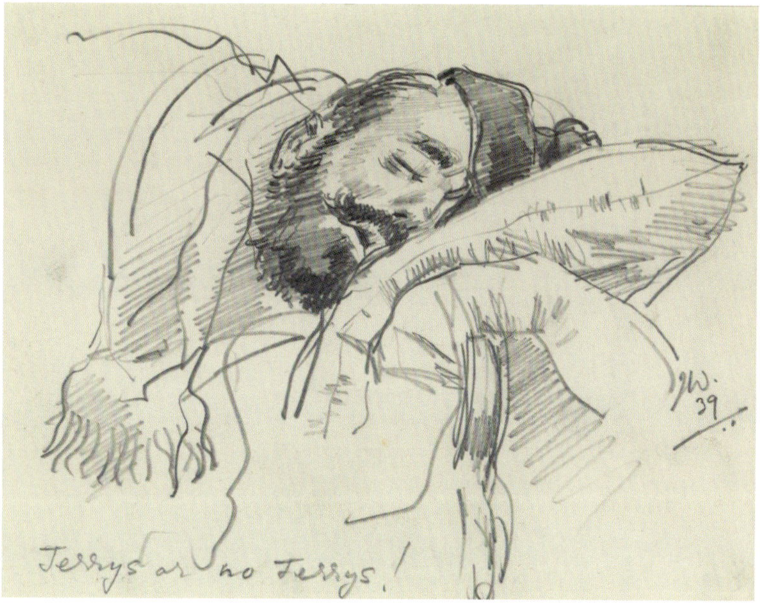

Plate 43 (left)
John Worsley
In Transit Germany Dec '43 Lieut. Guy Morgan RNVR (wounded and with kit), 1943
Graphite on paper
50.6 x 32.5 cm (19 ⅞ x 12 ¾ in)
PAI0532

Plate 44 (right)
John Worsley
'Jerrys or no Jerrys!' A leading seaman asleep after coming off the middle watch, 1939
Graphite on paper
12.1 x 15.5 cm (4 ¾ x 6 ⅛ in)
PAI0617

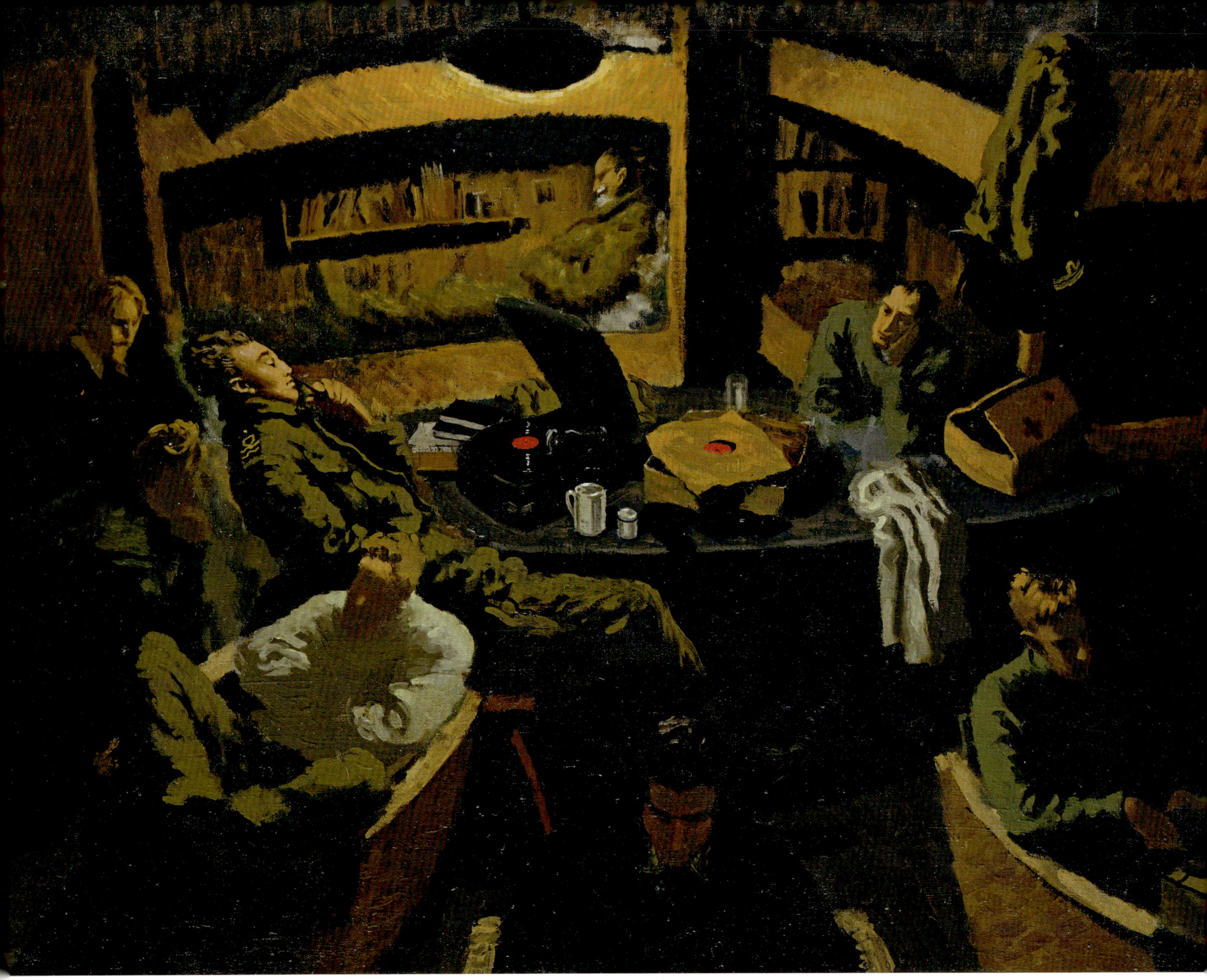

Plate 45
John Worsley
Naval officers room at Marlag 'O', prisoner of war camp, 1944–5
Oil on canvas
61 x 75 cm (24 x 29 ½ in)
BHC1672

Plate 46
John Worsley
Lieutenant (Basil Charles) Godfrey Place, VC, DSC, 1944
Oil on canvas
76.2 x 63.5 cm (30 x 25 in)
BHC2954

Plate 47
John Worsley
Lieutenant Commander Stephen Halden Beattie, 1944
Oil on canvas
76.2 x 63.5 cm (30 x 25 in)
BHC2536

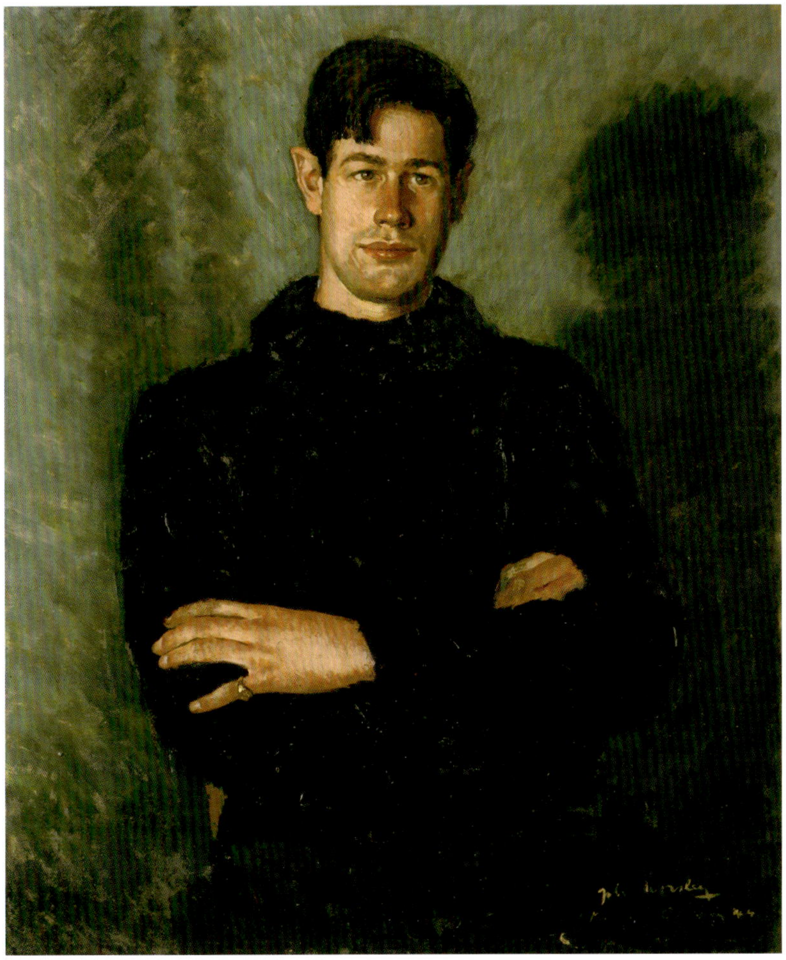

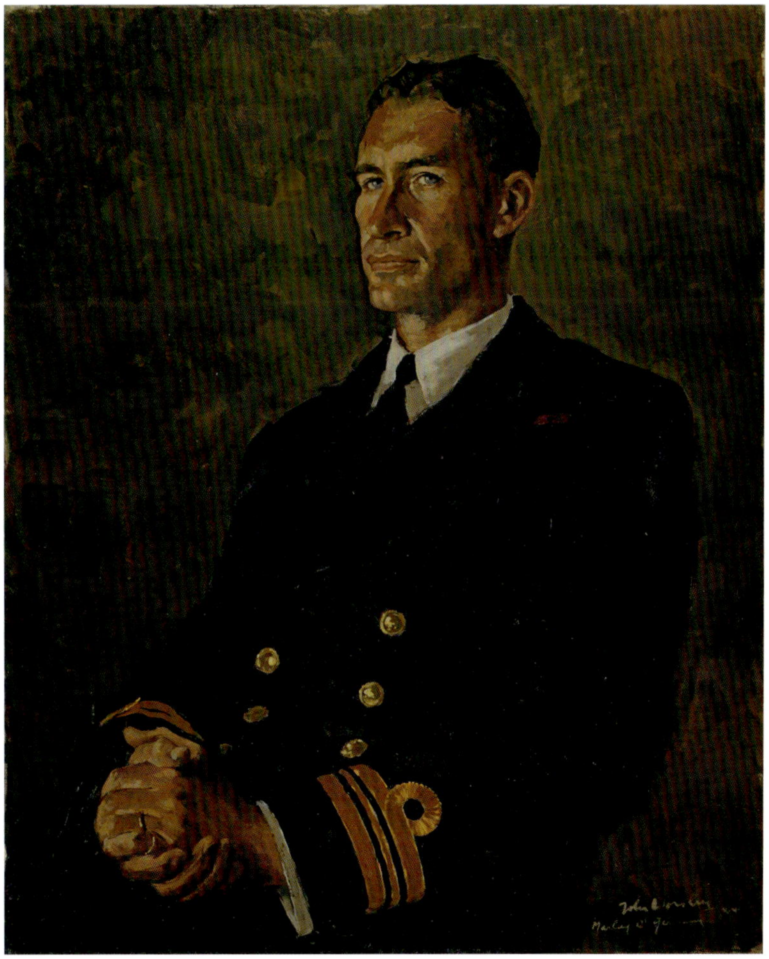

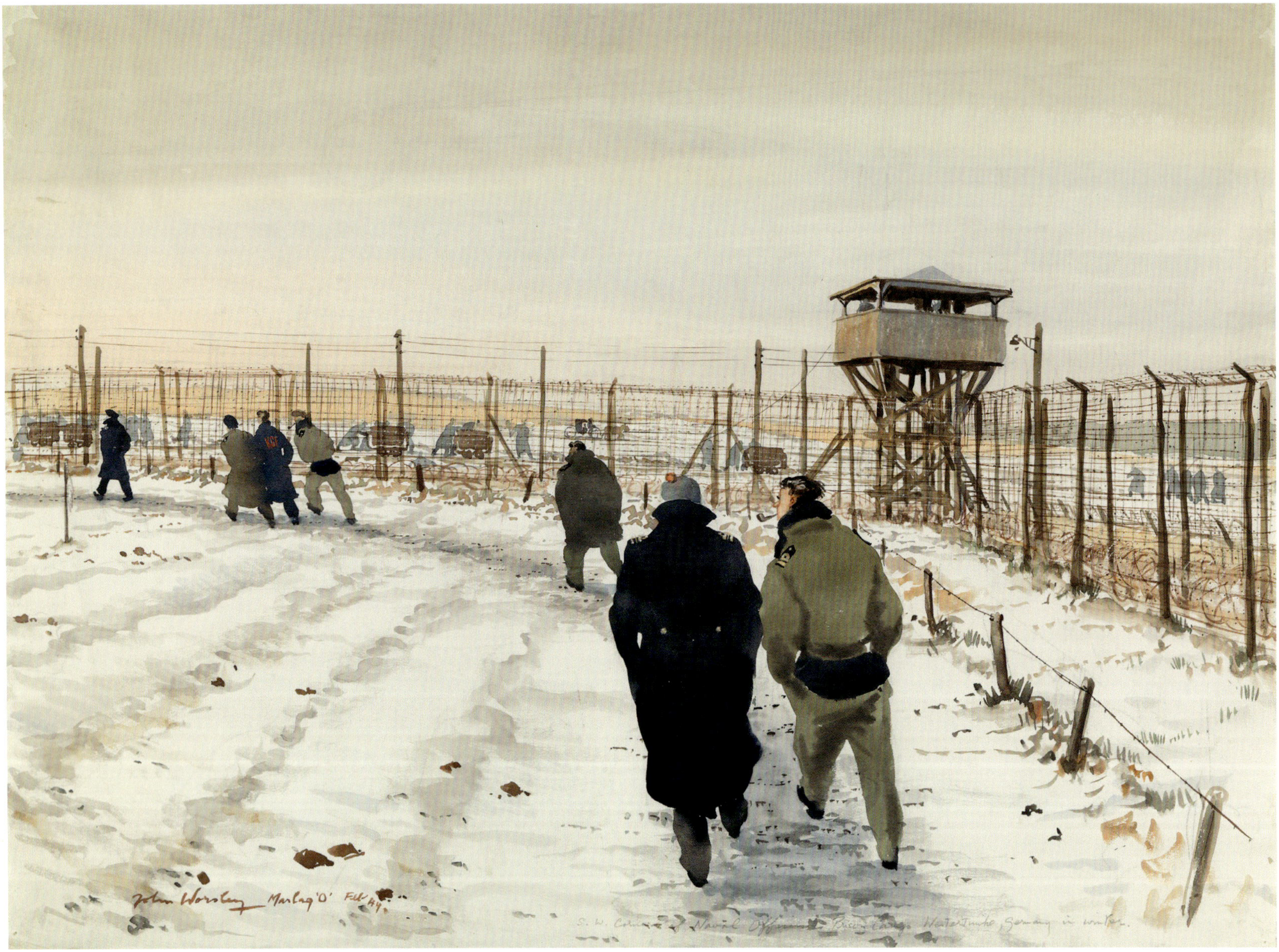

Plate 48
John Worsley
Marlag 'O' Feb '44 S.W. Corner of Naval Officers' Prison Camp, Westertincke, Germany, in winter, 1944
Watercolour on paper
49.8 x 65 cm (19 5/8 x 25 5/8 in)
PAI0527

Plate 49 (opposite)
John Worsley
Bomber formations, vapour trails and clouds. Marlag 'O' 1945, 1945
Watercolour on paper
37.8 x 27.5 cm (14 7/8 x 10 7/8 in)
PAF5723

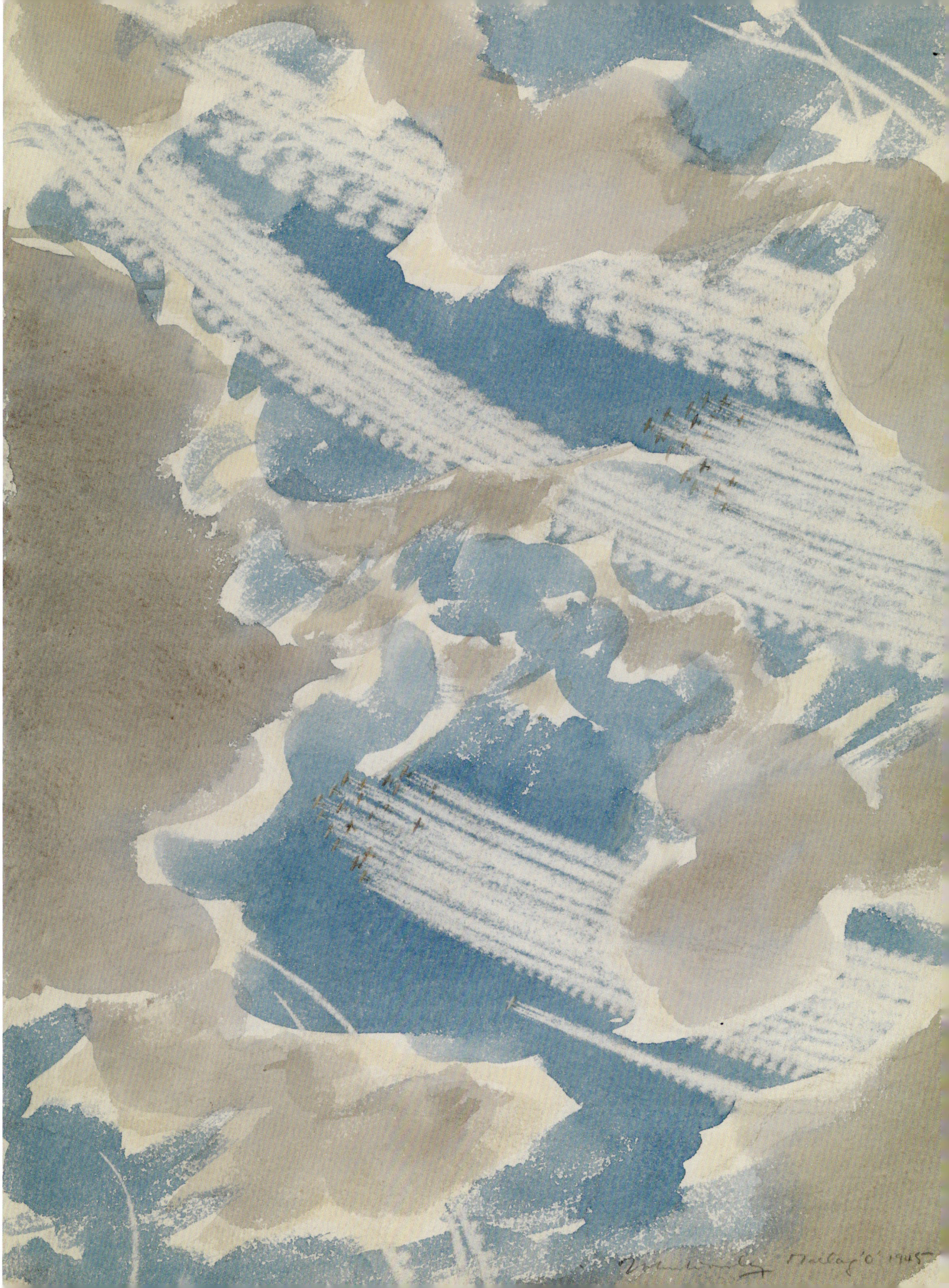

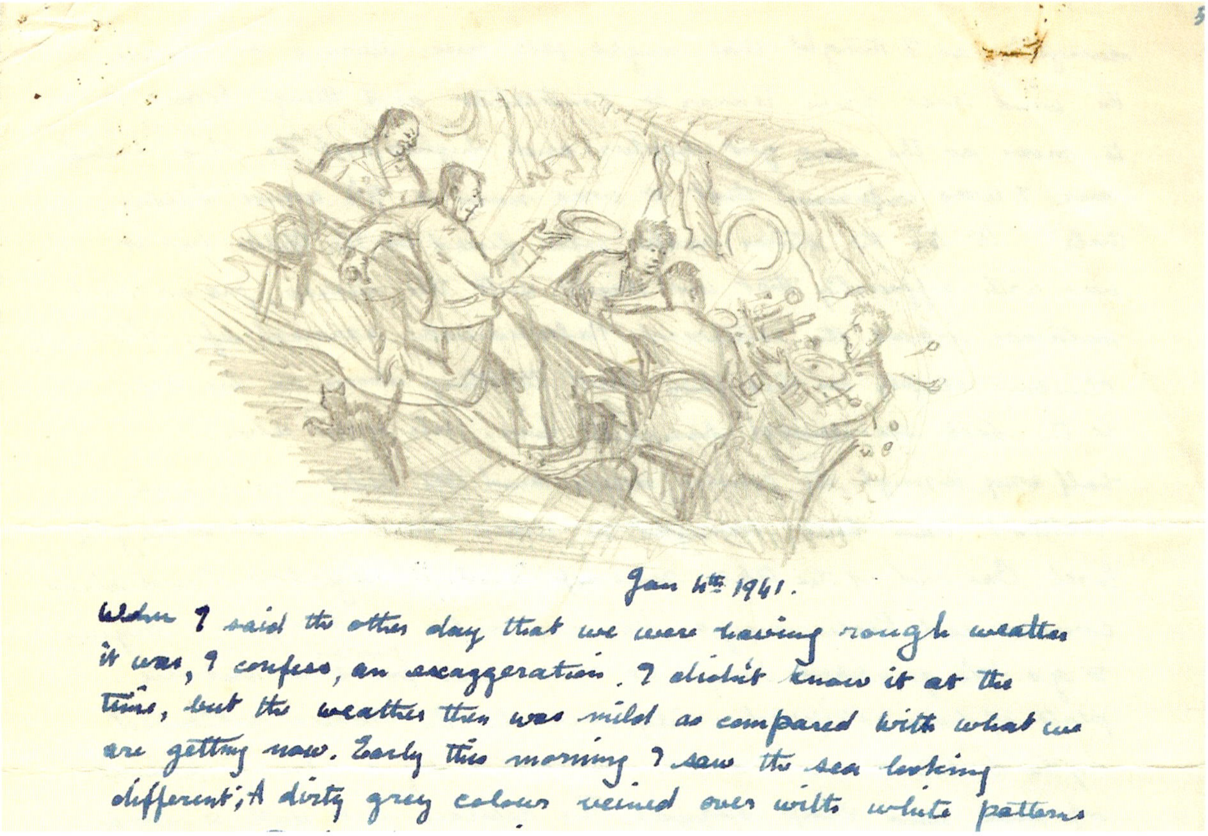

Jan 4th 1941.
When I said the other day that we were having rough weather it was, I confess, an exaggeration. I didn't know it at the time, but the weather then was mild as compared with what we are getting now. Early this morning I saw the sea looking different; A dirty grey colour veined over with white patterns

Plate 50
Page from John Kingsley Cook's logbook, 4 January 1941 (detail)
Private collection, image courtesy of Bridget Cook

'The steward laboriously [served up tea], alternately climbing steeply on his toes and trotting down on his heels as the deck see-sawed beneath him. We were about half way through this course [...] when there was an almighty lurch. One end of the table rose up and a regular landslide commenced. Plates, mugs, knives, forks and spoons began to go. We grabbed things as they went past us but the plate of ham skipped gaily over all the racks followed by the beetroot and cruet escorted by a strong formation of peas and lump sugar. The captain sat with a look of resignation while they all precipitated into his lap. The steward meanwhile had trodden on the sliding carpet and had disappeared through the door with a bang.'

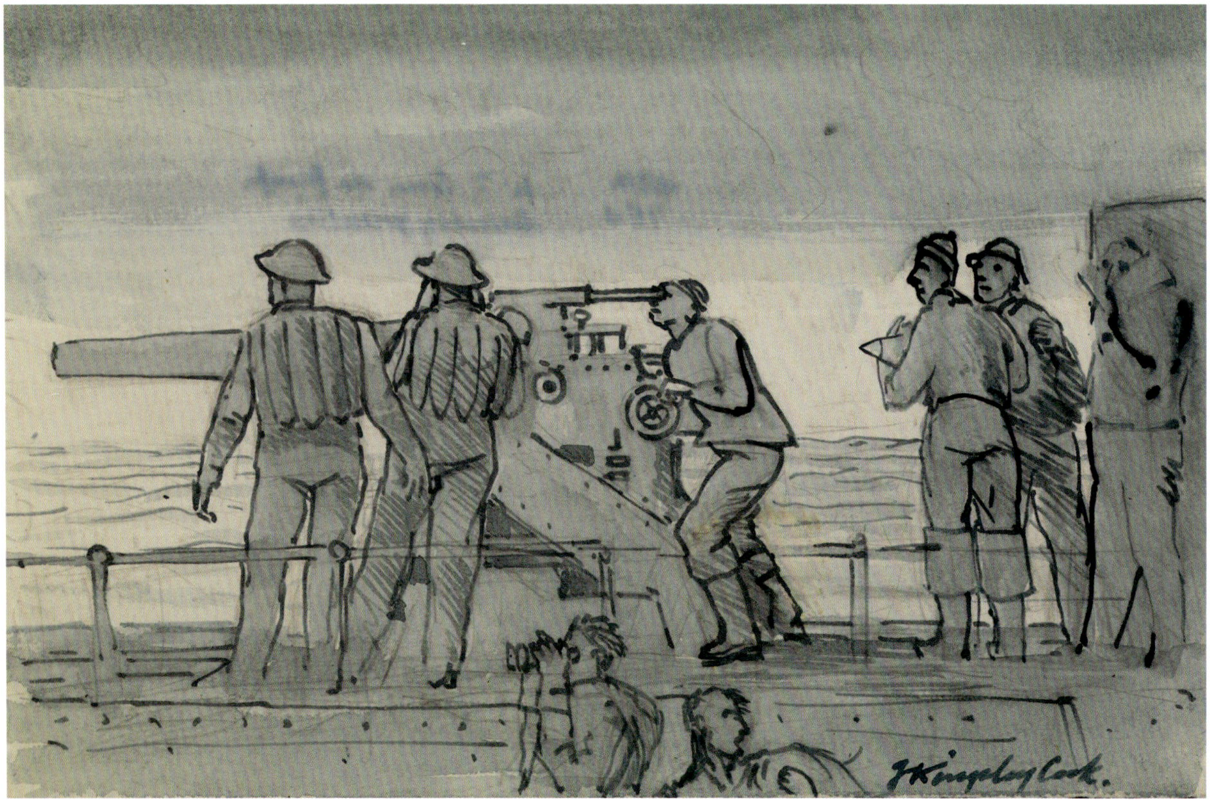

Plate 51
John Kingsley Cook
Gun on poop. Gunnery practice, 1941
Pen and wash on paper
12.2 x 18.4 cm (4 3/4 x 7 1/4 in)
ZBA5257

'At four o'clock we had firing practice. Our whole armament consists of two 'Tommy Guns' and a revolver! We might be able to keep a boarding party at bay for a while, but I'm afraid we'd be helpless if we were attacked by a plane or sub.'

John Kingsley Cook's logbook, 2 April 1941

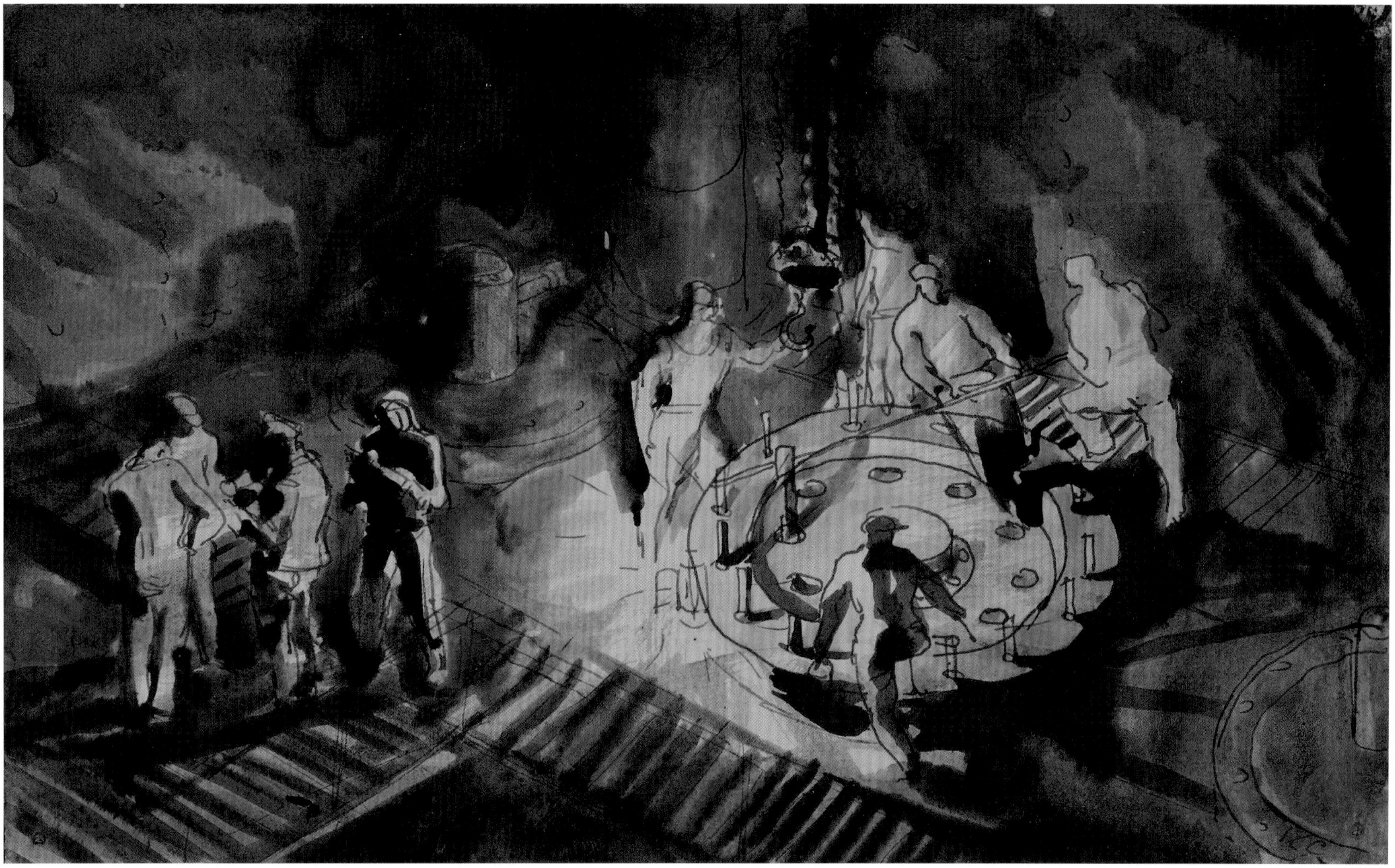

Plate 52
John Kingsley Cook
Breakdown in the engine room. The mate up top getting impatient, 1941
Pen and wash on paper
14.1 x 22.6 cm (5 ½ x 8 ⅞ in)
ZBA5280

'There, far below a group of sweating men were working by the light of an electric lamp. They were taking down the L.P. cylinder now, moving round this strange circular object, their shadows cast on the surrounding bulkheads, they looked like devotees of some devilish cult, performing their mysterious ritual.'

John Kingsley Cook's logbook, July 1941

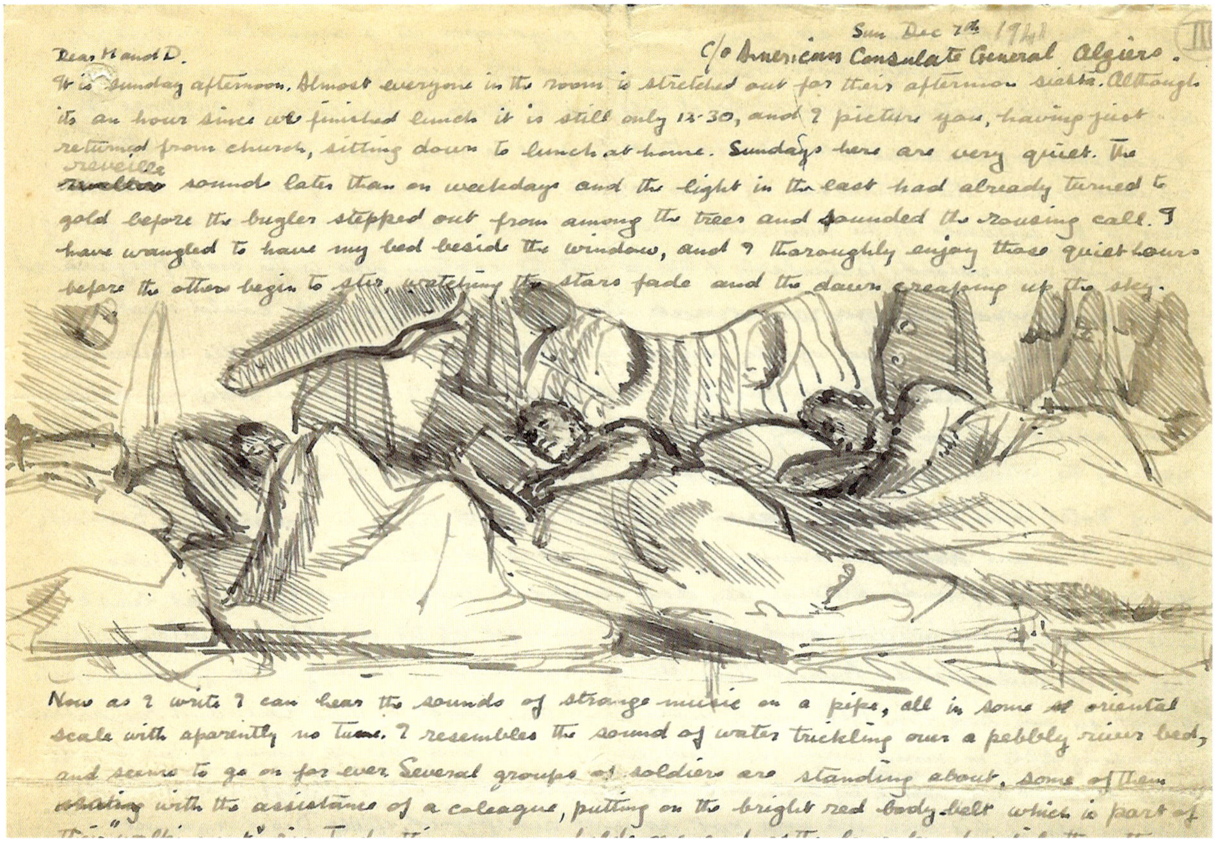

Sun Dec 7th 1941

Dear M and D. C/o American Consulate General Algiers.

It is Sunday afternoon. Almost everyone in the room is stretched out for their afternoon siesta. Although its an hour since we finished lunch it is still only 12-30, and I picture you, having just returned from church, sitting down to lunch at home. Sundays here are very quiet. The reveille sound later than on weekdays and the light in the east had already turned to gold before the bugler stepped out from among the trees and sounded the rousing call. I have wangled to have my bed beside the window, and I thoroughly enjoy these quiet hours before the others begin to stir, watching the stars fade and the dawn creeping up the sky.

Now as I write I can hear the sounds of strange music on a pipe, all in some oriental scale with apparently no tune. I resembles the sound of water trickling over a pebbly river bed, and seems to go on for ever. Several groups of soldiers are standing about, some of them assisting with the assistance of a colleague, putting on the bright red body-belt which is part of

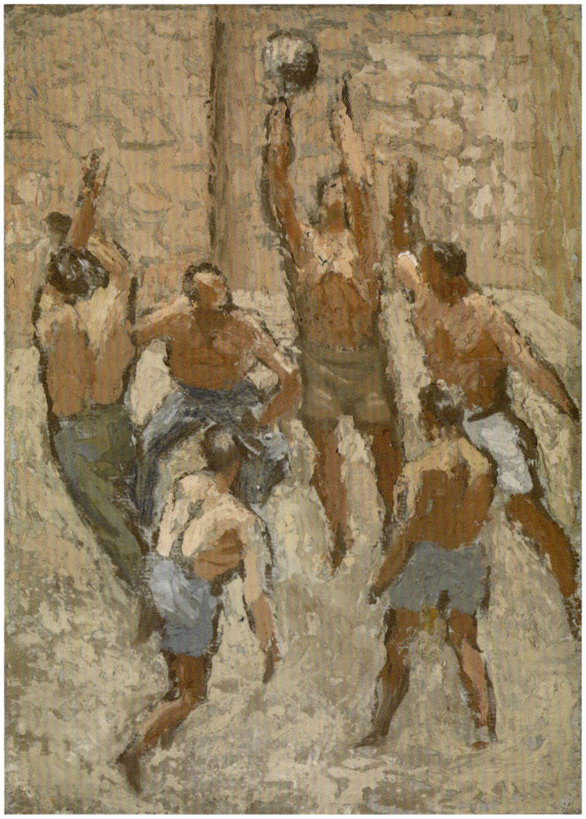

Plate 53 (above)
Letter from John Kingsley Cook to his parents, from Bône, 7 December 1941 (detail)
Private collection, image courtesy of Bridget Cook

Plate 54 (below)
John Kingsley Cook
Playing volleyball. Mécheria internment camp, 1942
Oil on board
32.1 x 22.8 cm (12 ⅝ x 9 in)
ZBA5459

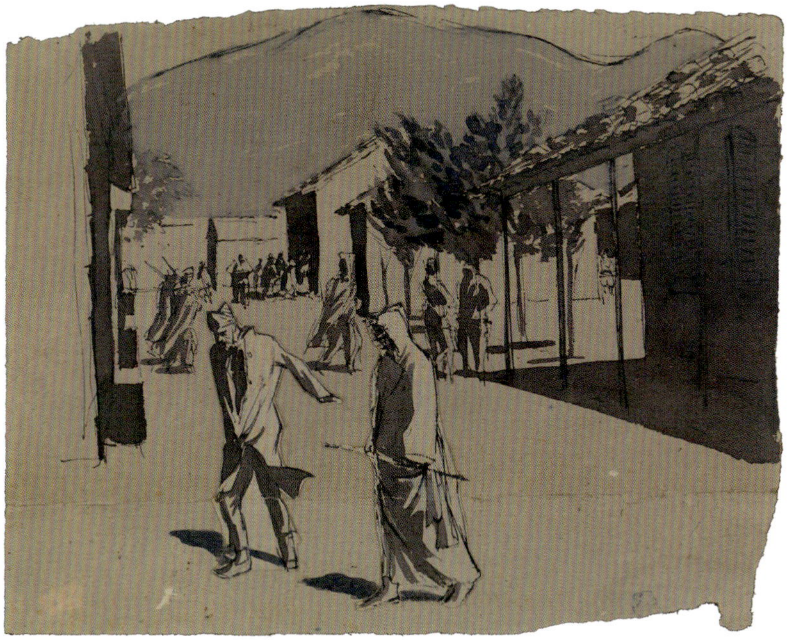

Plate 55 (above)
John Kingsley Cook
Spring day in the fort at Mécheria, 1942
Gouache on paper
27.7 x 44.3 cm (10 ⅞ x 17 ½ in)
ZBA5452

Plate 56 (below)
John Kingsley Cook
Guards and prisoners. Mécheria, 1942
Pen and wash on paper
18 x 22.2 cm (7 ⅛ x 8 ¾ in)
ZBA5339

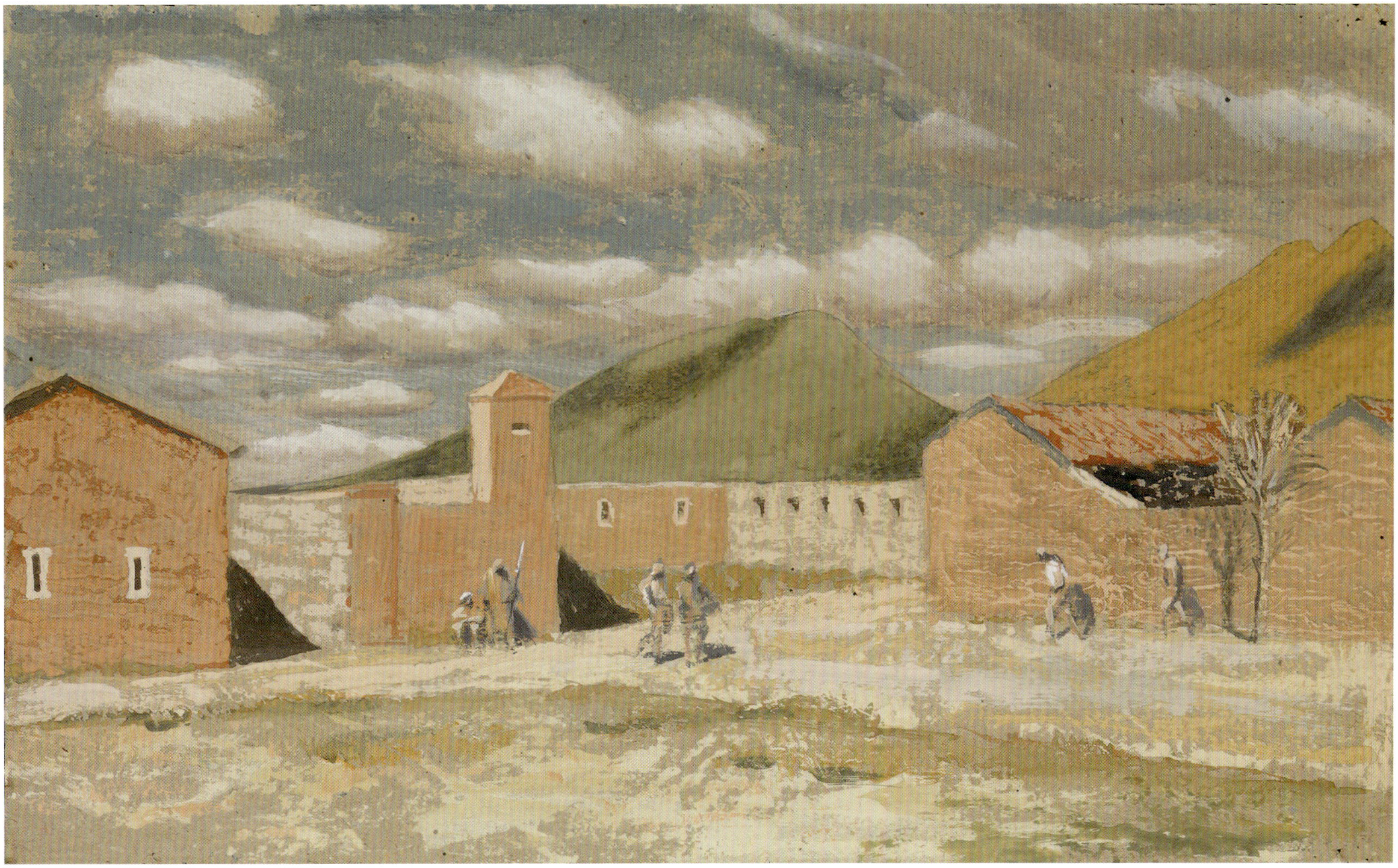

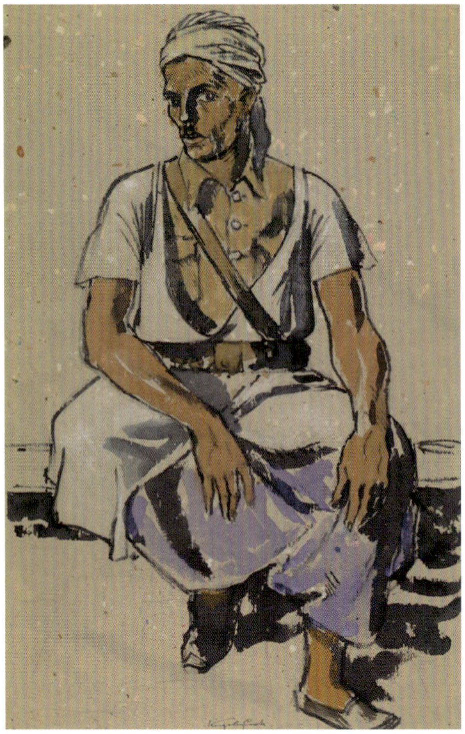

Plate 57 (above)
John Kingsley Cook
Shy Arab, 1942
Pen, wash and watercolour on paper
45 x 28.5 cm (17 ¾ x 11 ¼ in)
ZBA5456

Plate 58 (below)
John Kingsley Cook
Three inmates and a chameleon, 1942
Pen and wash on paper
16.6 x 21.6 cm (6 ½ x 8.5 in)
ZBA5393

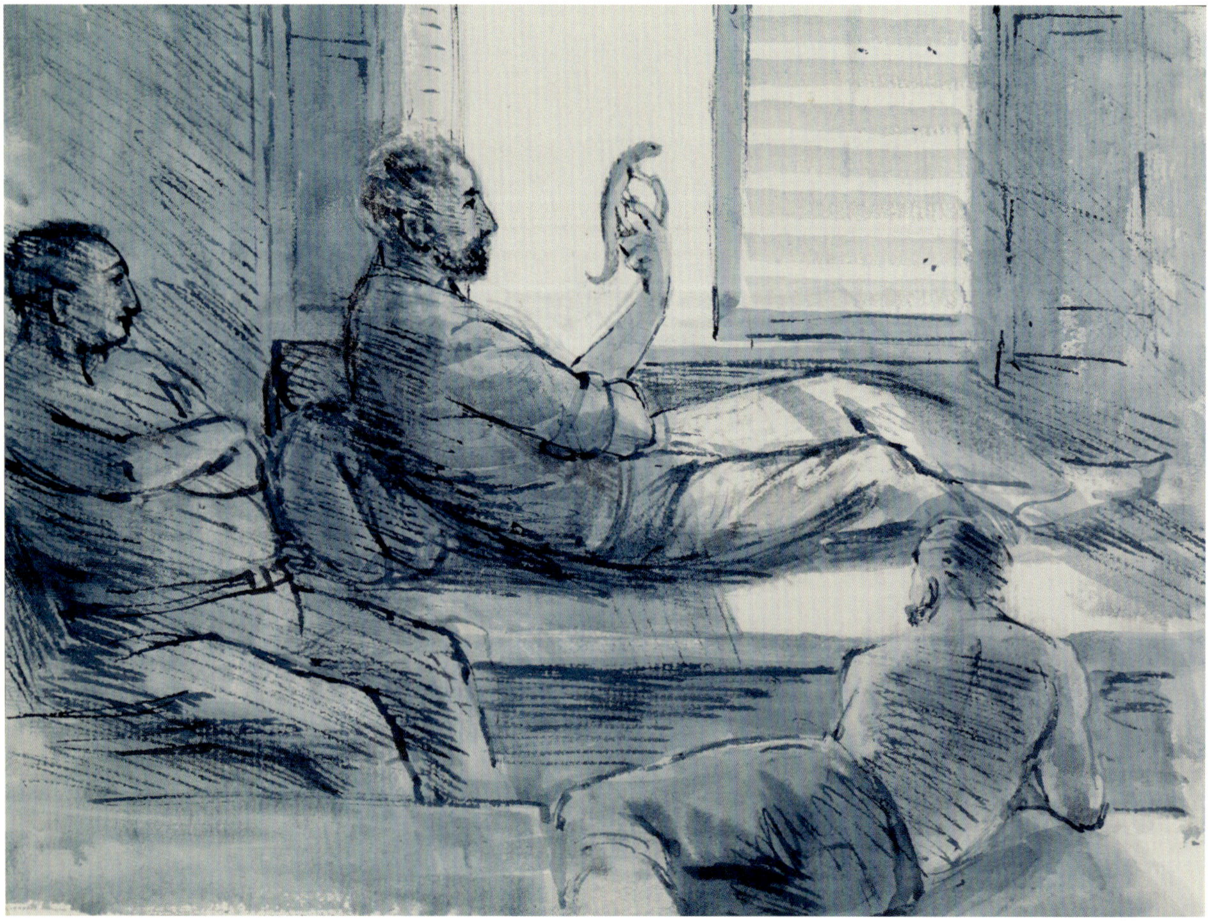

Plate 59
John Kingsley Cook
Spare propeller on Board. SS 'Esturia', 1944
Pen, wash and watercolour on paper
34.8 x 48.7 cm (13 ¾ x 19 ⅛ in)
ZBA5424

'The skies have been unusually expressive and I have been painting and painting. Yes. I've really been working! Pitchforth did me a lot of good, and has stimulated me to work in colour and to get onto larger sheets of paper. It had been years since I had had any contacts with artists and I realised just how much I had slipped that time, forgetting to use my eyes. I had unconsciously been developing the lazy attitudes to my surroundings and forgetting how to look at things. Now it has come back with a rush, and I see so much that I want to paint that I am at it all my spare time. It has already borne fruit in one or two watercolours [...] before I only saw pipes, girders, rusty decks and crumbling bulkheads which either dripped water on you, or tripped you up, or hit you across the shin in the blackout, now I see fascinating shapes, textiles and colours full of possibilities for painting.'

John Kingsley Cook, letter to parents, 21 May 1944

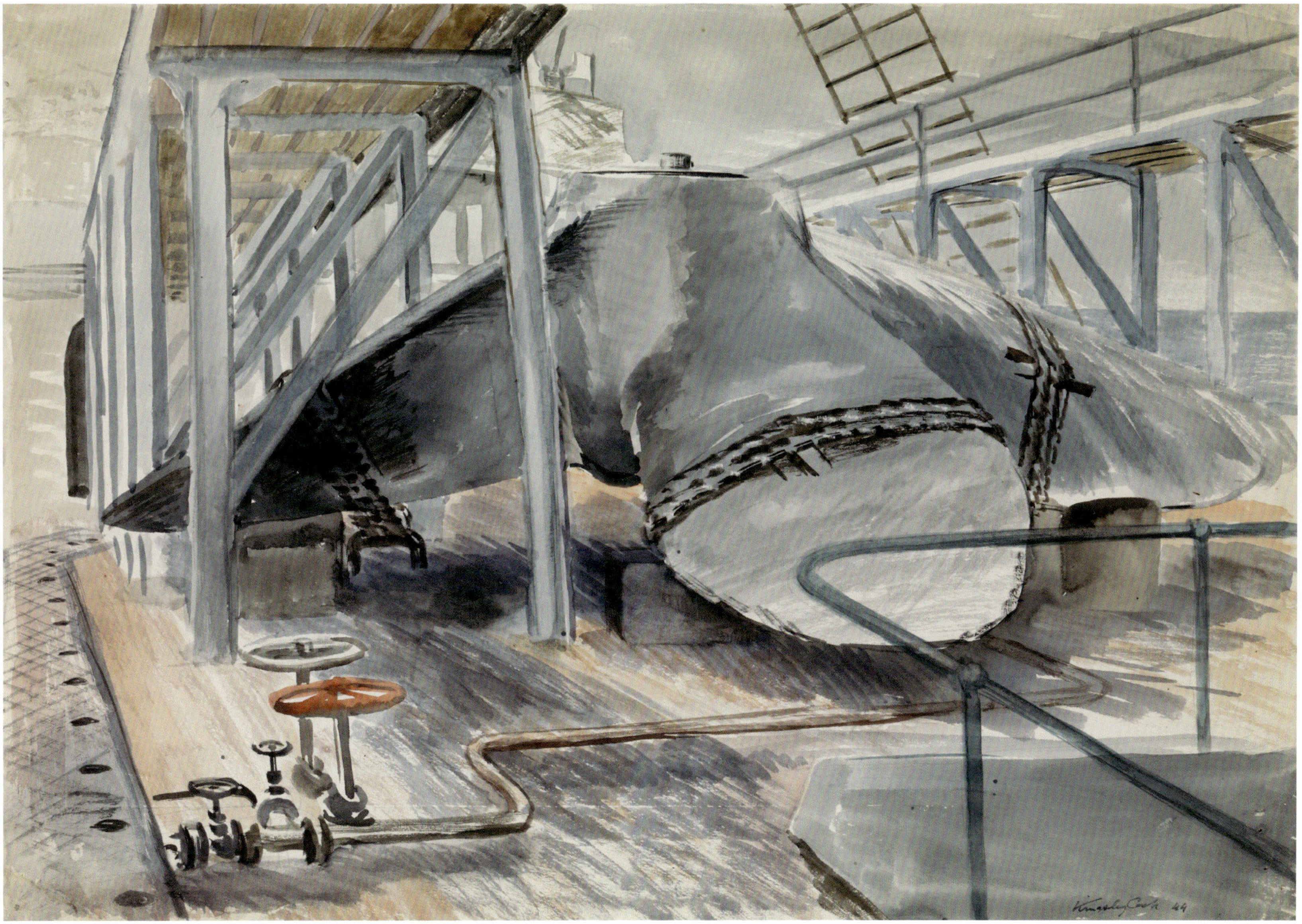

5

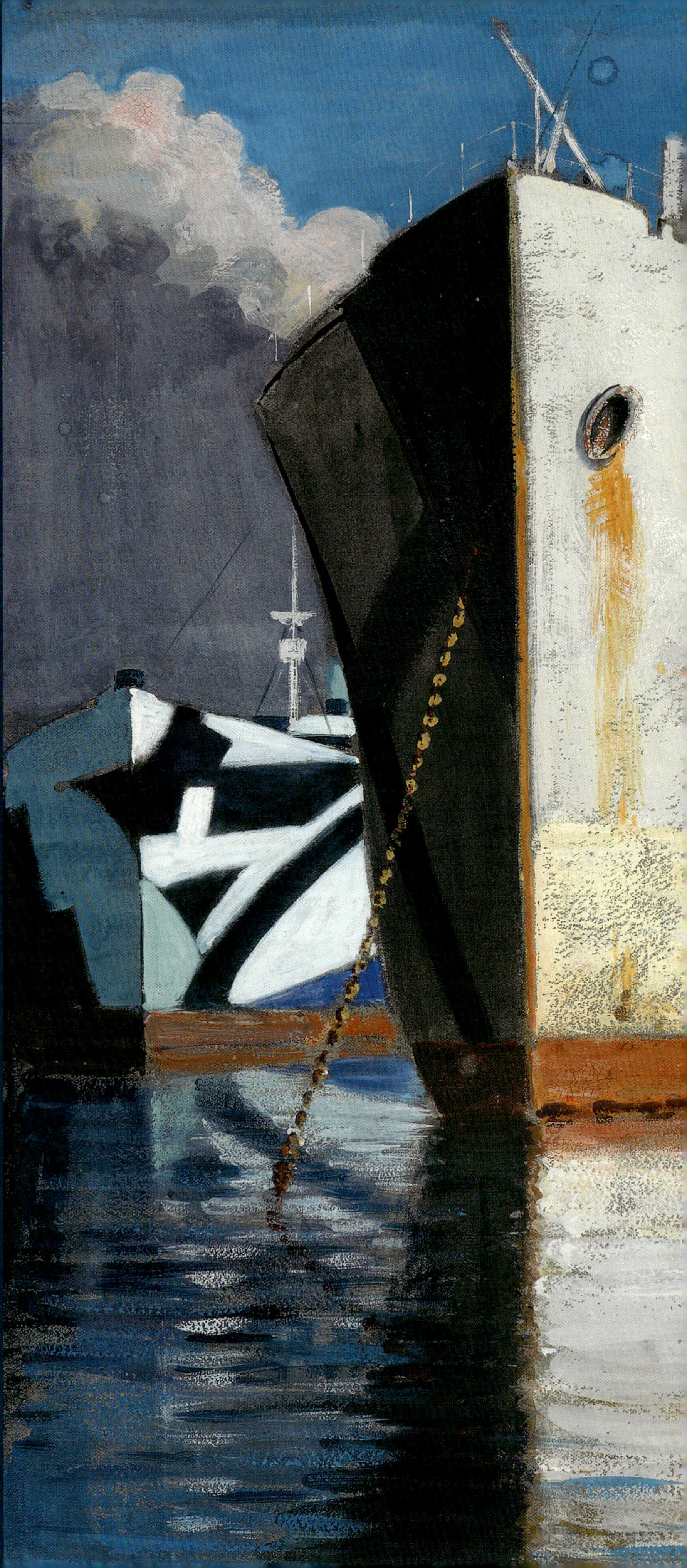

John Everett
Discharging flour, 1918
Gouache on board
38.6 x 51.2 cm (15 ¼ x 20 ⅛ in)
PAH6916

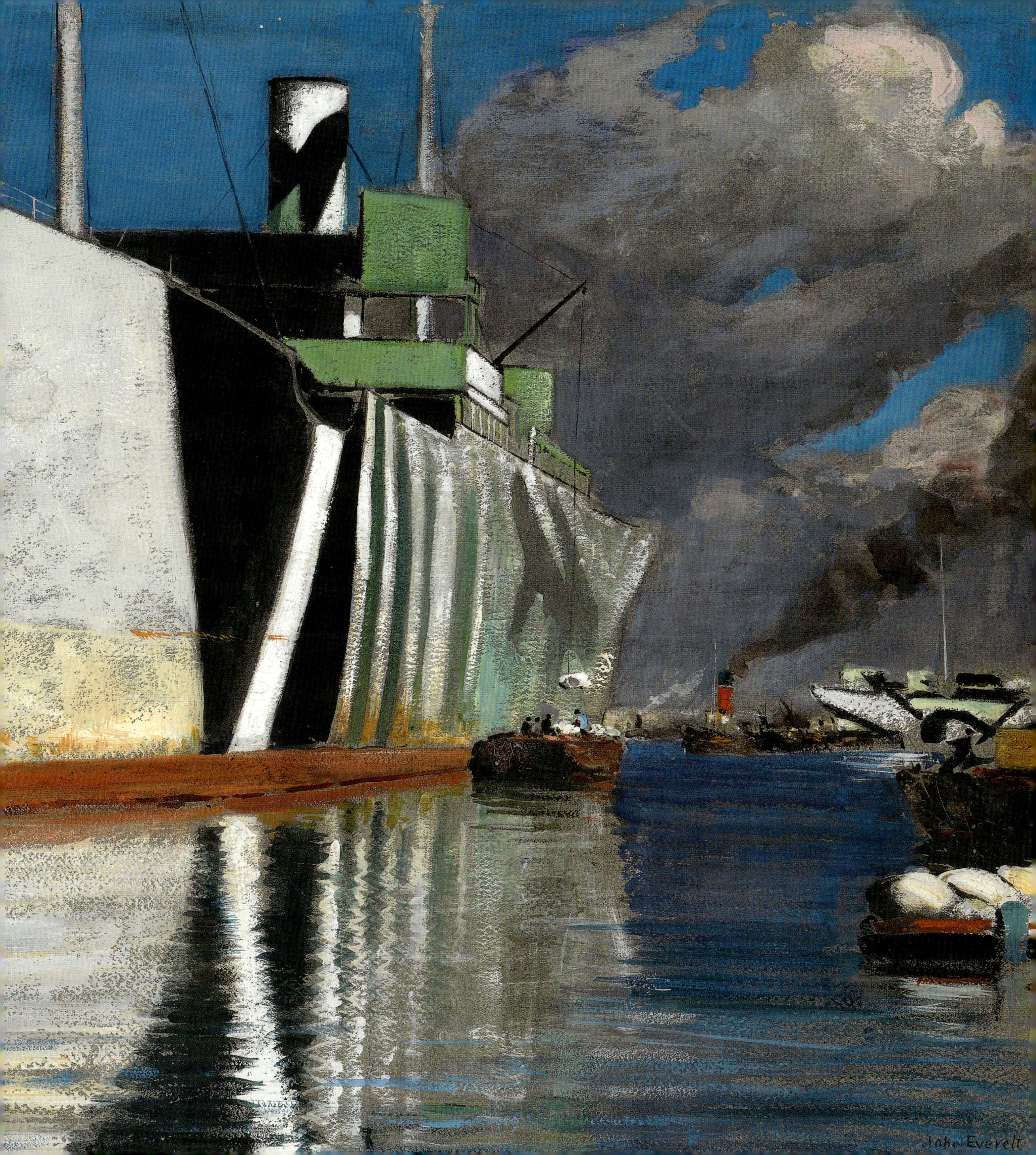
John Everett

5

Art, Artists and the Home Front

Amy Miller and Christine Riding

On 8 August 1914, just days after Britain formally entered the First World War, Parliament passed the Defence of the Realm Act (DORA). Intended for national security, DORA regulated aspects of daily life on the home front, including placing a ban on public discussion of 'military matters', the purchase of binoculars and spirits, the ringing of church bells and the melting-down of precious metals. It also gave the government the right to requisition any land, factory or workshop and made provision for censorship.[1] DORA indirectly drew attention to other key concerns: one clause, for example, banned feeding bread to birds and animals, which in turn made the point that the civilian food supply would be subject to disruptions from expected German threats, of whatever sort, to British merchant shipping.[2]

As with the Emergency (Defence) Powers Act of the Second World War,[3] DORA brought into sharp focus the expectations placed on civilian volunteers and the auxiliary and reserve forces that supported the war effort; for instance, the Women's Royal Naval Service (WRNS) and the Voluntary Aid Detachment (VAD). Their vital contribution was recorded by artists, whether on an official or independent basis. Artists were also called upon to use their training in more direct and practical ways, and with striking results, such as those engaged in sea-camouflage work and the highly distinctive style of 'dazzle'.

Importantly, the art representing the home front of both World Wars often served to highlight changing (and even conflicting) public perceptions and social attitudes, above all towards women.

The Art of Dazzle

It has been noted that the far-reaching effects of the First World War can be gleaned by comparing versions of the *Oxford English Dictionary* before and after the conflict.[4] New words and ideas entered common parlance, perhaps most notably in the present context the word 'camouflage'. Conceived by French artists and developed on the Western Front, camouflage schemes were first created for the Army, using painted canvas sheets to conceal artillery and personnel.[5] The concept was based around the idea of concealment through masking colour schemes, as first identified and employed in the 1890s by the American artist, Abbott Thayer (1849–1921), who 'looked to nature for examples, such as the protective colouring of moths and butterflies that enabled them to blend in with their surroundings'.[6] This principle was adopted in the disguising of trenches and gun positions in the First World War, and in the creation of camouflaged steel trees that were used for spying on the German front lines. These innovations were devised by the British artist, Solomon J. Solomon (1860–1927), who in 1916 had been sent, with the rank of lieutenant-colonel in the Royal Engineers, to set up a camouflage section in Flanders.

Of course, the idea of masking colouration was useful for combat on land but, for both the Royal Navy and merchant shipping, an open and continually changing seascape posed a far greater challenge. The merchant fleet sustained the British home and fighting fronts in both World Wars. It maintained indispensable lines of supply and communications but at the cost, in both conflicts – and worse in the second – of great losses to German U-boat attack. There were various attempts to make merchant ships less of a target, including one proposal to disguise them as floating islands complete with trees; while that proved impractical, the fact it was suggested at all shows the urgency of problem.[7]

In 1914, the zoologist John Graham Kerr (1869–1957) proposed employing camouflage at sea to Winston Churchill, then First Lord of the Admiralty. Kerr suggested, citing Thayer, that the precedents found in nature might be used in colour schemes designed specifically for shipping. Kerr went a step further and advised that, in the absence of suitable colouring, a ship should be painted white, diminishing the sharp silhouette it presented against the sky and making it more difficult to aim at accurately through a U-boat periscope. A number of similar camouflage proposals were tested – one recommended the

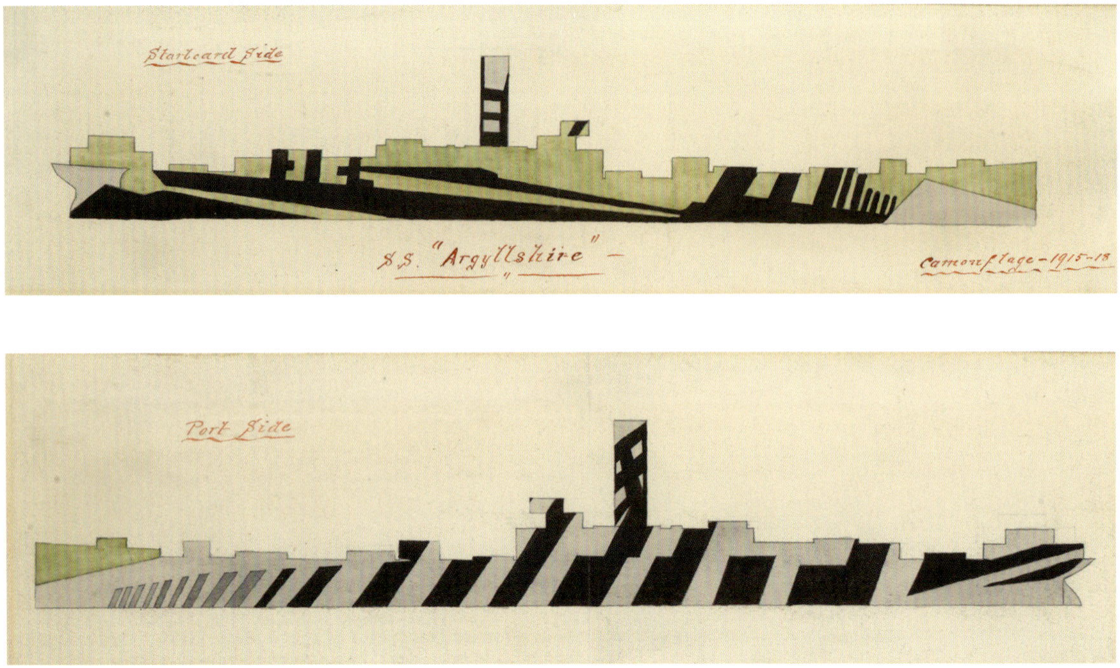

Fig.52
SS 'Argyllshire', starboard and port side silhouettes showing camouflage, 1917–18
Graphite and watercolour on paper
13.8 x 51.4 cm (5 3/8 x 20 1/4 in)/
13.8 x 45.2 cm (5 3/8 x 18 in)
PAH0415 and PAH0416

use of blue to 'paint submarines like high-swimming open sea fish' – but, on proving ineffective, they were not pursued.[8]

The scheme which was adopted in 1917, and which became known as 'dazzle painting' or just 'dazzle', was the brainchild of artist Norman Wilkinson (see Chapter 1: Pictorial Narratives of the War at Sea), at that time a lieutenant in the Royal Naval Volunteer Reserve and commanding a minesweeping launch working out of HM Naval Base Devonport, just north of Plymouth. Wilkinson was returning by train from weekend leave when he had the sudden inspiration that, at least as far as camouflaging ships from U-boats was concerned, 'the extreme opposite was the answer': that is, a vessel should be painted 'in such a way as to break up her form and thus confuse a submarine officer as to the course on which she was heading'. He quickly drafted such a proposal, with a sketch design, which he sent to the Admiralty Board of Inventions and Research, explaining that 'the idea is not to render the ship in any degree invisible, as this is virtually impossible, but to largely distort the external shape by means of violent colour contrasts'.[9]

Wilkinson's concept relied on a series of strong, contrasting geometric patterns that created false bow lines on the ship and broke up its natural silhouette (fig.52): as once explained to an objecting captain, the aim was not to turn it into 'an imitation of a West African parrot [but] rather to give the impression that the head is where your stern is'.[10] It was, above all, a scheme which took cognisance of the normal viewpoint from a hostile submarine, not surface ships: that is, what an attacking enemy commander could see in the limited view provided by a periscope from only a metre or so above the water. Crucially, any hesitation on his part, or further manoeuvring for a good torpedo shot, might give British crews the vital seconds needed to spot the threat and take evasive action. Wilkinson himself explained that 'the primary objective of this scheme was not so much to cause the enemy to miss his shot when in firing position, but to mislead him, when the ship was first sighted, as to the correct position to take up'.[11]

Wilkinson quickly gained cooperation to have the naval store ship *Industry* painted with a preliminary design at Devonport; while the experiment was being assessed, the next problem was where to set up what became the 'Dazzle Section' to develop, test and disseminate the range of patterns needed. This was solved when his friend, the sculptor and Royal Academician, Francis Derwent Wood (1871–1926), suggested using the Royal Academy Schools rooms in the basement of Burlington House, Piccadilly. That was soon agreed but ongoing delay in the Admiralty prompted Wilkinson (as recalled in his memoirs) to outline his scheme to 'a friend' in the Ministry of Shipping.[12] When they showed more rapid enthusiasm for it, oversight of the project was transferred to the Controller General of Merchant Shipbuilding and work got under way.

Because men were required for active service, most of the art students and artists who worked in the Dazzle Section with Wilkinson and his assistant, Cecil King, were women (fig.53): one of them, Evelyn Harriet McKenzie (1893–1968), also married Wilkinson in 1918. There was at least one 'Lady Modeller' employed and, as the programme gathered pace, a staff of 25 women, primarily engaged in transferring dazzle designs from models to ship

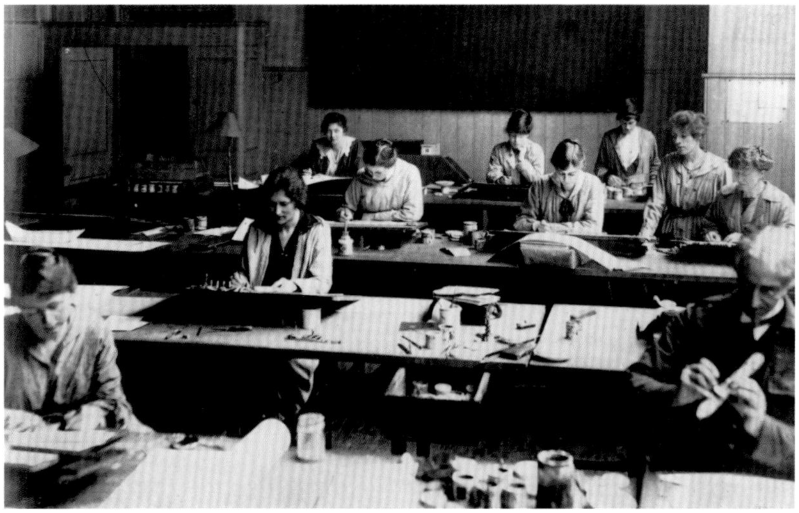

Fig.53
Reproduction of a photograph showing women working on 'dazzle' designs in a studio in the Royal Academy Schools, 1917. From 'A Brush With Life' by Norman Wilkinson, plate 25, 1917
Half-tone reproduction
11.5 x 17.7 cm (4 ½ x 7 in)
Royal Academy of Arts

plans. The process of selecting dazzle designs worked as follows: once the assistants had painted the ship models with dazzle patterns that Wilkinson, King and other artists devised, they were tested against a background simulating different weather conditions. The model was rotated on a turntable and viewed from all angles through a periscope. The dazzle patterns judged successful were sent as plans to merchant ports, initially Liverpool and Bristol, to be painted on to ships. Care was taken to make designs individual, and different on both sides of the vessel, to avoid U-boats becoming familiar with a recurring pattern.

By late 1917, the majority of merchant ships and some in the Navy were painted this way, and Wilkinson was soon giving advice to the US Navy Department on adopting the scheme. The principle was also revived in adapted form for British and American ships in the Second World War, and later, though never to the same extent.[13]

From Ship to Canvas

The Dazzle Section saw Wilkinson working in collaboration with one of the key proponents of Vorticism, the painter and printmaker Edward Wadsworth (1889–1949), who oversaw dazzle operations in Bristol and Liverpool. Vorticism – a modern art movement with links to French Cubism, German Expressionism and Italian Futurism – was, of course, not Wilkinson's starting point. However, its hard-edged definition and angularity was so similar to dazzle in practical terms that the two approaches clearly had strong visual affinities. Prominent Vorticists at the outbreak of the First World War also included the artists Henri Gaudier-Brzeska, William Roberts and the group's leader, Wyndham Lewis (1882–1957), who edited the magazine *BLAST*, published in July 1914. The second (and final) issue, subtitled 'War Edition', appeared the following year. Their boisterous and irreverent manifesto, as set out in the first issue, primarily constituted a long list of things to be 'Blasted' or 'Blessed', and broadly speaking offered a thorough blasting of 'Victorian' values and blessing of modernity, as embodied by technological and mechanical innovation. It was in this context that ships and ports were subjects of special focus ('BLESS ENGLAND FOR ITS SHIPS', 'BLESS ALL PORTS', 'BLESS THE GREAT PORTS [–] HULL, LIVERPOOL, LONDON, NEWCASTLE-ON-TYNE, BRISTOL, GLASGOW').[14]

By cruel irony, the launch of *BLAST* coincided with the outbreak of the First World War, which showed to murderous effect what the vaunted new technology could do and saw those involved in the movement drafted into the war effort, some becoming casualties. Lewis and Roberts were among the first official war artists; Gaudier-Brzeska was killed in the trenches in 1915, fighting for the French; Wadsworth, like Wilkinson, served in the Royal Naval Volunteer Reserve, in his case as an intelligence officer on the Greek island of Mudros until 1917.

Wadsworth's pre-war work was marked by a fascination with the industrial landscape of the north of England. It was one with which the artist was closely linked, since he was born in Cleckheaton, Yorkshire, the only son of an industrialist.[15] His early works, *Newcastle* (1913), which featured in *BLAST*, and *Cleckheaton* (1914),

Fig.54
Edward Wadsworth
Dazzle-ships in Drydock at Liverpool, 1919
Oil on canvas
304.8 x 243.8 cm (120 x 96 in)
National Gallery of Canada

depict stark northern landscapes transformed by industrialisation, the slanting chimneys and factories having an almost dazzle-like treatment.[16] Working for the Dazzle Section, Wadsworth arguably found the ideal forum via which his 'Vorticist' leanings could find their ultimate expression: the use of bold geometric patterns allied with the aesthetics of machinery and engineering to capture the spirit of industrialisation and technological advance, which contemporary ship design represented on a grand scale. Indeed, the art historian William Feaver has suggested that Wadsworth would have perceived his dazzle work on the RMS *Aquitania* as the opportunity to create 'the largest painting ever'.[17]

In the inter-war period, many of the Vorticists, worn down by the physical and psychological stresses of the conflict, returned to what could be seen as more traditional styles and figurative painting.[18] However, Wadsworth's post-war work clearly shows the ongoing influence of his employment in the Dazzle Section. One of his best-known post-war paintings, *Dazzle-ships in Drydock at Liverpool* (1919, fig.54) illustrates the use of geometric pattern to enhance the modern lines of the vessel and its monumental scale, the latter mirrored by the enormous size, at approximately 3 metres by 2.5 metres, of the canvas itself. His highly innovative series of woodcuts showing dazzle ships dispensed with clear outlines of them, instead relying on geometric shapes to suggest their form. Given the original purpose of dazzle, there was also some irony in one of these woodcuts being used as the poster image for the 1923 exhibition of English graphic art held in Germany.[19]

Dazzle was also one of the key artistic developments of the war that attracted the prolific marine painter John Everett (1876–1949), a fascinating figure who voyaged the world by sail and steam for the purpose, and had the benefit of inherited private income. Since he did not need to sell his output, he bequeathed most of it (over 1,500 paintings and drawings) to the National Maritime Museum. Unauthorised open-air drawing and sketching in sensitive areas, such as munitions factories, ports and naval bases, were forbidden under DORA, but the Ministry of Information approached Everett during the First World War and gave him permission to paint scenes in the London docks.[20] He spent the ensuing weeks outside, nearly every day, capturing the dazzle patterns on the ships, often within unconventional compositions that further accentuate their abstract quality. One canvas that he painted for the Ministry of Information in 1918, *A convoy, 1918* (plate 60), was possibly done to demonstrate how the asymmetry of dazzle tricked the eye, particularly the way in which the crazily slanting lines no longer offered a clear horizon. While Everett represents dazzle patterns in this painting, there is no evidence that these designs were ever applied to ships – unlike those shown in other examples of his dazzle work – and it is likely that the canvas was meant to convey its impression and effect rather than being a specific record.

Immediately after the war, an exhibition of Everett's work, showing the docks and particularly dazzle-painted ships, was held at the Goupil Galleries, London, in November 1918.[21] One of his dazzle-ship paintings was also included in the special post-war edition of the *Studio* magazine, which illustrated the conflict as represented by important artists: paintings by Wilkinson of the Gallipoli campaign (in which he had served) and another dazzle-ship work by Cecil King were also included.[22] The *Studio* publication is important, both as an early 'artistic review' of the war and because it covers all its theatres, including the work of some of the most influential and well-known names: Paul Nash's portrayals of the Western Front, Keith Henderson's extraordinary *Shell Explosion* and Muirhead Bone's images of soldiers on temporary leave. Charles Holme, founder and editor of the *Studio*, noted that the collected works were 'something more than mere renderings of scenes and events; rather should they be considered as the direct and personal impressions of men who have come into close contact with the realities of war, its emotions, its horrors, and its flood of human activity, and have given expression to them through the medium of their art'.[23] Everett was the only artist in this collection who had not actively served in the armed forces.

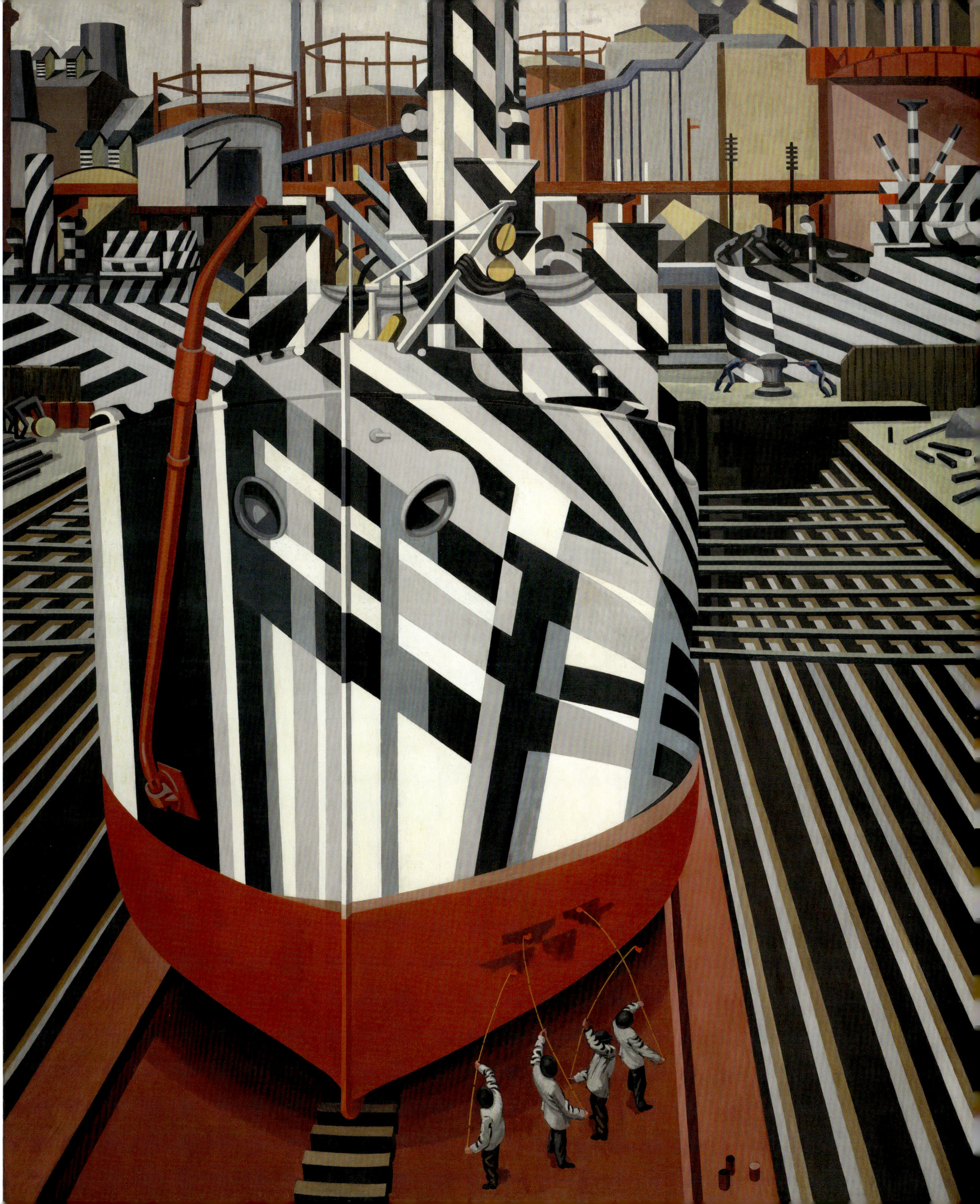

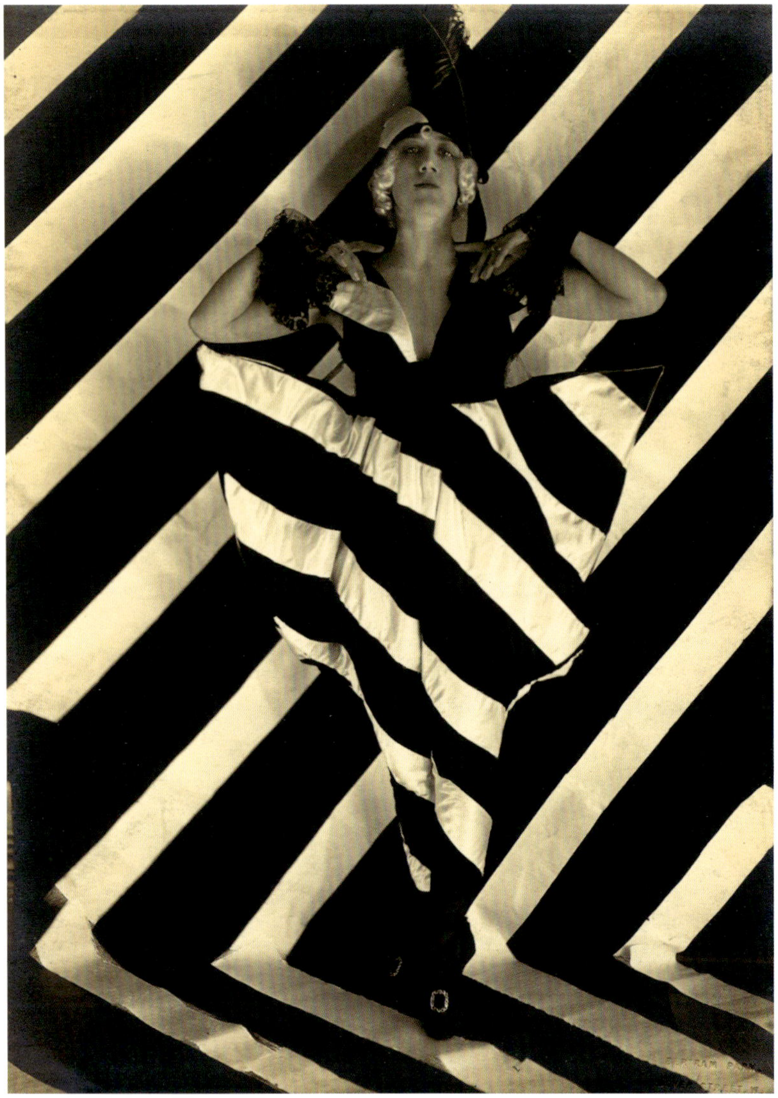

Fig.55
Bertram Park
Yvonne Gregory, 1919
Cream-toned bromide print
20.6 cm x 14.5 cm (8 1/8 in. x 5 3/4 in)
Given by June Mardall (née Park), 1977,
National Portrait Gallery
PG x11824

The work of the dazzle artists was also publicly celebrated in the post-war Chelsea Arts Club Dazzle Ball of 1919. Inaugurated in 1908 and in 1911 moved to the Royal Albert Hall because of over-subscription, the Chelsea Arts Club's ball became an annual fixture of the London social scene. It was not held during the war, the last preceding it being in March 1914.[24] This had been themed around 'Old England' and, in that regard, the Dazzle Ball marked a key departure in reflecting the wider impact of the war on British society. Appropriately, Wilkinson and King designed the event in a distinctive and boldly geometric style, as reported in the *Illustrated London News*:

> The scheme of the decoration for the great fancy dress ball given by the Chelsea Arts Club at the Albert Hall, the other day, was based on the principles of 'Dazzle', the method of 'camouflage' used during the war in the painting of ships to help them in escaping from the attacks of submarines. Many of the costumes were also designed specially for the occasion on 'Dazzle' lines, but here was also a great variety of fancy dress of the ordinary type. The total effect was brilliant and fantastic. During the evening a shower of 'bombs' in the shape of coloured balloons descended on the devoted heads of the dancers, and added greatly to the hilarity of the occasion.[25]

Record of one of these costumes survives in a photograph by Bertram Park of his wife and fellow photographer, Yvonne Gregory (fig.55). Gregory poses in a costume of angled stripes against a background of contrasting stripes, re-creating the false bow lines that were a visual hallmark of dazzle ships. Gregory, her husband and their business partner, Marcus Adams, were well-known society photographers at the 'Studio of Three' in Dover Street, London. Their use of dazzle illustrates the way in which something created for military purposes could be rapidly adopted and adapted into general social currency.

Women as Artists and Subjects

As already noted, women with formal artistic training played a significant role in the development and use of dazzle painting in 1917 and 1918. This kind of war work was to be repeated in the Second World War with the creation in 1940 of the Civilian Camouflage Directorate at Leamington Spa. There an art student, Victorine Foot (1920–2000), was both employed as a camoufleur and worked independently, sketching colleagues and their activities. Her painting, *Camouflaging a Cruiser in Dock* (1943, IWM) was acquired by the War Artists Advisory Committee (WAAC).

More generally women made vital contributions to the war effort in both conflicts through the various women's auxiliary corps, and in volunteer roles (see Chapter 5: Merchant Navy Comforts). Groups such as the Women's Auxiliary Air Force (WAAF), which existed for two years in 1918–20 and was re-formed in 1939, the Women's Auxiliary Army Corps and the Women's Royal Naval Service (WRNS), both created in 1917, provided support to the armed forces and, by taking on non-combatant roles previously held by men, liberated as many as possible for fighting service. Tellingly, the auxiliaries were founded or, like the WRNS, populated by women who had links to the suffragette movement.[26] Indeed, Vera Laughton Mathews (1888–1959), who had been an editor of the *Suffragette* (1913–14), joined the WRNS in 1918 and later became its director in 1939.

Initially the 'Wrens' (as they soon came to be known) were drawn from women living in significant ports around Britain, with the idea that they did not have to leave their home areas to join and participate. Enlistment across the United Kingdom was enthusiastic and consequently WRNS units were housed in dormitories near the key ports as well as (mainly for coding work) in Ireland, Malta, Gibraltar and Genoa. They also had a significant presence in the Humber, which was the hub of British anti-submarine warfare. The first Wrens appeared in uniform in early 1918 and took over dockyard roles traditionally occupied by men. They performed tasks of physical labour including portering and driving, worked as serving staff, and undertook clerical duties including the key wartime responsibility for coding. Such activities were recorded in paintings commissioned by the Women's Work Subcommittee (WWS) of the nascent Imperial War Museum (which was founded in early 1917) to ensure that there was official representation for women, both as artists and subjects.[27] Two examples of the latter are *Valve Testing: The Signal School, RN Barracks, Portsmouth* and *Boat-cleaning at the Coastal Motor Boat Base, Haslar Creek* by Arthur David McCormick (both 1919, IWM).[28]

An example of a female artist being commissioned by the WWS to work specifically on WRNS subject matter is Phyllis Keyes (born *c.*1881), who was sent to the naval base at Lowestoft for the purpose.[29] She produced six watercolours, each focusing on a particular task or occupation, both traditional and non-traditional, that were undertaken by the women. These include cooks and clerks, as well as sailmakers and depth-charge workers.[30] Thus, on the one hand, the Wrens motto, 'Never at Sea', underlined that they did not serve on naval ships; but, on the other, it embodied the inspiring ambition to be resilient, adaptable and ever-resourceful. That said, the first Wren casualty of the war, Josephine Carr, was on active duty when the mail boat in which she was travelling, the *Leinster*, was torpedoed in the Irish Sea in October 1918.[31]

Joyce Dennys (1883–1991), who was both an artist and naval nurse (VAD), was responsible for the design of the first Wrens recruitment poster (fig.56).[32] This shows a uniformed figure standing atop chalk cliffs with the sea and a lighthouse in silhouette behind her, gesturing for volunteers. A student at Exeter Art School, Dennys also designed the recruitment poster of 1915 advertising the VADS.[33] While the WRNS image may be viewed as emphasising the role of women as shore-bound – which for the most part they were – the iconic white cliffs and lighthouse can also be read as the Wrens taking an active role in the seaward defence of Britain, which both features symbolise.

Katharine Furse, the first Director of the WRNS, believed that there was 'no room for women in the Navy in peacetime'.[34] However, the inter-war years were a relatively short period and the Wrens were again mobilised in 1938. Their recruitment poster this time featured the slogan 'Join the WRNS and Free a man for the Fleet', despite the fact that women were increasingly taking on more traditional male roles. For example, in 1941 they began training as 'Boat Crew' (fig.4), and were soon serving on tugs and harbour launches as mechanics.

That trained artists counted among those serving is underlined by a reference made in J.B. Priestley's *British Women Go to War* (1944), where the author introduces 'the W.R.N.S. dispatch rider' featured in one of the photographic illustrations as a member of his family and 'a promising student of the Slade School of Art'.[35]

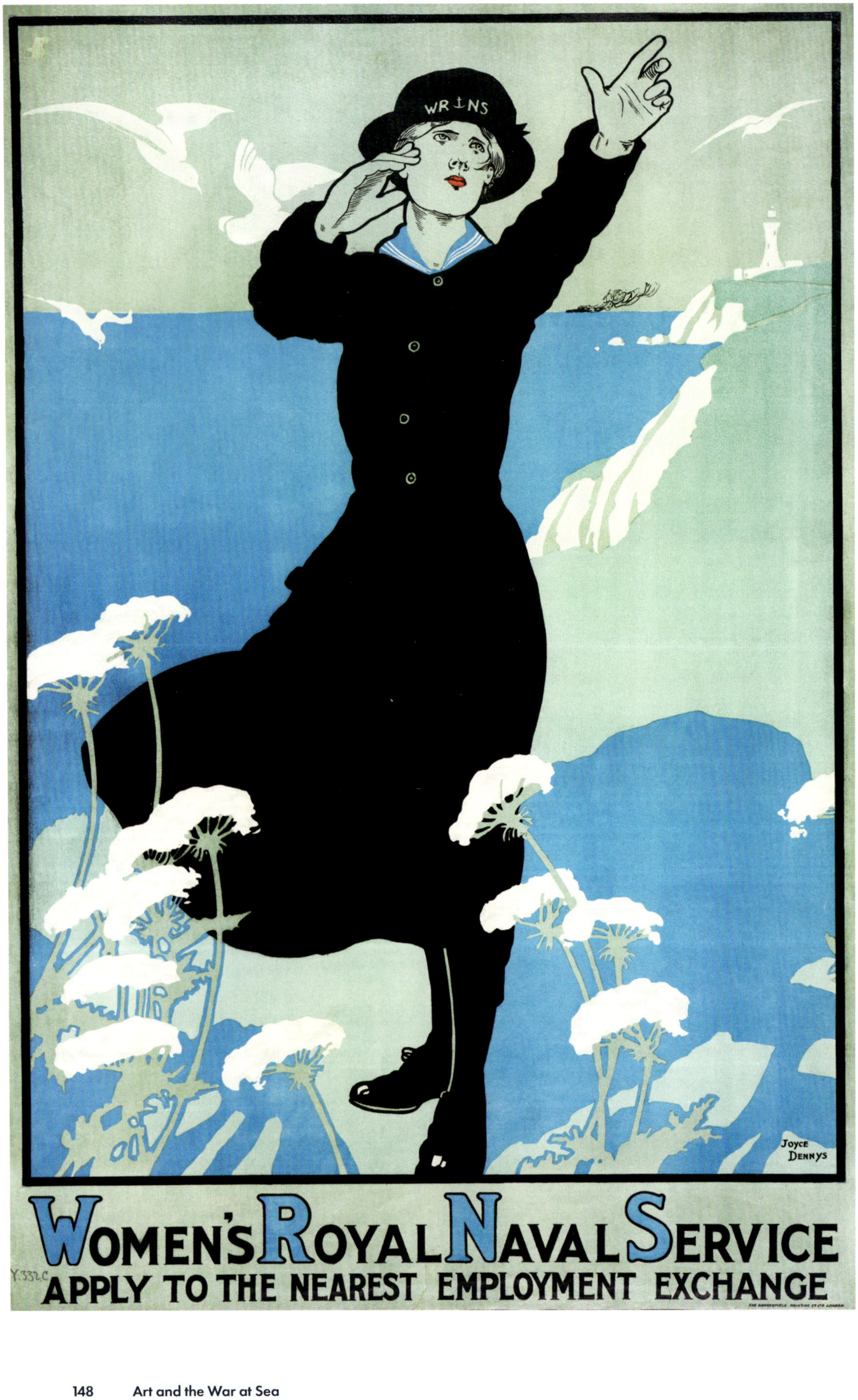

Fig.56
Joyce Dennys
Women's Royal Naval Service, 1918
Lithograph
75.6 x 49.3 cm (29 ¾ x 19 ⅜ in)
Imperial War Museums
ART.IWM PST 2766

Outside official commissions, therefore, female artists could and did work independently while on active duty in the WRNS.

One such artist, with an intimate knowledge of the Wrens' daily lives, was Gladys E. Reed (active 1943–4; also see Chapter 2: The Face of War and figs 4, 26, 27). While little is yet known about Reed herself, she trained at the Southern College of Art, Portsmouth, and is recorded as joining the WRNS in 1943 and serving as a Wireless Telegraph Operator at HMS *Eaglet* in Liverpool, the headquarters of the Commander-in-Chief of the Western Approaches. This shore base coordinated the British side of the Atlantic convoy system and monitored German U-boat activity with the aim of suppressing it. In the 14 drawings by her now in the National Maritime Museum collection, Reed shows Wrens engaged in diverse tasks such as telephone night duty, as radio mechanics and torpedomen, stripping and cleaning depth charges. She also captures the more domestic side of life, including 'dhobeying,' or washing out clothes in a hand basin. All are keenly observed and highly detailed studies.

One image (plate 65) shows a member of the WRNS boat crew repairing torpedo tubes. She is shown in Boat Crew uniform, which had only been added to the regulations in 1941; it is close to male Royal Naval ratings' dress and, instead of the customary Wrens' skirt and tailored jacket, Reed's image shows the distinctive bell-bottomed trousers, long fitted smock and a recognisably naval-pattern cap; in fact, the dress is nearly indistinguishable from that worn by the sailors. The physicality of the work the Wren is doing, and her unselfconscious, 'masculine' stance, certainly suggests the interchangeability between male and female roles on the home front. Indeed, the image really transcends gender: it is no longer either a man or a woman fixing torpedo tubes, it is a sailor.

In this regard, Reed's unsentimental, 'eyewitness' approach bears comparison with that of male artists, Stephen Bone, Leslie Cole and Vivian Pitchforth, among others, who were also creating images of everyday life, but on board Navy and merchant ships (see Chapter 3: Above and Below Deck). And similarly there are parallels with the work of Laura Knight, especially in her well-known painting *Ruby Loftus Screwing a Breech-ring* of 1943 (IWM). Perhaps above all, Reed's image offers a telling contrast with the more inhibited and conventionally posed Wren (torpedo branch) illustrated in *British Women Go to War* and the condescending tone and sentiment, by today's standards, of Priestley's text that accompanies it: 'it is part of the fascinating irony of our strange times,' he notes, 'that this fair and meditative maiden, who looks as if she might be dreamily contemplating a cluster of bluebells in a spring wood, is actually preparing for its dreadful task a thing that may soon blow a great hole in a ship's side and send hundreds of men to their deaths'.[36]

When she donated her drawings to the National Maritime Museum in 1947, Reed wrote to the then Director, Frank Carr, saying:

> I am afraid you will be more than a little shocked at the untidy state they are in. They were sketched under all sorts of conditions, have been carried wherever I have been stationed, and passed through many people's hands, so that since 1944 [they] have become very grubby. I console myself with the thought that they may still reflect a little of that busy, happy atmosphere that <u>did</u> exist in the WRNS – especially in the 'open air' categories.[37]

Despite her own reservations of their worth, Reed's drawings were evidently much admired: in response to the comments quoted above, Carr wrote 'we feel that these form a most useful and, if I may say so, a most graceful record of the WRNS work in the war, so much more telling than photographs'. In 1945 a number of Reed's drawings were also reproduced in the official Royal Navy magazine, the *Dittybox*, with the captions 'Two Wren Torpedomen chat during standeasy', 'Wren torpedomen at work on stripping and cleaning parts of depth charges' (plate 66), and 'Wren torpedoman repairing the sound power phones on board one of H.M. trawlers' (plate 67).[38]

Fig.57
Rosemary Rutherford
A Nurse reading, 1943–4
Graphite and wash on paper
60 x 48 cm (23 5/8 x 18 7/8 in)
Private collection

The Art of Healing

Another trained artist actively participating in the war effort, this time as a member of the Voluntary Aid Detachments, and whose war art has only recently come to light, is Rosemary Rutherford (1912–72). Trained at the Slade School of Art, and an exhibitor at the New English Arts Club, Rutherford volunteered in 1940 to join the VAD of the Red Cross and served as a nurse in the Royal Naval Hospitals at Chatham and Haslar (Gosport) and other RN auxiliary hospitals. At the same time the WAAC gave her permission to practise as an artist.

In a published account of her VAD service, Geraldine Horton recalls meeting Rutherford at Haslar, where they discussed her opportunities to paint. Referring to a previous posting to Yorkshire, Rutherford remarked that the patients in her care were 'Psychologically most interesting. We had poets, painters and musicians. Mostly very sensitive types.' 'I did dozens of portraits,' she continued, 'mostly pen and ink. The men enjoyed it as a rule, got them out of themselves a bit, but it was an exhausting struggle trying to be a good artist and a good nurse. In the end, I gave up being a good nurse.'[39] Her work as a whole captures the activities of doctors, nurses and orderlies, and the everyday experience of convalescing sailors and officers. Unlike the ratings portrayed by Eric Kennington (see plates 16–18), who very deliberately chose men from the lower ranks and women from the auxiliaries in their specific uniforms, Rutherford draws her naval subjects in their hospital dress: a simple blue jacket and white shirt. The men are thus stripped of rank and the accoutrements of war.

Some of her images have the same intimate, observational quality as those of Gladys Reed, such as her affectionate watercolour sketch of a nurse reading (fig.57) or the characterful pencil portrait of two sailors (plate 69). Others have an overtly religious tone, in particular the poignant representation of two nurses attending a patient, his prone, naked body resembling countless artistic representations of Christ's descent from the cross (plate 74).

This religious emphasis may simply reflect Rutherford's own beliefs as a devout Christian. However, there were precedents from the art of the First World War that may, in addition, have influenced her approach. Perhaps the most famous exponent of 'Biblical episodes in modern dress' was Stanley Spencer (1891–1959), who also trained at the Slade before serving in the Royal Army Medical Corps, first as an orderly in a Bristol hospital and then in the 68th Field Ambulance unit in Macedonia. As Robert Upstone has noted, Spencer viewed the wounded he encountered there in explicitly religious terms, describing them as 'so many crucified Jesus Christs'.[40] In his *Travoys Arriving with Wounded Soldiers at a Dressing Station at Smol, Macedonia* (1919, IWM), commissioned by the Ministry of Information, Spencer utilises the artistic conventions associated with the Nativity to suggest that the operation being performed by the Army surgeons is a kind of rebirth or resurrection.

That Rutherford viewed the convalescing sailors in similarly redemptive terms is underlined in two further works. The first is a portrait with the inscription, *'Chippy'– the carpenter on HMS Curacao, painted Cholmondeley Castle 1943*, and a further inscription *'then he recovered* [...] *Straightaway he was made whole'* (plate 70).[41] The second is an extraordinary watercolour (plate 75) showing hospital staff carrying a patient up the steps to a temporary operating theatre, their figures bathed in the light flooding through the open doorway. The latter certainly has affinities with Barbara Hepworth's celebrated National Health Service hospital series of 1947–9, especially in articulating in visual terms a common faith (to quote Chris Stephens on Hepworth) 'in the primary value of unselfish human cooperation and social responsibility'.[42]

Towards the end of the war, Rutherford travelled east on a troopship. Her related work, characterised by a brilliant colour palette, reflects what must have been an extremely exciting and liberating period of her life. Even so, one cannot help making the observation that the resulting images do not express the pathos and humanity of the scenes and portraits she executed at the naval hospitals of Chatham and Haslar.

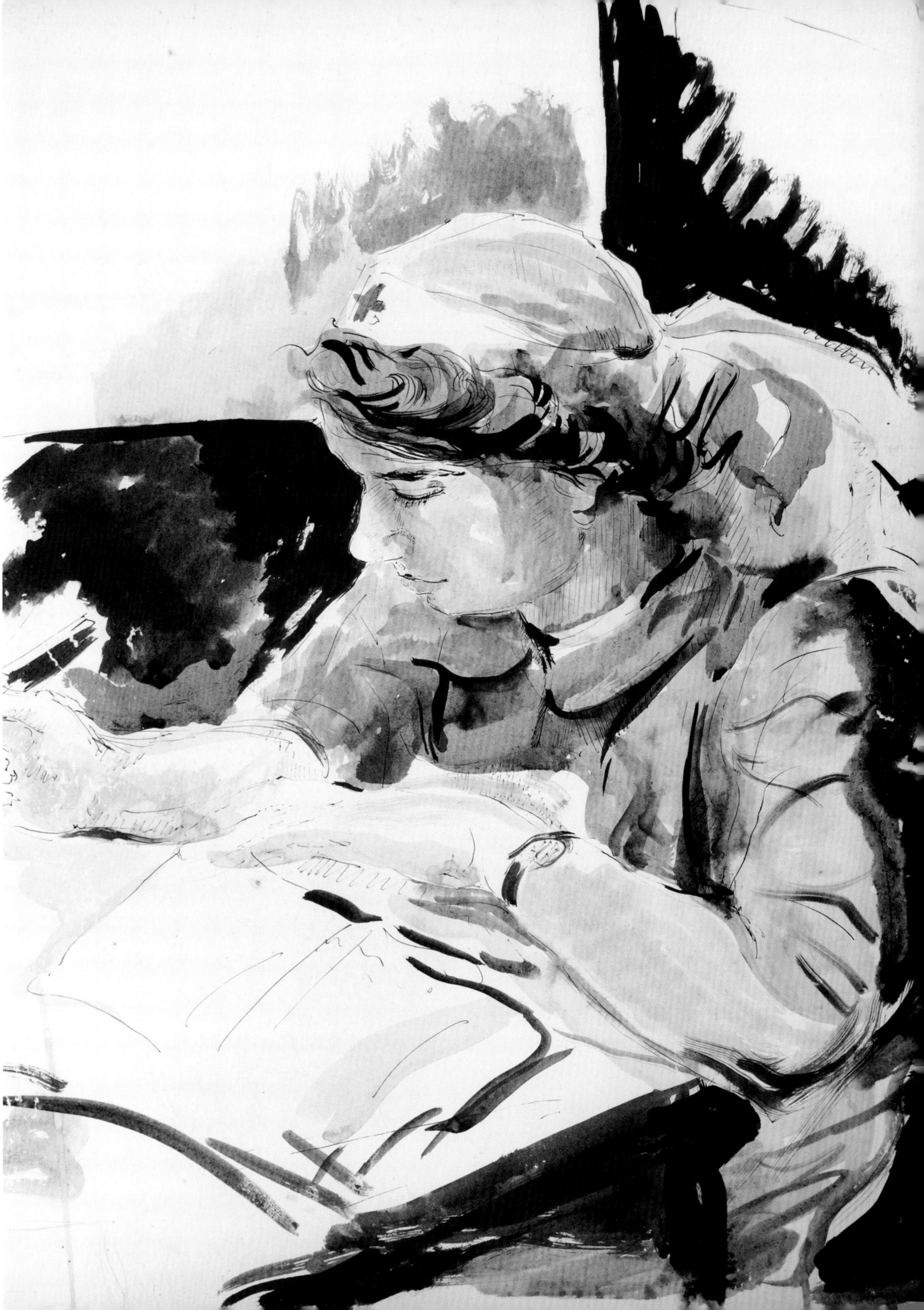

Merchant Navy Comforts

Amy Miller

Fig.58
Godfrey Philips
Captain Fryatt, 1916
Silk
Imperial War Museums
EPH 3666

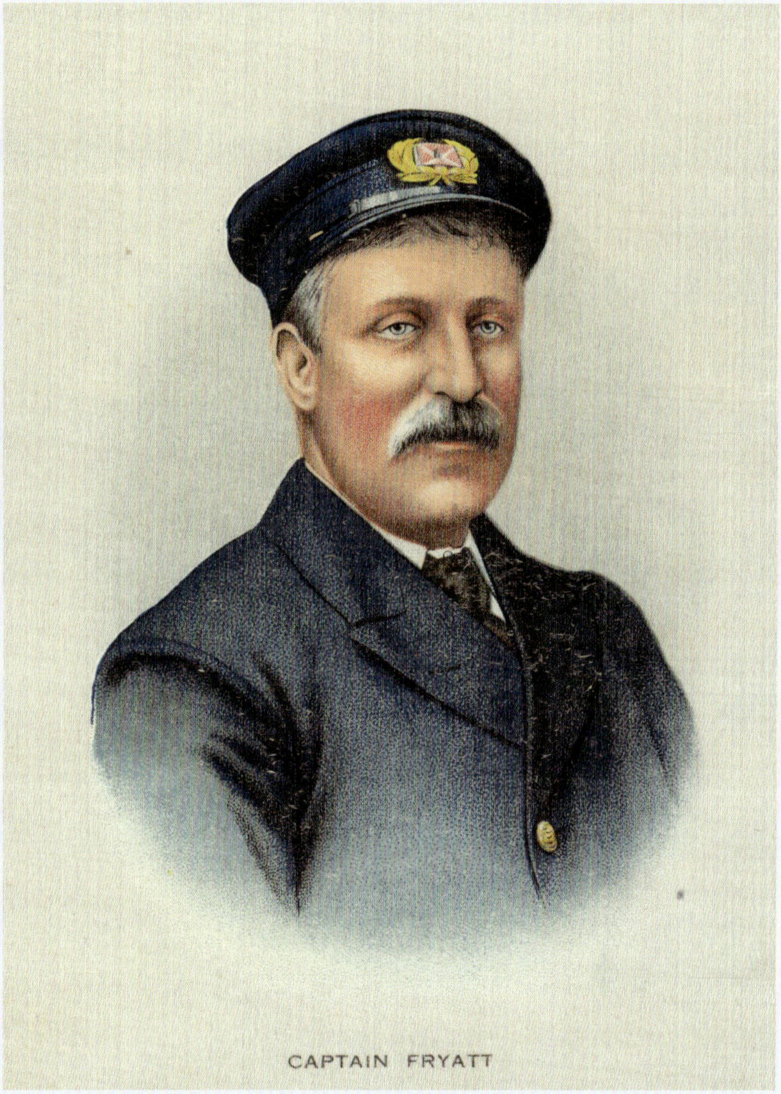

In 1914, Britain's mercantile marine consisted of a network of shipping companies, each with their own uniforms and, though all flying the red ensign, sailing under individual company flags. During the war, serving personnel not on active duty did not initially wear their uniforms, which led to a number of merchant seamen being handed white feathers, a mark of cowardice meant to shame able-bodied men into enlisting.[43] Even for those already in the armed forces this became such an issue that sailors on leave were told to wear their uniforms to avoid it. Similarly, shipping-company men were told to be in uniform even when off-duty, and specifically when they were in 'proximity to dock yards', to demonstrate they were actively part of the war effort.[44]

Without a generally shared uniform, or indeed being formally recognised as members of a legitimate non-combatant organisation, mercantile officers were also liable to charges of illegal acts of war. This was starkly illustrated in the case of Captain Charles Fryatt (fig.58), a master in the Great Eastern Railway's North Sea service. Early in March 1915 Fryatt was pursued by a U-boat but outran it. On 28 March, after another U-boat sank a British passenger vessel with great loss of life, Fryatt's ship, the SS *Brussels*, was ordered to stop by *U-33* off the Dutch coast, near the Maas Lightship. Too close to escape, he followed Admiralty instructions and tried to ram the submarine, forced it to dive and was five miles away by the time it resurfaced. The Admiralty awarded him a gold watch for his gallantry.[45]

Fryatt continued to sail between Britain and the Netherlands until 22 July 1916 when, again a short way past the Maas Lightship after leaving the Hook of Holland for Tilbury, the *Brussels* was captured by a German destroyer flotilla. In addition to his cargo of foodstuffs, Fryatt also had on board a number of Belgian refugees. The passengers and crew were detained and Fryatt, who was known to the Germans because of the earlier incidents, was imprisoned and charged with committing an illegal act of war against *U-33*. On 27 July 1916 he was tried by a military court, found guilty and shot two hours later, the German justification being that 'he was not a member of a combatant force' and therefore a *franc-tireur* – in effect, a pirate.[46] In an article titled 'Captain Fryatt's murder, retribution to be exacted' on 1 August 1916, *The Times* reported that Prime Minister H.H. Asquith had 'denounced the murder as an atrocious crime against the law of nations and the usages of war'.

Public outrage at Fryatt's execution was used propagandistically in much the same way as that of the nurse, Edith Cavell, which occurred the previous October.[47] In both cases this was part of attempts, along with the furore surrounding the sinking of the *Lusitania*, to lever the United States into joining the war. Cavell and Fryatt became the subject of poster campaigns – very effectively used in the First World War – to encourage recruitment across the

British Empire. While Cavell was shown as a frail martyr to German brutality, Fryatt was depicted as a stalwart figure whose unflinching gaze, adapted from a contemporary photograph, was seen below the headline, 'The Murder of Captain Fryatt'. The incident was also the subject of a pamphlet of the same title, published in 1916,[48] and of a silent film in Australia, written by Agnes Gavin and released in 1917 (the film was subsequently adapted into a stage play, *Captain Fryatt; or, For King and Country*). It achieved such notoriety that during the Battle of the Somme (1 July–18 November 1916), gunners chalked the messages 'Remember Capt Fryatt' on heavy artillery and 'To Capt Fryatt's Murderers' on the shells.[49]

It was in part owing to the Fryatt case that a uniform was created for officers in the 'Merchant Navy', a title then coming into gradual use but only formalised in 1928 (see Chapter 4: White Ensigns and Red Dusters). In 1918 a committee appointed by the Board of Trade both considered the issues around the creation of uniform and set out suggestions in a series of illustrated proposed regulations. The proposals highlighted the 'Order of the White Feather' problem, already mentioned, and the need to have a clear visual indicator that merchant seamen were in official war service. However, they went further in referring to the status and importance of the merchant fleet:

> the great majority of Mercantile Marine officers were strongly in favour of a Standard uniform. The principal reasons advanced by those witnesses in support of their views were that a Standard uniform would raise the status of its wearer; that the Mercantile Marine has proved its great value to the country during the present abnormal times, and consequently should be afforded some definite recognition in the shape of a national uniform.[50]

The uniform design was very nearly unanimously approved, although it was decided that the sleeve lace should feature a joined chevron, creating a lozenge shape, rather than the 'curl' or loop of gold lace on naval officers' dress. For although the Admiralty agreed the distinction and elevation of status implicit in uniform for the merchant service, in recognition of its wartime sacrifices and importance, it was by no means perceived as equal to that of the Royal Navy.

In the Second World War the Merchant Navy again proved its importance to the civilian population of Britain: the role of its members was summed up in a single line from an August 1943 debate in the House of Lords as 'those who, with such high courage and devotion to duty, have made possible our continuing to live by transporting food supplies across the oceans'.[51] This was certainly recognised on the home front, and supported during the inter-war period and the war itself by the creation of two key schemes: the British Ship Adoption Society (1936) and the Merchant Navy Comforts Service (1940). Both were established under the auspices of the Marine Society, a philanthropic organisation started in the mid-eighteenth century to clothe, train and prepare boys for the sea service.

The British Ship Adoption Society began on a small scale in 1933, allowing ships in the Merchant Navy to be adopted by schools. In 1936, it was unveiled on a national level when, according to an announcement in *The Times*, 'the scheme originated in an idea of the managers of an old-established British shipping company that there would be mutual advantages in bringing school boys in communication with the Captains and officers of British ships'.[52] Letters were initially exchanged with the pupils of a few London schools.

During the Second World War, the scheme expanded and the schools coordinated parcels of what were termed 'comforts', largely consisting of knitted long socks called 'sea stockings', hats and gloves. The children also maintained a correspondence with sailors on their adopted ship and, as crews were often international, they were soon corresponding with a wide group of seamen of different origins. A Norwegian sailor wrote of his experience with the British Ship Adoption scheme: 'May good [*sic*] bless the British people who so kind hearted think of the merchant seaman.'[53]

In many cases, the correspondence and sense of community created by the British Ship Adoption Society appears to have fulfilled the role of absent or non-existent family for seamen. The scheme was not without its issues, however, and the mass evacuation of children from key ports and cities at the beginning of the war, coupled with the wartime measure of a redistribution of shipping, led to a short-lived lapse. A 1942 article in *The Times* announced that 'some schools and ships have managed to maintain their association, in spite of all these obstacles, while others who were not so fortunate have revived their connexions'. The enthusiasm with which the scheme was backed by the public was apparent in another article in the same issue of *The Times*, which observed that there was a shortage of British ships to pair-up, with a waiting list of schools requesting one for adoption. The Society would shortly expand the scheme to include the adoption of Allied ships by British schools, and that (to quote *The Times* article again) 'So far representatives of every ally, except the U.S.S.R. whose ships are just coming here again, are linked up.'[54] A further expansion of the scheme was considered that would take in other countries within the British Empire.

The Merchant Navy Comforts Service was a voluntary organisation. It came into existence in February 1940 and began as a coordinated means of supplying woollen comforts to sailors. A posting in newspapers across the country from March to the end of May 1940 explained its work and issued a plea for supplies: 'The Merchant Navy Comforts Service, with the cooperation of the Legations and Consulates of Belgium and Holland has undertaken to supply the merchant officers and men of our new Allies, now cut off from their homes, with knitted comforts, books, and games. An appeal is made for funds and for gifts including urgently needed clothing.'[55]

These supplies, specifically wool, were obtained through donation and distributed to knitting groups throughout the United Kingdom. By 1943 it was estimated that there were between 6,000 and 7,000 knitting groups. The aim was to supply a small parcel of comforts to every sailor. They included two pairs of socks, a scarf, a sweater, gloves and a woollen helmet, while those going north in winter weather also received an additional pair of long socks. This benefit was also extended to the Royal Navy as women around Britain knitted garments for 'rescue kits' of warm clothing for men saved from the water after their ships sank. These garments, knitted as part of the war effort at home, would have been instantly recognisable and were clearly heavily utilised – especially by those on North Sea patrols and Arctic convoys – to the point that they became an almost 'unofficial' uniform.

One of the most iconic elements of the comforts was the woollen cap and this can clearly be seen in a sketch by John Kingsley Cook, a prolific but unofficial war artist who served in the Merchant Navy from 1940 to 1945, including a period as a Vichy French prisoner in Algeria (see Chapter 4: White Ensigns and Red Dusters). The image seems to have been executed in haste on the back of a chart.[56] It shows two figures, one in full foul-weather gear, and the other in the distinctive ribbed cap and woollen jumper that were the staples of the knitted comforts provided by the Society.

There was in fact little novel in these items themselves, since usually knitted to a standard traditional pattern. This is underlined by a number of sketches of 1939 and 1940 by John Worsley (fig.59), a war artist who served in the Royal Navy (see Chapter 4: From Service to Captivity). In *Dressing on Northern Patrol* (plate 42), we can readily identify the sea stockings, woollen jumpers and helmets that were essential to brave the cold, although in this case Worsley is making visual humour from the many layers needed to go on deck in freezing weather. And *'Jerrys or No Jerrys!'* (plate 44) shows a leading seaman who has collapsed into sleep on a couch almost immediately after coming off watch. He still wears his full cold-weather clothing, including woollen cap and scarf, none of which is Royal Naval regulation dress for the period. That such garments were, by the end of the Second World War, closely identified with the merchant service is clearly demonstrated by Charles Wheeler's monumental figures of an officer and a rating for the Merchant

Fig.59
John Worsley
Five Members of a Gun Watch
(seated, but ready for action), 1940
Wash and crayon on paper
30.1 x 34.8 cm (11 ⅞ x 13 ¾ in)
PAI0519

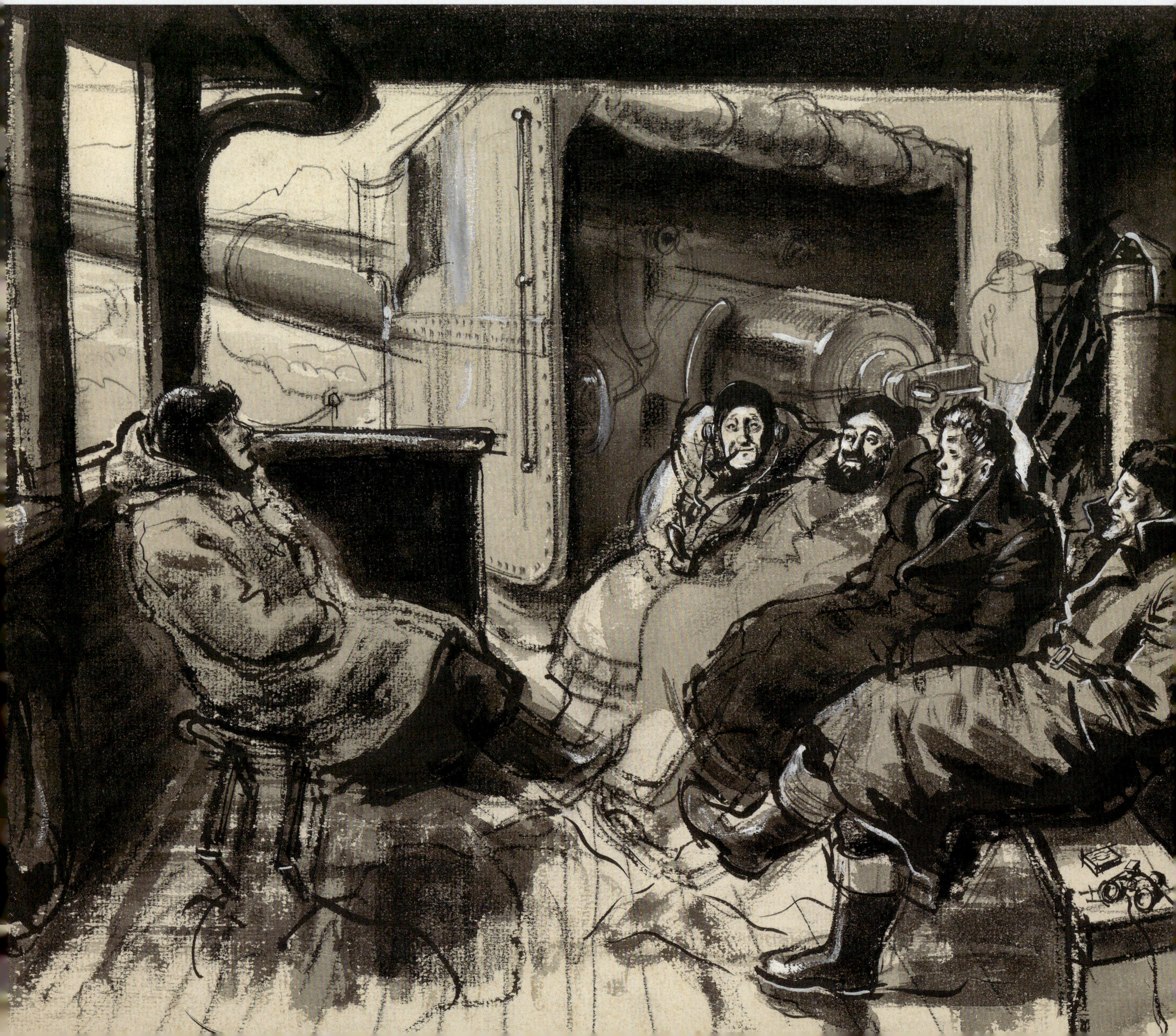

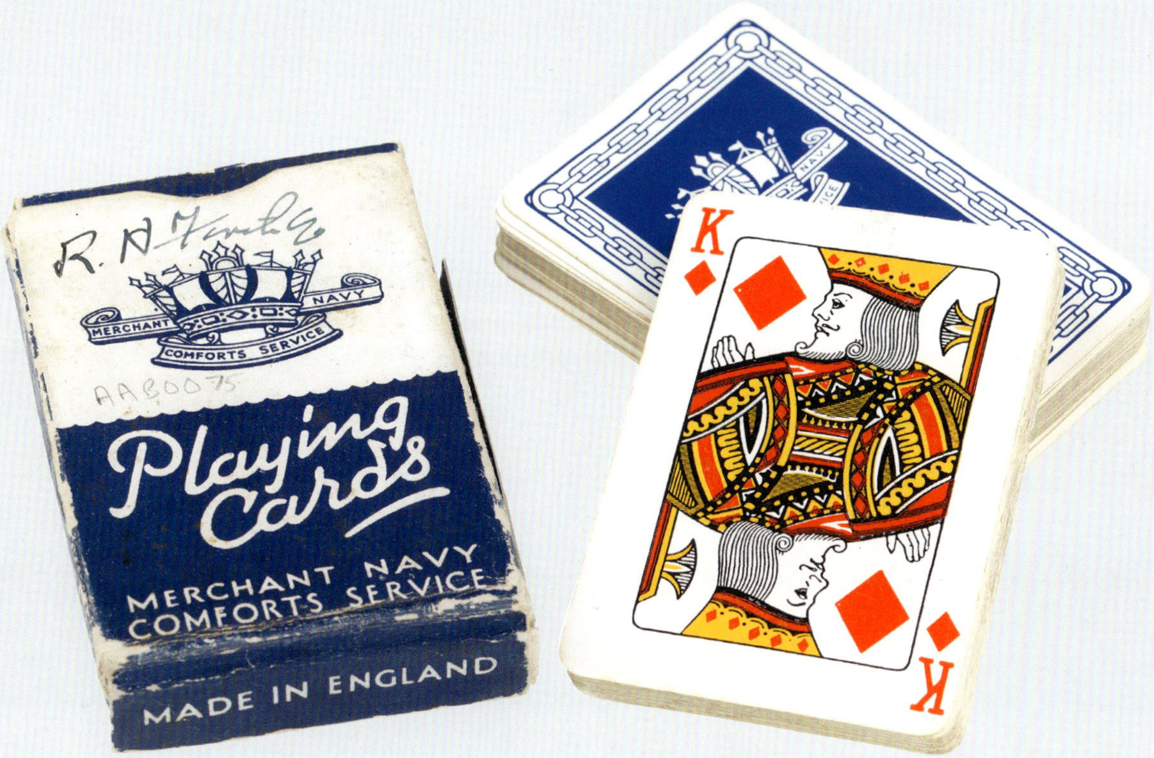

Fig.60 (left)
Playing cards, Merchant Navy Comforts Service
9.5 x 6.5 cm (3 3/4 x 2 1/5 in)
AAB0075

Fig.61 (below)
Merchant Navy lapel badge, 1939–45
Silver
2.3 x 2 cm (7/8 x 3/4 in)
UNI2045

Navy national memorial at Tower Hill, London, which were based (at Wheeler's insistence) on serving merchant seamen (plates 83 and 84).[57]

The Merchant Navy Comforts Society began to expand its services to include sending parcels to prisoners of war, undertaking 'to be next-of-kin of those who have no next-of-kin, so far as is known'.[58] The Society also sent Christmas parcels which, in addition to much-needed clothing, reflected the special nature of the occasion: they included playing cards, small domino sets, saccharine tablets, and toothbrushes and toothpaste.[59] Given the ephemeral nature of these parcels, very little survives in terms of material culture, but the National Maritime Museum has a pack of playing cards from a Christmas example (fig.60). The case bears the signature of the owner Captain R.H. Finch; he worked for the Port Line, which lost 13 ships in the war and suffered a commensurate number of casualties.

The symbols used on the Merchant Navy comforts give a very clear indication of the way in which its status had been enhanced between the First and Second World Wars, specifically in the use of the Royal Naval crown of alternating sails and sterns (fig.61) – previously solely reserved to the 'Senior Service'. Its use was extended to the Merchant Navy as an official recognition of its contributions, and losses, during wartime.

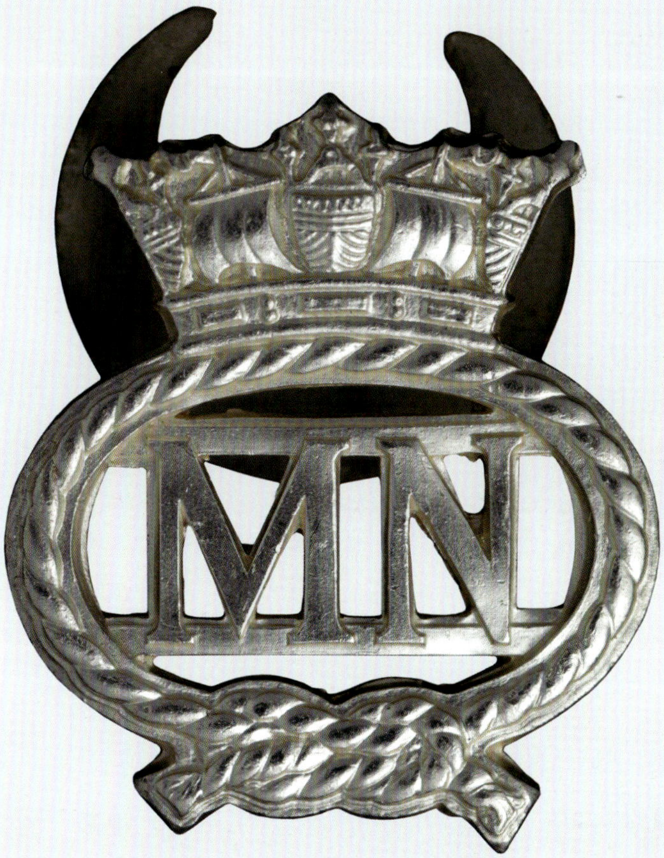

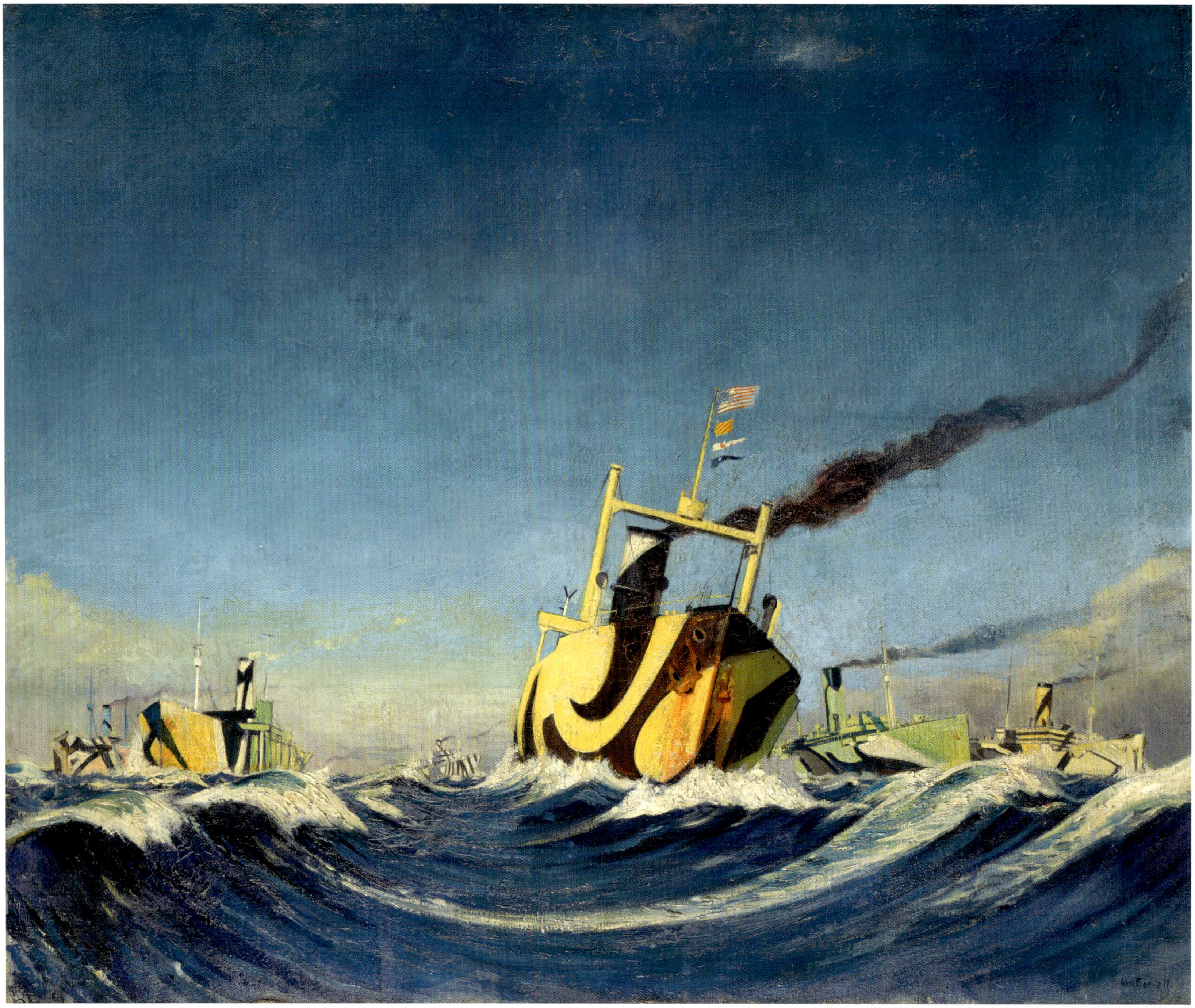

Plate 60
John Everett
A convoy, 1918, 1918
Oil on canvas
79.6 x 95.2 cm (31 3/8 x 37 1/2 in)
BHC1387

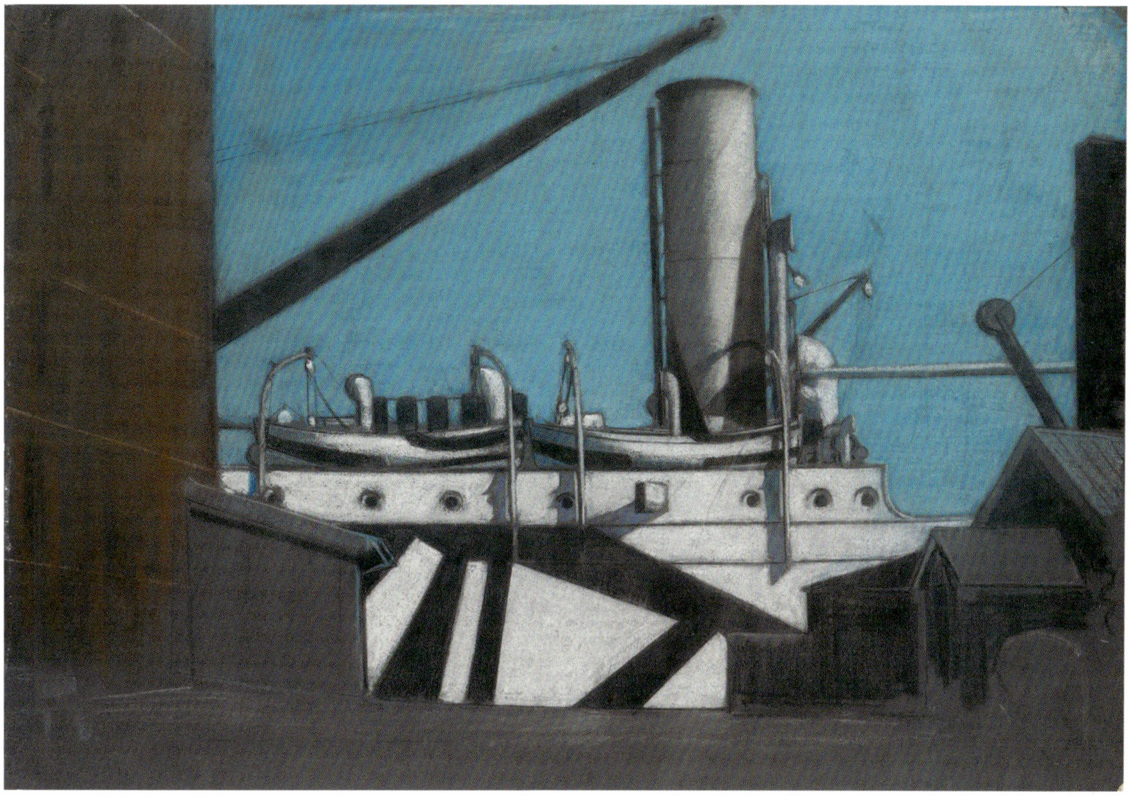

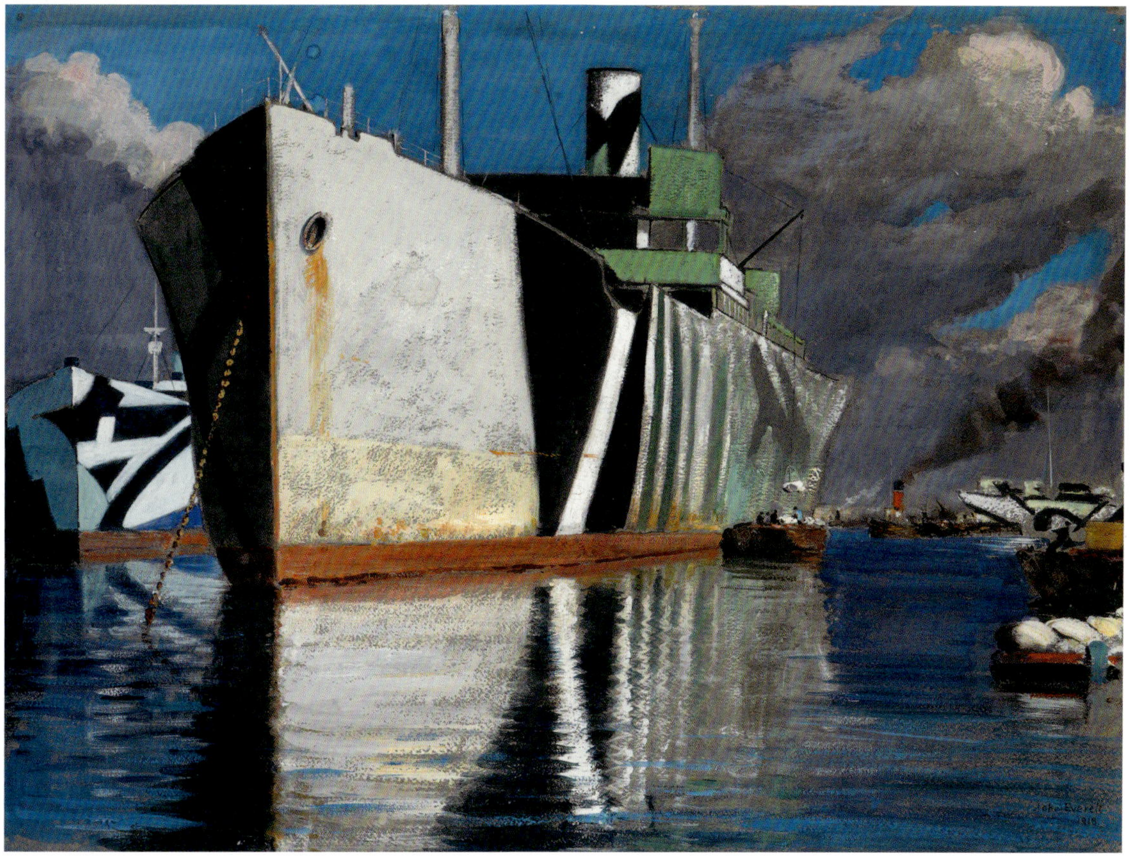

Plate 61 (above)
John Everett
Merchant ship, 1918
Pastel on paper
37.7 x 52.9 cm (14 ⅞ x 20 ⅞ in)
PAH6682

Plate 62 (below)
John Everett
Discharging flour, 1918
Gouache on board
38.6 x 51.2 cm (15 ¼ x 20 ⅛ in)
PAH6916

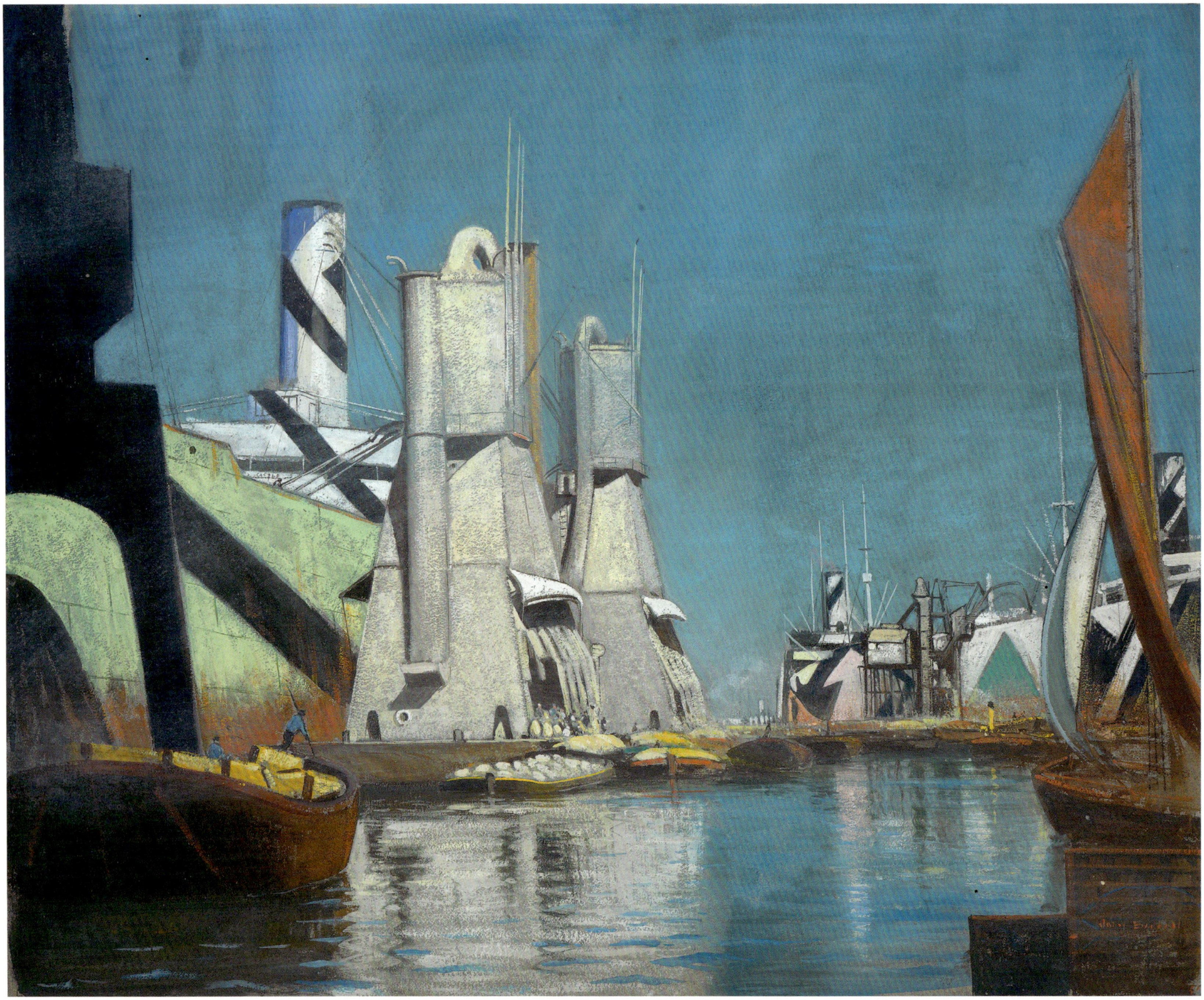

Plate 63
John Everett
The Grain Docks, 1918
Gouache on board
56.3 x 67.7 cm (22 1/8 x 26 5/8 in)
PAH6701

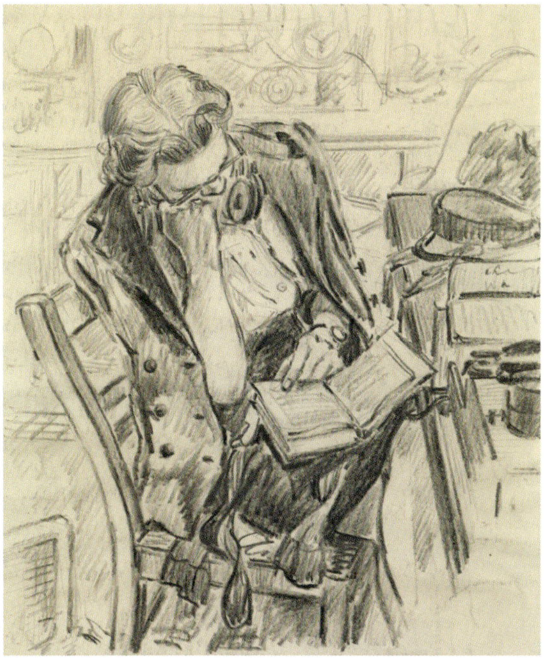

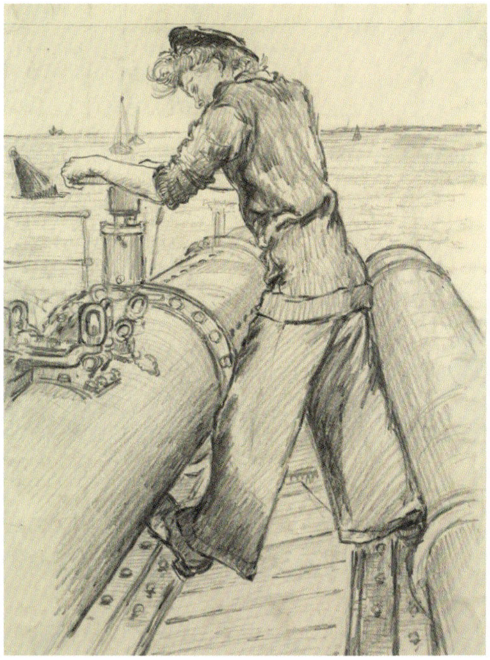

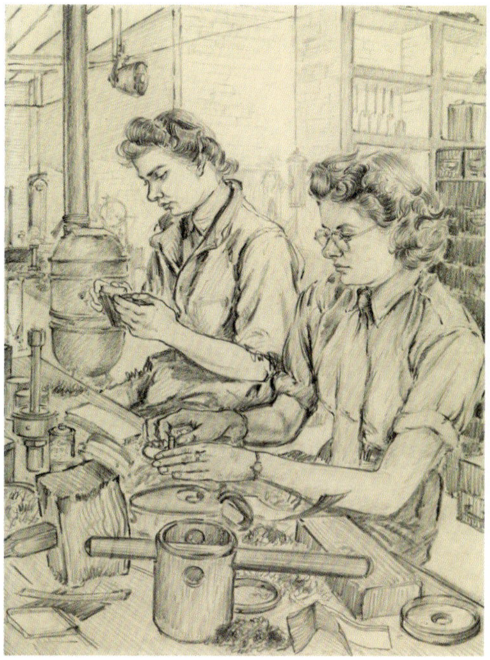

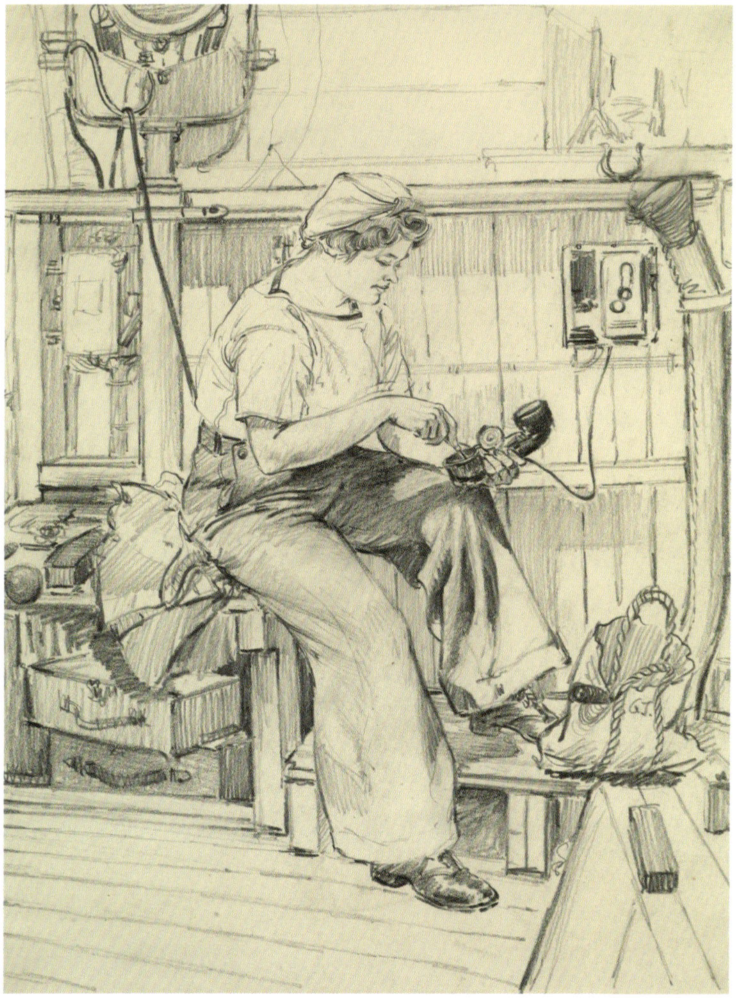

Plate 64 (above, left)
Gladys E. Reed
Night Watch. Wren on duty reading a Book, c.1943–4
Crayon on paper
25.6 x 21.3 cm (10 1/8 x 8 3/8 in)
PAH0088

Plate 65 (above, middle)
Gladys E. Reed
Wren Torpedoman servicing Torpedo Tubes, c.1943–4
Crayon on paper
38.8 x 27.7 cm (15 1/4 x 10 7/8 in)
PAH0090

Plate 66 (above, right)
Gladys E. Reed
Wren Torpedomen at Work on Stripping and Cleaning Parts of Depth Charges, c.1943–4
Crayon on paper
37.3 x 27 cm (14 5/8 x 10 5/8 in)
PAH0091

Plate 67 (right)
Gladys E. Reed
Wren Torpedoman repairing the Sound Power Phones on board one of H.M. Trawlers, c.1943–4
Crayon on paper
37.2 x 27.4 cm (14 5/8 x 10 3/4 in)
PAH0092

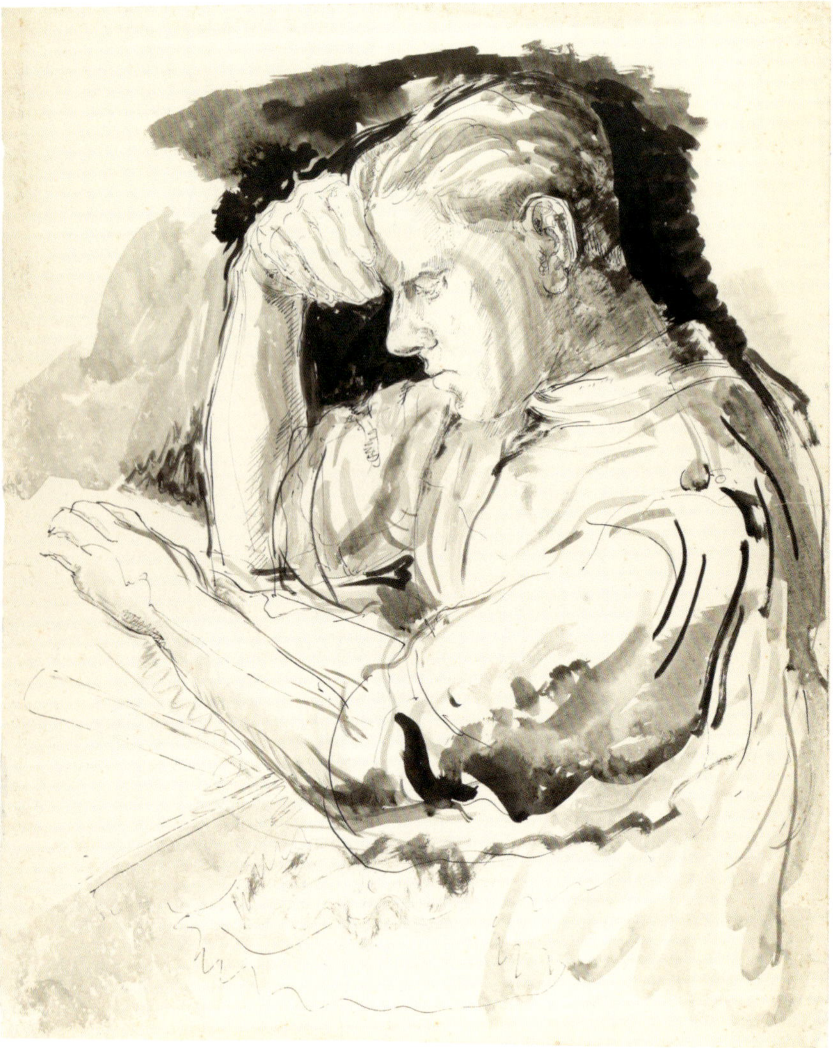

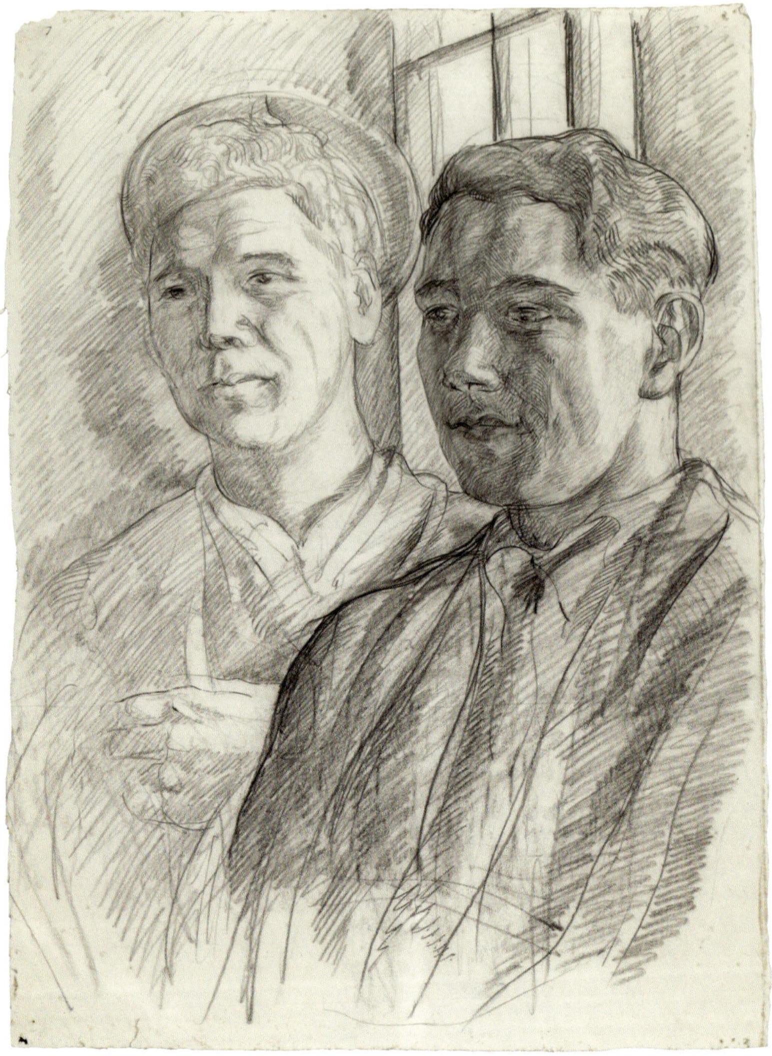

Plate 68 (left)
Rosemary Rutherford
A Doctor Reading, 1943–4
Graphite and wash on paper
60.2 x 48 cm (24 ½ x 18 ⅞ in)
ZBA7307

Plate 69 (right)
Rosemary Rutherford
Portrait of Two Sailors, 1943–4
Graphite on paper
53 x 39 cm (20 ⅞ x 15 ⅜ in)
ZBA7312

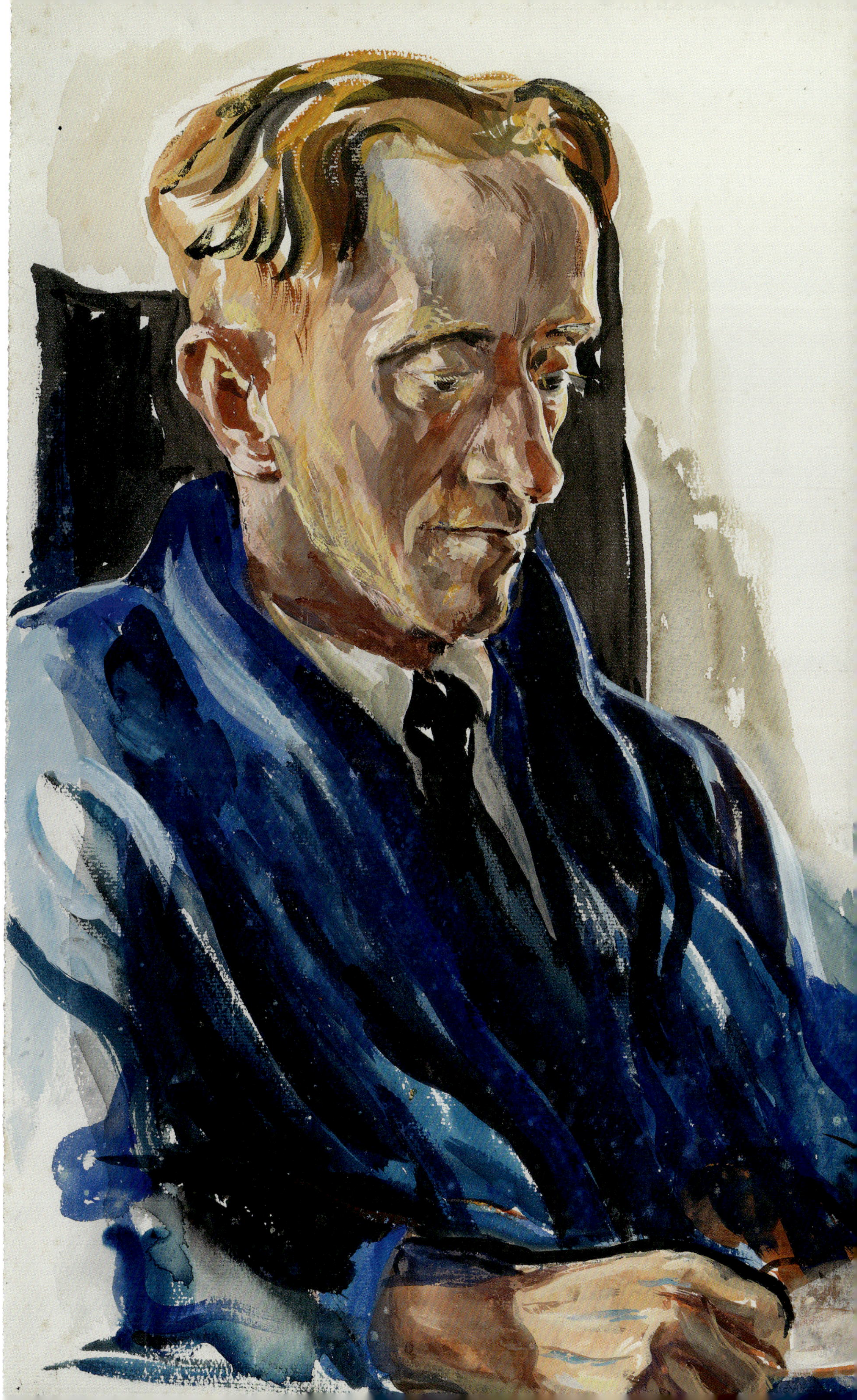

Plate 70
Rosemary Rutherford
'Chippy' – the Carpenter on HMS 'Curacao', 1943–4
Watercolour on paper
44 x 26.5 cm (17 ⅜ x 10 ⅜ in)
ZBA7310

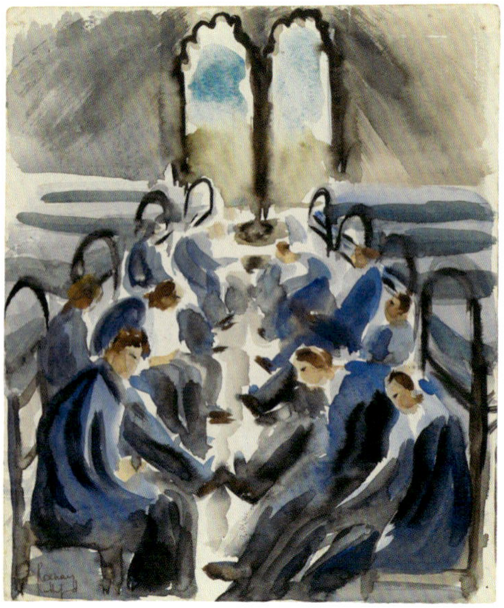

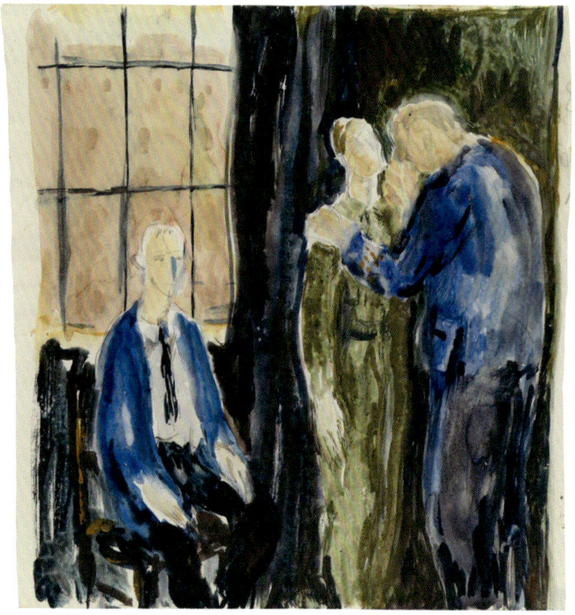

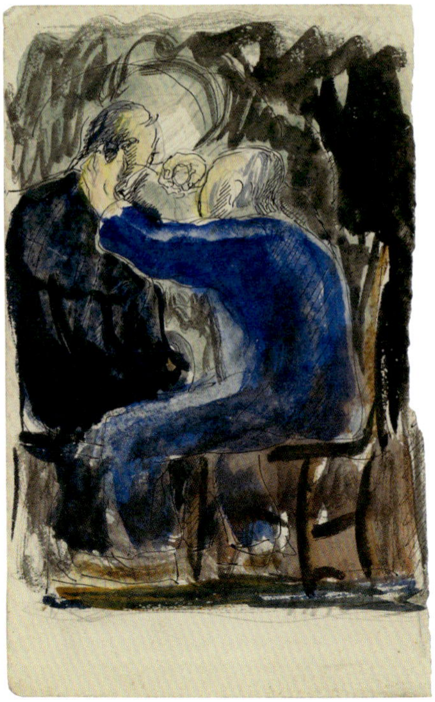

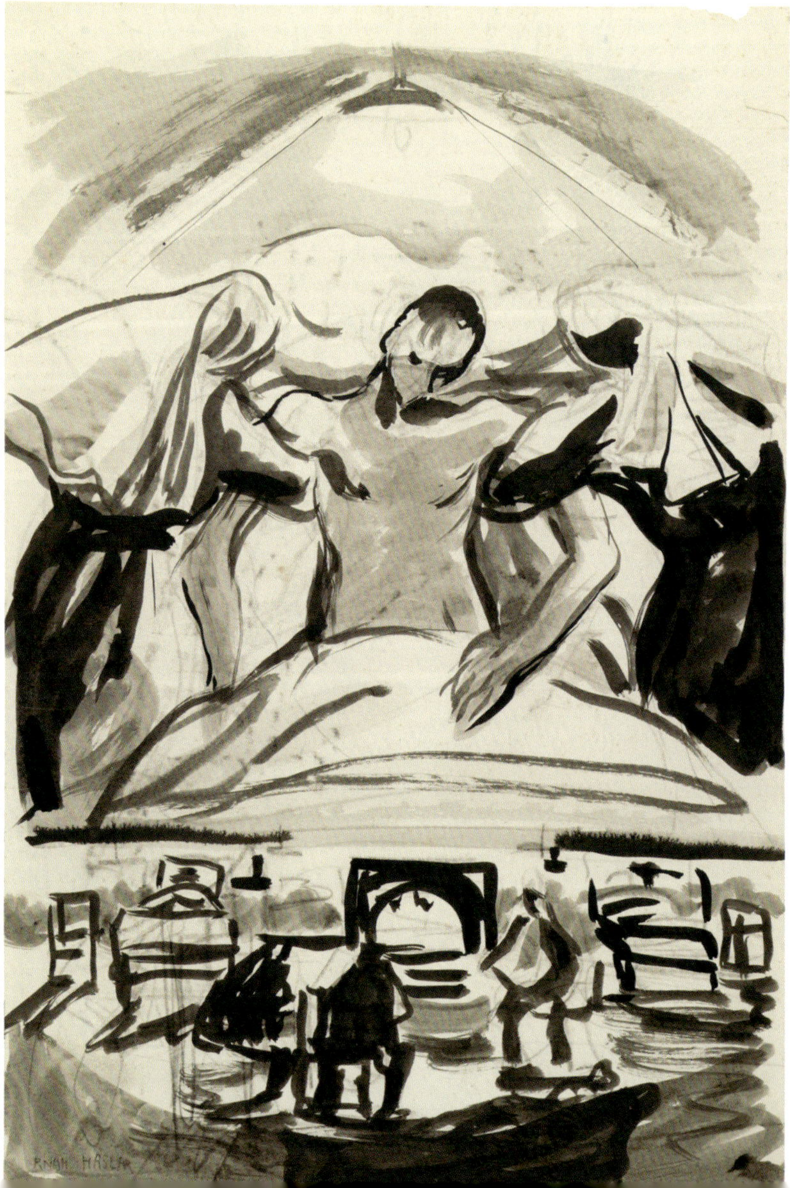

Plate 71 (above, left)
Rosemary Rutherford
A Hospital Ward, 1943–4
Watercolour on paper
27 x 21.5 cm (10 5/8 x 8 1/2 in)
ZBA7303

Plate 72 (above, middle)
Rosemary Rutherford
Eye examination, 1943–4
Watercolour on paper
23.5 x 21 cm (9 1/4 x 8 1/4 in)
ZBA7302

Plate 73 (above, right)
Rosemary Rutherford
Ear examination, 1943–4
Watercolour on paper
18 x 11.5 cm (7 1/8 x 4 1/2 in)
ZBA7301

Plate 74 (below, right)
Rosemary Rutherford
A Convalescing Sailor attended by Two Nurses, 1943–4
Graphite and wash on paper
44 x 29 cm (17 3/8 x 11 3/8 in)
ZBA7305

Plate 75 (opposite)
Rosemary Rutherford
The Operating Theatre, 1943–4
Watercolour, ink and graphite on paper
58.5 x 48 cm (23 x 18 7/8 in)
ZBA7299

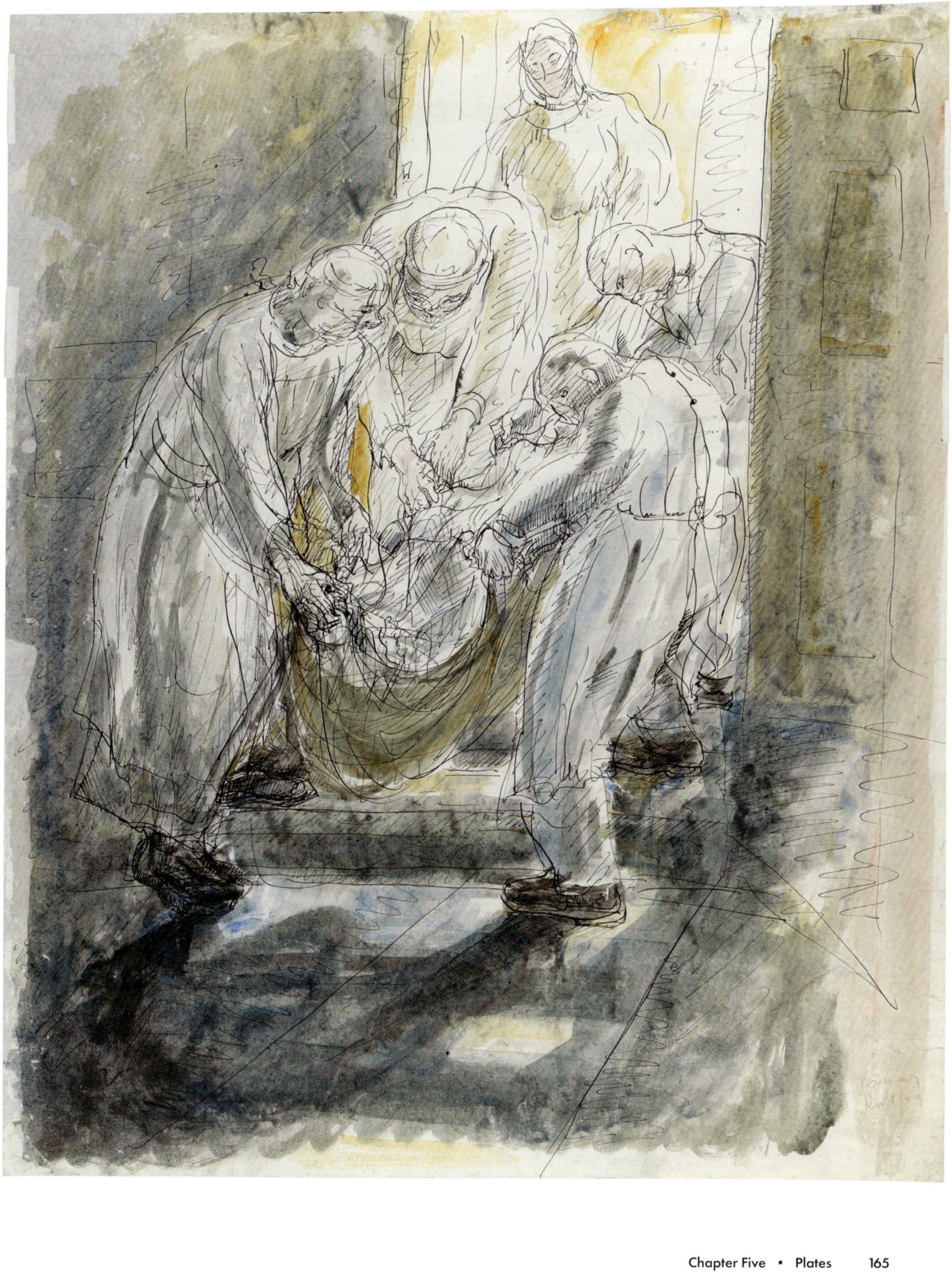

6

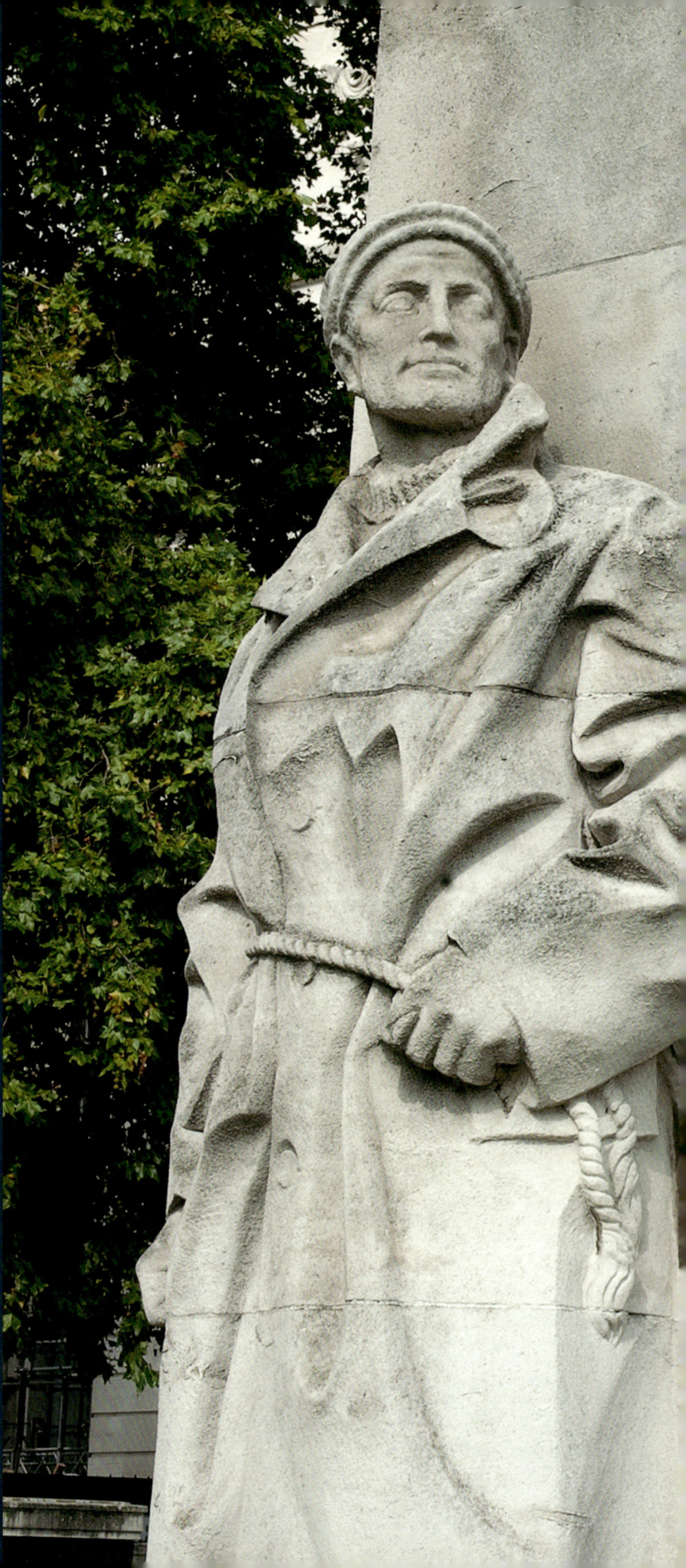

Charles Wheeler
Merchant Marine Memorial,
Tower Hill, London, 1952–5
Portland stone
206 cm (81 in) high
L7779-005

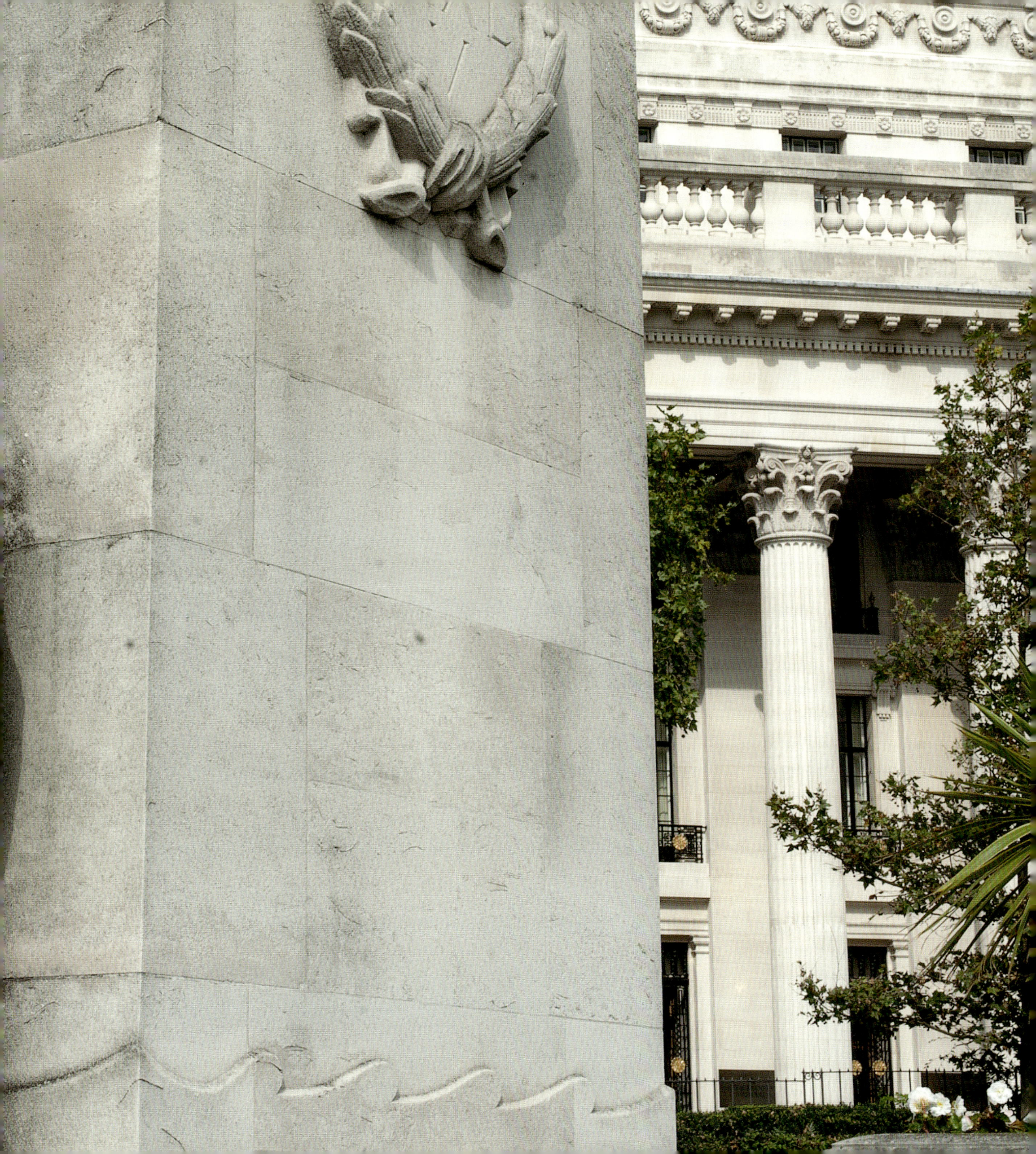

6

Public Memorials, Symbolic Spaces

Christine Riding

'If blood be the price of admiralty, Lord God, we ha' bought it fair!'

Rudyard Kipling, *The Song of the Dead*, 1893

It is often remarked that commemoration was a national preoccupation in Britain after the First World War. Although practical forms of remembrance – schools, hospitals, public gardens, and even art galleries and museums – were favoured by some, the vast majority of examples took the form of a passive, commemorative monument.[1] Indeed, as Geoff Archer has noted, the creation of public and private war memorials after 1918, was 'the greatest single project of public art the country has ever seen'.[2] On issues of style, format and location, there were many who felt that the lead should be taken at national level. While this was not forthcoming from the government, a number of national institutions, the Royal Academy of Arts, the Royal Institute of British Architects and the Victoria and Albert Museum to name a few, responded by setting up committees, staging exhibitions and publishing books.[3]

Sculpture was, by long-standing practice, associated with the commemorative, the architectural and the monumental, and was thus the art form of choice for memorials. It is therefore unavoidably true that the enormous number of war casualties directly translated into extraordinary professional opportunities for sculptors. Some measure of what the post-war period meant in this regard can be gleaned from the pages of *Modern British Sculpture: An Official Record of Some of the Works by Members of the Royal Society of British Sculptors*, published in 1922. Twenty-one sculptures for war memorials are included, by the likes of Charles Sargeant Jagger (1885–1934), Albert Toft, Gilbert Ledward and John Angel.[4]

It is equally true that designs which were highly experimental or abstract (as the word is specifically understood in art terms) were thought 'inappropriate for memorial art'.[5] Of course, that did not exclude abstract forms, such as obelisks or classical columns, the most famous example from the First World War being the Cenotaph in Whitehall, London, by Sir Edwin Lutyens (1869–1944), or the figurative representation of abstract ideas, such as truth, justice and sacrifice, all of which were employed *because* they were universally recognised and understood.[6]

On this level, one might suggest that commemorating the war at sea offered the sculptor greater artistic scope, from the realistic to the purely symbolic, than the Western Front. This is at least arguable given the plethora of pre-existing maritime symbols and motifs, and the long-standing tradition of allegorical and mythological representation associated with seafarers in general and the Royal Navy in particular, of which the preeminent example is the early eighteenth-century decorative scheme of the Painted Hall at what is now the Old Royal Naval College, Greenwich (see Introduction). As we shall see, these maritime allusions and associations were considered as relevant to memorials of the Second World War as to those of the First. In addition, artists well understood that a memorial could draw greater meaning from a specific setting. Consequently, location was often the very first question to be addressed.

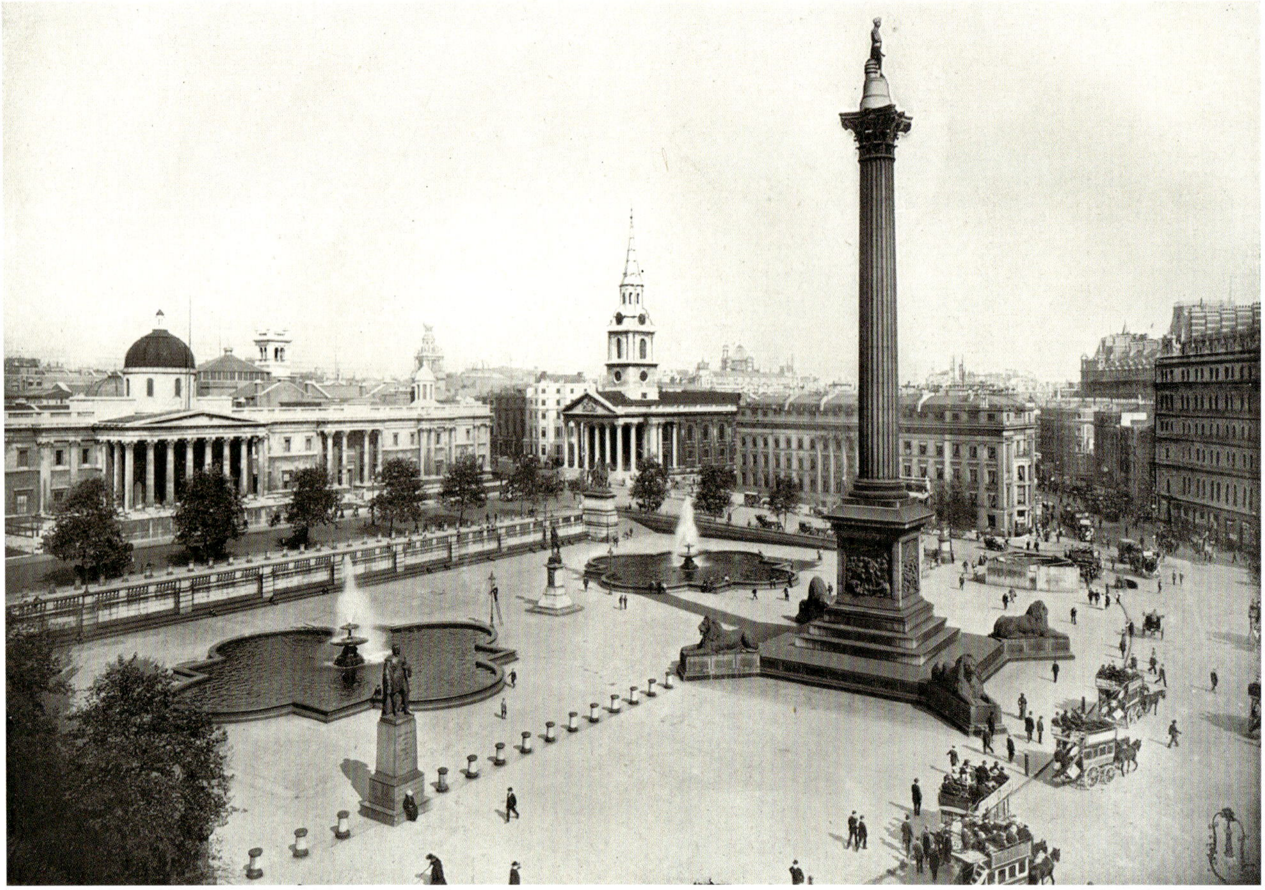

Fig.62
Peter Berthoud
View of Trafalgar Square,
London, 1908

The Power of Place

Concerning First World War burial sites, it was decided that the dead should rest where they had fallen; American casualties were the exception. In Britain the decision was founded on consideration of cost and equality, the result being the now iconic war cemeteries of France and Belgium, overseen by the Imperial (now Commonwealth) War Graves Commission.[7] The sea, of course, poses different commemorative problems: one cannot erect monuments on most of its battles sites and while some of its casualties reached shore graves, formally consigning far greater numbers to the deep has a long tradition, even when not implicit in the manner of their death. To a degree, this issue was addressed, in highly symbolic terms, on Armistice Day in 1920, with the interment of the 'Unknown Warriors' at Westminster Abbey and the Arc de Triomphe in Paris; many countries followed this example.

Some memorials relating to the war at sea were placed on the coast near the scene of tragedy. As examples, the crenulated tower on Mainland, Orkney, commemorates Lord Kitchener, the Secretary of State for War, who perished with almost all the ship's company when HMS *Hampshire* struck a German mine on 5 June 1916. The stone tower on the cliffs of the Mull of Oa, at the southern end of Islay, similarly remembers American soldiers who died after their troopship, *Tuscania*, was torpedoed by a U-boat in 1918.[8]

The wider question, therefore, was not just how but where to commemorate the Royal Navy, the Merchant Navy and the war at sea in general. Trafalgar Square (fig.62) was an obvious focus for the Navy, with the Admiralty Arch and Admiralty House (then the official residence of the First Lord of the Admiralty) in close proximity. During the war, the location's naval significance was underlined by the Navy League organising a service at St Martin-in-the-Fields, the official Admiralty church, for Trafalgar Day (21 October) in 1916, to be followed by the laying of wreaths at Nelson's Column in memory of those killed in the Battle of Jutland.[9] In the event, it was not the ordinary sailors that fought at Jutland but only its admirals who were permanently immortalised there. This continued the focus on naval leadership established when the square was laid out in the 1830s to mark the achievements and ultimate sacrifice of Vice-Admiral Horatio Nelson during the previous 'Great War' against Revolutionary and Napoleonic France (1792–1815).

Trafalgar Square also neatly underlined that the creative process of memorial making – as was the case with all examples discussed here – was a collaborative one between architect and artist. Nelson's Column was designed by the architect William Railton (1800–77) and constructed between 1840 and 1843, with the figure of Nelson by Edward Hodges Baily (1788–1867). The column's pedestal displays bronze bas-reliefs, added in 1849, representing scenes from the Battles of Cape St Vincent, the Nile, Copenhagen and the death of Nelson at Trafalgar (respectively by Musgrave Watson, William F. Woodington, John Ternouth and John Edward Carew). In all four panels the other naval officers, sailors and marines take a supporting role around the central figure of Nelson, in line with contemporary history paintings of their period.[10] The bronze lions *couchant* by Sir Edwin Landseer were installed in 1867.

The granting of a national memorial to Admiral Lord Jellicoe by Parliament after his death on 19 November 1935 was thus highly appropriate, given his position as Commander-in-Chief of the Grand Fleet in 1914–16. Combining this with one to his successor in the role, Admiral Lord Beatty, was not without controversy, and violently opposed by Jellicoe's family and supporters.[11] Over and above any personal rivalries or animosities, the tense juxtaposition of Trafalgar and Jutland, for the public at least, cannot have gone unrecognised, even in the mid-1930s. Notwithstanding that Jutland was the Navy's most significant fleet action since Trafalgar, it is possible that the decision to introduce the 1916 battle into such a powerfully symbolic space was, in part, to counter any lingering disputes or disappointments surrounding it.

The completed memorial is a significant yet comparatively modest intervention, given the scale of the site, and involved the remodelling by Lutyens of the two large-scale fountains from 1845 (designed by Sir Charles Barry) with new sculpture groups in bronze of mermaids, Tritons and dolphins. These were executed by Charles Wheeler (1892–1974) and William McMillan (1887–1977) who also, respectively, provided the bronze portrait busts of Jellicoe and Beatty that were placed on stone plinths on the north side of the square. The installation was delayed by the outbreak of the Second World War and was finally unveiled on Trafalgar Day in 1948.

If Trafalgar Square broadly remained a place of commemoration for high-ranking naval officers, where would the Navy as a whole be remembered? After 1918, the Naval Memorials Committee decided that members of the service who had died at sea with no known grave were to be commemorated on three coastal sites at or near the naval manning ports of Chatham, Portsmouth and Plymouth: those who sailed from each were named there, and at Plymouth sailors from Australia and South Africa were also included. The Committee recommended that the memorials should be identical, with their main feature to be an obelisk: this was an ancient form frequently used for memorials in Britain from the eighteenth century onwards, and also much favoured by naval opinion because the structure could serve as a leading mark for shipping.[12] Sir Robert Lorimer (1864–1929), the Scottish architect famed for his work in the Baronial style, designed the obelisks as tall, tapering pylons, stepped at the apex. Sculptural details were provided in stone, bronze and copper by Henry Poole (1873–1928). Perhaps intentionally, the base of the columns includes four (stone) lions in a similar pose and position as those by Landseer in Trafalgar Square. All three memorials were unveiled during 1924.

Other more challenging decisions concerned sites commemorating those elements of the war that were new or previously unacknowledged, namely the Royal Navy's submarine service and the Merchant Navy. In the event, the first completed national monument relating specifically to the war at sea was the National Submarine War Memorial in 1922 (fig.63). Located on the Thames Embankment in London, it is composed of a granite plinth by the architect Arthur Heron Ryan-Tenison, which is set into the Embankment wall on the riverside, with a large central bronze bas-relief and other sculptural details by Frederick Brook Hitch (1897–1957).

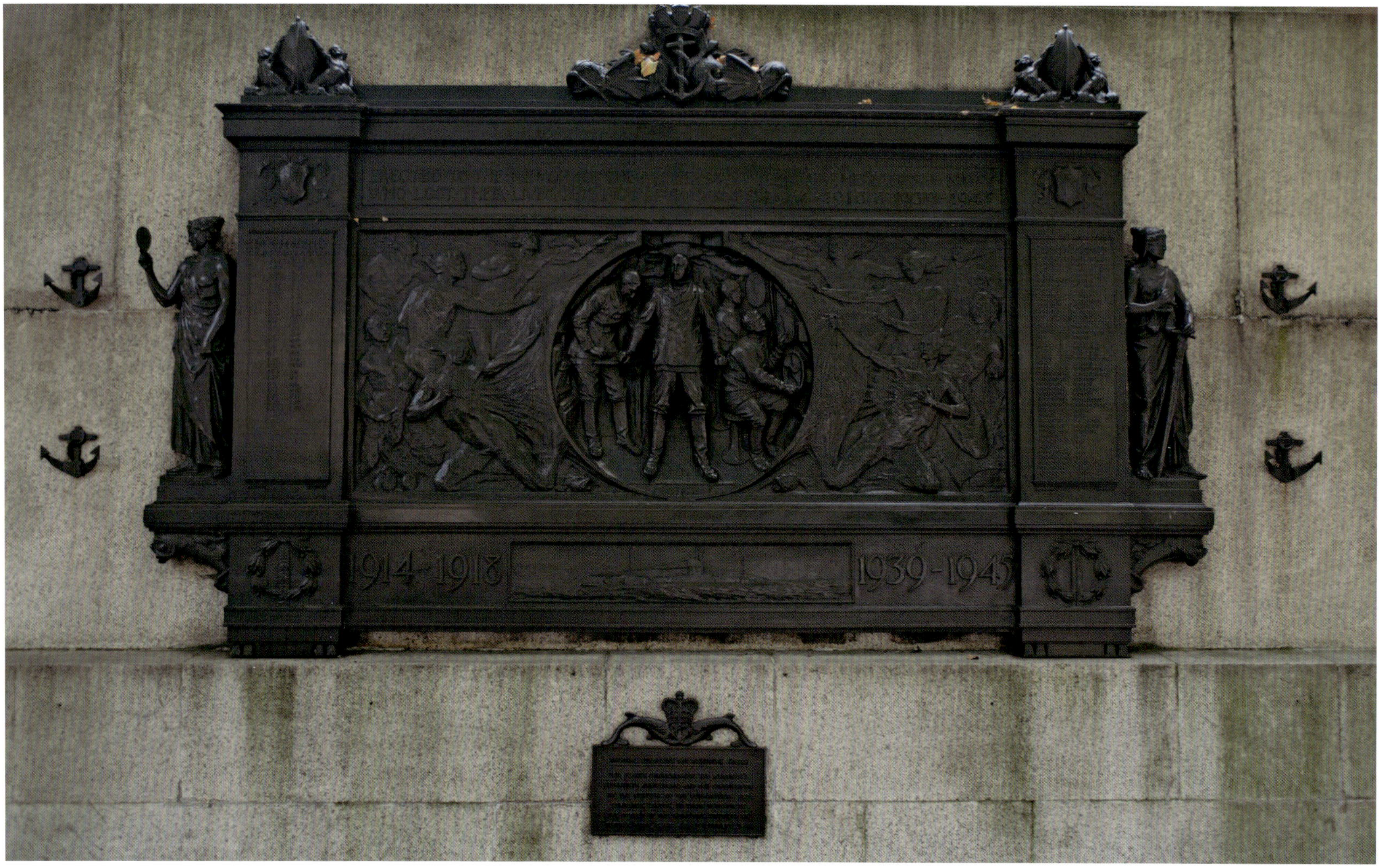

Lutyens' initial idea for the location of a memorial to the merchant service also focused on the Embankment near Temple Gardens, perhaps because he too considered a Thames-side site as wholly appropriate to seafarers. That this idea did not materialise may simply have resulted from the submariners having got there first. However, Tim Skelton and Gerald Gliddon have argued that it was the Royal Fine Art Commission (RFAC) that thwarted the plan, much to the annoyance of Lutyens (who was a RFAC member). The Commissioners suggested an alternative location downriver at Tower Hill, an area 'devoted to sea-going occupations' and, in their estimation, highly suitable to the lower social status of merchant seamen and the lesser standing of the merchant marine, in comparison to that of the Royal Navy.[13]

In response, Lutyens designed a pavilion in the shape of a long, vaulted corridor of Portland stone – an imposing structure that draws parallels with his larger-scale shelters in British cemeteries of the Western Front – with sculptural work by Sir William Reid Dick (1879–1961).[14] The bronze plaques are engraved with the names of some 12,000 individuals, each one positioned under the ship in which they served (a convention also employed on the Royal Naval monuments). Despite the evident awkwardness of the site, Lutyens' memorial displays grandeur and dignity. This was no doubt deliberate given his sensitivity towards issues of equality and inclusiveness, and his conviction that all war cemeteries and memorials, no matter where located, should be universal and non-denominational. The memorial was unveiled in December 1928, which by chance or design was also the year in which the appointment of the Prince of Wales as 'Master of the Merchant Navy and Fishing Fleets' (in February) had, de facto, finally established 'Merchant Navy' itself as the formal title of the British merchant fleet.

There is an assumption today that the overwhelming energy behind monument building after the First World War had exhausted itself by the end of the Second. Hence the relative paucity of monuments devoted specifically to the 1939–45 conflict. Given the

Fig.63
The National Submarine War Memorial, 1922, Embankment, London
L7780-003

sheer volume of existing memorials, more practical issues may well have had a bearing, as well as more subjective concerns that were raised in various quarters about artistic merit.

Of greater influence was the chronological proximity and devastating nature of the two conflicts which, to quote Jay Winter, resulted in the widely held view that 'the dead [...] formed one community of fallen'.[15] Lutyens was certainly of this opinion. In correspondence with Sir Fabian Ware about new war graves, he stated, 'keep the same headstones, the same monuments, i.e. extend the existing cemeteries where possible [...] In a hundred years time 1914 and 1939 will be all part of the one war. It is certainly the same sacrifice for the same cause.'[16]

The national memorials of the Second World War described here were thus extensions to those of the First (as were more local ones, which often simply had 1939–45 inscriptions added). Sir Edward Maufe (1883–1974), who served in the Royal Naval Volunteer Reserve in 1914–15, was chief architect for the Imperial War Graves Commission in the UK, and therefore responsible for the extensions to Lorimer's memorials at Chatham, Portsmouth and Plymouth, and to that by Lutyens at Tower Hill. Maufe's designs for the naval memorials were all broadly similar in format, following the example of the existing monuments, and comprised a Garden of Remembrance with a long perimeter wall displaying bronze plaques listing names, terminating with domed pavilions at each end. The stone figures of naval officers and ratings, and other sculptural motifs, were provided by Wheeler, McMillan and, in addition at Portsmouth, Esmond Burton (*c.*1886–1964). The Duke of Edinburgh, a Commander in the Royal Navy during the war, unveiled the Chatham memorial in October 1952, with ceremonies at Portsmouth and Plymouth following in April 1953 and May 1954 respectively.

The men and women of the Merchant Navy, fishing fleets and the lighthouse and pilot services, who have (as the inscription confirmed) 'no grave but the sea', were commemorated at Tower Hill.[17] Here the new memorial extends beyond Lutyens' pavilion and takes the form of a long platform with obelisks, leading to a sunken Garden of Remembrance with a curved perimeter wall, on which are bronze panels recording 23,765 names. The carved figures of an officer and a rating positioned in front of the obelisks, a series of seven large-scale reliefs representing the 'Seven Seas', and other carved Merchant Navy and nautical motifs are by Wheeler.

The obvious result of this extension is that it absorbed the First World War memorial and substantially increased the physical area and the visual impact of the commemorative site, thus giving it greater parity with those created for the Navy. It was unveiled on 5 November 1955, attended by some 16,000 relatives and comrades, with buglers of the Royal Marines sounding 'The Last Post'.[18] The dedication ceremony ended with the sound of a ship's siren from the nearby Pool of London.

Between Tradition and Modernity

Other than the national memorials, the vast majority of First World War monuments involving figurative sculpture commemorate the casualties of the Western Front but some are more inclusive. While Jagger's famous *Soldier Reading a Letter* dominates the Great Western Railway War Memorial (1921–2) at Paddington Station, the Navy, Merchant Navy and Air Force are represented through the carved motifs of a fouled anchor and an eagle. Other examples incorporate a sailor figure or representations of ships, submarines and so on, thus visually commemorating the war at sea, such as the memorial of 1927 by Sydney and Vincent March, located in The Diamond, Londonderry, which includes a sailor arriving hurriedly on to the deck of a ship while pulling on his oilskin.[19] And in Exeter, John Angel (1881–1960) created a memorial that has a central pedestal with a soldier, a sailor (seated on the miniaturised ship), a VAD nurse in uniform and, unusually, a prisoner of war.[20] Allegorical representations of the Navy also exist. Birmingham's Hall

Fig.64
Albert Toft
Navy, 1925
Hall of Memory, Birmingham
Cast bronze
Approx. 140 cm (55 ⅛ in) high

of Memory (1925), an impressive domed Portland stone octagon in Centenary Square, has four figures – modern variations on the theme of Michelangelo's tomb sculptures – by Albert Toft (1862–1949), all on external plinths, representing the Army, Navy (fig.64), Air Force and women's services.[21]

The national memorials associated with the war at sea brought together a number of standard commemorative themes, as well as specifically maritime ones. Henry Poole's work on the Royal Navy memorials for the First World War, for example, included a cluster of different traditional maritime and naval forms at the apex, comprising the prows of four ships situated below female figures representing the four winds, with the latter supporting a sphere signifying the world.

In this context, the near-contemporary National Submarine War Memorial is additionally noteworthy in combining allegorical and realistic representations in a single design (fig.63). The main part shows the interior of a submarine's control room, in cross section, with the central figure of a captain flanked by three submariners at work. Unusual for the early 1920s, such on-board representations were far more common during the 1940s and were often similarly framed within a circular field to suggest both the submarine's cylindrical body and the confined interior space (see Chapter 3: Above and Below Deck). In the memorial, the captain's pose and expression suggest his alertness to the dangers lurking outside. Rather than being represented by enemy ships or submarines, or the explosions of mines and torpedoes, these are alluded to by a group of naked figures, perhaps representative of the Elements, or of Nereids and Tritons, the last two being mythological creatures associated with the classical god of the sea, Poseidon (or Neptune). These figures surround the submarine, actively trying to disrupt or disable it with large fishing nets. Thus the submariners are represented as threatened by external forces, rather than posing a threat themselves.[22] Below this scene, a further bas-relief shows a surfaced submarine in profile. To left and right, the main panel is supported by conventional female figures, in the classical style, representing Peace and Victory. Finally, the granite plinth sports bronze hooks in the form of anchors, on which commemorative wreaths are hung annually.

This complex interplay between the allegorical, the mythological and the contemporary not only acts as a summary of the different components employed in war memorials across the country, but (appropriately enough) complements the relief representations of contemporary medal design – sculptures in miniature – which often combined myth and allegory with contemporary scenes and portraiture. Two sculptors discussed here, William McMillan and Charles Wheeler, were actively engaged in this demanding art form, producing designs for commemorative and service medals during and after the First World War.[23] By the time they were commissioned in November 1936 to participate in the Jellicoe and Beatty memorials project (1937–48), they were established artists with reputations for public and architectural sculpture.[24]

The initial discussions around the redevelopment of Trafalgar Square, and the iconography to be employed, made the assumption that more statues would be installed. The RFAC even suggested returning to this 'commonplace solution', well after the commission had begun, in 1938. However, the notion was given short shrift by Sir Philip Sassoon, First Commissioner of Works, who stated – no doubt responding to the proliferation of figurative memorials in Britain during the 1920s and early 1930s – that everyone was 'tired of statues of men in uniform that offer no scope to the artist's imagination and skill'.[25] This may well explain why one part of the commission, the bronze portraits of Jellicoe and Beatty in contemporary naval uniform, were executed as life-size busts (plates 76 and 77) and given a discreet location against the north wall of the square.

The sculptor Sir William Reid Dick suggested fountain memorials, an idea endorsed by the Admiralty, and the RFAC opted for group compositions within the fountain basins. These, it was proposed, would be designed employing 'Baroque themes', which

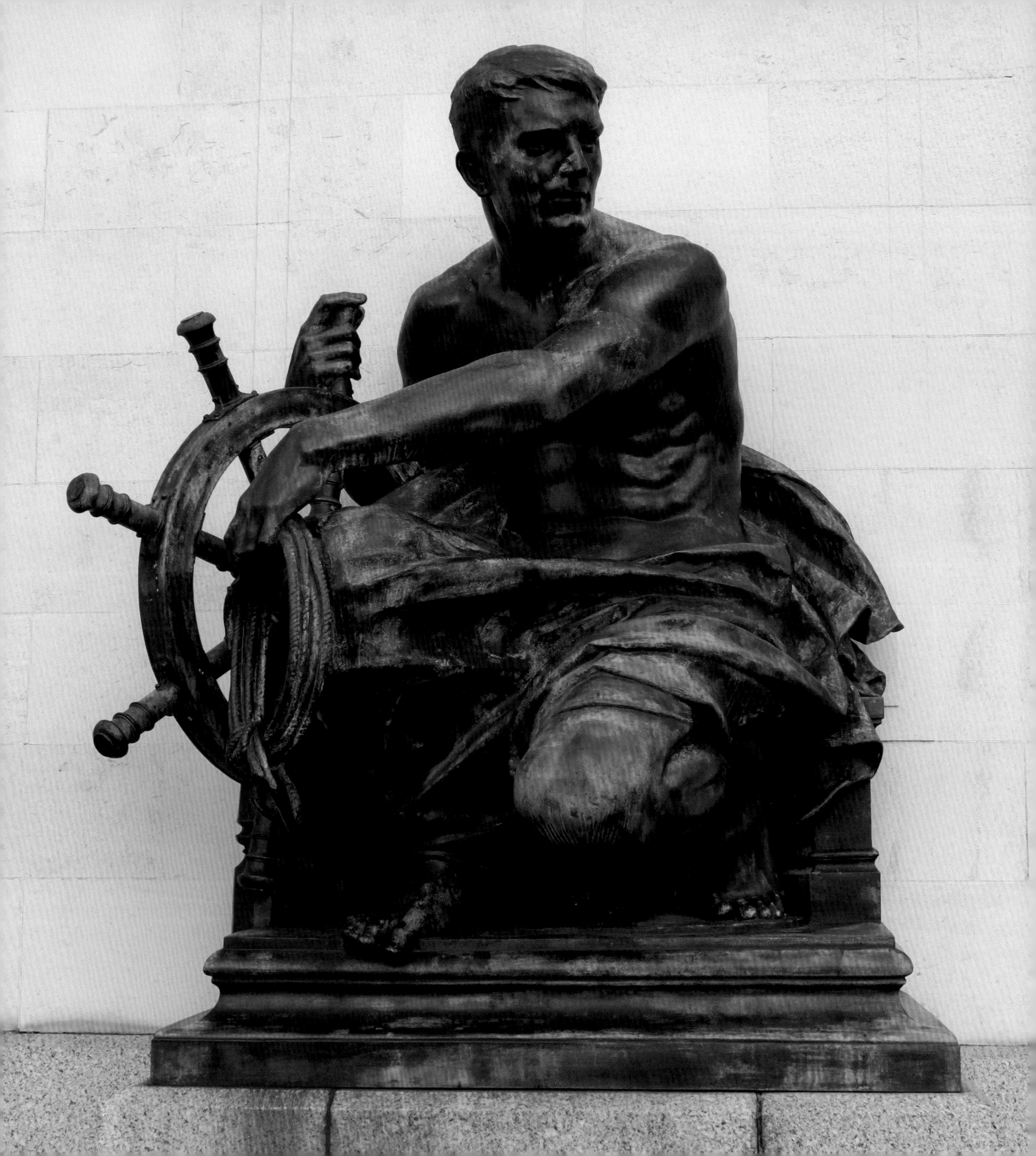

Fig.65
Charles Wheeler
The Royal Naval Memorial,
Second World War extension,
1946–52, Chatham

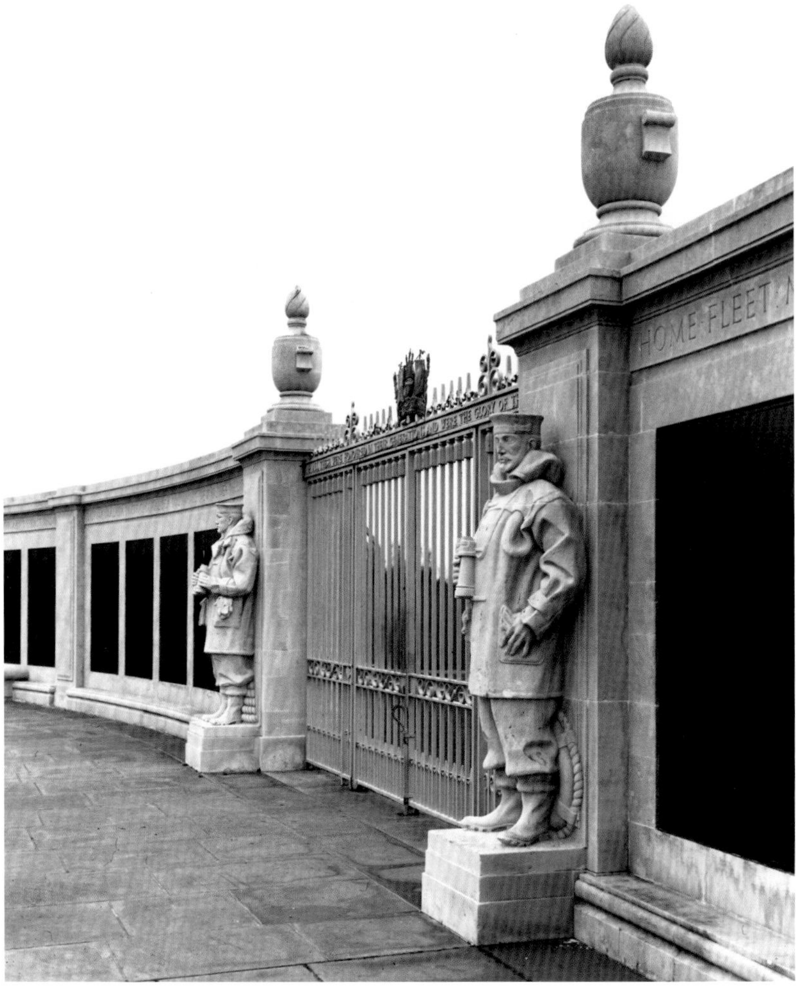

were 'justified by the site and plastic nature of the composition' and 'would give a note of variety and liveliness to Trafalgar Square as a whole, in pleasing contrast to the many vertical features which dominate'.[26] Given these comments, it is unsurprising that Lutyens' earlier suggestion of two cenotaph pylons was rejected.

The remit for the fountain sculptures, in particular the reference to 'Baroque themes', and the focus on designs, as requested by the Admiralty, of a 'sufficiently nautical character' (by which was meant 'tritons or something of the kind' and 'dolphins etc.'), certainly played to Wheeler and McMillan's strengths.[27] As students, they had been contemporaries at the Royal College of Art (RCA) at a time when the college was promoting Arts and Crafts principles and the New Sculpture. The college also promoted the in-depth study of ancient, medieval and Renaissance art, in particular carved and cast reliefs, examples of which could be found in the collections of the British Museum, the Victoria and Albert Museum and the Royal Academy, which has Michelangelo's celebrated marble *Taddei Tondo (The Virgin and Child with the Infant St John)* of *c.*1504–5. Appropriate baroque artworks were also near at hand, preeminent among which was Bernini's sculptural group, *Neptune and Triton* (1622–3), on exhibition at the Royal Academy in 1938 and subsequently acquired by the Victoria and Albert Museum in 1951. Given the broad interest in baroque art at the time, there were important contemporary sculptors who had drawn inspiration from this tradition. They included the Swede, Carl Milles (1875–1955), whose work had been displayed at the Tate Gallery in 1927.[28] Two projects by him that would have been of particular relevance here were the *Tritons* fountain (*c.*1920–25) in Stockholm and *Poseidon* fountain (*c.*1927) in Gothenburg, both of which, in focusing on mythological sea creatures, made allusions to Sweden's maritime heritage.

The finished groups (plates 78–81) by Wheeler and McMillan are a distillation of such past and present influences but interpreted from a highly individual perspective. Both artists designed a Triton and a mermaid group, Wheeler's situated in the fountain on the west side and McMillan's on the east. Each group is fluid, dynamic and playful, in the spirit of baroque theatricality but with the smooth surfaces and pared-down detailing associated with the modern 'archaising' style. That both artists were sensitive to the integration of the sculptures into their watery setting is underlined by Wheeler's comment in his memoirs that they had 'spent many hours experimenting with different nozzles in order to get the jets of water [projecting from the figures] to our liking'. In Wheeler's opinion, the Jellicoe and Beatty memorial fountains succeeded because both artists worked 'sympathetically together'.[29]

He and McMillan collaborated again during the 1950s on the naval memorial extensions at Chatham, Portsmouth and Plymouth. In contrast to Trafalgar Square, the main elements of the commission were not mythological and marine creatures (although these are represented at all sites) but four over-life-size figures in contemporary dress: two ratings by Wheeler (fig.65, plate 82) and a commando and a marine by McMillan, collectively representing 'The Royal Navy on the Alert'. The inspiration behind

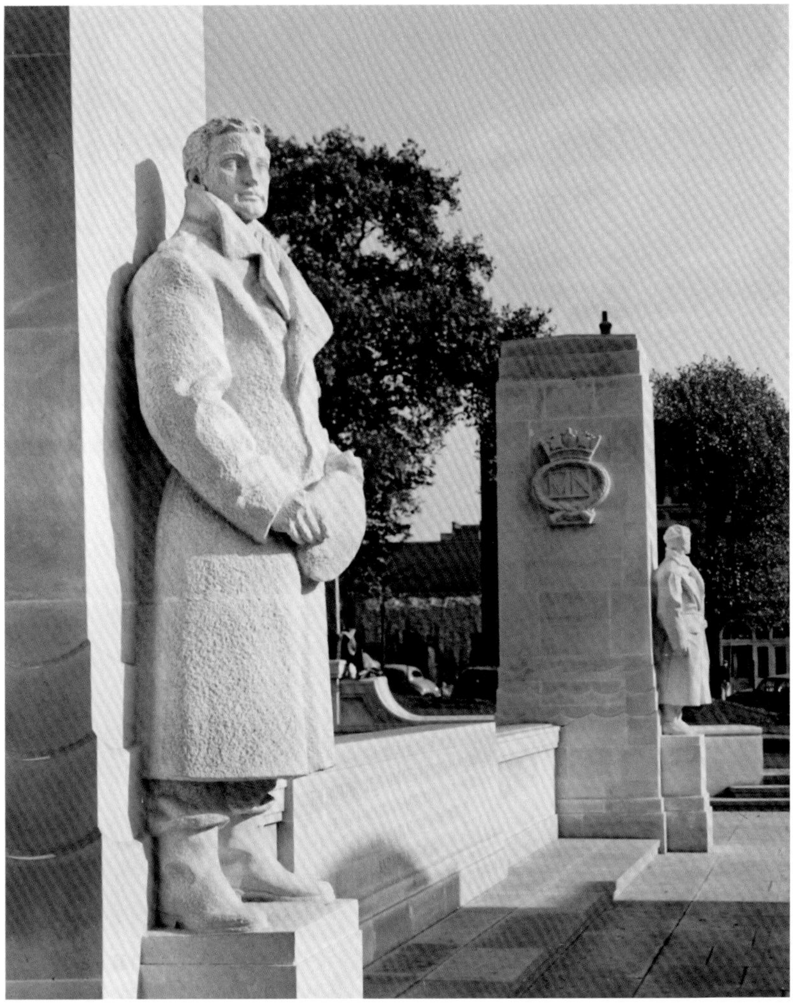

Fig.66
Charles Wheeler
The Merchant Marine Memorial,
Second World War extension, 1952–5,
Tower Hill, London

these figures came in part from First World War memorials, above all the imposing sentinel figures by Jagger and Gilbert Ledward (1888–1960).[30] A more recent exemplar was Ledward's Second World War memorial dedicated to 'the Submarine Service, Commandos, Airborne Forces and Special Air Service', which was unveiled at Westminster Abbey by Sir Winston Churchill in May 1948. This includes three bronze figures – submariner, commando and parachutist – placed in stone niches. As with Wheeler's near-contemporary naval figures, the submariner is shown on watch holding binoculars.[31]

The initial intention was to cast the naval memorial sculptures in bronze. In the event, concerns around mounting costs meant that they were carved in Portland stone. While this may seem a relatively minor change, the aesthetic advantages and disadvantages of bronze and stone were widely discussed in the art world, in part because of the need to represent contemporary uniforms. In *War Memorials*, published in 1946, Arnold Whittick noted that 'One of the chief difficulties [...] in making effective statues of soldiers, sailors and airmen is to treat the uniform in an artistic manner and in sculptural terms.' 'Bronze,' he continues, 'generally lends itself to more realistic treatment than stone, and because of this I think it is more of a handicap to artistic treatment. The comparative intractability of stone is an aid rather than a handicap in this matter.' Whittick pointed to the example of 'early Egyptian' and 'early Greek sculptures' as a guide to the paring down of modern details. His comments are certainly borne out when one compares the meticulous representation of Jellicoe's and Beatty's features and uniforms in the Trafalgar Square busts and the relative minimalism of the naval figures at Chatham, with the stone surface playing (to use Whittick's words) 'a bigger part in the effect'.[32] While acknowledging that these are not portraits of particular individuals but representations of 'everymen', there is enough contemporary detail for the viewer to discern modern binoculars, machine guns, the toggles of a duffle coat or the texture of knitted scarves and gloves protruding from a pocket (see Chapter 5: Merchant Navy Comforts).

Wheeler repeated this approach in his sculptures of an officer and a seaman for the Merchant Marine Memorial at Tower Hill (fig.66, plates 83 and 84). Here too, the figures stand watch, at once contemporary and universal, carved in Portland stone. In fact, Wheeler reduced the detail still further, allowing the pitted stone surface to suggest the texture of the greatcoats, knitted hats and other garments. He seems also to have given the figures more softness and movement in the folds of the garments and in the turn of the sailors' heads. Their quiet dignity presents a striking contrast to the other major element by Wheeler on the site, a series of carved relief panels representing the 'Seven Seas' (fig.67, plates 85–89). Here Wheeler gave full rein to his imaginative powers and skill as a carver. While the compositions and subject matter relate to the Triton and mermaid groups in Trafalgar Square, they far exceed them in range, complexity and ambition. Indeed, the 'Seven Seas' represents a roll-call of deities, marine creatures and motifs,

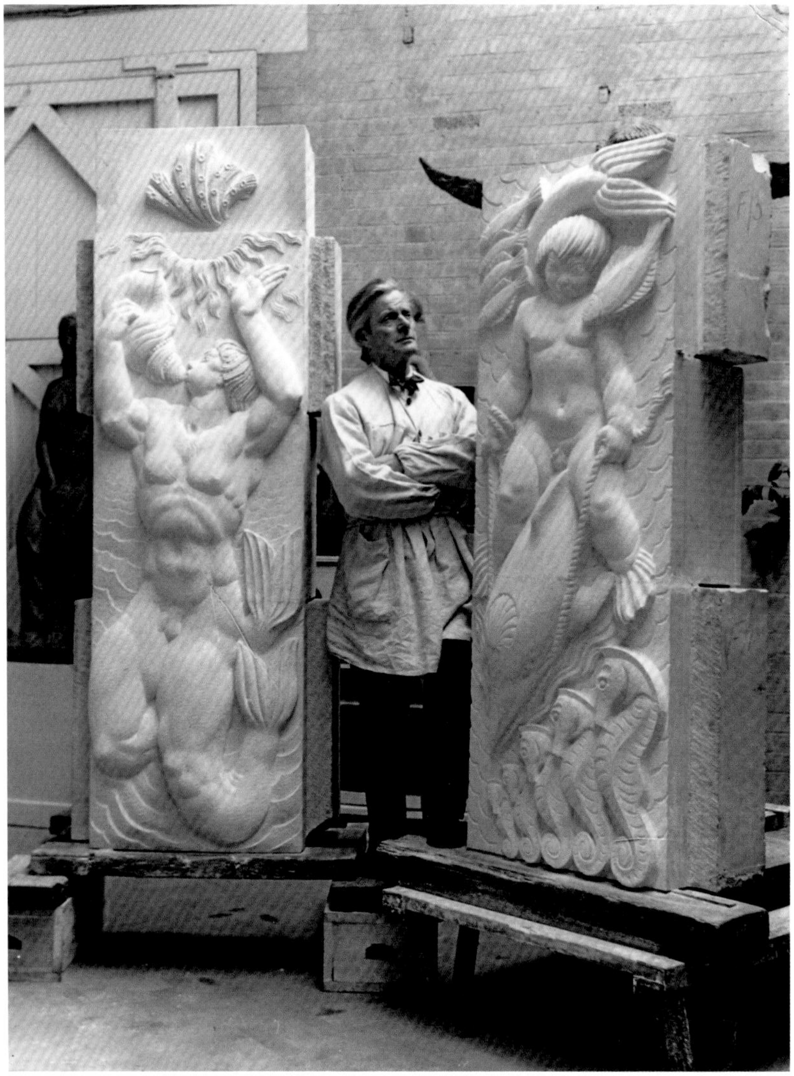

Fig.67
Charles Wheeler in his studio with 'Triton' and 'Merchild' panels, 1955

including Triton, Venus (Aphrodite), Neptune, Zephyr, a mermaid and merchild, shells and fish, dolphins and seahorses.

While the art-historical references are too diverse and wide ranging to be fully explored here, one artist from whom Wheeler seems to have developed ideas is Botticelli, whose *Birth of Venus* (Uffizi, Florence, *c.*1486), with its relationship to the sea, finds echoes in the *Zephyr* and *Venus* panels (plate 87): it is also worth noting here that Wheeler had previously executed a series of Aphrodite figures, one of which was acquired by the Tate Gallery in 1943. The boldness of Wheeler's figuration also chimes with that of William Blake (1757–1827), whose reputation was high during and after the First World War. This was primarily through the staging of a number of exhibitions devoted to his works, from 1913 to 1947, and well-publicised sales and acquisitions for public collections, such as the sale of Blake's 102 illustrations to Dante's *Divine Comedy* in 1918–19, and the donation of nine 'Large Colour Prints' to the Tate Gallery in 1939 (of which Wheeler was appointed a trustee in 1942).[33] As the art historian Colin Trodd has observed, Blake's 'noble, simple, sincerity' was appreciated by artists and critics alike as a bridge between the Gothic and Renaissance traditions (with various commentaries linking him to Giotto, Fra Angelico and Michelangelo) and twentieth-century art.[34]

But perhaps the key to understanding the meaning and relevance of the 'Seven Seas' panels, both to the artist and to the memorial project, comes via a near-contemporary sculpture that Wheeler described as 'a work of great subtlety, originality and charm'.[35] This was Gilbert Ledward's *Monolith* (1936), a piece acquired by the Tate Gallery that also featured in Whittick's *War Memorials*, alongside other historic and contemporary examples demonstrating 'rhythmical unity in sculpture'.[36] Importantly, Ledward was directly responding to the highly influential 1934 publication, *Stones of Rimini* by Adrian Stokes, in which the 'Stones' of the title were the fifteenth-century relief carvings at the Tempio Malatestiano in Rimini by Agostino di Duccio.[37] Both Stokes' analysis and the accompanying photographic illustrations foreground the rhythmic nature of the Italian artist's style, the inventiveness of the compositions and the playful sensuousness of the subject matter, largely drawn from mythology, astrology and the arts. In fact, his promotion in *Stones of Rimini* of direct carving was to have a profound impact on British sculptors who, like Wheeler, worked in that manner.[38]

Beyond these points of artistic interest, Stokes made a further allusion that has direct relevance to the Merchant Navy memorial's location at Tower Hill and the occupations of those it commemorates. In a chapter called 'Stone and Water', he describes stonework as 'the sea [...] petrified', and later how 'in Quattro Cento carving [...] marine decoratives [*sic*], principally in the shape of dolphins, attained a paramount exuberance'. Thus, in his opinion, Duccio's sculptures 'reflect, and even concentrate, the common Mediterranean fantasies of stone and water'. 'Even the port of London,' he continues:

has its Mediterranean aspect, where at Wapping or Limehouse the stout warehouses are steeped in the river. The Genoa-like passages between them are narrow and tall; at their ends you emerge into the light and into the open, discover an array of steps, or a quay that locks the river in a seething stone or brick embrace. The stones retain an equal warmth if the sun is out, an equal radiance that contrasts with the polyp-like elongations and contractions of the water's glassiness.

'Of such sort,' he concludes, 'is the scenery of maritime commerce.'[39]

On one level, the 'Seven Seas' panels simply express (to quote Catherine Moriarty) the artist's 'creative pleasure in marine forms'.[40] On another, they are a commemoration of civilians, represented by Wheeler's officer and seaman, who died 'devoted to sea-going occupations' in the two World Wars. Combined with the carved service badges located nearby, sporting the Admiralty crown and 'MN' monogram, these diverse yet connected art forms are both original and ambitious in artistic terms and powerful allusions to the growing status and prestige of the Merchant Navy.

Museums as Memorials

As previously noted, some First World War memorials took the form of public museums and art galleries. The Aberdeen Art Gallery, for example, was extended to incorporate a 'Memorial Court' and war memorial; in Kirkcaldy, Fife, the public memorial comprised a new art gallery and museum, a long dedicatory wall and cenotaph at its centre, and a public garden.[41] In March 1917, the War Cabinet gave formal approval for the foundation of the National War Museum, which from January 1918 was renamed the Imperial War Museum (IWM). The National War Museum Committee (NWMC) included representatives of the Admiralty, War Office and Ministry of Munitions. Concerning the new museum, the Committee agreed 'that the very heart and focus of the building should be of a memorial character'. This, it was suggested, 'might take the form of a Hall of Honour as rich and beautiful in character as artists can devise, and adjacent to it a Gallery devoted to the separate memorials of the Navy and the Army by ships, regiments and contingents'. The Director General, Sir Martin Conway, summarised the Committee's thoughts in stating: 'It is therefore suggested that the proposed Museum be adopted as the War Memorial.'[42]

In 1936, the Imperial War Museum moved to its present location in Southwark, in the building previously occupied by the Bethlem Royal Hospital. The following year, the National Maritime Museum (NMM) opened to the public, in the buildings previously housing the Royal (formerly Greenwich) Hospital School. While not conceived as a 'war memorial', the long-standing royal, naval and broader maritime associations of the site were of paramount importance in the decision to establish the Museum at Greenwich. It was this 'spirit of place' that led to the commissioning in 2013 of a new artwork, *Full Fathom Five* (fig.71), by the artist Rozanne Hawksley (see Chapter 6: Rozanne Hawksley). This was conceived as a memorial to the 'unknown sailor' and installed in a ground-floor parlour of the Queen's House as part of a retrospective exhibition of Hawksley's work. The tremendous poignancy of this location not only derived from the role of the House as the centre of the Royal Hospital School at the time of the First World War, but also because a war memorial bearing the names of some 150 boys who had lived and trained there had been installed in the Great Hall of the House in 1919.[43] Removed, with the School, to Suffolk in the 1930s and later effectively lost, the remnants of the memorial were recently rediscovered and, on Remembrance Day 2014, were briefly returned to their original setting. Thus the Queen's House was transformed once more into a place of commemoration.

Rozanne Hawksley: War, Memory and Commemoration

Amy Miller

Hooded in angry mist, the sun goes down:
Steel-gray the clouds roll out across the sea:
Is this a Kingdom? Then give Death the crown,
For here no emperor hath won, save He.

Herbert Asquith, 'Nightfall', 1915

Rozanne Hawksley was born in Portsmouth in 1931. Growing up in a major naval port, she saw first-hand the physical and psychological impact of war on those who returned home. Eight years old when the Second World War began, she was evacuated to Wiltshire. In the 1950s she trained first at the Southern College of Art, Portsmouth, and then at the Royal College of Art, where her circle included Lucian Freud, Francis Bacon and John Minton. After graduating, she moved to Washington, DC, in 1964, where she undertook embroidery and design commissions, including for the Kennedy family. In the 1970s she began developing her work as an artist with one of her early pieces, *Please look after Mr. Sid*, employing printmaking, stitch and found objects. However, the work that established her reputation as regards war art was *Pale Armistice: in Death only are we United* (1987, Embroiderers' Guild), a memorial wreath of white gloves. For the artist these represent both the range of human emotions (a hand may be extended in friendship, to comfort or in anger, to push away or strike) as well as the physical presence of the individual as the glove moulds itself to the hand. This piece is a meditation on the way that war affects everyone: it comprises worn gloves as well as those that are stiffly new, bridal gloves and gloves belonging to officers. A second version, titled simply *Pale Armistice*, was commissioned by the Imperial War Museum (IWM) in 1991.[44]

In 2014, the National Maritime Museum commissioned Hawksley to create a new work as part of commemoration of the centenary of the First World War. This installation, *Full Fathom Five*, was shown in the Queen's House at Greenwich, with *Pale Armistice: in Death only are we United*, *The Seamstress and the Sea* (2003–6), the sweetheart pieces entitled *He Always Wanted to be a Soldier I* and *II* (2006), and *Prisoner* (begun 1988, completed *c.*1995). The last is one of her bleakest and most challenging sculptural pieces, conveying the physical and emotional impact of conflict on those caught up in war zones.

The Seamstress and the Sea

One of Hawksley's most autobiographical works, *The Seamstress and the Sea*, reflects a childhood spent in the Royal Navy's principal home port. It incorporates naval ephemera that were part of everyday life: sailors' collars, cap tallies and 'Fleet Day' cards. It is also a poignant tribute to her grandmother, Alice Hunter, who was an outworker sewing sailors' collars for Bourne's, a local naval outfitters, and who was killed when her home and workplace in Hay Street was destroyed during an air raid in July 1944. Associated pieces to *The Seamstress and the Sea* serve as a personal memorial

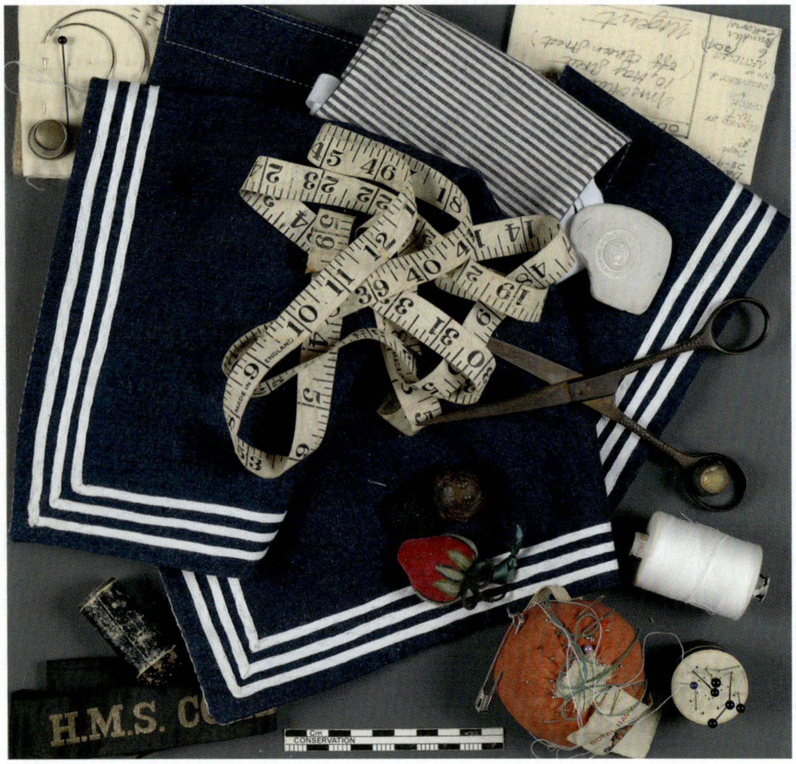

Fig.68 (left)
Rozanne Hawksley
For Alice Hunter, 2003
Various media
39 x 39 x 6.5 cm
(15 3/8 x 15 3/8 x 2 1/2 in)
ZBA6940

Fig.69 (opposite, left)
Robert Austin
Stitches out, man who lost his fingers – Leading Seaman P.A. McDougall, 1944
Charcoal on paper
55 x 76.5 cm (21 5/8 x 30 1/8 in)
PAJ2884

Fig.70 (opposite, right)
Installation image of *War and Memory* (2014) at the Queen's House, Royal Museums Greenwich, showing *Stretcher and Body Bag*, 2003
ZBA6977

to the experience of war, as in *Flossie and Me* (created for the 'Children and War' gallery at the IWM, 2007), which is a response to Hawksley's childhood experiences as a wartime evacuee, and her knowledge of separation, loss and uncertainty. Apart from the death of her grandmother, her parents were displaced by heavy enemy air raids on Portsmouth, while uncles and cousins went to fight and returned with their own psychological traumas. The series of pieces created for *The Seamstress and the Sea* uses the medium of stitch as a narrative device to follow Alice Hunter's life, and that of an imagined sailor for whom she sewed. They track the changing identity of the person sewing, from Alice to the naval surgeon, to the sailor himself, to explore the loss of loved ones – whether family or comrades.

Alice's work as a seamstress supported her six children, from the time of her husband's death in the influenza pandemic of 1919 until her own in the 1944 air raid. Her work is represented in *The Seamstress and the Sea* series by a grouping of sewing implements called *For Alice Hunter* (2003, fig.68), including her ball of tailor's wax, which survived the destruction in Hay Street. The Royal Navy is at the centre, in the shape of a sailor's collar, as indeed it was at the centre of daily life in Portsmouth. In creating these, the artist recalled her grandmother at work surrounded by 'great piles of cloth; the sound of her needle drawing the waxed thread through the tough cloth [...] of her singing sad and jolly songs of the First World War as she sewed'.[45]

The women in Rozanne's family played an active part during the Second World War: in addition to supplying the Navy with clothing, as Alice did, Rozanne's aunt Ella was a nurse with Queen Alexandra's Royal Naval Nursing Service (QARNNS). This role is also captured by a series of highly sensitive drawings by Robert Austin (1895–1973), a noted artist and illustrator who taught at the Royal College of Art, and was an official war artist during the Second World War, recording the work of women in the Royal Air Force and nursing. When viewed with Hawksley's work, as it was in the Queen's House, his drawing (fig.69) of a QARNN using scissors to remove a sailor's stitches, undoing the work of needle and thread, makes a parallel between the changing identity of the sewer in Hawksley's personal history and in her work as an artist. Austin has added the inscription at the bottom of his drawing, 'Stitches out, man who lost his fingers – Leading Seaman P.A. McDougall'. This link between the seamstress and the more medical side of stitching is also raised by a diagrammatical drawing that Hawksley created, entitled *Stitches: Means & Methods & Stitching* (2003), which explores the surgeon's use of needles nearly identical to those employed by Alice Hunter and the techniques used to stitch wounds, which did not vary markedly from those of domestic needlework. In the final piece of *The Seamstress and the Sea*, entitled *Stretcher and Body Bag* (2003, fig.70), it is the sailors themselves who sew. The artist has re-created a stretcher and shroud used for burial at sea, with the needle and thread left at the point where, by tradition,

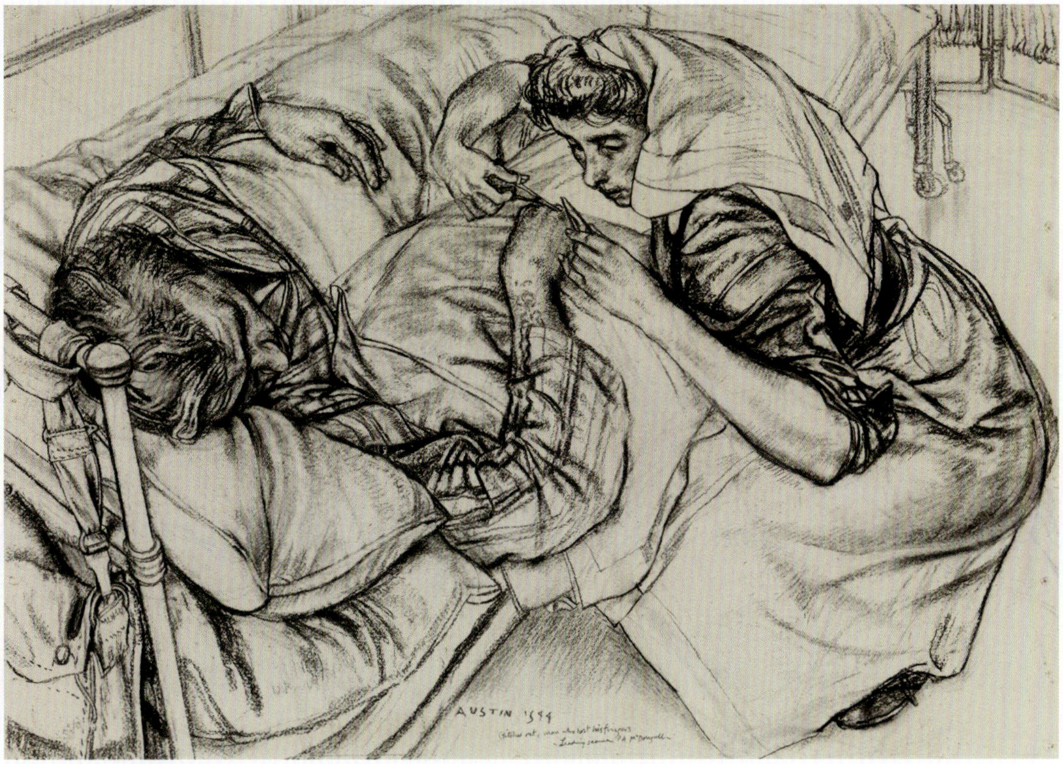

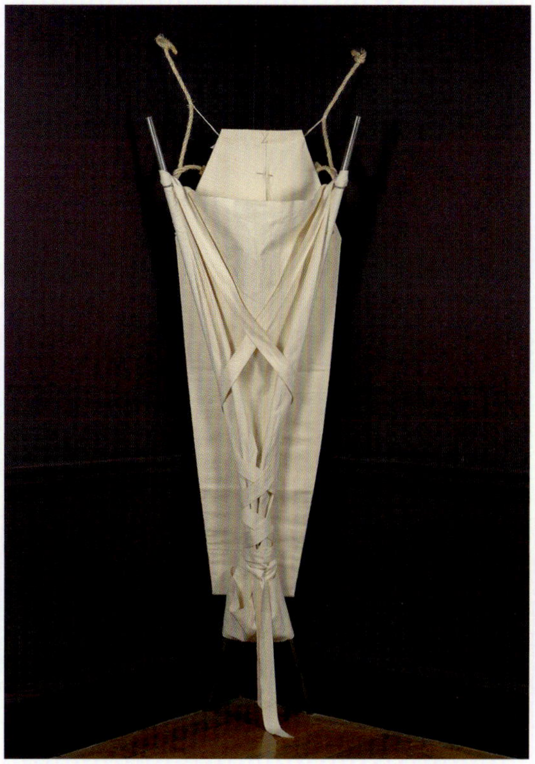

the last stitch was made through the nose of the deceased. Here the act of stitching is carried out by the shipmates of the dead.

The emotional scars left by the experience of war examined by Hawksley can be considered in juxtaposition to the work of Eric Kennington (1888–1960), an official war artist who produced a series of detailed portraits of airmen, seaman and soldiers during the Second World War. The contrast gives the viewer the opportunity to contemplate what trauma or war-induced inner turmoil may be masked by the stoic exteriors and 'stiff upper lips' of the latter's subjects. Kennington produced these portraits, in part, to illustrate the heroic qualities of those who were not officers. Of one sitter, Stoker Martin (plate 17), he wrote, 'Man of action: instantaneous: 100 per cent reliable: expert technician. Much humour under thorough camouflage. Very gentle, sensitive, and great physical strength.'[46] The telling comment here is 'under thorough camouflage' – the sailor masks his true character and emotions. This extraordinary stoicism, hiding untold agonies within, is explored in a drawing Rozanne Hawksley created for *Seamstress and the Sea*, titled *We Jolly Sailor Boys: Remembering* (2003). It shows a decorated sailor haunted by the events of war. In the background, ships are being bombed and a wounded shipmate writhes in agony, attended by death.

Similarly, *Halt! Who goes there?* (early 1990s) is a moving and disturbing image of Hawksley's uncle Harry, who joined the war because he thought he 'would have a smart red coat'. Instead he found himself a prisoner of war in Poland and was also part of the British evacuation from Dunkirk in 1940. Hawksley recalled that 'he had a bad war like pretty well everyone and his last days were very sad [...] he could never settle'.[47] The image captures this psychological destruction.

While much of *The Seamstress and the Sea* finds its roots in family history and personal reminiscences, the work also became, to quote Mary Schoeser, 'a memorial to hundreds of men and women who served or died at sea.' It is both autobiographical and universal.[48]

Full Fathom Five

In 1919 a set of oak memorial panels was installed in the Great Hall of the Queen's House (as mentioned in Chapter 6: Public Memorials, Symbolic Spaces), then the centre of the Royal Hospital School premises at Greenwich. It bore the names of over 150 boys who died in the First World War and in other conflicts and incidents going back to the late nineteenth century. These boys had trained and lived in the buildings which, from 1937, opened to the public as the National Maritime Museum. The memorial itself was removed to the School's new premises at Holbrook, Suffolk, when it left Greenwich in 1933. There its purpose was at some point 'lost' by being overpainted with later School honours. In more recent times

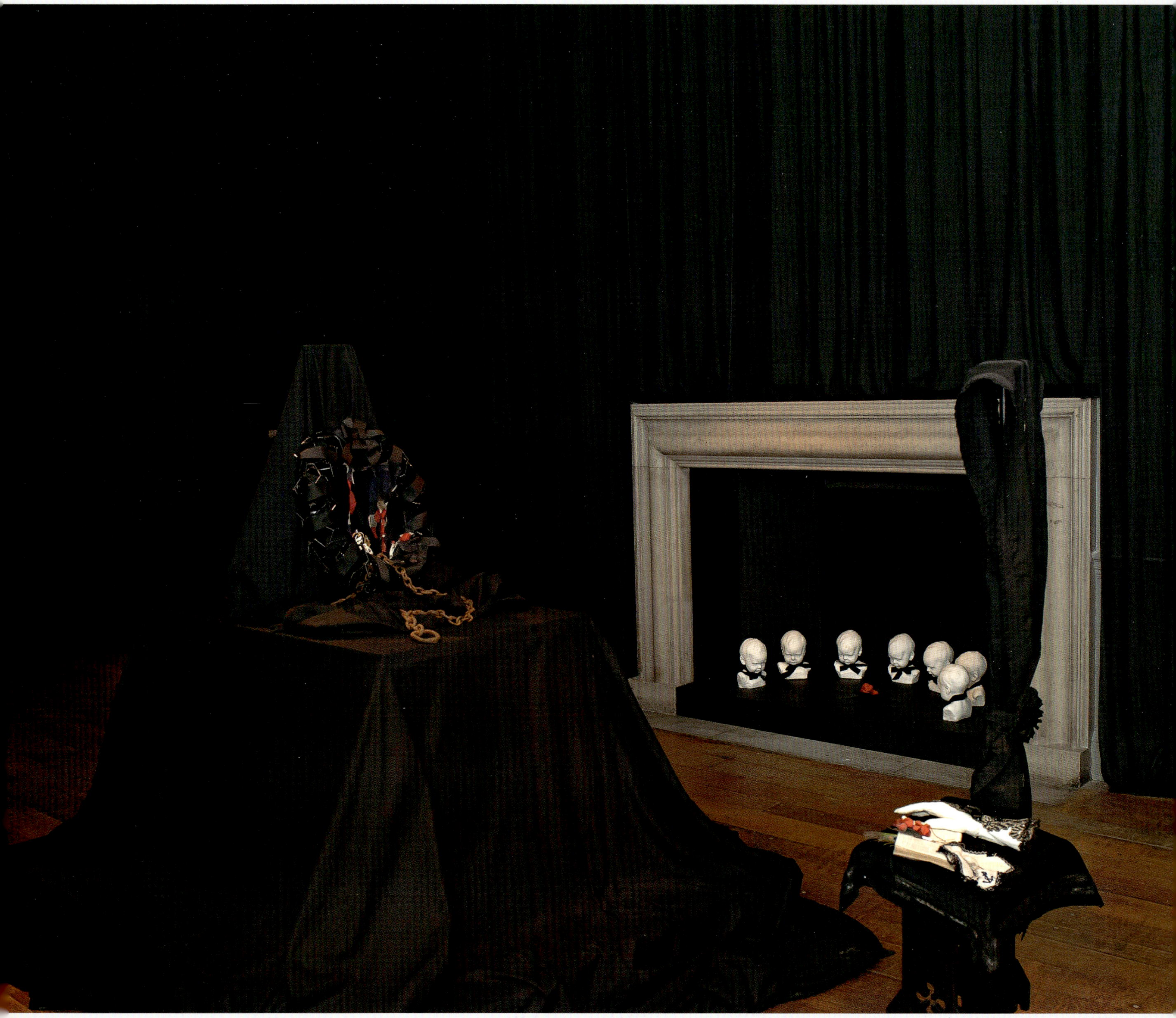

Fig.71
Installation image of *War and Memory* (2014) at the Queen's House, Royal Museums Greenwich, showing *Full Fathom Five*
L7469-024

it was dismantled, though the individual panels survived and, almost miraculously, recent stripping has retrieved the 'ghost' names of those originally commemorated.

Hawksley's 2014 commission for the Queen's House sought temporarily to reintroduce the memorial's message there but with a wider scope, not only to commemorate the former boys of the School but also the 'unknown sailor' casualties of war. The new memorial, *Full Fathom Five* (fig.71), was situated in the north-west parlour on the ground floor of the House, which the artist shrouded in black muslin to create the dramatic effect of deepest mourning. At the centre of the room she placed an empty catafalque, with a jet memorial wreath from the First World War. This was set against a rusted cross of iron, salvaged from the sea and tied with sailors' silks, cap tallies, fragments of a Union Jack and cloth poppies – the symbols of service, duty and sacrifice, and remembrance.

At the foot of the wreath was a crowned death's head, a visual acknowledgement of the poem 'Nightfall' by Herbert Asquith, one of a series he wrote on his First World War experiences: 'Then give Death the crown | For here no emperor has won, save He.'[49] At the bottom of the catafalque was a place for the mourner, a black prie-dieu on which rested the mementoes of mourning: a glove (which for the artist also represents the physical presence of the mourner) and an embroidered handkerchief, rent between the words 'hope' and 'ever'. This installation was intended as a kind of dialogue between the living and the dead. A rusted chain was placed on the catafalque, leading towards the mourner, while below the prie-dieu (featuring a kneeler with the word 'Sacrifice' embroidered in red – one of the only points of colour in the room) a dull black-and-silver mourning ribbon led back to the catafalque. Overall it represented the sacrifice of those who went to war and lost their lives, and the sacrifice by the living of those they held dear.

Although Hawksley initially envisioned a dramatically draped room that was almost extravagantly baroque in its expression of mourning, work on the installation prompted a sparser approach to focus the visitor on the catafalque and the mourner. However, the artist introduced seven 'cherubs' in the form of plaster-cast portrait busts of an unknown child, adorned with black ribbons, representing mourners, the lost generation of young men who died in the First World War and those children who would never be born.

On Remembrance Day 2014, students from the Royal Hospital School returned the memorial panels to the Queen's House in a procession that included Rozanne Hawksley. After the students placed the panels in the Hall, a student bugler signalled 'The Last Post', just prior to the bell at the Old Royal Naval College striking 11 o'clock. The panels were positioned against the east wall, below the point where they were originally mounted after the war's end, nearly a century before: thus the memorial was restored to the House but only for a day. During that time, Hawksley worked with the students finally to complete *Full Fathom Five*. The students had already researched the names on the memorial to re-create the biographies of those it commemorated, and had uncovered the story of Charles Ernest Timmins, a bugler and the youngest boy from the School to die in the First World War. Aged just 14, he was killed when shrapnel pierced his bugle in action off Heligoland in November 1917. The artist felt that, in Timmins, she at last had the identity of her 'unknown sailor' and that the 'conversation' of the living and the dead in *Full Fathom Five* was between mother and son. In collaboration with Hawksley, the students added poppies with their names inscribed on one petal and that of Timmins on the other.

The fact that this work was only a temporary memorial, pointing to the former presence in the Queen's House of one intended as permanent but long ago removed and nearly irretrievably lost, highlights the almost ephemeral quality of memorialisation: that the names and events on such monuments only hold meaning as long as the memory of those who knew the dead, or those who experienced the war, survives.

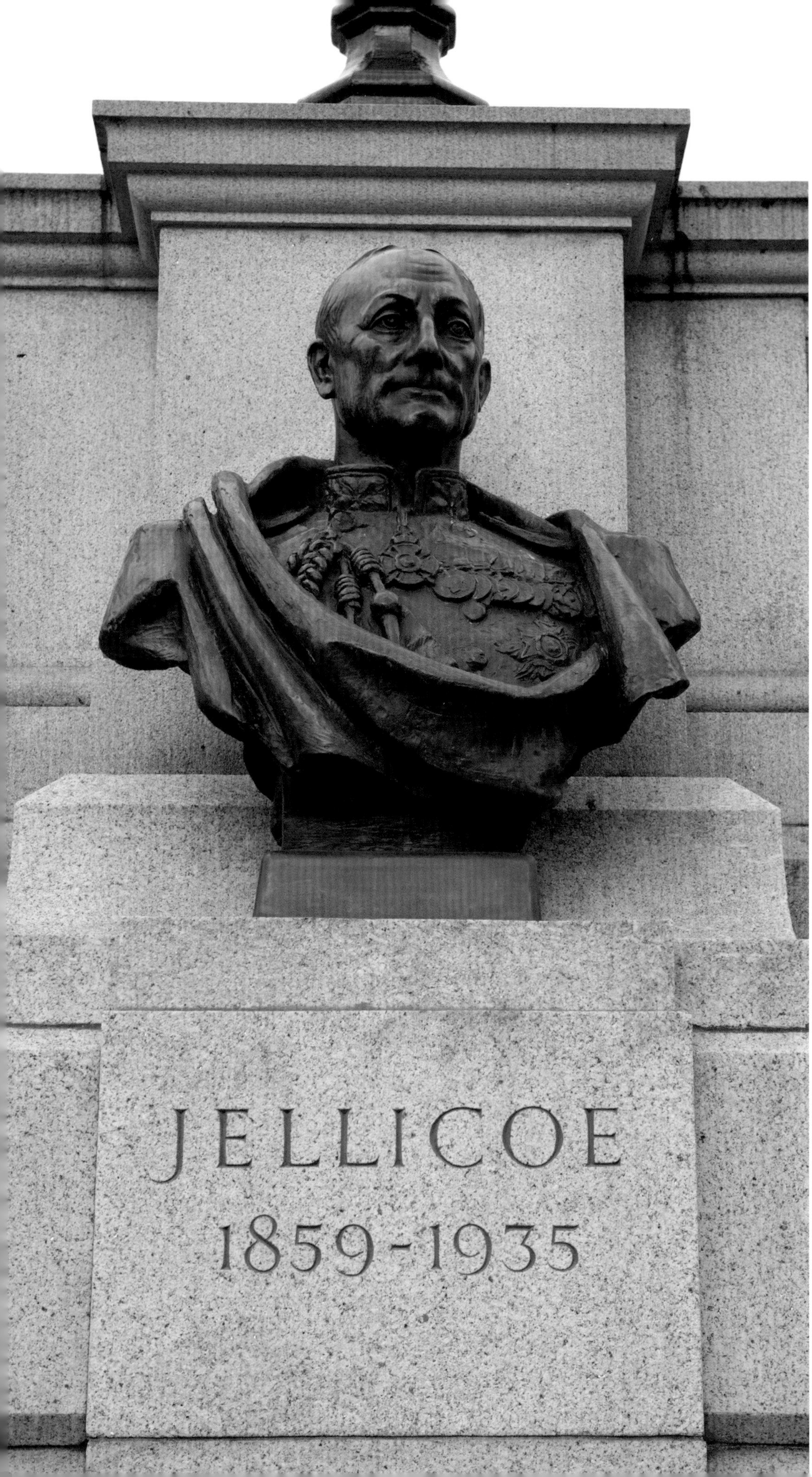

Plate 76 (left)
Charles Wheeler
Portrait Bust of Admiral Lord Jellicoe,
1937–48, Jellicoe Memorial,
Trafalgar Square, London
Cast bronze
Approx. 100 cm (39 in) high
L7781-001

Plate 77 (opposite)
William McMillan
Portrait Bust of Admiral Lord Beatty,
1937–48, Beatty Memorial,
Trafalgar Square, London
Cast bronze
Approx. 100 cm (39 in) high
L7782

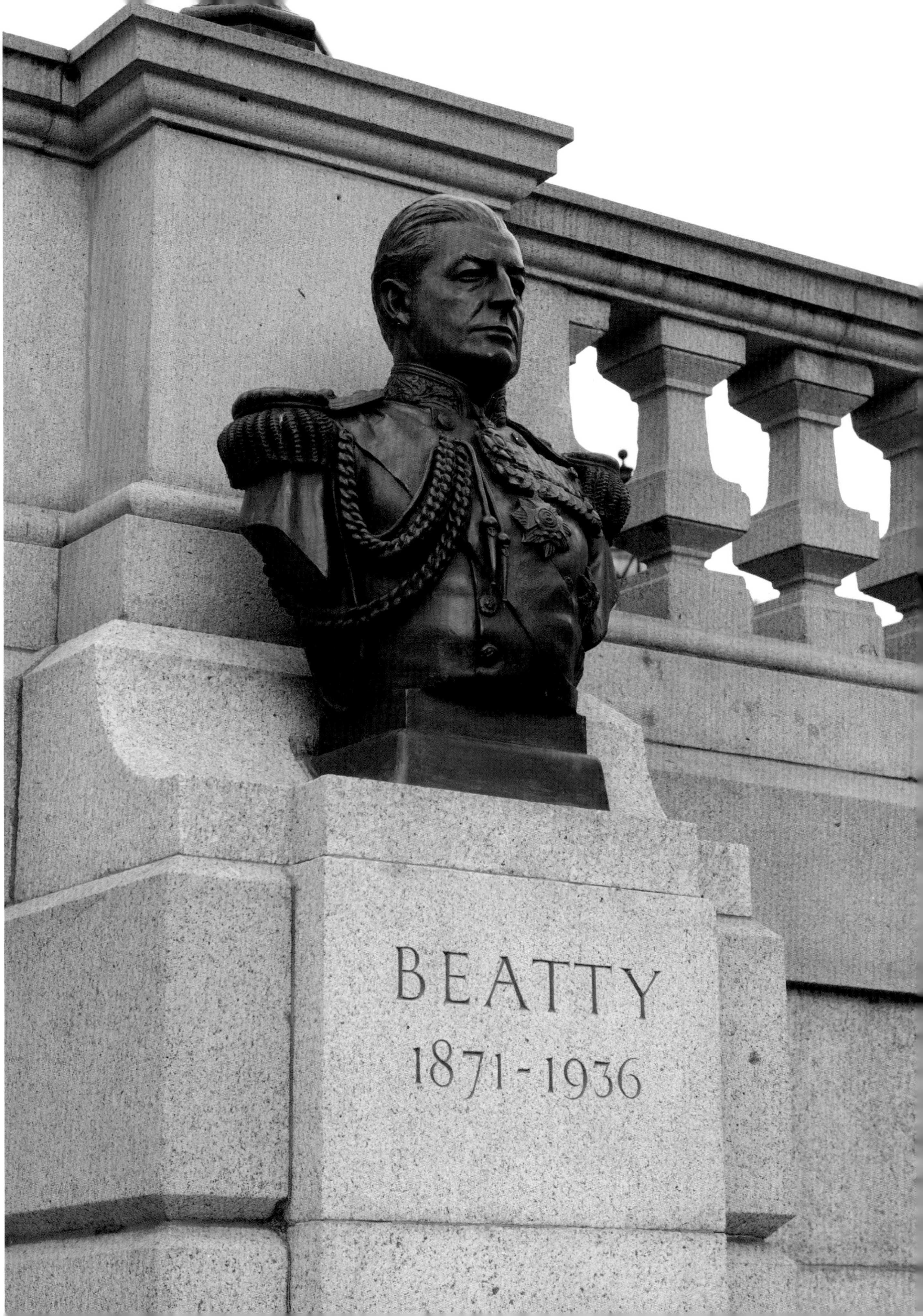
BEATTY
1871-1936

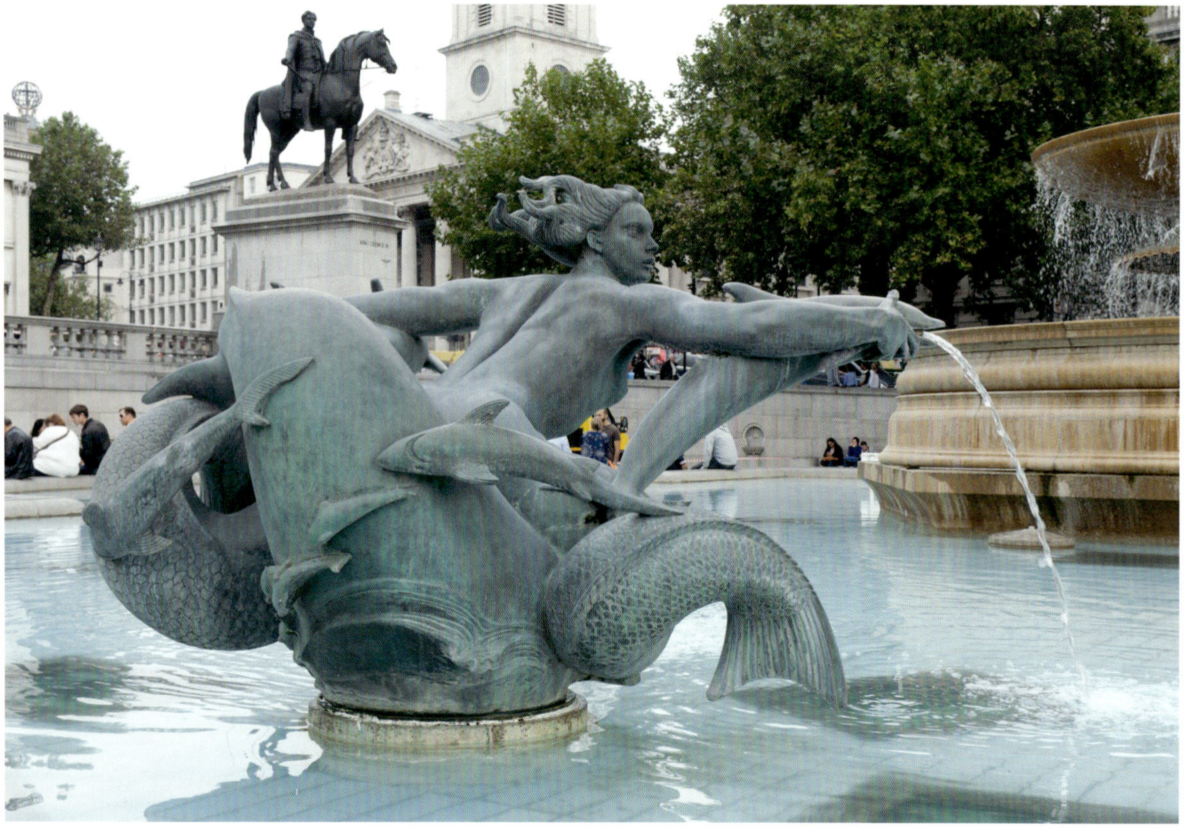

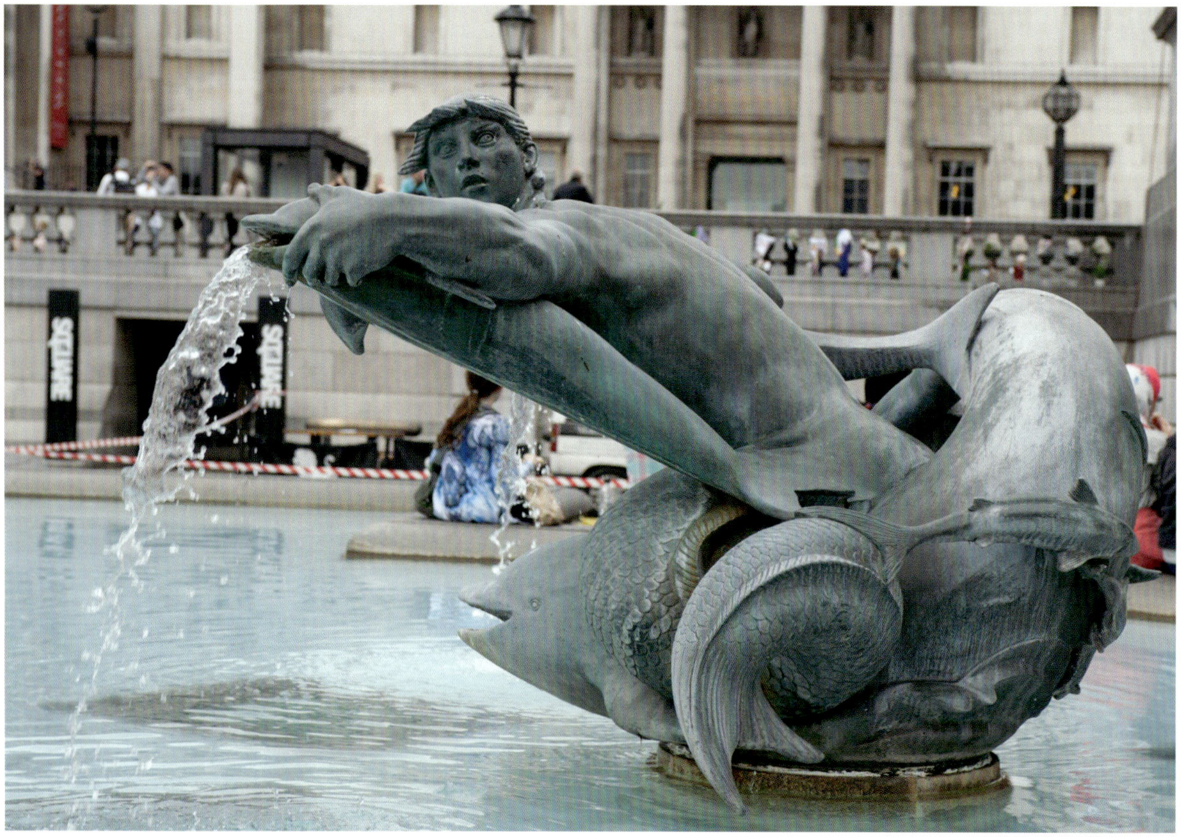

Plate 78 (above)
William McMillan
Mermaid fountain group, 1937–48
Beatty Memorial, Trafalgar Square, London
Cast bronze
150 x 250 cm (59 x 98 in)
L7786-002

Plate 79 (below)
William McMillan
Triton fountain group, 1937–48
Beatty Memorial, Trafalgar Square, London
Cast bronze
150 x 250 cm (59 x 98 in)
L7784-002

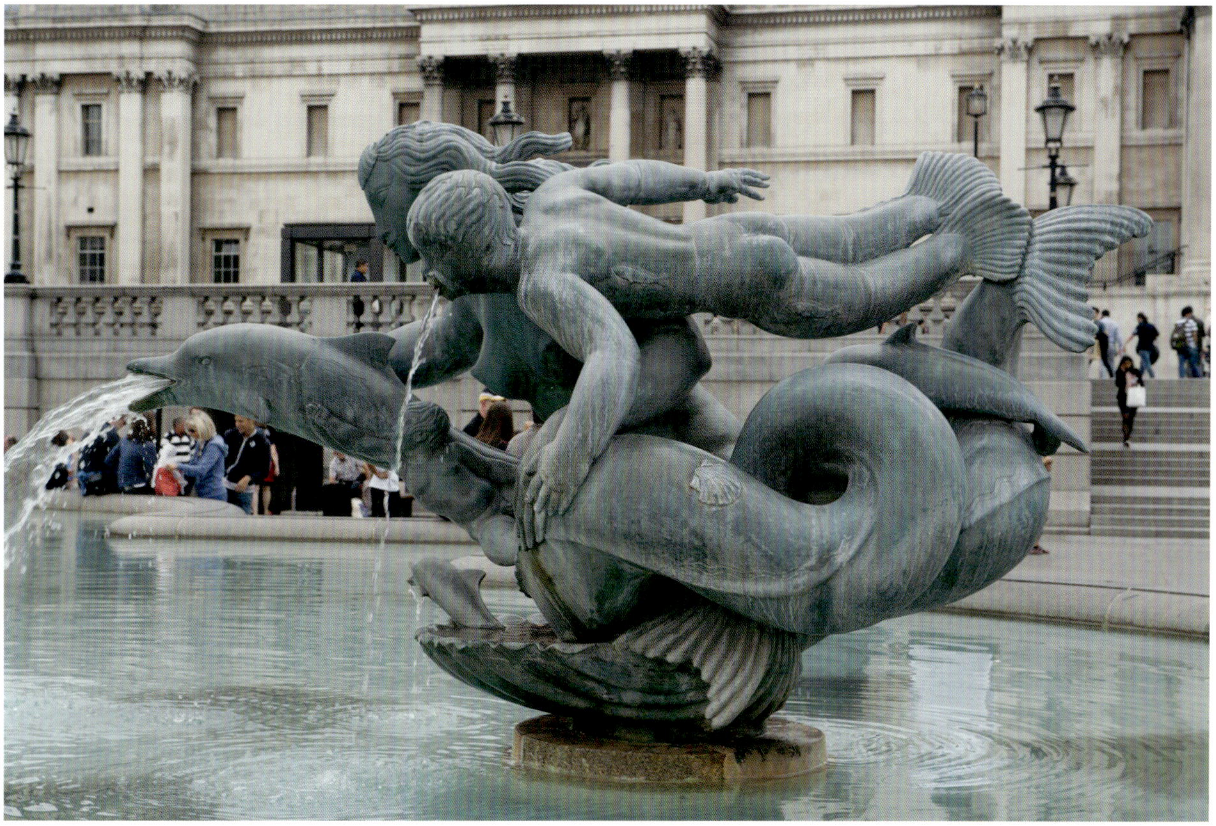

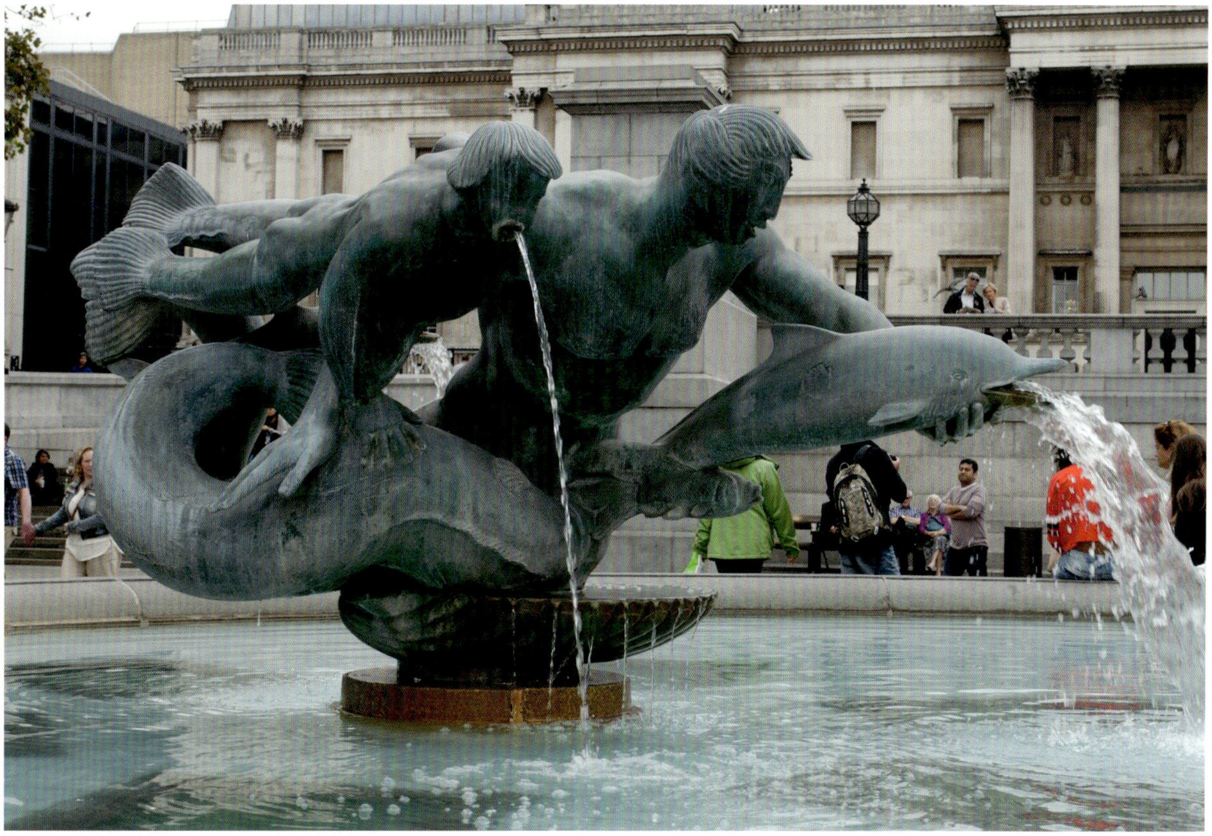

Plate 80 (above)
Charles Wheeler
Mermaid fountain group, 1937–48
Jellicoe Memorial, Trafalgar Square, London
Cast bronze
150 x 250 cm (59 x 98 in)
L7783-001

Plate 81 (below)
Charles Wheeler
Triton fountain group, 1937–48
Jellicoe Memorial, Trafalgar Square, London
Cast bronze
150 x 250 cm (59 x 98 in)
L7785-001

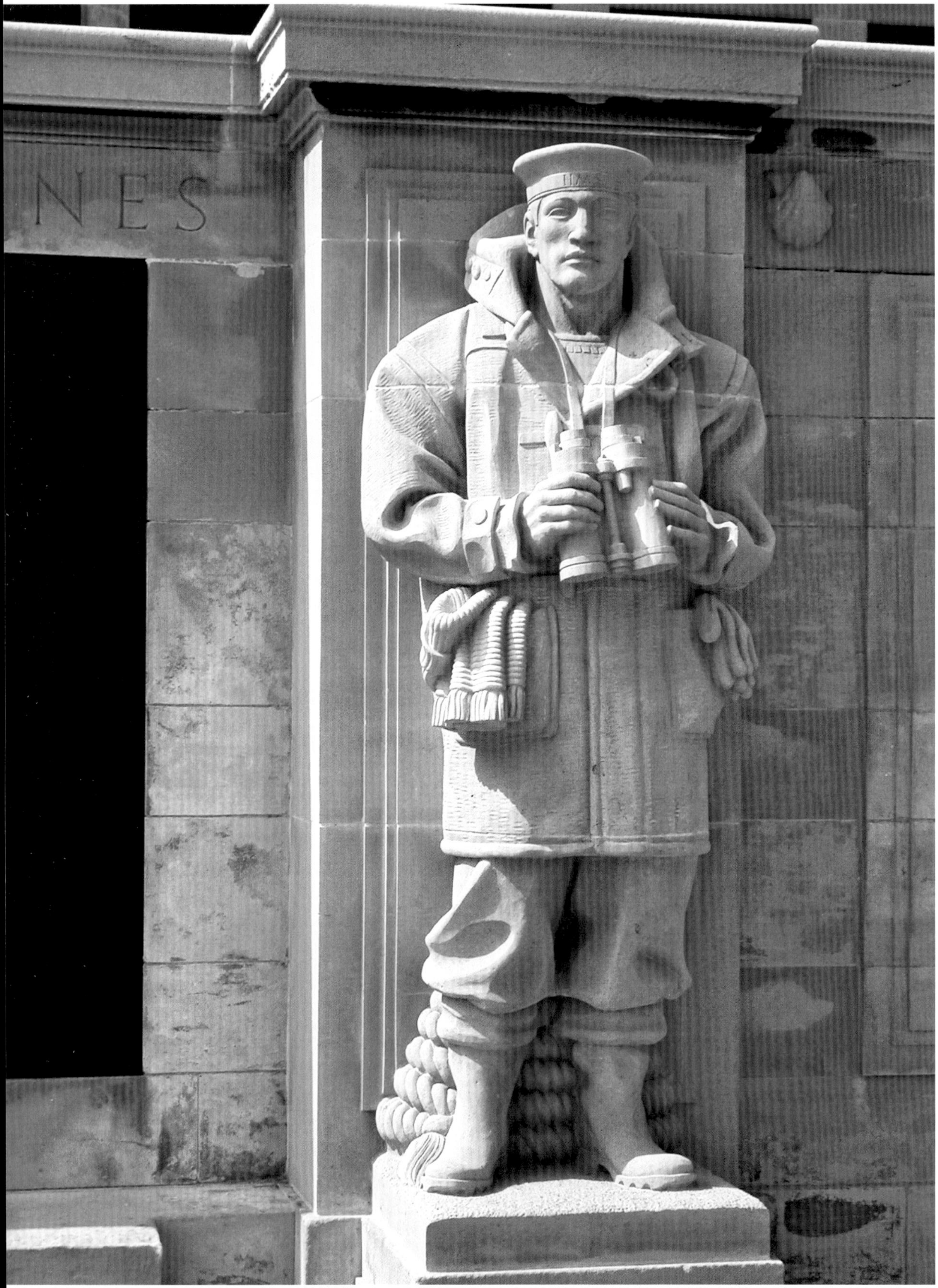

Plate 82 (left)
Charles Wheeler
Sailor (The Royal Navy on the Alert), 1946–52
Royal Naval Memorial, Portsmouth
Portland stone
214 cm (84 ¼ in) high

Plate 83 (opposite, left)
Charles Wheeler
Merchant Marine Officer, 1952–5
Merchant Marine Memorial, Tower Hill, London
Portland stone
206 cm (81 in) high
L7779-004

Plate 84 (opposite, right)
Charles Wheeler
Merchant Marine Rating, 1952–5
Merchant Marine Memorial, Tower Hill, London
Portland stone
206 cm (81 in) high
L7779-005

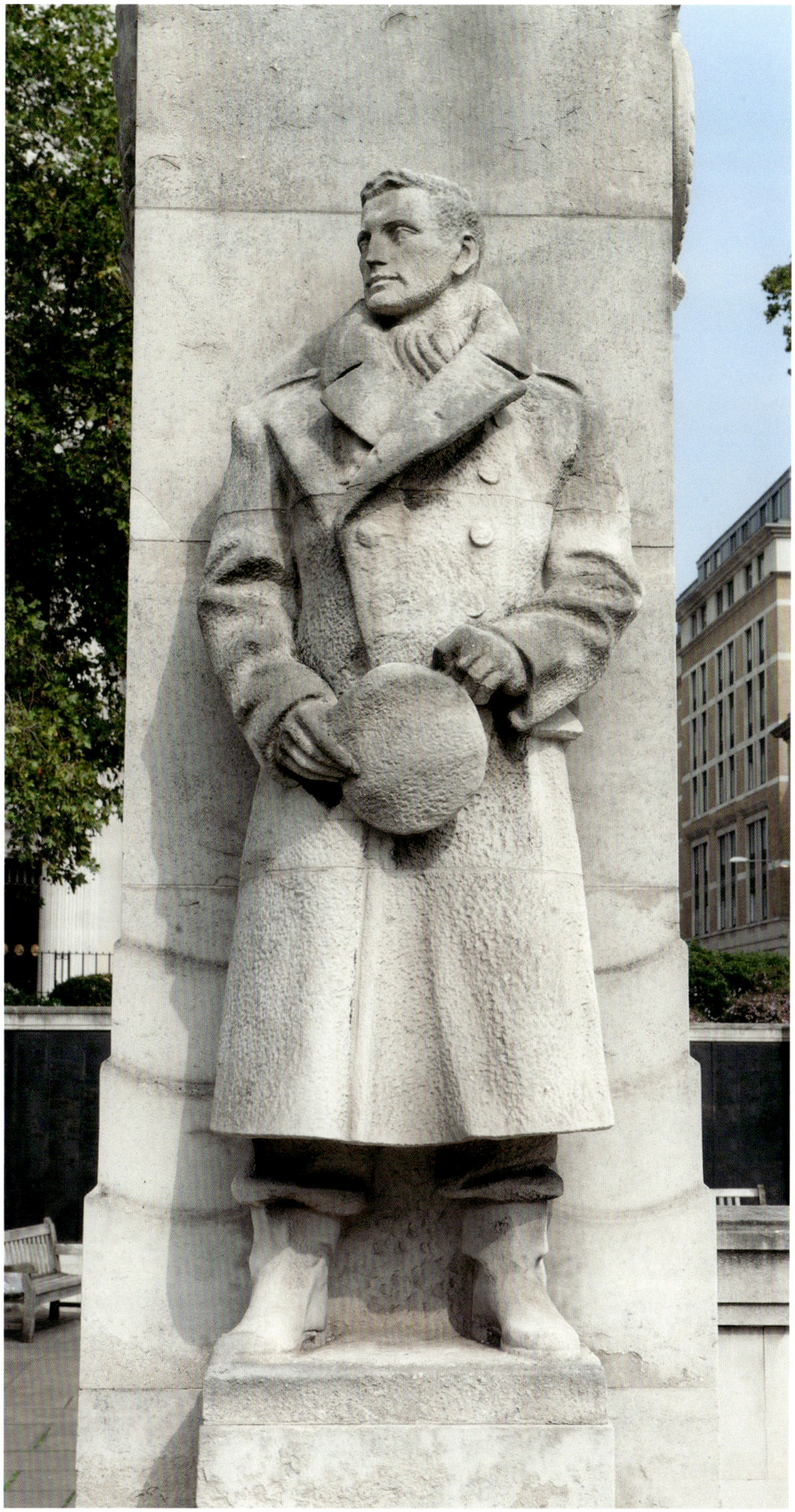

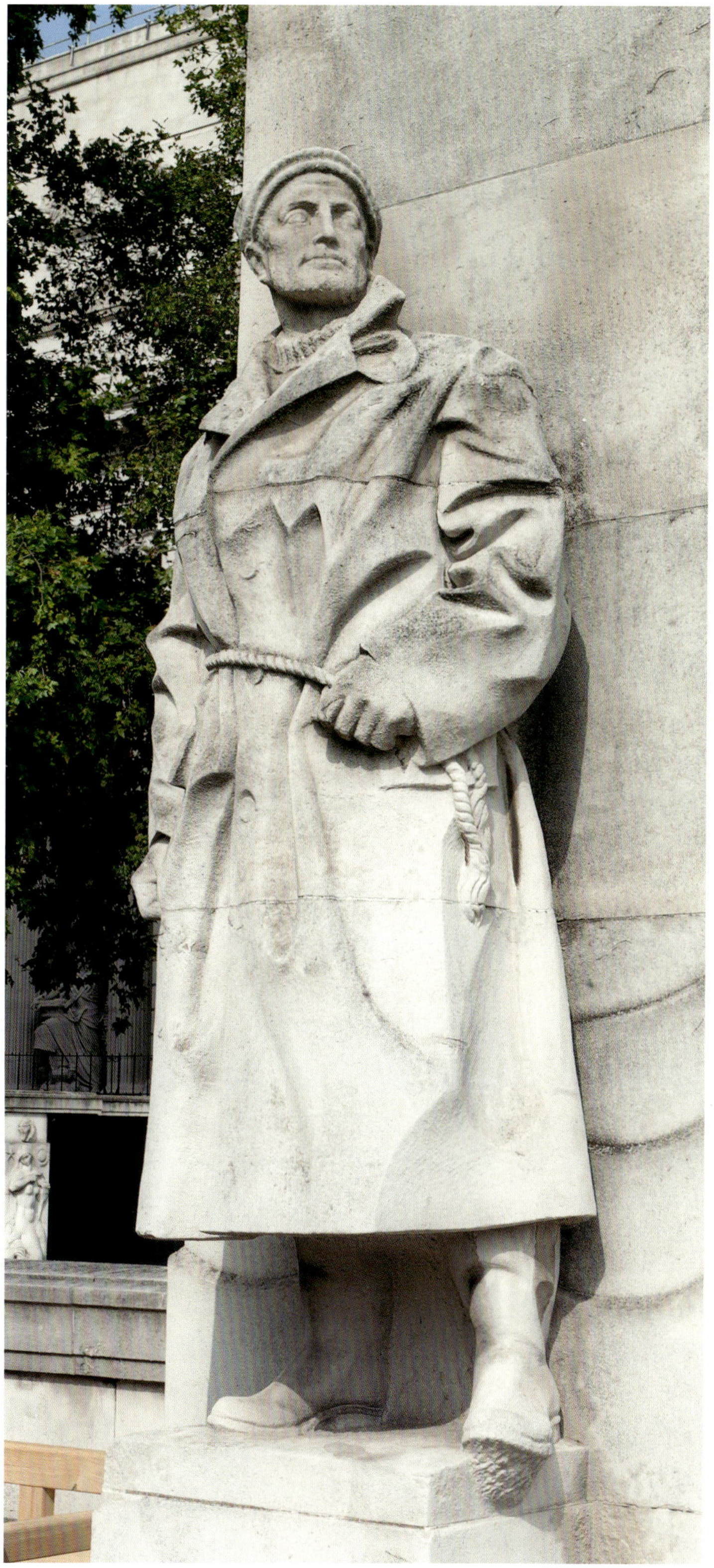

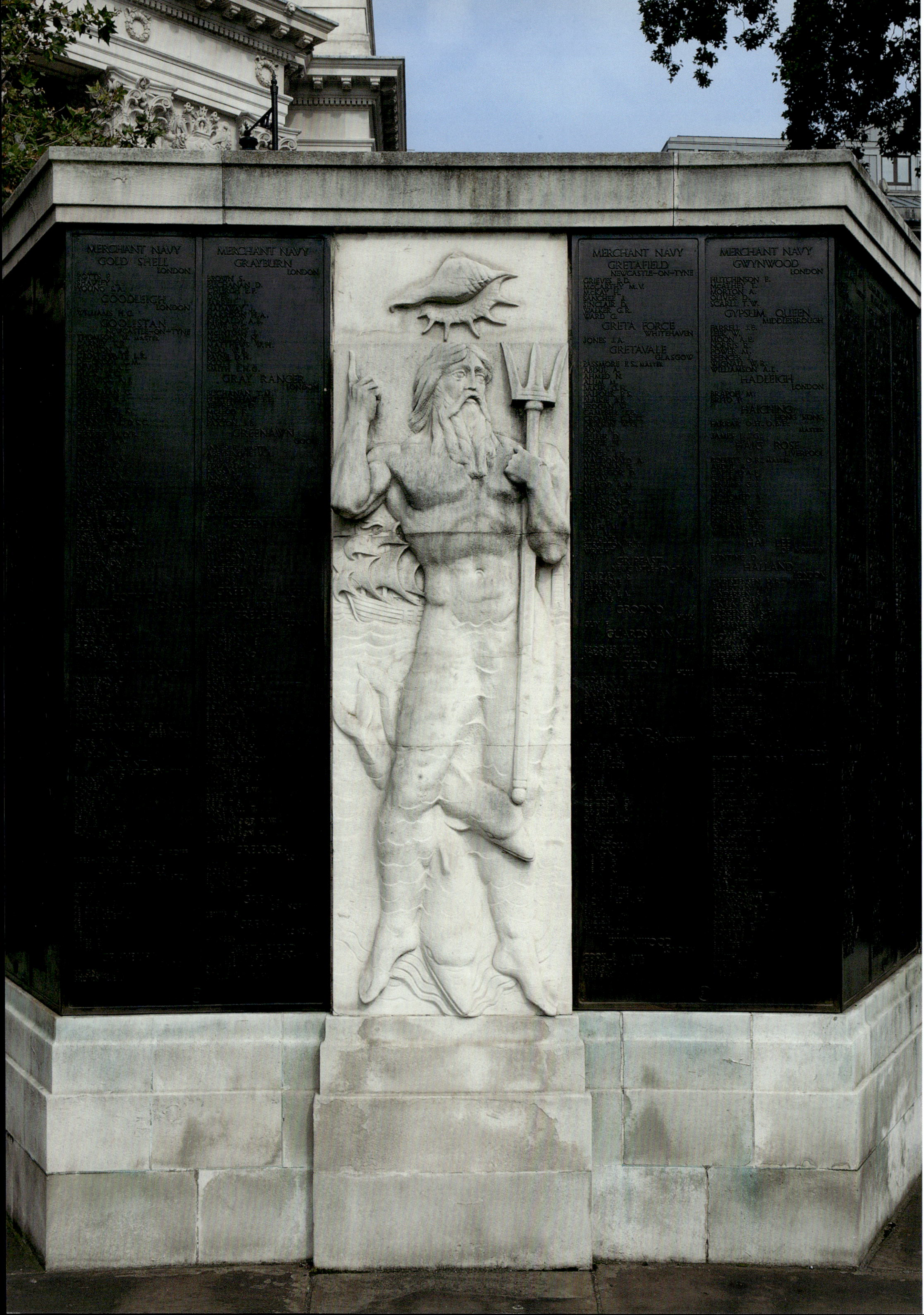
MERCHANT NAVY
GOLD SHELL
LONDON
MERCHANT NAVY
GRAYBURN
LONDON
MERCHANT NAVY
GRETAFIELD
NEWCASTLE-ON-TYNE
MERCHANT NAVY
GWYNWOOD
LONDON
GRETA FORCE
WHITEHAVEN
GRETAVALE
GLASGOW
GYPSUM QUEEN
MIDDLESBROUGH
HADLEIGH
LONDON

Plate 85 (opposite)
Charles Wheeler
Neptune ('The Seven Seas'), 1952–5
Merchant Marine Memorial,
Tower Hill, London
Portland stone
203 x 62 cm (79 7/8 x 24 3/4 in)
L7779-010

Plate 86 (above, left)
Charles Wheeler
Female Wind ('The Seven Seas'), 1952–5
Merchant Marine Memorial,
Tower Hill, London
Portland stone
203 x 62 cm (79 7/8 x 24 3/4 in)
L7779-008

Plate 87 (above, right)
Charles Wheeler
Venus ('The Seven Seas'), 1952–5
Merchant Marine Memorial,
Tower Hill, London
Portland stone
203 x 62 cm (79 7/8 x 24 3/4 in)
L7779-013

Plate 88 (below, left)
Charles Wheeler
Triton ('The Seven Seas'), 1952–5
Merchant Marine Memorial,
Tower Hill, London
Portland stone
203 x 62 cm (79 7/8 x 24 3/4 in)
L7779-017

Plate 89 (below, right)
Charles Wheeler
Mermaid ('The Seven Seas'), 1952–5
Merchant Marine Memorial,
Tower Hill, London
Portland stone
203 x 62 cm (79 7/8 x 24 3/4 in)
L7779-014

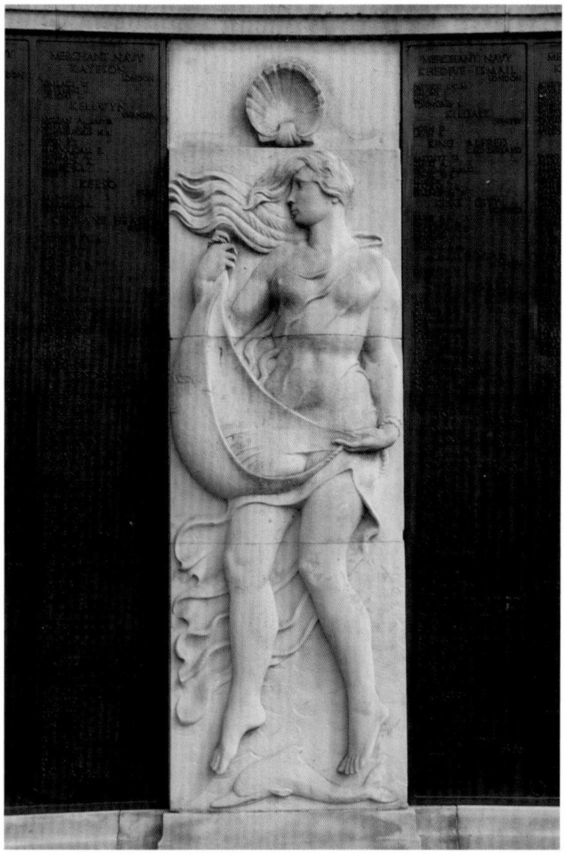

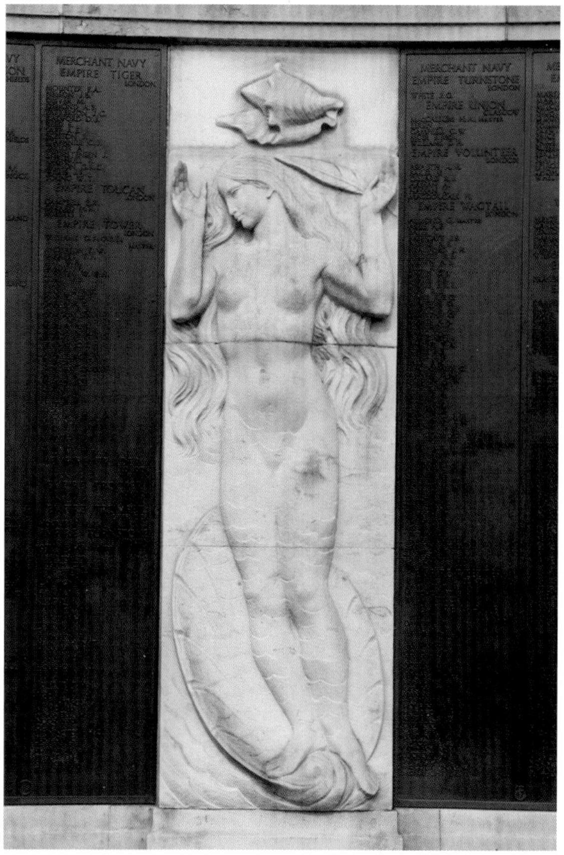

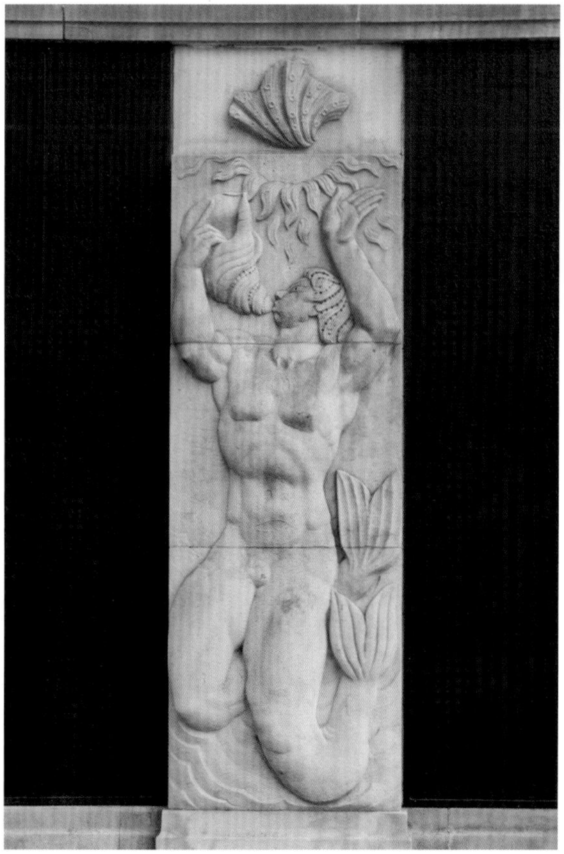

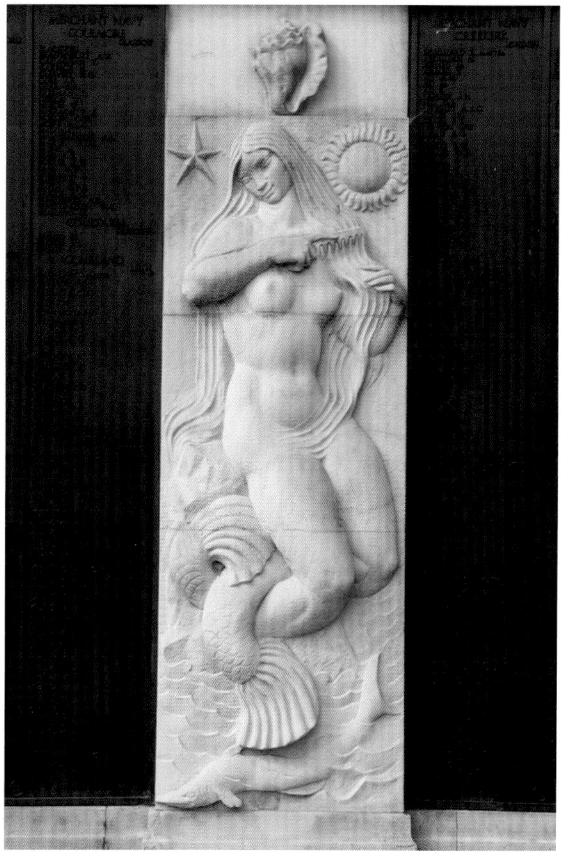

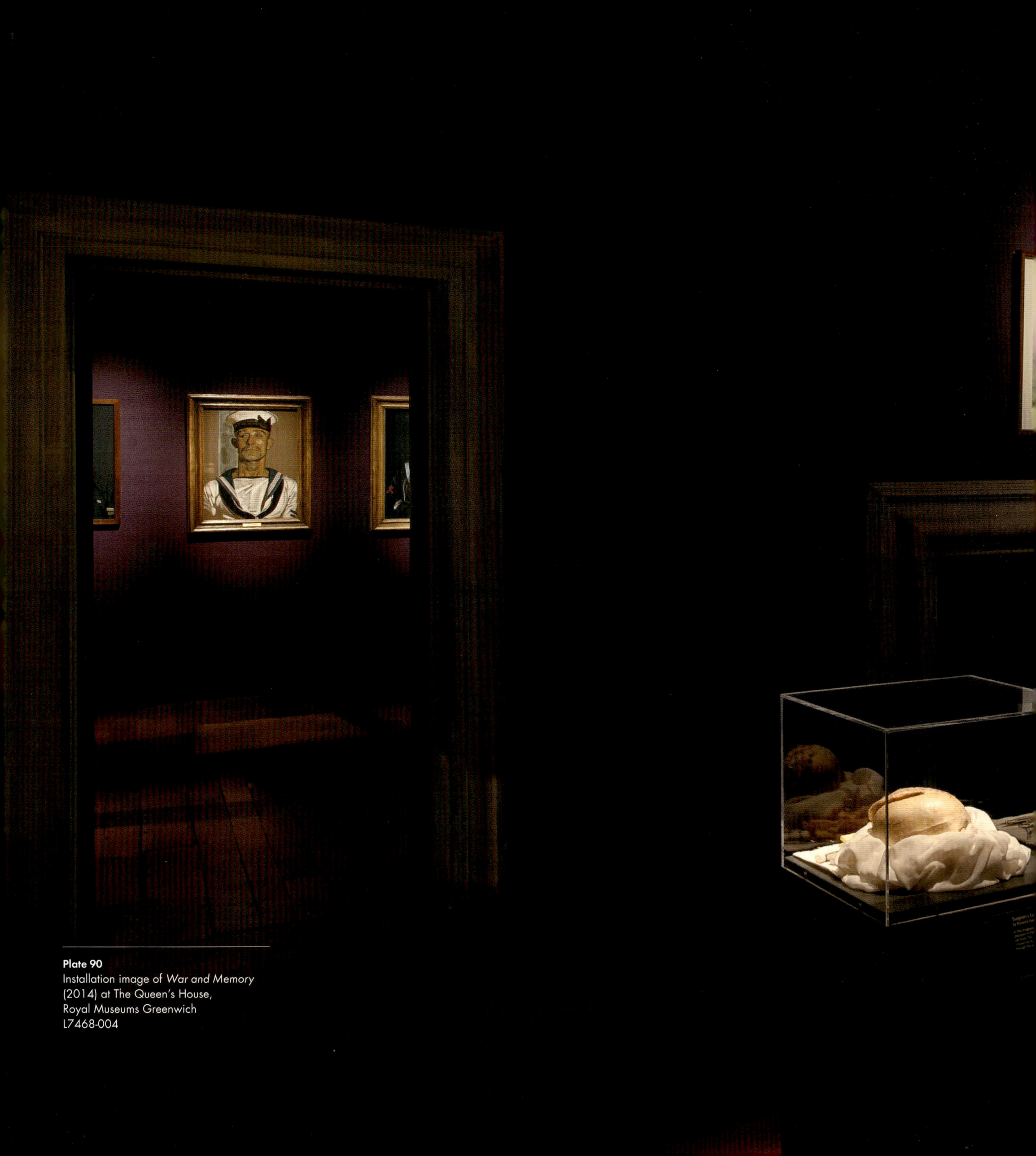

Plate 90
Installation image of *War and Memory* (2014) at The Queen's House, Royal Museums Greenwich
L7468-004

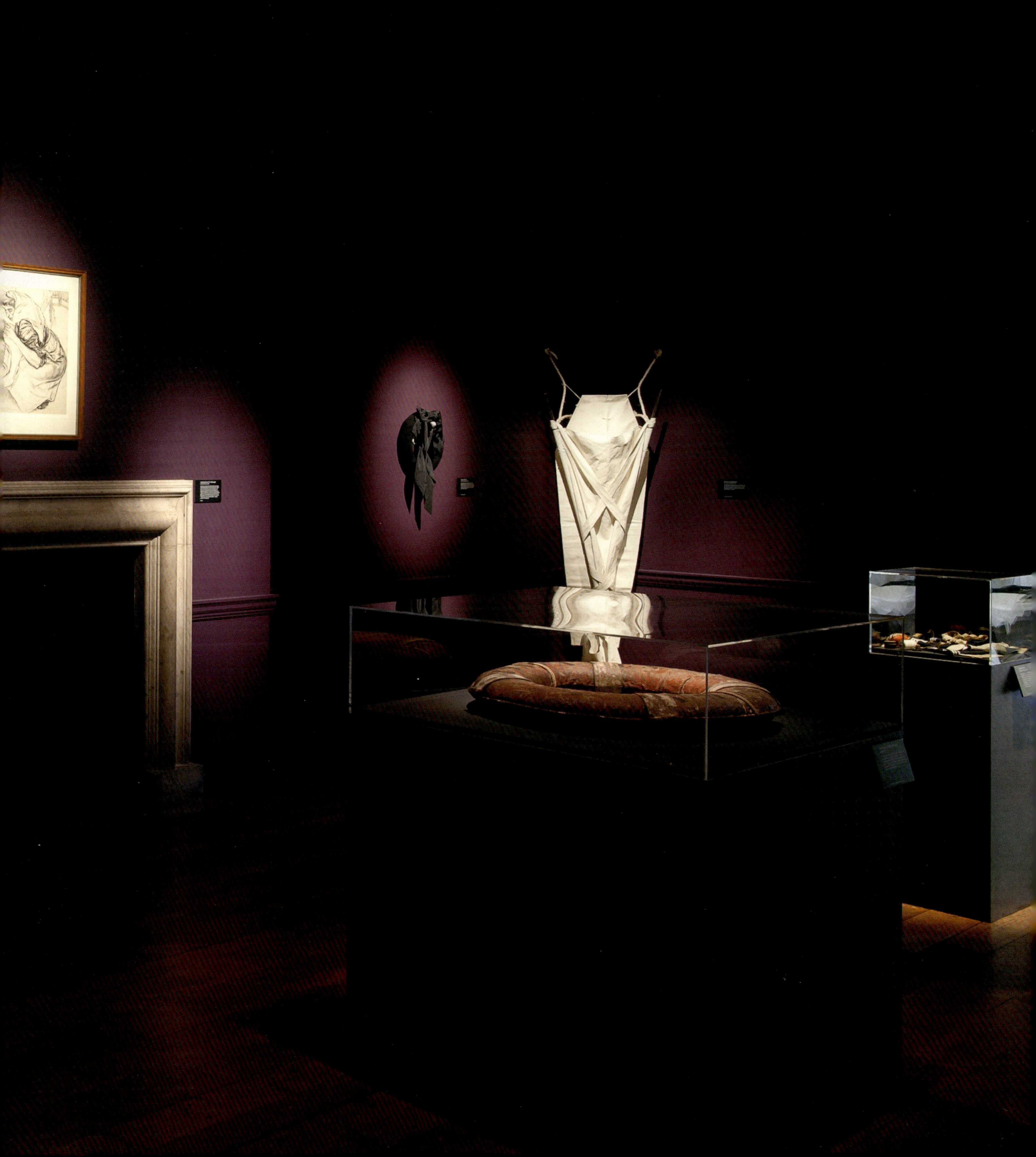

Notes

Introduction

1. James Baikie, *Peeps at the Royal Navy*, 3rd ed., London, 1921, p.88. The book was first published in 1913.
2. Richard Woodman, *The Real Cruel Sea: The Merchant Navy in the Battle of the Atlantic, 1939–1943*, London, 2004, p.1.
3. Sir Herbert Richmond, 'Introduction', in *War at Sea: War Pictures by British Artists*, Oxford, 1942, p.7.
4. Sue Malvern, *Modern Art, Britain and the Great War*, New Haven and London, 2004, p.13.
5. Ibid., pp 41–4. For National Maritime Museum (NMM) collections of Charles Pears' *Transport by Sea* prints, see PAG9452.
6. 'The Western Front: Drawings by Muirhead Bone', *Country Life*, March 1917, p.LXXXIII.
7. See Malvern, *Modern Art*, pp 188–9 for artists supported by the Bone Fund.
8. Sylvester Bone, *Sir Muirhead Bone: Artist and Patron*, London, 2009, p.104.
9. Paul Gough, *A Terrible Beauty: British Artists in the First World War*, Bristol, 2010, p.25; John Bonehill, '"For the national cause": Art, Britishness and the War Artists Advisory Committee, 1939–45', in Geoff Quilley (ed.), *Art for the Nation: The Oil Paintings Collections of the National Maritime Museum*, London, 2006, pp 115–7.
10. Gough, *A Terrible Beauty*, pp 21–2.
11. See Malvern, *Modern Art*, pp 178–97, for a breakdown of artists involved with the various art schemes during and after the First World War.
12. Gaynor Kavanagh, *Museums and the First World War: A Social History*, London and New York, 1994, pp 138–9.
13. Charles Wheeler, *High Relief: The Autobiography of Sir Charles Wheeler, Sculptor*, Feltham, 1968, p.103.
14. See, for example, Geoff Quilley and John Bonehill (eds), *William Hodges, 1744–1797: The Art of Exploration*, New Haven and London, 2004; David Hempleman-Adams, Sophie Gordon and Emma Stuart, *The Heart of the Great Alone: Scott, Shackleton and Antarctic Photography*, London, 2009.
15. Christine Riding and Richard Johns, *Turner and the Sea*, London, 2013, pp 248–9; Geoff Quilley, 'The pen in the first person: The artist as eyewitness on voyages of exploration', in *Empire to Nation: Art, History and the Visualization of Maritime Britain, 1768–1829*, New Haven and London, 2011, pp 15–51.
16. Richmond, *War at Sea*, p.6.
17. L. Swinburne and Norman Wilkinson, *The Royal Navy*, London, 1907, p.x.
18. Gough, *A Terrible Beauty*, p.33, note 61.
19. Richard Johns, 'James Thornhill and Decorative History Painting in England after 1688', unpublished PhD thesis, University of York, 2004, pp 183–4.
20. Sarah Crellin, *The Sculpture of Charles Wheeler*, Farnham, 2012, p.72.
21. Kevin Littlewood and Beverley Butler, *Of Ships and Stars: Maritime Heritage and the Founding of the National Maritime Museum, Greenwich*, New Brunswick, 1998, p.116.
22. Jan Rüger, *The Great Naval Game: Britain and Germany in the Age of Empire*, Cambridge, 2009, p.1.
23. Both are now in the collections of the NMM; BHC2894 and UNI0024.
24. Swinburne and Wilkinson, *The Royal Navy*, p.xi; Harold F.B. Wheeler, *Stirring Deeds of Britain's Sea-dogs in the Great War*, London, 1916, p.14.
25. J.B. Priestley, *British Women Go to War*, London, 1944, p.24.
26. Geoffrey Callender, *The Story of H.M.S. 'Victory'*, 2nd edition, London, 1929, p.7.
27. Quoted in Richard Stein, *Victoria's Year: English Literature and Culture, 1837–1838*, Oxford, 1987, p.253.
28. Richmond, *War at Sea*, p.59.
29. Baikie, *Peeps at the Royal Navy*, 1913, p.88.
30. Mary A. Conley, *From Jack Tar to Union Jack: Representing Naval Manhood in the British Empire, 1870–1918*, Manchester, 2009, pp 1, 3, 5, 8.
31. Christopher McKee, *Sober Men and True: Sailors Lives in the Royal Navy, 1900–1945*, Cambridge and London, 2002, p.47.
32. Wheeler, *Stirring Deeds*, pp. 13, 16, 17.
33. Quintin Colville, 'Jack Tar and the gentleman officer: The role of uniform in shaping the class- and gender-related identities of British naval personnel', *Transactions of the Royal Historical Society*, 6th Series, vol.13, 2003, pp 105–29.
34. McKee, *Sober Men*, p.53.
35. Colville, 'Jack Tar', p.128.
36. McKee, *Sober Men*, p.48.
37. Brian Foss, *War Paint: Art, War, State and Identity in Britain, 1939–1945*, New Haven and London, 2007, p.120.
38. Richmond, *War at Sea*, pp 9–10.
39. For further information, see the NMM website entry for N2676: http://collections.rmg.co.uk/collections/objects/14149.html.

Chapter 1

1. The Dardanelles is the strait linking the Aegean to the Sea of Marmara, and beyond it (through the Bosphorous) the Black Sea: the long Gallipoli peninsula of Turkey, including that port town, forms its northern shore. The 1915 Allied landings were on its north-western side.
2. Neutral ships could only be searched for war materials and a fully effective blockade did not start until the USA joined the war in April 1917: reasons are summarised in Max Hastings, *Catastrophe: Europe Goes to War, 1914*, London, 2013, pp 259, 385.
3. Winston Churchill, *The World Crisis, 1916–1918*, London, 1927, pt 1, p.112.
4. 'Q' stood for Queenstown (now Cobh, Ireland) where most of the ships were based; a few were also used in the Second World War.
5. Drawings in the NMM collection include, for example, advertising work for P&O (PAE1065–66), White Star Line (PAE2088), the *Royal Naval Exhibition* of 1891 (PAE1068) and the Coronation Naval Review of 1911 (PAF2125).
6. A.J. Balfour (First Lord of the Admiralty, May 1915–December 1916) sanctioned Wyllie's invited presence on 'certain ships of the Grand fleet and [for him to] make studies of them under actual war conditions' (W.L. Wyllie *et al., More Sea Fights of the Great War, Including the Battle of Jutland*, London, 1919, p.75). His wife's biography of him (M.A. Wyllie, *We Were One*, London, 1935, p.119) suggests that in 1915 he went north as guest of Rear-Admiral Arthur Leveson, second in command of the 2nd Battle Squadron.
7. Wyllie, *More Sea Fights*, pp 61–3; probably but not certainly during his 1915 visit.
8. Wilkinson also saw the surrender from *Revenge*, as did Madden's son Charles (1906–2001) whom Wyllie taught watercolour while on board. He too became an admiral, a good amateur painter and Chairman of Trustees of the NMM: for his brief recollections of the episode see Roger Quarm and John Wyllie, *W.L. Wyllie: Marine Artist*, London, 1981, pp 109–10.
9. Wyllie eventually painted a large panorama of Trafalgar for the Victory Museum (now the National Museum of the Royal Navy), opened by George V in 1930.
10. The Naval Gallery was founded by Greenwich Hospital for Seamen (as it then was) in 1824: the separate Naval Museum opened alongside the Royal Naval College in 1873.

11. He also made some striking Western Front images, including of air combat: he lost two sons in the Army and a third, Harold, also a painter, was in the Royal Flying Corps before becoming an infantry officer.
12. For a specific example, see Wyllie, *More Sea Fights*, p.121, and the related image of HMS *Southampton* at Jutland.
13. Willem van de Velde the Elder (1611–93) was exceptional in being an official documenter of naval actions for both the Dutch and British navies. Subsequent professional artists who depicted sea battles first-hand were few: Nicholas Pocock appears to have witnessed the Battle of the 1 June, 1794, G.P. Reinagle was with the fleet at the Battle of Navarino in 1827, and from May to October 1855 J.W. Carmichael covered the Baltic campaign in the Crimean War for the *Illustrated London News*.
14. The prefaces credit 'many authors' and 'naval friends' for help but the co-writers were principally M.F. Wren for the first book and W.D. Kirkpatrick and Charles Owen for the second. Owen, in fact, seems to have fulfilled a significant role in both. Nothing is known of Wren but Kirkpatrick was a naval engineer and author of several papers in the *Transactions of the Liverpool Engineering Society*, 1921–34.
15. There are also nine maps and battle plans in the first book by W. Bevan (who also did two line plates, reducing Wyllie's total to ninety-eight) and five Jutland plans by Wyllie in the second.
16. For example, *Bringing in the Wounded 'Lion'* (Wyllie, *More Sea Fights*, p.36) was a Royal Academy work in 1915 and *Old Portsmouth: Minesweepers Putting to Sea* (ibid., p.68) is apparently from the etching (NMM PAF0732) replicating an oil also shown there that year.
17. *The Times*, 2 December 1919.
18. *Prince of Wales*, a King George V-class battleship, first saw action in the Denmark Strait against the *Bismarck*, when the latter sank the battle-cruiser *Hood*, 24 May 1941; *Repulse* was also a battle-cruiser.
19. 'Pedestal', the most heavily protected convoy of the war, comprised just 14 merchant vessels defended by 39 warships, including 5 aircraft carriers. Only 5 merchantmen got through, most famously (in sinking condition) the tanker *Ohio*, while 4 warships lost included the carrier HMS *Eagle*.
20. Eurich to E.M.O'R. Dickey, Secretary of the WAAC, 10 June 1940, IWM, WAAC archives, ART/WA2/03/069.
21. Jan Gordon, 'Art and artists', *Observer*, 8 September 1940.
22. Douglas Hope, *Burlington Magazine*, vol.77, October 1940, pp 128–33.
23. See E. Chaney and C. Clearkin, *Richard Eurich (1903–1992): Visionary Artist*, London, 2003, p.62 (ill.).
24. The *Illustrated London News* pictorial report leads (p.303) with the four marine paintings by Eurich, one by Henry Carr and two by Stephen Bone. The subsequent spread (pp 304–5) shows works by R.V. Pitchforth, Edward Ardizzone, Henry Lamb, Charles Cundall, 'J. Perry' (John Berry) and John Worsley, of which only Worsley's *Hit-and-run day raid on Port Augusta ... 1943* is in the NMM (PAI0616).
25. Wilkinson's first advertisements were for the Liverpool Steamship Co. in 1903 and the London and North Western Railway in 1905, but he became best known for his work for the London Midland and Scottish Railway in the inter-war years.
26. Wilkinson to Wallcott (Admiralty representative, IWM), 11 December 1917 (IWM ART/WA1/342). Christian commanded the landings at Suvla Bay and told Wilkinson, 'I had no idea you were an artist. I shan't have much for you to do so you had better spend some of your time making sketches of operations.' Norman Wilkinson, *A Brush with Life*, London, 1969, p.65.
27. *Illustrated London News*, 27 November 1915. These were his final war illustrations in the publication until his view of the German fleet surrender in the 30 November 1918 issue.
28. A second impression followed in 1916. If it did not directly prompt Wyllie's *Sea Fights* books, it was a precedent for them.
29. Norman Wilkinson, *The Dardanelles: Colour Sketches from Gallipoli*, 1919, p.1. While acknowledging that 'many professional artists' were fighting in France and elsewhere he less presciently thought this would produce little artistic record as 'life in the trenches is so arduous'.
30. The money (granted on application in 1922) was from the Royal Commission on Awards to Inventors. A dismissive reference to dazzle-type camouflage in Wyllie's *More Sea Fights* (pp 92–4) is to an unsuccessful alternative proposal by Percyval Tudor-Hart, one of several listed in a naval summary reprinted in Wilkinson, *Brush with Life*, pp 84–6.
31. Excepting the *Queen Elizabeth* purchase (IWM ART 249) the naval war group are now IWM ART 2326, 2450–53 and 2572: these six are oil versions of watercolours in Wilkinson's *Dardanelles*. After he failed to deliver any of the works commissioned by late 1918 – all being painted in scarce free time – the IWM drew a line on more and also limited his proposed dazzle set to two (IWM ART 4029–30). He also completed at least one large official sea-piece for the Canadians (*Canada's Answer*, *c.*1919, Canadian War Museum, Ottawa).
32. Wilkinson, *Brush with Life*, p.132.
33. The WAAC only accepted gifts from seven artists, and had paid dealings with five of those seven, including Wilkinson. The other two were Martin Hardie and Herbert A. Olivier; a work by Phyllis Ginger was also presented by the Goldsmiths' Company. See Brian Foss, *War Paint: Art, War, State and Identity in Britain, 1939–1945*, London, 2007, pp 196–204, which lists all the WAAC artists by category of their engagement.
34. See Wilkinson, *Brush with Life*, p.134, for his short and less than reliable account of the donation. Foss who discusses the set's public reception, wrongly says there were 52 and also that the WAAC bought one work, which Wilkinson does not mention (Foss, *War Paint*, p.163). Records in the IWM (ART/WA2/03/485) suggest it was of a 1939 air raid on Wilhelmshaven, purchased in January 1942: if so its present whereabouts are not clear.
35. Ibid.
36. Wilkinson, like Wyllie, exhibited at the Academy (though not a member) across 63 years, 1907–70, and died aged 92. Eurich, elected full a full Academy member in 1953, showed work there across 52 years (1937–89); he died aged 89, Wyllie at 79.
37. *New York Times*, 1 May 1915.
38. See, for example, *New York Times*, 10 May 1915.
39. On the sinking of the *Lusitania* see, for example, David Ramsay, *Lusitania: Saga and Myth*, London, 2001; Diana Preston, *Wilful Murder: The Sinking of the Lusitania*, London, 2002. The casualty numbers vary between sources but all agree that just short of 1,200 were killed and that between 761 and 768 escaped the ship. The most commonly quoted figures are used here.
40. *The Times*, 8 May 1915.
41. *The Times*, 10 May 1915.
42. Ibid.
43. Nicoletta F. Gullace, 'Friends, aliens, and enemies: Fictive communities and the *Lusitania* riots of 1915', *Journal of Social History*, vol.39, 2005, pp 345–67.
44. *New York Times*, 8 May 1915; Thomas A. Bailey, 'The sinking of the *Lusitania*', *American Historical Review*, vol.41, 1935, pp 54–73.
45. *American Art News*, 13 May 1916, p.3.
46. *Burlington Magazine*, July 1916, p.173. On German medals, see Thomas Hockenhull, '"Mediocre essays in medallic vituperation": German First World War medals and the British Museum', *Medal*, no.64, 2014, pp 16–31.
47. NMM MEC2677.1.
48. Wyllie, *More Sea Fights*, p.48.

Chapter 2

1. Frank O. Salisbury, *Sarum Chase*, London, 1944, rev. ed. 1953, pp 33–5.
2. *London Gazette*, second supplement, 15 September 1916; *The Times History of the War*, vol.IX, London, 1916, p.158.
3. Mary A. Conley, *From Jack Tar to Union Jack: Representing Naval Manhood in the British Empire, 1870–1918*, Manchester, 2009, pp 160–92.
4. 'Funeral of naval hero John Travers Cornwell 1916', *British Pathé*, http://www.britishpathe.com/video/funeral-of-navy-hero-john-travers-cornwall/query/travers [accessed 10 February 2015].
5. Conley, *From Jack Tar*, p.162.
6. *Spectator*, 15 July 1916, p.68, quoted by Richard Davenport-Hines, 'Cornwell, John Travers (1900–1916)', *Oxford Dictionary of National Biography*, Oxford, 2004, online ed., May 2008, http://www.oxforddnb.com/view/article/45719 [accessed 30 June 2014]. This request echoed a letter to *The Times*, 11 July 1916.
7. Bonham's, London, 'First World War' sale, 1 October 2014, lot 97, p.48, on the preparatory sketch.
8. On the hagiographic casting of Cornwell as a Christian as well as Nelsonian figure, see Conley, *From Jack Tar*, pp 160–92.
9. IWM file: Ambrose McEvoy, ART/WA1/288/2. Founded as the 'National War Museum' in March 1917, it was renamed 'Imperial' in November to reflect the Empire's contributions.
10. Meirion and Susie Harries, *The War Artists: British Official War Art of the Twentieth Century*, London, 1983, p.131. Fourteen of the completed portraits from the IWM collection were included in the exhibition *Sea Power* in aid of King George's Fund for Sailors at the Grosvenor Gallery, London, December 1918. Two more portraits, in the Canadian War Museum, were shown at the *Exhibition of Canadian War Pictures* at Burlington House, London, December 1918 and January 1919. See C. Johnson, *The Works of Ambrose McEvoy from 1900 to May 1919*, London, 1919, vol.1, pp 9–10, and IWM archives, ART/WA1/288/1. McEvoy hoped to have the portrait of Cornwell ready for exhibition (letter to Curator and Secretary of IWM, 29 July 1918) but it was left unfinished, remained in the artist's family and was not shown until it came on loan to the NMM in 1966.

11. Letters from McEvoy to Yockney, 17 March 1919 and 12 October 1919, in the IWM, ART/WA1/288/2.
12. Quote from the critic of *Colour*, June 1917, as reproduced in Harries, *The War Artists*, p.131. McEvoy's technique involved first painting the general forms in neutral monochrome, as suggested by Reginald Gleadowe, *Ambrose McEvoy*, London, 1924, p.28.
13. On mourning photographs and later practices to picture the dead, see Audrey Linkman, *Photography and Death*, London, 2011.
14. Identifiable portraits of ratings before the First World War are rare and, when they exist, usually as part of groups, such as John Burnet's *Greenwich Pensioners commemorating the Battle of Trafalgar* (c.1835, Apsley House, London).
15. IWM file: The Western Front, ART/WA1/455.
16. Bone to Masterman, 12 November 1916, IWM, ibid.
17. Dodd also made a large numbers of drawings of scenes of daily life on board ship, all at the IWM.
18. According to Harries, *The War Artists*, p.18, home sales were between 4,000 and 4,500 copies per volume; 1,500 copies of each volume were distributed free to libraries, clubs and other public spaces, and 5,000 of each were printed for circulation in the United States. Exhibitions held in 1918 of the original drawings for Bone's *Western Front* and Dodd's *Generals* and *Admirals* also had very high attendance.
19. Andrew Lambert, 'Jellicoe, John Rushworth, first Earl Jellicoe (1859–1935)', *Oxford Dictionary of National Biography*, Oxford, 2004, online ed., May 2013, http://www.oxforddnb.com/view/article/34171 [accessed 30 June 2014].
20. Gerard T. Meynell to Wellington House, 1 January 1918, in IWM file: Francis Dodd, ART/WA1/108, quoted in Harries, *The War Artists*, p.18.
21. Judy Egerton, 'Monnington, Sir (Walter) Thomas (1902–1976)', *Oxford Dictionary of National Biography*, Oxford, 2004, http://www.oxforddnb.com/view/article/31455 [accessed 30 June 2014]. The NMM purchased the portrait from Monnington in 1960.
22. Charles Wheeler, *High Relief: The Autobiography of Sir Charles Wheeler, Sculptor*, Feltham, 1968, p.104.
23. Evelyn Silber and Terry Friedman (ed.), *Jacob Epstein, Sculpture and Drawings*, exh.cat., Leeds City Art Galleries/Whitechapel Art Gallery, London, 1998, p.172. Originally conceived in 1913, *Rock Drill*, as completed, was exhibited in the March 1915 London Group exhibition. The drill was then removed and the figure dismembered by the time it was shown in 1916 and became a symbol of the horror of war.
24. Paul G. Halpern, 'Fisher, John Arbuthnot, first Baron Fisher (1841–1920)', *Oxford Dictionary of National Biography*, Oxford, 2004; online ed., September 2010, http://www.oxforddnb.com/view/article/33143 [accessed 7 July 2014].
25. Jacob Epstein, 'How I sculptured Lord Fisher', *Weekly Dispatch*, 24 December 1916; see also Jacob Epstein, *Let There Be Sculpture: An Autobiography*, London, 1940, pp 105–6.
26. Leicester Galleries, *The Sculpture of Jacob Epstein*, exh. no. 238, February–March 1917. Also exhibited were *The Tin Hat* and his portrait of Muirhead Bone, given by the latter, together with the bronze version of Fisher and another bust, to the IWM.
27. F. Rutter, *The Sunday Times*, 25 February 1917; Laurence Binyon, 'The Art of Jacob Epstein', *New Statesman*, 17 March 1917, pp 567–8.
28. Anon., 'A master of portraiture', *The Times*, 26 February 1917, p.11.
29. Silber and Friedman, *Jacob Epstein*, p.172; Evelyn Silber, *The Sculpture of Epstein: With a Complete Catalogue*, Lewisburg, 1986, p.33, no.63.
30. The painting, originally titled *A Child's World* (1886) and subsequently known as 'Bubbles' is on loan at the Lady Lever Art Gallery, Port Sunlight.
31. Sarah Crellin, *The Sculpture of Charles Wheeler*, Farnham, 2012, p.20.
32. The costs for Dobson's and Wheeler's busts were discussed at length in the correspondence between Gleadowe, E.M.O'R. Dickey and the Morris-Singer Company of founders, in October–November 1941. The final foundry estimates to Gleadowe, 21 and 24 October 1941, were £28 for James (at first judged too expensive) and £15 for Creasy; IWM, WAAC archives, Correspondence with Artists: Charles Wheeler, ART/WA2/03/198.
33. NMM SCU0067 and 0068.
34. Wartime sculpted portraits in the IWM fall into the following categories: high-ranking officers, Victoria Cross winners, politicians, artists and other notables such as doctors (with thanks to Claire Brenard, IWM, for this summary).
35. Jonathan Black, *The Face of Courage: Eric Kennington, Portraiture and the Second World War*, exh.cat., RAF, Hendon, June 2011–June 2012, p.21; Silber and Friedman, *Jacob Epstein*, p.172; Dring to Dickey, 4 September 1940, IWM, WAAC archives, Correspondence with Artists: William Dring, ART/WA2/03/172.
36. Paul Gough, *A Terrible Beauty: British Artists in the First World War*, Bristol, 2010, p.20.
37. WAAC minutes, 30 November 1939, IWM, quoted in Black, *The Face of Courage*, p.20.
38. Four of these portraits are naval: Leading Seaman Vearncombe of HMS *Vernon*, Captain F.S. Bell of HMS *Exeter*, Able Seaman Povey and Stoker H. Martin of HMS *Exeter*.
39. Black, *The Face of Courage*, p.26.
40. Eric Kennington and J.B. Priestley, *Pilots, Workers, Machine*, Luton, 1941, unpaginated, quoted in Black, *The Face of Courage*, p.26.
41. Charles Holme, *Studio*, November 1940, pp 148–9, quoted in Black, *The Face of Courage*, p.29.
42. *Connoisseur*, August 1940, p.78, quoted in Black, *The Face of Courage*, p.31.
43. Mrs Ella Hart to Celandine Kennington, 23 December 1943, letter in the family of the artist, quoted in Black, *The Face of Courage*, p.29.
44. Kennington and Priestley, *Pilots*, unpaginated.
45. Dring to Dickey, 4 September 1940, this and subsequent Dring correspondence are from the IWM, WAAC archives, Correspondence with Artists: William Dring, ART/WA2/03/172.
46. Walter Lamb, Secretary of the Royal Academy, to Dickey, 6 May 1941, IWM.
47. Dring's correspondence with Gleadowe, 5 August and 21 September 1941, IWM.
48. Correspondence between Southampton school, WAAC, Board of Education and Dring, March 1942, IWM. After Dring was called up in April 1944, the WAAC successfully argued he should remain a war artist; he was reassigned to the RAF, by then judged in more urgent need of recording.
49. *The Times*, 5 March 1943.
50. 'Art. Miscellaneous exhibitions', *Time and Tide*, 13 March 1943, IWM, WAAC archives, Publicity file, 9 August 1943–11 May 1945, ART/WA2/01/093.
51. Evans developed a chronic infection in his ankle bone, which led to his naval discharge and some years later to amputation of the leg below the knee. See *Lives of the Fellows of the Royal College of Physicians*, vol.VIII, Oxford, 1989, p.145.
52. 'Obituary: Commander Bill King', *Daily Telegraph*, 23 September 2012.
53. Correspondence held in the WAAC archives, October–November 1943, reveals Bridgman sat for Dring, and, most poignantly, that Dring was requested to make a replica portrait for his widow so she could have a lasting souvenir of her husband's features.
54. Very little is known about Gladys E. Reed, but it seems she was born on 19 June 1917, according to a birth record from the district of Portsmouth, vol. 02B, page 534. She is mentioned in *The Evening News*, Portsmouth, as having passed the examination in Drawing at the Municipal School of Art, 14 October 1936, and as having been appointed as teacher of dress and design at the Ashton-under-Lyne School of Art, 11 July 1939. She served in the Wrens in 1943–4, and wrote to the National Maritime Museum from Southsea in 1947. We lose her trace after that. Grateful thanks are owed to Alec Leggatt, who knew her in the late 1930s and early 1940s, and to Penny Allen, Bethany Wright, and especially to Tom Long, for their research.
55. At an uncertain date Reed offered to sell her drawings to the WAAC, which it declined (IWM, WAAC archives, Correspondence with Artists: General, Ra-Ri, ART/WA2/03/024). She presented them to the NMM in 1947, acquisition file NMM6 719/3/47.
56. 1941, NMM PAJ3130
57. Freedman enjoyed spending time with the crews, as described in his correspondence with the WAAC, July–August 1941 (IWM, WAAC archives, Correspondence with Artists: Barnett Freedman, ART/WA/03/040). He set up a studio in *Repulse*, and spent three months on board *Tribune* (Marita Ross, 'Britain's artists go to war', *Evening Gazette*, 3 April 1944). On the popularity of Freedman's 'albums' with the WAAC, see Harries, *The War Artists*, p.215.
58. Robert K. Massie, *Castles of Steel: Britain, Germany and the Winning of the Great War at Sea*, London, 2003, p.93.
59. John Irving, *The Smoke Screen of Jutland*, New York, 1967; see p.143 for an explanation of Admiral Jellicoe's cautious approach and the Admiralty's approval of his methods.
60. Massie, *Castles of Steel*, p.565.
61. Bernard Ireland and Eric Grove, *Jane's War At Sea, 1897–1997*, London, 1997, pp 88–91.
62. George Bonney, *The Battle of Jutland, 1916*, Stroud, 2010, p.151.
63. Peter Hart and Nigel Steel, *Jutland 1916: Death in the Grey Wastes*, London, 2004, p.107.
64. A. MacLean and H.E.R. Stephens, 'Surgical experiences in the Battle of Jutland', *Journal of the Royal Naval Medical Service*, vol.2, no.4, October 1916. This and two other articles in the same volume describe in detail the horrific effects of combat injuries and efforts to cope with them.
65. Claire E.J. Herrick, 'Casualty care during the First World War: The experience of the Royal Navy', *War in History*, vol.7, no.2, April 2000.

66. Massie, *Castles of Steel*, p.657.
67. N.J.M. Campbell, *Jutland: An Analysis of the Fighting*, London, 1986, p.352.
68. Hart and Steel, *Jutland 1916*, p.150.
69. Ibid., p.222.
70. Gordon Taylor, *The Sea Chaplains: A History of the Chaplains of the Royal Navy*, Oxford, 1978, p.356.
71. Bonney, *The Battle of Jutland*, p.193.
72. British ship losses (113,300 tons) were three modern battle-cruisers, three older armoured cruisers and eight destroyers. The Germans lost 62,300 tons: one battle-cruiser, one pre-dreadnought battleship, four light cruisers and five torpedo boats.
73. V.E. Tarrant, *Jutland: The German Perspective*, London, 1995, pp 250–51.
74. Hart and Steel, *Jutland 1916*, pp 418–24.
75. Richard Woodman, *The Victory of Seapower: Winning the Napoleonic War, 1806–1814*, London, 1998, pp 9–13.
76. David C. Evans and Mark R. Peattie, *Kaigun: Strategy, Tactics and Technology in the Imperial Japanese Navy, 1887–1941*, Annapolis, 2012, pp 131–2. As the majority of the participating Japanese ships were British-built, the Royal Navy took a keen interest in the Russo-Japanese War and this engagement in particular.
77. Conley, *From Jack Tar*, ch.5.
78. W. Jameson, *The Fleet that Jack Built*, London, 1962, p.199.
79. G. Bennett, *The Battle of Jutland*, Ware, 1999, p.190.
80. J. Jellicoe, *The Grand Fleet 1914–16: Its Creation, Development and Work*, London, 1919, p.415.

Chapter 3

1. Sylvester Bone, *Sir Muirhead Bone: Artist and Patron*, London, 2009, p.86.
2. Bone's first-hand experience of the war was a regular feature in the press at the time. A now-famous photograph of him at the Western Front, his legs and walking stick pressed in the mud, was published as 'Mr Muirhead Bone on Active Service', *Manchester Guardian*, 24 November 1916.
3. The rapid genesis of the publication is clear in Bone's related letters from October to December 1917 in the IWM file, 'The Western Front', ART/WA1/455. Original bound sets are usually found in two volumes under the imprints of *Country Life* or Doubleday, New York. In addition to the regular issue of 20 lithographs, they were issued in groups, including as a 'luxury' large format, in portfolios of six and as individual prints. See also, Sue Malvern, *Modern Art, Britain and the Great War: Witnessing, Testimony and Remembrance*, New Haven and London, 2004, pp 17, 24–9, 38–41; Paul Gough, *A Terrible Beauty: British Artists in the First World War*, Bristol, 2010, p.51. Aside from the Colnaghi & Obach exhibition, drawings were shown at the Royal Academy and the Whitechapel Gallery. 'War landscapes: Mr Bone's realism', *The Times*, 27 January 1917; 'Art & artists: the Royal Academy Winter Exhibition', *Observer*, 21 January 1917.
4. 'The Artist at the front: Mr Muirhead Bone's pictures', *The Times*, 24 January 1917. As Bone also discovered, artistically useful ruins were not common: front-line structures had often been completely flattened by shelling.
5. 'H.T.', 'Mr Muirhead Bone's war drawings', *Manchester Guardian*, 21 June 1917. They had returned to Bond Street after a tour to Edinburgh, Glasgow, Aberdeen and Newcastle upon Tyne.
6. Meirion and Susie Harries, *The War Artists: British Official War Art of the Twentieth Century*, London, 1983, p.132. For Wyllie's access see Chapter 1: Pictorial Narratives of the War at Sea.
7. Advert for part five of *The Western Front*, *The Times*, 9 May 1917.
8. Gough, *A Terrible Beauty*, pp 46–8; see 'The official drawings of the war', *Manchester Guardian*, 24 January 1917, in which the journalist suggests that Bone's vision is truer than photography, for 'Mr Bone is not only accurate, he is also truthful, and he is most truthful when most accurate.'
9. Harries, *The War Artists*, p.9; Gough, *A Terrible Beauty*, p.46. Pre-war, Bone had acquired notoriety in London for his drawings for the *Architectural Review*, edited by D.S. MacColl, a lifelong friend. The *Manchester Guardian* critic wrote: 'The old Piranesi-Bone has here asserted himself unhesitatingly in the ruined buildings, and the architect-Bone in the drawings at Hesdin and Cassel', 'H.T.', 'Mr Muirhead Bone's war drawings'.
10. 1917, NMM PAI0684.
11. On Bone's significant role in the First World War official commissions and beyond, see Malvern, *Modern Art*, pp 13–14 and Bone, *Sir Muirhead Bone*, pp 104–18.
12. Harries, *The War Artists*, p.209, claims they were 'the most widely reproduced of all official war art'.
13. NMM PAD9697–98, PAF5719–20, PAJ2957, PAJ3141, PAJ3143.
14. Sylvester Bone, *Panel Sketches in Oil by Stephen Bone, 1904–1958*, exh.cat., Abbott and Holder, London, 2010, p.6.
15. For lists of potential subjects sent by Stephen Bone to the WAAC, see letters to E.M.O'R. Dickey, 4 May 1942, suggesting experiments with rocket aircrafts, underground factories, or to record the ensemble of a town's wartime effort, and to Elmsie Owen, 18 May 1943, reiterating the above as well as conscientious objectors, railways, gas workers and chemical factories. Both letters in IWM, WAAC archives, Correspondence with Artists: Stephen Bone, ART/WA2/03/233.
16. Bone, *Panel Sketches*, pp 6–7.
17. WAAC press release, 'New war pictures at the National Gallery', 2 March 1944, quoted exactly in 'War artists anniversary', *Birmingham Post*, 6 March 1944; see also 'New war pictures', *Yorkshire Observer*, 4 March 44. Original in IWM, WAAC archives, Publicity file, 9 August 1943–11 May 1945, ART/WA2/01/093.
18. Bone, *Panel Sketches*, p.6.
19. IWM, WAAC archives, Correspondence with Artists: Stephen Bone, ART/WA2/03/233.
20. Bone, *Panel Sketches*, p.7. For instance, the 1945 drawing of the boiler room of HMS *Norfolk* by Stephen Bone, NMM PAI0539, is very close in subject, style and composition to Muirhead Bone's 1917 lithograph of *The Boiler Room of a Battleship*, NMM PAI0685.
21. Stephen Donovan, 'What lies beneath: The submarine shipwreck in Anglo-American culture, 1880–1920', in Carl Thompson (ed.), *Shipwreck in Art and Literature: Images and Interpretations from Antiquity to the Present Day*, London, 2013, pp 150–70.
22. His *Irish Troops in the Judean Hills Surprised by a Turkish Bombardment* (1919, IWM) was commissioned by the British War Memorials Committee of the Ministry of Information in February 1918, but only begun after the war.
23. Gleadowe to Ravilious, 23 December 1939, and Ravilious to Colonel Garwood, 24 December 1939, in Anne Ullmann (ed.), *Ravilious at War: The Complete Work of Eric Ravilious, September 1939–September 1942*, Upper Denby, 2002, vol.2, nos 463–4, p.511. On Ravilious' keenness to 'take part in the war and try to get it over', see Christine Nash's diary, 31 October 1939, in Ullmann, *Ravilious at War*, p.502, no.454, and Ravilious to Dickey, 17 January1940; this and subsequent letters quoted here to the WAAC are in the IWM, WAAC archives, Correspondence with Artists: Eric Ravilious, ART/WA2/03/037.
24. Ravilious to Dickey, 15 February 1940 and 5 July 1940, IWM.
25. Ravilious to Dickey, 19 July 1940, 2 August 1940, 24 September 1940, IWM.
26. Ravilious to Binyon, 2 August 1940 and 8 August 1940, in Ullmann, *Ravilious at War*, nos 107, 109, pp 109–10. A number of preparatory drawings and photographs are in private collections; some are on long-term loan at the Towner Gallery, Eastbourne.
27. Ravilious to Dickey, 24 January 1940, IWM.
28. Ravilious to Binyon, 29 October 1940, Ullmann, *Ravilious at War*, no.132, p.130. He concluded: 'It is actually a very clever idea if it can be done well. Which such books never are.'
29. Ravilious to Dickey, 12 November 1940, IWM.
30. Ravilious to Tuely, 4 January 1941, in Ullmann, *Ravilious at War*, no.149, p.140. See also Ravilious to Binyon, 26 December 1940, in Ullmann, *Ravilious at War*, no.145, p.138.
31. Ravilious to Tuely, 1 April 1941, in Ullmann, *Ravilious at War*, no.161, p.147. The WAAC purchased the preparatory drawings, at £2, 10 shillings each. While there is no record of the WAAC acquiring the prints, two sets from the Admiralty Library were transferred to the NMM in 1957.
32. A close-up drawing of the tools is on long loan at the Towner Gallery, Eastbourne.
33. 1943, NMM PAI0548.
34. 1941, NMM PAD8075.
35. Dring to Dickey, 2 December 1941, IWM, WAAC archives, Correspondence with Artists: William Dring, ART/WA2/03/172.
36. Public Record Office, reference AIR 27/1566, in Ullmann, *Ravilious at War*, no.278, p.262.
37. 'War pictures', *Eastern Daily Express*, 21 October 1942; 'Nation's war pictures', *Daily Telegraph*, 23 October 1942; *Scotsman*, 23 October 1942; T.W. Earp, 'Fewer robots in war pictures. Human note first', *Daily Telegraph*, 23 October 1942; *Manchester Guardian*, 24 October 1942. Some 70 works by Ravilious were acquired by the WAAC; unpublished research report by Thomas Heal, NMM, 2010.
38. Marita Ross, 'Britain's artists go to war', *Evening Gazette*, 3 April 1944.
39. 'Let's face it', *Yorkshire Observer*, 29 May 1942.
40. On Weston being an eyewitness, see 'New war pictures at the National Gallery', *Shipbuilding and Shipping Record*, 11 June 1942, p.625. The sole painting by Weston in the WAAC collection, it was bought for ten guineas in February 1942, IWM, WAAC archives, Correspondence with Artists: Garth Weston, ART/WA2/03/251.

41. 'Let's face it', *Yorkshire Observer*, 29 May 1942. By contrast, in 'The Connoisseur Divan: Our new war pictures', *Connoisseur*, no.110, 1942, pp 74–6, H. Granville Fell, compared Coxon's picture favourably to Théodore Géricault's *Raft of Medusa* (1819, Musée du Louvre, Paris). The painting was purchased for 35 guineas, IWM, WAAC archives, Correspondence with Artists: Raymond Coxon, ART/WA2/03/070.
42. Eurich interview, 1978, IWM, cat. no.3818, reel 3.
43. Paul Kennedy, *The Rise and Fall of British Naval Mastery*, London, 2001, pp 243–6, for wider discussion.
44. See N.A.M. Rodger, *Command of the Ocean: A Naval History of Britain, 1649–1815*, London, 2005, for discussion of the period.
45. Captain E. Hawkes, *Britain's Wonderful Fighting Forces*, London, *c.*1940, pp 205–9.
46. H.L. Hitchins to his mother, 11 June 1916, NMM REG13/000566.
47. Peter Hart and Nigel Steel, *Jutland 1916: Death in the Grey Wastes*, London, 2004, pp 415–6.
48. William James, *Admiral Sir William Fisher*, London, 1943, p.62.
49. Le Mesurier to his wife, 26 August 1916, in Harriet Bachrach (ed.), *Jutland Letters, June–October 1916*, Salisbury, 2006, p.64.
50. Peter Liddle, *The Sailor's War, 1914–18*, Poole, 1985, pp 113, 140.
51. Filson Young, *With the Battle Cruisers*, Edinburgh, 2002, pp 122, 86.
52. Liddle, *The Sailor's War*, p.133.
53. Peter Hore, *The Habit of Victory*, London, 2005, p.304, quoting Walter Cowen, NMM, COW17/1–6.
54. Le Mesurier to wife, 23 August 1916, in Bachrach, *Jutland Letters*, p.61. Rear-Admiral Sir Robert Arbuthnot commanded the 1st Cruiser Squadron, with *Defence* as his flagship: he died in her at Jutland.
55. Le Mesurier to wife, 21 July 1916, in Bachrach, *Jutland Letters*, p.46.
56. Liddle, *The Sailor's War*, pp 133–4.
57. Young, *With the Battle Cruisers*, p.127.
58. Victor Hayward, *HMS Tiger at Bay*, London, 1977, pp 73–4.

Chapter 4

1. Worsley's wartime experiences are recounted in a 1978 audio interview (IWM, cat. no.3173) and described in John Worsley and Kenneth Giggal, *John Worsley's War*, Shrewsbury, 1993.
2. E.M.O'R. Dickey to Worsley, 22 May 1940; this and following Worsley correspondence are from the IWM, WAAC archive, Correspondence with Artists: John Worsley, ART/WA2/03/082.
3. Worsley to Dickey, undated, probably July 1940.
4. Correspondence between Dickey and Worsley, 1, 8 and 12 August 1940.
5. His first eight drawings were displayed in the first War Artists exhibition in July 1940; see WAAC to Worsley, 1 June 1940.
6. 'Exhibition of British War Artists at the Modern Museum of Art, New York: personal notes on the exhibitors'; in IWM, WAAC archive, War Artists Biographical Material N–Z, ART/WA2/01/065.
7. Worsley represented the wreck in *The Last of the Laurentic*, acquired by the WAAC for 30 guineas, Dickey to Worsley, 24 April 1941. The painting was lost through enemy action as the War Artists exhibition was on its way to South America and Worsley was commissioned to paint a replica; Dickey to Worsley, 28 September 1942.
8. Worsley to Dickey, 3 May 1941. Worsley provided illustrations for his crewmate John Fernald's *Destroyer from America* (1942); 2 drawings for 6 guineas, Dickey to Worsley, 2 January 1942; 8 drawings for 20 guineas, Dickey to Worsley, 23 July 1942.
9. Letter certifying appointment, 27 July 1943, IWM.
10. Worsley and Giggal, *John Worsley's War*, p.48.
11. *Illustrated London News*, 11 March 1944, p.305, IWM and NMM. One was displayed in the National Gallery's War Artists exhibition of March 1944.
12. Martin D.W. Jones, 'Into the lion's mouth: John Worsley, War Artist', *Country Life*, vol.179, 20 February 1986, pp 448–9; also discussed in Worsley and Giggal, *John Worsley's War*, pp 50–51. In his audio interview with the IWM, Worsley said: 'I felt that because I was a war artist, I was like a referee, I was on the touchline, watching, and therefore nobody would hurt me. It was a curious psychological approach.'
13. Worsley audio interview, IWM, reel 2.
14. Thanks are owed to Claire Brenard for clarifying that while John Worsley was the only full-time salaried artist to be held as a prisoner of war for an extended period, Edward Bawden was briefly held captive in the Vichy internment camp in Casablanca for two months in 1942.
15. Letter from Worsley's mother to Irene D. Neville, WAAC, 18 May 1944, IWM. Painting LD5155.
16. See letter Winsor & Newton to Neville, WAAC, 11 May 1944, IWM.
17. Worsley audio interview, IWM, reel 2; Worsley and Giggal, *John Worsley's War*, p.81.
18. Worsley audio interview, IWM, reel 3; Worsley and Giggal, *John Worsley's War*, pp 84–5.
19. IWM, LD5128, LD5129, LD5149, LD5127.
20. These drawings are at the IWM; Worsley and Giggal, *John Worsley's War*, pp 93–102. Worsley's dummy was the subject of a feature film, *Albert RN*, directed by Gilbert Lewis in 1953.
21. Eric Newton, *A Record of War by British War Artists, Selected and Introduced by Eric Newton*, London, 1945, p.67. Worsley audio interview, IWM, cat. no.3173, reel 3. Morgan's wartime experiences are recorded in his *Only Ghosts Can Live*, London, 1945, illustrated by Worsley.
22. Worsley to Gregory, 8 October 1945, and response, 9 October 1945. Forty-eight works were acquired for 200 guineas, see memo from Gregory to Miss Dodd, Finance Division of the WAAC, 22 May 1945, and a further three paintings for 75 guineas, 5 July 1945, IWM.
23. Cook to his parents, Galveston, 21 February 1941; Cook's logbook, January–February 1941. The letters, logbook and unpublished memoir are held by Bridget Cook, whose help is gratefully acknowledged.
24. Cook's logbook, March–April, July 1941.
25. Cook to his parents, West Caddoa, Port Arthur, Texas, 26 February 1941.
26. Cook's logbook, 1, 2 and 4 April 1941.
27. Cook's memoirs, unpaginated.
28. Cook's logbook, uncertain dates and 14 July 1941.
29. NMM ZBA5321–24.
30. According to Cook's notes, his parents received news from Marconi that he was a survivor on 11 December 1941 and a letter from the Red Cross giving his whereabouts on 6 January 1942; they received his first letter, written on 5 November 1941, two days later. He received his first letter from them on 16 February 1942.
31. Cook to his parents, Bône, 5, 10 and 25 November 1941.
32. Cook to his parents, Bône, 7–18 December 1941. The letter's sketch formed the basis for a drawing, later acquired by the WAAC and now in the Aberdeen Art Gallery, LD2818. It was displayed in a War Artists exhibition in 1945; Newton, *War through Artists' Eyes, Paintings and Drawings by British War Artists*, p.40.
33. Cook to his parents, Mécheria, Algeria, 25 September 1942. He occasionally received art supplies from friends; letter to his parents, Mécheria, 19 July 1942.
34. Cook to his parents, Mécheria, 16 February and 6 March 1942. A schematic drawing shows the location of Cook's studio within the compound.
35. Cook to his parents, Mécheria, 27 April 1942.
36. Cook to his parents, Bône, 7–18 December 1941. This inspired a drawing, NMM ZBA5332.
37. Cook to his parents, from Bône, 7–18 December 1941; from Mécheria, 15 October 1942.
38. Cook to his parents, Mécheria, 27 April and 13 August 1942.
39. Cook's memoirs, unpaginated. Letters to his parents, 10, 18 May 1942; 13, 19 August 1942; notebook kept in Algeria, undated.
40. Cook's memoirs, unpaginated. Cook to his parents, Mécheria, 11 April 1942. Drawing NMM ZBA5362.
41. For instance, Cook to his parents, Mécheria, 29 March 1942.
42. IWM, LD2816, LD2817, LD2819, and Aberdeen Art Gallery, LD2818. WAAC to Cook, 11 March 1943; this and further correspondence with the WAAC, IWM, WAAC archives, Correspondence with Artists: John Kingsley Cook, ART/WA2/03/169.
43. John Kingsley Cook's Certificate of Discharge, in the artist's family.
44. Cook to his parents, December 1943–July 1944.
45. Cook to Gregory, WAAC, 6 December 1943, IWM.
46. Purchased for 12 guineas and now in the IWM and Aberdeen Art Gallery. Gregory to Cook, 16 December 1943, IWM.
47. Cook to his parents, SS *Esturia*, 21 April 1944.
48. Cook sent the resulting drawings made in Gibraltar to the WAAC but only one was purchased, *Convoy on a Grey Day*, for 6 guineas and now at Aberdeen Art Gallery. Cook to Gregory, WAAC, 27 July 1944, IWM.
49. Cook's memoirs, unpaginated.
50. The Royal Navy was the principal advocate of the modern convoy system, using it for escorting troopships before its 1917 extension to cargo vessels.
51. *The Times*, 14 February 1928; *London Gazette*, 14 February 1928, p.1048. While *The Times* of 30 July 1919 reported that the King spoke of 'the recreation of our Merchant Navy' [*sic*] at a London event on the 29th, frequent claims that he 'granted' the title itself, and just for First World War service, are misleading: as the phrase 'merchant navy' was common by 1900.
52. Ian Friel, *The British Museum Maritime History of Britain and Ireland*, London, 2003, p.245.
53. Richard Woodman, *Arctic Convoys*, London, 1994, p.17.
54. The red ensign, previously the 'senior' Royal Naval and British merchant flag, became that of merchant shipping only in 1864 when the Navy took exclusive use

of the white ensign. Reserve and other auxiliary forces took blue.

55. Woodman, *Arctic Convoys*, p.176.

56. The equivalency of ranks is borne out by Statutory Instrument 1949 No.1852, *The War Pensions (Mercantile Marine) Scheme 1949*, and Statutory Rules and Orders 1946 No.1640, *War Pensions (Naval Auxiliary Personnel) Scheme*.

57. Examples are officers' uniforms of the Peninsula and Oriental Steam Navigation Company (P&O) and the Orient Line.

58. Creighton served as Commodore of ocean convoys for the first three years of the Second World War. He took part in 25 convoys, mainly in the North Atlantic, and was twice sunk.

59. Paul Kemp, *Convoy! Drama in Arctic Waters*, London, 1999, p.93.

60. Kemp, *Convoy!*, p.93.

61. L.S. Saunders's memoirs, 1941–42, NMM MSS/88/009.0.

Chapter 5

1. Parliamentary Archives, HL/PO/PU/1/1914/4& 5G5c29, Defence of the Realm Act, c.29.

2. Kevin D. Stubbs, *Race to the Front: The Material Foundations of Coalition Strategy in the Great War*, Westport, CT, 2002, p.24.

3. The details of the first regulations of the Emergency (Defence) Powers Act of 1939 were published in *The Times*, 29 August 1939, under the headline 'Safety of the realm', outlining measures intended to protect the security of the state, public safety, ships and aircraft, essential supplies, general provisions, etc.

4. Nicholas Rankin, *Churchill's Wizards: The British Genius for Deception, 1914–1945*, London, 2008, pp 34–41.

5. Spencer C. Tucker (ed.), *The European Powers in the First World War: An Encyclopedia*, New York and London, 1996, pp 160–61.

6. Thayer published a paper on 'The Law which Underlies Protective Coloration' in 1896, followed by a book co-authored with Gerald Thayer, *Concealing Coloration in the Animal Kingdom*, London, 1909.

7. Nearly 7,000 Allied ships were sunk by German U-Boats with the loss of approximately 15,500 on board, according to the Commonwealth War Graves Association.

8. An undated naval memorandum briefly summarising the schemes is reprinted in Norman Wilkinson, *A Brush with Life*, London, 1969, pp 84–6. Entitled 'Dazzle' it may be the first formal record of the term.

9. Ibid., pp 79–80.

10. Rankin, *Churchill's Wizards*, p.190.

11. Tim Newark, *Camouflage*, 2007 p.74.

12. Ibid., pp 83, 79. Wood used his own talents in modelling towards facial reconstruction of those who had been horribly wounded in the First World War.

13. Ibid.

14. Wyndham Lewis (ed.), *BLAST: Review of the Great English Vortex*, no.1, June 1914, pp 22–3.

15. Jonathan Black, '"Constructing a Chinese-puzzle universe": Industry, national identity and Edward Wadsworth's Vorticist woodcuts of West Yorkshire, 1914–1916', in Mark Antliff and Scott W. Klein (eds), *Vorticism: New Perspectives*, Oxford, 2013, p.90.

16. Ibid., pp 91–3.

17. William Feaver, *The Listener*, vol.92, British Broadcasting Corporation, 1974, p.183.

18. Richard Cork, *Vorticism and its Allies*, 1974, p.91.

19. Roy R. Behrens (ed.), *Ship Shape: A Dazzle Camouflage Sourcebook*, Iowa, 2012, p.54.

20. From the NMM's typed copy of Everett's manuscript memoir, p.111 ('Memoirs of John Everett, which he called "Wicked Devils, Wicked Devils", and which he began on 4th December, 1945 and finished sometime in the year of his death in 1949'). The original manuscript is in a private collection.

21. 'Camouflaged ships', *The Times*, 16 December 1918.

22. The *Studio* ran from 1893 to 1964 and special-topic editions (of which it published 117 between 1894 and 1940) were normally published three times a year.

23. Charles Holme (ed.), 'The war depicted by distinguished British artists', *Studio*, London and New York, 1918.

24. 'Artists' revelries', *Observer*, 1 March 1914.

25. 'The art of naval "camouflage" applied to fancy dress: The Chelsea Arts Club "Dazzle" Ball', *Illustrated London News*, 22 March 1919, pp 414–15.

26. Marjorie H. Fletcher, *The WRNS: A History of the Women's Royal Naval Service*, Annapolis, 1989, p.11.

27. Ibid.

28. IWM ART 2619 and 2620.

29. Catherine Speck, *Beyond the Battlefield: Women Artists of the Two World Wars*, London, 2014, pp 27, 235.

30. IWM ART 2306–11.

31. Speck, *Beyond the Battlefield*, p.23.

32. Ibid., p.15.

33. In addition to her WRNS recruitment poster, Dennys wrote and illustrated a VAD alphabet.

34. Fletcher, *The WRNS*, p.24.

35. J.B. Priestley, *British Women Go to War*, London, 1944, p.24.

36. Priestley, *British Women*, p.24.

37. Quoted from NMM acquisition file NMM6 719/3/47.

38. 'Two torpedomen' was the February 1945 back-cover image of the *Dittybox*: the other drawings appeared in the October issue, p.23.

39. Geraldine Horton, *No Nightingale Sang*, Hythe, 1996, pp 138–9.

40. Timothy Hyman and Patrick Wright (eds), *Stanley Spencer*, exh.cat., Tate, London, 2001, p.102.

41. Ibid.

42. Chris Stephens, 'Preface', in Nathaniel Hepburn, *Barbara Hepworth: The Hospital Drawings*, London, 2012, p.7.

43. Admiral Charles Fitzgerald founded the Order of the White Feather in conjunction with Mrs Humphrey Ward in August 1914. Its aim was to shame able-bodied men into enlisting after they were presented with the white feather, a symbol of cowardice.

44. Committee on Mercantile Marine Uniform, *Report of the Committee Appointed by the Board of Trade to Advise as to the Uniform to be Adopted as the Standard Uniform for the Mercantile Marine*, London, 1918, p.3.

45. The watch is now in the Imperial War Museum, EPH10291.

46. Charles F. Horne (ed.), *Source Records of the Great War*, vol.IV, New York, 1923.

47. Edith Cavell was matron of her own hospital in Belgium. During the First World War, she helped men to avoid service by giving them jobs in the hospital and also aided some in finding safe passage through the Netherlands. She was discovered, put on trial for treason and executed. On news of her death, enlistment in the British Army doubled. Diana Souhami, *Edith Cavell*, London, 2011.

48. Anon., *The Murder of Captain Fryatt*, London, 1916.

49. See photographs Q4101 and Q943 in the IWM collection. In 1919, both Fryatt's and Cavell's bodies were repatriated and public funerals held for them at St Paul's Cathedral and Westminster Abbey respectively. There is a bronze and marble memorial to Fryatt at Liverpool Station, London, the former headquarters of the Great Eastern Railway.

50. Committee on Mercantile Marine Uniform, *Report*, p.3.

51. House of Lords Debate, 3 August 1943, *Hansard*, vol.128, cc.955–75.

52. 'Schools and ships,' *The Times*, 25 March 1936.

53. House of Lords Debate, 3 August 1943, *Hansard*, vol.128, cc.955–75.

54. 'Ships adopted by schools', *The Times*, 24 January 1942, p.2.

55. 'Merchant Navy Comforts Service', *Observer*, 31 March 1940; *Guardian*, 31 March 1940; *The Times*, 17 May 1940.

56. NMM ZBA5264.

57. Sarah Crellin, *The Sculpture of Charles Wheeler*, Farnham, 2012, p.172.

58. House of Lords Debate, 3 August 1943, *Hansard*, vol.128, cc.955.

59. These parcels were supplied or funded by many companies across Britain who had staff or family members serving in British forces or the Merchant Navy. One record in the Northern Assurance papers held in the Aviva Archive at Norwich mentions that Christmas parcels 'are again being sent to all members of the London staff serving in the forces. Each parcel will contain: pair of socks, packet of playing cards, pocket set of dominates, saccharine tablets, razor blades or medicine pack, toothbrush and toothpaste. It is possible to obtain as much wool as we require from the various organisations, so if you will find more knitters we will promise to produce the wool (and patterns).'

Chapter 6

1. Alan Borg, *War Memorials from Antiquity to the Present*, London, 1991, p.69.

2. Geoff Archer, *The Glorious Dead: Figurative Sculpture of British First World War Memorials*, Kirstead, 2009, p.10.

3. Borg, *War Memorials*, p.71. The Royal Academy (RA) in London and Royal Scottish Academy in Edinburgh both set up committees on war memorials. As early as autumn 1916, the Royal Institute of British Architects held *The Design of War Memorials* exhibition. The Victoria and Albert Museum and RA War Memorials Committee followed suit, collaborating on an exhibition from October 1919 to November 1920.

4. *Modern British Sculpture: An Official Record of Some of the Works by Members of the Royal Society of British Sculptors, London*, 1922, see pp 23, 41, 52 and 83.

5. Borg, *War Memorials, p.70.*

6. Lutyens was one of three principal architects for the Imperial (now Commonwealth) War Graves Commission. The Cenotaph was first installed in 1919, in Whitehall, as a temporary structure of wood and plaster for the year's Victory (or Peace) Parade; it was replaced in 1920 with the present version in Portland stone. The format was adapted in other cities. The Whitehall monument comprises a tall, stepped pylon at the top of which is a cenotaph (an empty tomb), with carved wreaths by Francis Derwent Wood.

7. For an in-depth analysis of the style and location of the British war memorials of the Western Front, see Jeroen Geurst, *Cemeteries of the Great War by Sir Edwin Lutyens*, Rotterdam, 2010.

8. More recently sunk naval vessels have been designated official war graves: the two at Scapa Flow are HMS *Vanguard* and *Royal Oak*.

9. *Evening Standard*, 3 October 1916.

10. For discussion of contemporary history painting in the late eighteenth and early nineteenth century and its impact on representations of Nelson and the Battle of Trafalgar, see Christine Riding, 'Trafalgar Squared', in *Turner and the Sea*, London, 2013, pp 103–12.

11. Sarah Crellin, *The Sculpture of Charles Wheeler*, Farnham, 2012, p.71.

12. Borg, *War Memorials*, pp 87–8.

13. Tim Skelton and Gerald Gliddon, *Lutyens and the Great War*, London, 2008, p.94; David Crane, *Empires of the Dead*, London, 2014, p.198.

14. Geurst, *Cemeteries*, p.56. Geurst draws parallels between the Merchant Marine (or Merchant Navy) Memorial and the pavilions of two Western Front cemeteries, Hooge Crater Cemetery and Serre Road Cemetery. See also the discussion on pavilions and shelters, pp 80–93. The Merchant Marine Memorial is illustrated on pp 54, 88.

15. Jay Winter, *Sites of Memory, Sites of Mourning: The Great War in European Cultural History*, Cambridge, 1998, p.9.

16. Quoted in Christopher Hussey, *The Life of Sir Edwin Lutyens*, London, 1950, p.566.

17. The inscription on the memorial at Tower Hill reads 'Twenty four thousand of the Merchant Navy and fishing fleets whose names are honoured on the walls of this garden gave their lives for their country and have no grave but the sea.'

18. A.H. Joyce, 'The Merchant Navy War Memorial', *Ships Monthly*, June 1993, p.15.

19. Another example of a sailor figure is the Exchange News Room War Memorial (1924) in Liverpool by Joseph Phillips, which has bronze sculptures of three soldiers, a sailor and a nurse, with a summit figure of Britannia protecting a child.

20. Archer, *Glorious Dead*, p.309. Archer suggests that a prisoner-of-war figure may have been included because of the relief work for prisoners in Germany carried out by Lady Owen, wife of the then Mayor of Exeter. The memorial was unveiled in 1923 by Admiral Sir David Beatty (Archer, *Glorious Dead*, p.182).

21. See Michelangelo's tomb sculptures of Guiliano di Lorenzo, Duke of Nemours, and Lorenzo di Piero, Duke of Urbino (Medici Chapels, Basilica di San Lorenzo, Florence, 1521–4), and his *Moses* for the tomb of Pope Julius II (San Pietro in Vincoli, Rome, *c.*1513–15).

22. Archer, *Glorious Dead*, p.97.

23. McMillan won the competition for the British War Medal, Wheeler being runner-up, and designed the Allied Victory Medal (both dated 1919). Wheeler made designs for the International or King's Medal (not struck), and a joint design with Walter Gilbert for a commemorative Jutland medal (struck in 1916), which was sold in aid of the Royal Navy Relief Fund. Both McMillan and Wheeler submitted competition designs for the Next of Kin Memorial Plaque ('The Dead Man's Penny').

24. For example McMillan had executed war memorials in Aberdeen and Manchester (both 1919) and Wheeler had already begun a major sculptural project for the Bank of England (1927–42).

25. Crellin, *Charles Wheeler*, pp 72, 154. Crellin's in-depth study of the Jellicoe and Beatty memorial project is indispensable for the history of the commission, in particular the discussions around the appropriate themes for the site.

26. Ibid., p.72.

27. Ibid., p.154.

28. Carl Milles was particularly admired by Wheeler. Ibid., pp 16–18.

29. Charles Wheeler, *High Relief: The Autobiography of Sir Charles Wheeler, Sculptor*, Feltham, 1968, pp 48, 47.

30. See for example, the bronze figures, *Wipers* (IWM, 1919–20), *Soldier on Defence* (Hoylake War Memorial, 1919–22), *Sentry* (Memorial to Employees of S. & J. Watts and Co., c.1919–22) and the Royal Artillery memorial (1921–5) by Jagger, and the Guards' Division Memorial (1922–6) by Ledward. Wheeler and McMillan's pared down approach in stone particularly chimes with that of Jagger in his representation of a British and Belgian infantrymen in the centre of the Anglo-Belgian War Memorial (1921–3), Brussels.

31. Catherine Moriarty, *The Sculpture of Gilbert Ledward*, Farnham, 2003, p.86. The figure of the submariner was exhibited at the Royal Academy in 1950, ibid., p.121.

32. Arnold Whittick, *War Memorials*, London, 1946, pp 70–1.

33. For a timeline of sales, exhibitions and acquisitions of Blake's work see 'William Blake: William Blake at Tate timeline', *Tate*, http://www.tate.org.uk/whats-on/tate-britain/display/william-blake-display/william-blake-william-blake-tate-timeline [accessed 11 December 2014).

34. Colin Trodd, *Visions of Blake: William Blake in the Art World 1830–1930*, Liverpool, 2012, pp 439, 444, 447.

35. Quoted in Moriarty, *Gilbert Ledward*, p.113.

36. Whittick, *War Memorials*, p.142.

37. Moriarty, *Gilbert Ledward*, pp 64–6.

38. Adrian Stokes, *Stones of Rimini*, London, 1934.

39. Stokes, *Stones of Rimini*, pp 19–22, 157.

40. Catharine Moriarty, *'The Sea Goeth It All About': Maritime Themes in British Public Sculpture*, Brighton, 2011, p.5, http://arts.brighton.ac.uk/__data/assets/pdf_file/0003/73290/seagoeth.pdf [accessed 15 December 2014].

41. Gilbert Torrence Bell, 'Monuments to the fallen: Scottish war memorials of the Great War', unpublished PhD thesis, University of Strathclyde, 1993, p.200.

42. Gaynor Kavanagh, *Museums and the First World War: A Social History*, London and New York, 1994, pp 124, 134.

43. A photograph of the war memorial *in situ* is in the NMM photographic archive D9469, and is reproduced in Val Horsler (ed.), *The Royal Hospital School: Celebrating 300 Years*, London, 2012, p.57.

44. IWM ART 16410. The first version of *Pale Armistice* (1987) was shown in *The Subversive Stitch* exhibition at the Cornerhouse, Manchester, in 1988.

45. Mary Schoeser, *Rozanne Hawksley*, Farnham, 2009, p.26.

46. Eric Kennington, W.O. Kennington and J.B. Priestley, *Pilots, Workers, Machines*, Luton, 1941, unpaginated.

47. Schoeser, *Rozanne Hawksley*, pp 48, 89.

48. Ibid, p.23.

49. Herbert Asquith, *The Volunteer and Other Poems*, London, 1915, p.46.

Select Bibliography

Archer, Geoff, *The Glorious Dead: Figurative Sculpture of British First World War Memorials*, Kirstead, 2009

Bachrach, Harriet (ed.), *Jutland Letters, June–October 1916*, Salisbury, 2006

Behrens, Roy R. (ed.), *Ship Shape: A Dazzle Camouflage Sourcebook: An Anthology of Writings About Ship Camouflage During World War I*, Iowa, 2012

Bennett, Geoffrey, *The Battle of Jutland*, Wordsworth Military Library edn, Ware, 1999

Binyon, Helen, *Eric Ravilious: Memoir of an Artist*, Guildford, 1983

Black, Jonathan, *The Face of Courage: Eric Kennington, Portraiture and the Second World War*, exh.cat., RAF, Hendon, June 2011–June 2012

Bohm-Duchen, Monica, *Art and the Second World War*, Princeton, NJ, 2013

Bone, Sylvester, *Panel Sketches in Oil by Stephen Bone, 1904–1958*, exh.cat., Abbott and Holder, London, 2010

Bone, Sylvester, *Sir Muirhead Bone: Artist and Patron*, London, 2009

Bonney, George, *The Battle of Jutland, 1916*, Stroud, 2010

Borg, Alan, *War Memorials from Antiquity to the Present*, London, 1991

Bosman, Suzanne, *The National Gallery in Wartime*, London, 2008

Cantwell, John D., *Images of War: British Posters 1939–45*, London, 1989

Chaney, Edward and Clearkin, C., *Richard Eurich (1903–1992): Visionary Artist*, London, 2003

Colville, Quintin, 'Jack Tar and the gentleman officer: The role of uniform in shaping the class- and gender-related identities of British naval personnel', *Transactions of the Royal Historical Society*, 6th Series, vol.13, 2003, pp 105–29

Conley, Mary A., *From Jack Tar to Union Jack: Representing Naval Manhood in the British Empire, 1870–1918*, Manchester, 2009

Cork, Richard, *A Bitter Truth: Avant-garde Art and the Great War*, New Haven and London, 1994

Creighton, Rear-Admiral Sir Kenelm, *Convoy Commodore*, London, 1956

Crellin, Sarah, *The Sculpture of Charles Wheeler*, Farnham, 2012

Edwards, Bernard, *The Quiet Heroes: British Merchant Seamen at War, 1939–1945*, Barnsley, 2010

Epstein, Jacob, *Let There Be Sculpture: An Autobiography*, London, 1940

Foss, Brian, *War Paint: Art, War, State and Identity in Britain, 1939–45*, New Haven and London, 2007

Friel, Ian, *The British Museum Maritime History of Britain and Ireland*, London, 2003

Gleadowe, Reginald, *Ambrose McEvoy*, London, 1924

Goodden, Henrietta, *Camouflage and Art: Design for Deception in World War 2*, London, 2007

Gough, Paul, *A Terrible Beauty: British Artists in the First World War*, Bristol, 2010

Grove, Eric J. and Ireland, Bernard, *Jane's War At Sea, 1897–1997*, London, 1997

Harding, Stephen, *Great Liners at War*, Stroud, 2007

Harries, Meirion and Susie, *The War Artists: British Official War Art of the Twentieth Century*, London, 1983

Hart, P. and Steel, Nigel, *Jutland 1916: Death in the Grey Wastes*, London, 2004

Hawkes, Captain Ellison, *Britain's Wonderful Fighting Forces*, London, *c.*1940

Hayward, *HMS Tiger at Bay*, London, 1977

Hore, Peter, *The Habit of Victory*, London, 2005

James, William, *Admiral Sir William Fisher*, London, 1943

Jellicoe, Admiral Viscount [John Rusworth], *The Grand Fleet 1914–16: Its Creation, Development and Work*, London, 1919

Johnson, C., *The Works of Ambrose McEvoy from 1900 to May 1919*, London, 1919

Kemp, Paul, *Convoy! Drama in Arctic Waters*, London, 1999

Kennedy, Paul, *The Rise and Fall of British Naval Mastery*, London, 2001

Kennington, Eric and Priestley, J.B., *Pilots, Workers, Machine*, Luton, 1941

Knott, Richard, *The Sketchbook War: Saving the Nation's Artists in World War II*, Stroud, 2013

Liddle, Peter, *The Sailor's War, 1914–18*, Poole, 1985

Littlewood, Kevin and Butler, Beverley, *Of Ships and Stars: Maritime Heritage and the Founding of the National Maritime Museum, Greenwich*, New Brunswick, 1998

Mallmann Showell, Jak P., *The U-Boat century: German Submarine Warfare, 1906–2006*, London, 2006

Malvern, Sue, *Modern Art, Britain and the Great War: Witnessing, Testimony and Remembrance*, New Haven and London, 2004

Massie, Robert K., *Castles of Steel: Britain, Germany and the Winning of the Great War at Sea*, London, 2003

McKee, Christopher, *Sober Men and True: Sailors Lives in the Royal Navy, 1900–1945*, Cambridge and London, 2002

Moorhouse, Paul, *The Great War in Portraits*, exh.cat., National Portrait Gallery, London, 2014

Morgan, Guy, *Only Ghosts Can Live*, London, 1945

Newton, Eric, *War through Artists' Eyes, Paintings and Drawings by British War Artists*, London, 1945

Phillips, Lawrie, *The Royal Navy Day by Day*, 4th edn, Stroud, 2011

Powers, Alan, *Eric Ravilious: Artist and Designer*, Farnham, 2013

Powers, Alan, *Eric Ravilious: Imagined Realities*, London, 2003

Preston, Diana, *Lusitania: An Epic Tragedy*, New York, 2003

Preston, Diana, *Wilful Murder: The Sinking of the Lusitania*, London, 2002

Priestley, J.B., *British Women Go to War*, London, 1944

Quarm, Roger and Wyllie, John, *W.L. Wyllie: Marine Artist*, London, 1981

Quilley, Geoff (ed.), *Art for the Nation: The Oil Paintings Collections of the National Maritime Museum*, London, 2006

Ramsay, David, *Lusitania: Saga and Myth*, London, 2001

Richmond, Admiral Sir Herbert, *War at Sea: War Pictures by British Artists*, Oxford, 1942

Russell, James, *Ravilious Submarine*, Norwich, 2013

Salisbury, Frank O., *Sarum Chase*, London, 1944

Silber, Evelyn and Friedman, Terry (eds), *Jacob Epstein, Sculpture and Drawings*, exh.cat., Leeds City Art Galleries/ Whitechapel Art Gallery, London, 1998

Slader, John, *The Red Duster at War: A History of the Merchant Navy During the Second World War*, London, 1988

Speck, Catherine, *Beyond the Battlefield: Women Artists of the Two World Wars*, London, 2014

Ullmann, Anne (ed.), *Ravilious at War: The Complete Work of Eric Ravilious, September 1939–September 1942*, Upper Denby, 2002

Webb, Brian (ed.), *Eric Ravilious, Submarine Dream. Lithographs and Letters*, London, 1996

Wheeler, Charles, *High Relief: The Autobiography of Sir Charles Wheeler, Sculptor*, Feltham, 1968

Whittick, Arnold, *War Memorials*, London, 1946

Wilkinson, Norman, *A Brush with Life*, London, 1969

Wilkinson, Norman, *The Dardanelles: Colour Sketches from Gallipoli*, London, 1919

Woodman, Richard, *Arctic Convoys*, London, 1994

Woodman, Richard, *The Real Cruel Sea: The Merchant Navy in the Battle of the Atlantic, 1939–1943*, London, 2004

Worsley, John and Giggal, Kenneth, *John Worsley's War: An Official War Artist in World War II*, Ramsbury, 1993

Wyllie, M.A., *We Were One: A life of W.L. Wyllie, RA, RE, RI*, London, 1935

Wyllie, William Lionel, Owen, Charles and Kirkpatrick, W.D., *More Sea Fights of the Great War, Including the Battle of Jutland*, London, 1919

Wyllie, William Lionel and Wren, M.F., *Sea Fights of the Great War: Naval Incidents during the First Nine Months*, London, 1918

Young, Filson, *With the Battle Cruisers*, Edinburgh, 2002

Acknowledgements

The editor would like to thank the following colleagues: Emily Churchill, Photographic Studio Co-ordinator, Kara Green, Publishing Project Manager, and curators Quintin Colville, Robert J. Blyth and Pieter van de Merwe for their editorial input and suggestions concerning the texts, Melanie Vandenbrouck for her considerable contribution to the project, and to Robert J. Blyth, Andrew Choong, John Graves, Jeremy Michell, Amy Miller, Melanie Vandenbrouck and Pieter van de Merwe for their engaging and authoritative essays.

Special thanks are also due to Bridget Cook and the John Kingsley Cook family, Ken Eaton, Peter Nash and the Society for Nautical Research, Joshua Akin, Penny Allen, Hugh Antram, Tom Barrow, Laurence Birnie, Claire Brenard, Elizabeth Campbell, Elisabeth Carr, Paul Cook, Karen Eden-Tuxford, Jennifer Foot, Anupam Ganguli, Elizabeth Hamilton-Eddy, Rozanne Hawksley, Thomas Heal, Nick Jellicoe, Richard Johns, Emma Lefley, Alec Leggatt, Margarette Lincoln, Tom Long, Sarah Maisey, Clara de la Pena McTigue, Meredith More, Albert Neher, Richard Norris, Rebecca Nuotio, William Punter, Nigel Rigby, Martin Salmon, Nick Savage, Andrew Sim, Louise Simkiss, Simon Stephens, Bob Todd, Barbara Tomlinson, Tina Warner, Tracey Weller, David Westwood, Annette Wickham, Camilla Wilkinson, Bethany Wright and Yukiko Yoshii.

Image Credits

Illustrations in this publication appear by kind permission of the following:

Peter Berthoud: Fig. 62
Estate of Bertram Park / National Portrait Gallery, London: Fig. 55
Christophe Finot (CC BY-SA 3.0): Fig. 64
Imperial War Museums: Figs 1, 6, 19, 41, 56, 58
National Gallery of Canada, Ottowa. Transfer from the Canadian War Memorials, 1921 Fig. 54
Estate of Frank O'Salisbury. All rights reserved, DACS 2015: Fig. 20
Private collection: Fig. 57
Private collection, image courtesy of Bridget Cook: Fig. 47, Plates 50, 53
Private collection / Photo: National Maritime Museum, Greenwich, London: Fig. 29
Royal Academy of Arts, London: Fig. 53
Estate of Charles Wheeler: Figs 65, 66, 67; Plate 82

Pictures in the National Maritime Museum collection are listed below. Images can be ordered from the Picture Library, National Maritime Museum, Greenwich, London, SE10 9NF (telephone: 020 8312 6704/6631) or online at images.rmg.co.uk

© National Maritime Museum, Greenwich, London: Figs 8, 9, 11, 12, 16, 17, 18, 21, 28, 31, 33, 48, 51, 52, 60, 61, 63, 68, 70, 71; Plates 1, 2, 3, 4, 14, 60, 61, 62, 63, 76, 77, 78, 79, 80, 81, 83, 84, 85, 86, 87, 88, 89, 90
© National Maritime Museum, Greenwich, London. Presented by the artist's family, 2012: Figs 45, 46; Plates 51, 52, 54, 55, 56, 57, 58, 59
© National Maritime Museum, Greenwich, London. Caird Fund. Reproduced with kind permission of the Artist's Estate: Fig. 22
© National Maritime Museum, Greenwich, London. Captain P. L. Gunn Collection: Figs 38, 40
© National Maritime Museum, Greenwich, London. Earl Howe Collection: Figs 30, 39, 41
© National Maritime Museum, Greenwich, London. Purchased for the Museum by the Society for Nautical Research Macpherson Collection Endowment Fund: Plates 68, 69, 70, 71, 72, 73, 74, 75
© National Maritime Museum, Greenwich, London. Presented by the War Artists Advisory Committee: Figs 2, 3, 5, 7, 10, 13, 23, 24, 25, 32, 34, 35, 36, 37, 42, 43, 44, 49, 50, 59, 69; Plates 5, 6, 7, 15, 16, 17, 18, 19, 20, 21, 22, 23, 24, 25, 26, 27, 28, 29, 30, 31, 32, 33, 34, 35, 36, 37, 38, 39, 40, 41, 42, 43, 44, 45, 46, 47, 48, 49
© Norman Wilkinson Estate, from the Collection at the National Maritime Museum, Greenwich, London: Figs 14, 15; Plates 8, 9, 10, 11, 12,
© On loan to the National Maritime Museum, Greenwich, London. Kindly lent by Mrs Mona McEvoy: Plate 13
© National Maritime Museum, Greenwich, London. We regret that Museum enquiries have not been able to identify the copyright holder and would welcome any information that would help us update our records. Please contact the Picture Library: Figs 4, 26, 27; Plates 64, 65, 66, 67

Contributors

All contributors are curators at Royal Museums Greenwich:

CHRISTINE RIDING is Head of Arts and Curator of the Queen's House. She was previously Curator of Eighteenth- and Nineteenth-century British Art at Tate Britain, and was Deputy Editor of *Art History* (The Journal of the Association of Art Historians). She is co-author of *Turner & The Sea* (2013) which was published to accompany a major exhibition at the National Maritime Museum.

ROBERT J. BLYTH is Senior Curator of World and Maritime History, and editor of the *Journal for Maritime Research*. Among his publications, he is co-editor (with Andrew Lambert and Jan Rüger) of *The Dreadnought and the Edwardian age* (2011).

ANDREW CHOONG is Curator of Historic Photographs & Ship Plans. He specialises in naval warfare from 1860 to 1945 with particular focus on the Royal Navy, the US Navy and Japan's Teikoku Kaigun. He curated the *Arctic Convoys, 1941–45* exhibition (2011) at the National Maritime Museum.

JOHN GRAVES is Curator of Ship History and is an acknowledged expert on British passenger ships and shipping from the steam age to the present day. His publications include *Waterline: Images from the Golden Age of Cruising* (2005).

JEREMY MICHELL is Curator of Historic Photographs & Ship Plans. He was Curator of *The Last of the Tall Ships* exhibition (2009) based on the photographic work of Alan Villiers and has contributed to numerous National Maritime Museum exhibition catalogues, including *Nelson & Napoleon* (2005).

AMY MILLER is Curator Emeritus and former Curator of Decorative Arts & Material Culture. She curated *Sailor Chic* (2007) at the National Maritime Museum and *Rozanne Hawksley: War and Memory* at the Queen's House (2014). She is the author of *Dressed to Kill: British Naval Uniform, 1748–1857* (2007).

MELANIE VANDENBROUCK is Curator of Art, post-1800. She curated *War Artists at Sea* (2014) in the Queen's House, an exhibition of the National Maritime Museum's collection of art from the First and Second World Wars. She previously was an assistant curator in the Sculpture Department, Victoria & Albert Museum.

PIETER VAN DER MERWE is the General Editor and Greenwich Curator and has published on various aspects of maritime history and art, and theatre history. He is Vice-Chairman of the Turner Society and on the editorial board of the *Mariner's Mirror* (Journal of the Society for Nautical Research).

Index

Numbers in *italics* indicate illustrations.